Fair and Unfair Trials in the British Isles, 1800–1940

Fair and Unfair Trials in the British Isles, 1800–1940

Microhistories of Justice and Injustice

Edited by
David Nash and Anne-Marie Kilday

BLOOMSBURY ACADEMIC
LONDON • NEW YORK • OXFORD • NEW DELHI • SYDNEY

BLOOMSBURY ACADEMIC
Bloomsbury Publishing Plc
50 Bedford Square, London, WC1B 3DP, UK
1385 Broadway, New York, NY 10018, USA

BLOOMSBURY, BLOOMSBURY ACADEMIC and the Diana logo
are trademarks of Bloomsbury Publishing Plc

First published in Great Britain 2020

Copyright © David Nash and Anne-Marie Kilday, 2020

David Nash and Anne-Marie Kilday have asserted their rights
under the Copyright, Designs and Patents Act, 1988, to be identified
as Authors of this work.

Cover design: Terry Woodley
Cover Image © rclassenlayouts/Getty Images

All rights reserved. No part of this publication may be reproduced or transmitted in any form or by any means, electronic or mechanical, including photocopying, recording, or any information storage or retrieval system, without prior permission in writing from the publishers.

Bloomsbury Publishing Plc does not have any control over, or responsibility for, any third-party websites referred to or in this book. All internet addresses given in this book were correct at the time of going to press. The author and publisher regret any inconvenience caused if addresses have changed or sites have
ceased to exist, but can accept no responsibility for any such changes.

Every effort has been made to trace copyright holders and to obtain their permissions for the use of copyright material. The publisher apologizes for
any errors or omissions and would be grateful if notified of any corrections
that should be incorporated in future reprints or editions of this book.

A catalogue record for this book is available from the British Library.

Library of Congress Cataloging-in-Publication Data
Names: Nash, David, 1973- editor. | Kilday, Anne-Marie, editor.
Title: Fair and unfair trials in the British Isles, 1800-1940 : microhistories of justice and injustice / edited by David Nash and Anne-Marie Kilday.
Description: London ; New York, NY : Bloomsbury Academic, 2020. | Includes bibliographical references and index.
Identifiers: LCCN 2020027577 (print) | LCCN 2020027578 (ebook) | ISBN 9781350050945 (hardback) | ISBN 9781350050952 (ebook) | ISBN 9781350050969 (epub)
Subjects: LCSH: Trials–England–History | Trials–Scotland–History | Trials–Ireland–History. | Fair trial–England–History | Fair trial–Scotland–History | Fair trial–Ireland–History.
Classification: LCC KD8362 .F35 2020 (print) | LCC KD8362 (ebook) | DDC 347.41/0709034–dc23
LC record available at https://lccn.loc.gov/2020027577
LC ebook record available at https://lccn.loc.gov/2020027578

ISBN:	HB:	978-1-3500-5094-5
	PB:	978-1-3501-9243-0
	ePDF:	978-1-3500-5095-2
	eBook:	978-1-3500-5096-9

Typeset by Integra Software Services Pvt. Ltd.

To find out more about our authors and books visit www.bloomsbury.com
and sign up for our newsletters.

*In memory of Rebecca Henderson (1994–2019).
Our colleague, friend and continuing inspiration.*

Contents

List of Illustrations	viii
Notes on Contributors	ix
Acknowledgements	xi

Introduction Contextualizing the Unfair Trial in the Age of Public Criticism
Anne-Marie Kilday and David Nash ... 1

1. 'A Monstrous Innovation on the Laws': Murder and Double Jeopardy at the Old Bailey *Heather Shore* ... 17
2. Legislating to Ensure 'Impartial' Justice: Palmer's Act of 1856 *Katherine D. Watson* ... 35
3. 'All That They Had Heard, All That They Had Read, All That They Had Seen': Questions of Fairness and Justice in the Trial of George Vass *Helen Rutherford, Northumbria University and Clare Sandford-Couch, Newcastle University* ... 53
4. The Trials of Peter Barrett: A Microhistory of Dysfunction in the Irish Criminal Justice System *Niamh Howlin* ... 73
5. The Maamtrasna Murders: The Trial of Myles Joyce *Conor Hanly* ... 99
6. The Bedborough Case, 1898: 'A Curious Gonfalon Round Which to Fight' *Lesley A. Hall* ... 117
7. 'Circumstances of Unexplained Savagery': The Gilchrist Murder Case and Its Legacy, 1908–1927 *Anne-Marie Kilday* ... 137
8. 'Police Fiasco', 'The Black Army', 'Devil Dodgers' and 'Humbug': The Apparent 'Inevitably' of Unfair Blasphemy Trials up to 1922 *David Nash* ... 175
9. The Bobbed-Haired Bandit and the Smash-and-Grab Raider *Alyson Brown* ... 195

Bibliography	212
Index	229

Illustrations

Figures

2.1	'William Palmer at 'The Oaks', 1854	38
7.1	Photograph of Marion Gilchrist (undated)	138
7.2	Crime Scene Photograph, Glasgow – 1908	140
7.3	Mortuary Photograph of Miss Marion Gilchrist – 1908	142
7.4	Photographs of Oscar Slater – 1909 and 1927	154
7.5	Newspaper Photograph of Detective-Lieutenant John Thomson Trench, 1914	158

Tables

2.1	*Appendix:* Significant Events in the Prosecution of William Palmer	49
5.1	Crown challenges to the appointment of jurors in the trials of P & M Joyce and P & M Casey	109

Contributors

Alyson Brown is Professor of History at Edge Hill University. She has conducted extensive research into prison history and heritage and into the history of crime. She has published several monographs, including *Inter-war Penal Policy and Crime in England* (2013) and numerous articles and chapters. Her current monograph project is on motor bandits and criminal mobility in Britain during the inter-war period.

Lesley A. Hall, FRHistS, PhD, DipAA, was formerly Senior Archivist, Wellcome Library. She is now Wellcome Library Research Fellow and Honorary Senior Lecturer, Department of Science and Technology Studies, University College London. She has published extensively on questions of sexuality and gender in Britain from the nineteenth century to the present and is currently working on a study of inter-war progressive individuals and movements.

Conor Hanly is Lecturer in Law at the National University of Ireland Galway. He received his primary law degrees from the National University of Ireland Galway. He received a first-class honours LL.M. from University College Dublin, and LL.M. and J.S.D. degrees from Yale Law School. His main research interests lie in the fields of criminal law and legal history. He has written extensively on Irish criminal law, and was lead researcher on a groundbreaking study of attrition in rape cases in Ireland. He is a regular contributor to the Irish national media on criminal law issues. In legal history, he won the Joseph Parker Prize in Roman Law and Legal History from Yale Law School in 2004, and is primarily interested in the history of the jury.

Niamh Howlin is Associate Professor at the Sutherland School of Law, University College Dublin. She has published extensively in the area of legal history; her most recent monograph is *Juries in Ireland: Laypersons and Law in the Long Nineteenth Century* (2017). She is also the joint editor, with Dr Kevin Costello, of two collections of essays, *Law and the Family in Ireland, 1800–1950* and *Law and Religion in Ireland 1695–1950*.

Anne-Marie Kilday is Professor of Criminal History at Oxford Brookes University. She has published widely on the history of violence and the history of female criminality in Britain, Europe and North America from 1600 to the present. Her most recent volume is *Crime in Scotland 1660–1960: The Violent North* (2019). She is currently working on two monograph projects: one on the history of homicide in Britain and one on nineteenth-century criminal women (with David Nash).

David Nash is Professor of History at Oxford Brookes University. He has published widely on the history of atheism, secularism, the history of blasphemy and the history of shame. He has also advised NGOs, international organizations and governments about the issue of blasphemy law repeal. He is currently working on two edited books and two monograph projects: one on the history of atheist narratives in Britain and one on nineteenth-century criminal women (with Anne-Marie Kilday).

Helen Rutherford is Solicitor and Senior Lecturer in the Law School at Northumbria University. She is also carrying out PhD research at Newcastle University. She has published on legal history and the English Legal System. Her research interests focus on the life and work of the Victorian Coroner for Newcastle upon Tyne and nineteenth-century crime with a North East England focus.

Clare Sandford-Couch is Visiting Lecturer in the Law School at Newcastle University. She has published on legal history, art history and the role of the arts and humanities in legal education. Her research interests largely address interactions of law and visual culture and late medieval Italian art history. Her current research focus includes crime histories in nineteenth-century Newcastle upon Tyne.

Heather Shore is Professor of History at Manchester Metropolitan University. She is the author of monographs, *Artful Dodgers: Youth and Crime in Early Nineteenth Century London* (1999) and *London's Criminal Underworlds, c. 1720 to c. 1930: A Social and Cultural History* (2015), and a number of other co-edited and co-authored books. Her research interests have focused on the history of juvenile delinquency and youth justice, the idea of the 'criminal underworld' and the history of organized crime, and more recently the history of victims of crime.

Katherine D. Watson is Reader in History at Oxford Brookes University. Her research focuses on areas where medicine, crime and the law intersect, and includes *Poisoned Lives: English Poisoners and Their Victims* (2004), *Forensic Medicine in Western Society: A History* (2011) and the forthcoming *Medicine and Justice: Medico-Legal Practice in England and Wales, 1700–1914* (2020). She is completing a book on acid attacks in Britain 1790–1975, and her next major project will investigate poisoning crimes in Scotland since the early eighteenth century.

Acknowledgements

The editors would like to thank the numerous people who have helped in the writing of this book. Firstly, we would like to express our thanks to staff at the National Archives of Ireland, the National Library of Ireland, the National Archives at Kew, the London Metropolitan Archives, the British Library, the National Archives of Scotland, the Mitchell Library, the archives of the University of Glasgow and the Bodleian Library of the University of Oxford for their patience and helpful advice. We would also like to thank each of the contributors to this volume for their hard work and, in particular, their patience and grace when dealing with our many queries.

Special and grateful thanks also go to James Hamilton, Research Principal of the Society of Writers to Her Majesty's Signet (The Signet Library, Edinburgh) for his hospitality and for allowing us access to the William Roughead collection. Also to Pam Fortescue for all her administrative support and expertise with the preparation of this volume.

We would also like to thank those involved at Bloomsbury publishing in the production of this book from embryonic idea to published work. Thanks go to our commissioning editor Emily Drew and to our various editorial contacts including Maddie Holder, Beatriz Lopez, Dan Hutchins and Abigail Lane. We would also like to thank our anonymous reviewers for their helpful and important contributions.

Introduction
Contextualizing the Unfair Trial in the Age of Public Criticism

Anne-Marie Kilday and David Nash
Oxford Brookes University

Arguably, the period 1820–1940 was when the modern criminal trial that we would recognize today began to evolve. During this period legal procedures including the role of counsel, juries and the judge began to fuse into a fully fledged legal system where 'fairness' was to become a part of the public discussion of their function. Before this point in time, the law was an arena in which ' … social relations were forged, and in which its reciprocities and fissures were reflected.'[1] As Peter King argues, the judicial process up until 1820 should be regarded as both opaque and often regulated by custom alongside vested interest. Significantly it was without regularized procedures where the likelihood of particular outcomes could be predicted on the basis of fair judgement alone. King suggested that the late eighteenth-century legal procedures (especially around property crime) constituted an endless series of ' … layer upon layer of negotiation opportunities and discretionary choices.'[2] King's metaphor for this system, such as it was, portrayed it as a series of connected, but also separate rooms through which cases would progress at varying speeds. The speed of such progress and the trial outcomes would be dictated, according to King's metaphor, by facets of the building's design and the anticipation of what would happen to a case when it progressed to a subsequent room. This mechanism could seem capricious and arbitrary and at its best was a ' … complex multidimensional set of decision-making processes.' Andrea McKenzie has foregrounded both the real and imagined frustration with court proceedings and their relationship to justice which had a dimension in popular culture. A fixation with the gallows in biographies, dying speeches and accounts of criminal trials made it a portent of judgement and true justice in the hereafter. Something regularly contrasted with the fallibility of the temporal criminal trial in England.[3]

---

[1] P. King (2000) *Crime, Justice and Discretion in England 1740–1820* (Oxford: Oxford University Press), pp. 4–5.
[2] Ibid., pp. 124–5.
[3] A. McKenzie (2007) *Tyburn's Martyrs: Execution in England, 1675–1775* (London: Hambledon).

Contrasting with this apparent arbitrariness, J.M. Beattie has argued that the development of the criminal trial was more progressive and that this 'reform' commenced at an earlier period than the late eighteenth and early nineteenth centuries, with London and its needs operating as a significant catalyst for change.[4] Commercial and moral interests pushed the case for greater systematization of prosecution and justice. Beattie argues that the eighteenth century witnessed a series of schemes to make the conscious use of court proceedings more attractive. This period also secured a measure of balance by the middle of the century, through the formalization of defence counsel presence in court. Taken together, Beattie sees here the origins of a recognizably modern system of criminal administration.[5] This theme was also investigated by Allyson May who also saw a process of modernization at work. She examined the 1836 Prisoners' Counsel Act as a pivotal moment in making the criminal trial a balanced and autonomous procedure – thus laying a claim to the idea in the public's imagination of the trial as supposedly 'fair'.[6]

Yet the arrival of this phenomenon was scarcely immediate, nor was this transition accomplished without difficulty. We might also consider that the phenomenon of the 'unfair' trial in the period after 1820 is problematic for the existing historiography which sees the eighteenth-century conduct of trials as arbitrary, something to be marginalized by the early nineteenth-century modernization of legal practice and presumption. In this respect, one premise behind this book is to suggest that a new perspective upon the history of this change might be opened up by examining the mistakes, bungled procedures, anomalies, corruption and problematic elements that characterized some criminal trials from the era after 1820. These might suggest that expectations, customs and the realm of unofficial action to 'steer' the law changed its form or translated itself into other narratives. By placing unfair trials together, we can study a range of factors and compose a wider history of the issues that adversely influenced major trials and their outcomes in the 1820–1940 period. We can also uncover how effectively authorities reacted in order to limit the damage caused, or to close the loopholes that had seemingly been created for defendants or those with vested interests. As such, this potentially qualifies some former and cruder modernization narratives, whilst suggesting the possibility of continuity, at least in respect of expectation of the law's outcomes, if not necessarily in the mechanisms and procedures to achieve these.

In doing so, we contend that some high-profile and famous British trials that are often considered by both public and scholarly opinion, with the benefit of hindsight, to have been unfair deserve placing in a broader context. This takes two forms. We contend that placing these cases (or case studies) together can indicate a collection of places where the law and legal proceedings fail. As such, this writes an unwitting history of societies confronting the inadequacy of their systems for upholding and

---

[4] J.M. Beattie (1986) *Crime and the Courts in England 1660–1800* (Princeton: Princeton University Press), pp. 623–5.
[5] J.M. Beattie (2001) *Policing and Punishment in London 1660–1750* (Oxford: Oxford University Press) preface pp. vi–vii.
[6] A. May (2003) *The Bar and the Old Bailey, 1750–1850* (Chapel Hill: University of North Carolina Press).

promoting moral behaviour and the law. This shines a light upon the process of negotiating the consequences of that failure and all that this entails. In addition, the notoriety of some unfair trials means that past coverage of them has too often focused squarely upon personalities, and as such these trials have only ever been considered in this isolated and limiting context. Examination of these with a wider framework makes them obviously reflective of other issues beyond the law.

This context for the concept of the 'age of public criticism' outlines a chronology of the growth of public interest in the affairs of justice and the courtroom.[7] This can be examined through a consideration of developments in the burgeoning mass media of the age. These include (in the earlier period) radical and unstamped newspapers, the growth of a local press and later developments that diversified the content of such publications as well as their readership. Alongside these, changes in journalism brought the courtroom and the exploits within it into the lives of thousands who resided outside these premises. As such, courtrooms and cases became both an entertainment medium and an acknowledged part of the public sphere which reflected divergent attitudes, accepted norms and (sometimes) emerging values.[8] The press were also conduits for a considerable range of social and political causes that found themselves represented in the pages of a growing and more accessible press media. In some instances, these were championed, or criticized, through the medium of reporting upon specific court cases. This is something which, on occasion, highlighted injustice, intolerance, corruption or the pursuit of nefarious and vested interests.

The 'age of public criticism' ostensibly signals the importance of the media as a quintessentially vital player in the concept of the unfair trial. In some trials described in this book, the media itself is the instrument of prejudicial opinion, damaging the process of providing a fair trial. Pre-trial publicity and its depiction of the defendant in a pejorative light are demonstrated to be fundamental in at least two of the case studies where trials produced unfair verdicts and outcomes. Thus, chronologically, the 'age of public criticism' serves to describe the period (roughly from 1820 to 1940) in which the criminal prosecution, trial and its outcome became a fundamental staple of newspaper and periodical reporting. Trials became stories upon which social and cultural agendas were hung, as well as being the more spontaneous products of episodic moral panics.[9] But they could, as one episode in the book particularly demonstrates, be the central and only mechanism at work in the miscarriage of justice. In this particular trial, which we encounter in Chapter IX, the press coverage brought together presumption, moral panic and criminal archetype (fed by fictional portrayal) to produce a publicly available 'trial' of its own. Certainly, the concept of trial by journalism had been well established in the closing decades of the nineteenth century. However, the momentum of this can be seen to carry on energetically into the twentieth century, when both fact

---

[7] This has been traced for the early period in the essays contained in D. Lemmings (2012) (ed.) *Crime, Courtrooms and the Public Sphere in Britain, 1700–1850* (Farnham: Ashgate).
[8] For more on this, see J. Rowbotham, K. Stevenson and S. Pegg (2013) *Crime News in Modern Britain: Press Reporting and Responsibility 1820-2010* (London: Palgrave).
[9] For evidence of this in the earlier period, see R. Crone (2012) 'Publishing Courtroom Drama for the Masses, 1820–1855' in Lemmings (ed.) *Crime, Courtrooms and the Public Sphere*, pp. 193–216.

and fictional portrayal created social and criminal outcasts. These moral constructs, and the stereotypes associated with them, were peddled to readerships who used them explicitly to think deeply about the concepts of disorder. In instances of this nature, the final and eventual appearance in court, though anticipated as the culmination of this trial by journalism, regularly became something of a contrary and lacklustre anti-climax, when compared to the sensational event anticipated by press coverage.

The unfair trial – Justice under scrutiny?

The unfair trial is a genre capable of opening out the courtroom for scrutiny where otherwise this might not happen. Trials that run their course without the intervention of an impasse, a stumbling block, or a significantly notable error simply do not attract this sort of attention. In such cases, which we should acknowledge amount to an overwhelming majority of those tried, the court and the courtroom are simply processes, legal methodologies and a fundamental means to an obvious end. The existence and knowledge of the unfair trial upsets this balance and suddenly turns the courtroom into an ambivalent and contested space. No longer do the scales of justice loom as an omnipotent and trusted entity. Instead legal proceedings in unfair trials can become a context, in which newly created narratives can produce conceptions of innocence and guilt (and indeed right and wrong) for different audiences.

Alongside mainstream media coverage, new forms of popular culture were involved in creating and recreating stereotypes and in establishing impressions drawn from supposition and constructed narratives. These emerged in everything from the Penny Dreadful to the sensational waxworks exhibits that characterized mid- and late Victorian England. Then, in the new century, both photography and radio also added further dimensions to this clamorous debate. Public criticism also became a species of activism, since the public sometimes involved themselves in trying to rectify miscarriages of justice to an extent not seen before. Thus, the wider public in this period frequently communicated with government and authority to complain about certain trial outcomes. On other occasions, they appealed for clemency for individuals they considered wrongfully convicted (especially if sentenced to death). Others initiated public campaigns for retrials, or to free convicted individuals, often enlisting the opinion and support of powerful political, cultural or literary figures to do so.

Supposedly, one of the hallmarks of the transition to modern society is the rational organization and codification of many customs, behaviour and structures. Law is a major component, and indeed an engine of this, so its use and application have been a major bargaining chip in battles between the rulers and the ruled in many cultures and societies. Out of such battles, modern societies have come to expect systems of law to be regularly re-codified, rational, predictable and, most importantly, fair on a considerable range of levels. Achieving this goal was regularly seen by individuals as the passport to citizenship, civilization and advancement within modern society. It was also a comprehensible rational yardstick alongside which conceptions of relative freedom were measured. One needs only look at the English obsession with both the truth and the imagined truth of Magna Carta to substantiate this claim. Whilst a simple temporary declaration, this document has come to have a peculiar life of its own, living on in the English imagination to be invoked as securing and maintaining the freedom of the individual against the pretensions of legal tyranny. Such a powerful argument could also cross the water to influence American jurisprudence, as well as protests in Northern Ireland about internment without trial.[10]

One other important aspect of modernization has been the principle that the law should be homogenous. According to this logic, anomalies should not persist since the law should be impartial and capable of persuading all of a conception of equity as a principle for its enactment. This is because the law, as an abstract idea, appears in the mind of individuals as a stable, unswerving and powerful entity to which individuals hold up an imagined idea of justice. It is easy to consider this to have been a regular part of popular culture, manifesting itself in differing attitudes to offenders both popular and unpopular. However, we must also remember that the aspiration for the proper treatment of criminal offenders has also been a benchmark of civilization for theorists of social development.

Optimists like Norbert Elias (1897–1990) saw rules, and the acceptance of them, as indicative of the progress of civilization, with an emphatically obvious benefit to those living through a process of change, as by adhering to regulations they could eventually arrive at modernity.[11] Within this paradigm, everyone 'knew where they stood' because the rational application of behavioural rules reinforced concepts of correct and incorrect behaviour. The growing sophistication of society progressed alongside the development of rules to govern the regulation of new areas of life, providing confidence for populations in their personal investment for the future, whether this be psychological or material. Optimism related to the law and its associated directives is also evident elsewhere in the work of theorists, although these potentially take us in a different direction and potential conclusion. Jurgen Habermas, for instance, expressed approval of the English courtroom's facility and capability for enhancing and promoting his beloved 'public sphere'. He saw this as some guarantor of 'good governance'.[12] Yet here the unfair trial is double-edged. It might positively stimulate (and indeed dramatically multiply) the further discussion and participation of individuals and groups in a thriving public sphere. However, the problematic nature of such cases producing this dialogue has the capacity to potentially undermine the credibility of 'good governance'.[13] Beyond this the fear emanating from Habermas, that participation in trials eventually dissolves into a less active and valuable consumption of them, may equally need revision when confronted with the unfair trial.[14] The evidence of this book seems to demonstrate that it is a wider respect for 'fairness' in

---

[10] For an example of Magna Carta's history considered to have a lasting and popular relevance, see D. Jones (2016) *Magna Carta: The Birth of Liberty* (Penguin, London).
[11] This is substantially the argument in N. Elias (2000 edition) *The Civilising Process* (London: Wiley Blackwell).
[12] See D. Lemmings (2012) 'Introduction: Criminal Courts, Lawyers and the Public Sphere' in Lemmings (ed.) *Crime, Courtrooms and the Public Sphere* (Farnham: Ashgate), pp. 1–21 at p. 17.
[13] Ibid., p. 17.
[14] Ibid., p. 18.

the administration of justice that keeps dialogues about the justice or injustice of the law alive and well into the twentieth century.

Conversely, pessimists like Michel Foucault (1926–1984) came to problematize the notion of the trial and its fairness in some new ideological ways. Foucault saw rules and their justification under the expertise of rational specialists as a curb upon human freedom.[15] Such experts and specialists effectively queued up to provide the ideological justification for regimes of sentencing and punishment. Sometimes such experts also provided the evidence which the judicial system would use to try and convict individuals. For Foucault this produced a type of justice, which wholly served the interests of elites who used knowledge and regulation as a form of power. This was supposedly used to suppress a variety of forms of dissidence from conventionally promoted morals, behaviour and expectations. For Foucault, the successful application of justice, and its widespread acceptance, was often an assault upon the subjectivity of individuals who became subjugated and defined by regimes of discipline. Marxist historians who critiqued the operation of the English legal system would see in it a much cruder form of control and suppression. The historians of *Albion's Fatal Tree*, for example, famously saw parliamentary legislation, trials for a range of misdemeanours and felonies and their outcomes, as the naked expression of property seeking to defend itself against encroachment, in an age of social upheaval. Indeed, the authors of this work saw this as a concerted and deliberate action by a whole class to use the ultimately coercive measure of the death penalty. Although quarrelling with this monolithic description of an entire class involved in a dark enterprise, even the critics of *Albion's Fatal Tree* did acknowledge that the law could be manipulated by individuals of that class to further their own individual ends.[16]

It is easy to see how the fair trial is a phenomenon which underpins and nurtures popular acceptance and embracement of the law, alongside assent to the authority that enforces it. Yet we should also note how many theorists and commentators of both law and human behaviour build squarely upon the public trust in the fair trial, and the coherent acceptance of the law and its logic. Optimists like Norbert Elias saw rules, their coherence, logic and rational enforcement as having a benign transformative power. They were, for him, a motor of beneficial social and cultural change that drove society towards modernity through the medium of consent. Ironically, even pessimists like Michel Foucault and Karl Marx (1818–1883) built their conception of a surveillance (or capitalist) society upon the utterly efficient functioning of its mechanisms of

---

[15] Although at times contradictory, the bulk of Michel Foucault's thoughts on sexuality, the prison and other institutions foregrounded his distrust of the enlightenment. This, for him, was the occasion at which specialist knowledge (such as the law, psychology and criminology through their narratives) achieved unrivalled power in the West. This occurred at the expense of the 'subjectivity' of the individual who was thereafter the prisoner of objectivity.

[16] See D. Hay, P. Linebaugh, J. Rule, E.P. Thompson and C. Winslow (2011 edition) *Albion's Fatal Tree: Crime and Society in Eighteenth Century England* (London: Verso). The critique of this offered by John Langbein saw draconian legislation as only piecemeal, and in response only to specific threats to individual pieces of property. These were the initiative of only singular individuals who were in Parliament or had connections with those who were. See J. Langbein (1983) 'Albion's Fatal Flaws', *Past and Present*, 98, pp. 96–120.

apparent repression. We should also note that the historiography of how justice worked is built entirely on observing the 'standard' trial and administration of justice. Such an assumption led Robert Shoemaker to assert that as the eighteenth-century judicial system had seemingly exemplary intent, this encouraged crime reporting, which in turn relied upon the verdict as somehow just and incontestable.[17] Yet in the picture of nineteenth-century unfair trials, it becomes obvious that crime reporting had evolved to play a significantly more ambivalent role by that time.

Within all paradigms of how justice 'works', in its very widest sense, the 'unfair' trial is a worryingly but often transitory 'fly in the ointment', although occasionally it seems to be more than this. The unfair trial, or miscarriage of justice, can subtly (and sometimes boldly) question broader popular narratives of legitimate authority and its impartiality. In this book, we can see a variety of such instances which unravelled in different ways, and produced different narrative effects. Some appeared to be unfair even as they proceeded to court. In others, courtroom mechanisms appeared to prevent the achievement of justice and there are examples that see both defence *and* prosecution actively disadvantaged by this. We also see instances where the creation of the prosecution case, and the actions of policing authorities in compiling such cases, was highly questionable. Then there are further instances where legal technicalities enable the guilty, indeed those guilty of the most heinous of crimes, to escape justice. The law itself was also indicted on some occasions where it became the medium under scrutiny. This scrutiny can expand and envelope the personalities and opinions of those who preside over the law and its operation. This factor can also produce instances where such predilections or apparent whims overturn others' expectations of justice and envisaged outcomes.

We should also be aware that, as time went on, the courtroom became increasingly open to the evidence and opinion of experts. This obviously appears to go along with both the modernization of the law and the urge to use still more methods of reaching a just conclusion. Notwithstanding Foucault's warning about the consequences of co-opting specialists and professionals to classify and pronounce, some instances of the unfair trial also display the fallibility of such experts and the evidence that they present. As such, the progress of justice and its development in the British context can thus emerge as a somewhat bumpier ride than we might have expected.

From fair trial to unfair trial

There are a considerable variety of audiences for the unfair trial. This further fuels discussion of them, sometimes considerably beyond their immediate context. Some of these audiences are apparently more obvious than others. Press coverage, a phenomenon which often ironically actively contributes to some 'unfair trials', is also a deeply interested and avid consumer of miscarriages of justice. It is scarcely

---

[17] See R. Shoemaker (2012) 'Representing the Adversary Criminal Trial: Lawyers in the Old Bailey Proceedings, 1770–1800' in Lemmings (ed.) *Crime, Courtrooms and the Public Sphere*, pp. 71–91.

surprising that newspapers and periodicals should interest themselves in court cases, especially when they somehow go wrong. They constitute mediums of intelligence gathering and opinion that can influence the procedures and conduct of policing and legal agencies. They also influence, and reflect, public opinion in a relationship that historians are discovering appears to be increasingly complex. The media has consistently toyed with narratives of the fair trial, something which itself breeds confidence in the more important overarching narrative of 'British Justice'. This symbiotic relationship between the media and this narrative means that such expectations of this as the status quo regularly impact upon popular conceptions of the rule of law and its purpose. Arguably, this creates confidence in the function of wider culture and individual conceptions of personal security, alongside the safety of the person and their personal estate.

All of these issues present problems for the popular and philosophical conceptions of justice and its logical, rational operation. Unfair trials instantly remove the abstract and idealizing qualities from the idea and practice of justice. Instead this is unsatisfactorily replaced with images of fallibility, frailty and incoherence. Justice's previously abstract and superhuman nature becomes replaced with the all too visible characteristics of human frailty. These less desirable qualities appear as incompetence, bias and actions that appear wilful and sometimes obsessive. Such instances also seemingly expose a variety of malevolent vested interests that seemingly hijack the legal process and the very notion of justice itself. Equally the exposure of these unsavoury truths can persuade the concerned that the capacity for human bias, incompetence and wilful misbehaviour in the application of justice indicates that there is a dark figure of human action overriding the apparently rational operation of justice. In this way, the narrative of 'British Justice' can rapidly dismiss ideals of fair judgement by peers, to resemble an enterprise ruled by circumstance and chance.

This range of concerns all seem startlingly visible in this volume as factors bringing the law into disrepute. They appear as government misuse of the legal system to place it in furtherance of political ends and policy. They also appear as inadequacies in the framing and compilation of the law, as well as in specific instances of its implementation. Policing and agents of authority can also appear to deviate from ideals of service to emerge publically as, by turns, inept, partisan and fallible. Still worse, they appear capable of corruption and the misuse of resources, all in pursuit of unpalatable and unacceptable goals. These emerge in everything from the ignoble closing of ranks, through to the careless and indifferent indulgence of excepted archetypes that influence policing itself. When such instances get as far as the courtroom, they become simplistic stereotypes of who should be in the dock to face the due process of law.

The unfair trial, as has been suggested, exposes and illuminates the fallibility of legal systems which are, after all, implemented and in many senses 'used' by fallible humans. Modern work by psychologists and criminologists, as well as by historians, has satisfactorily established that judicial outcomes can be heavily influenced by the particular characteristics of protagonists. Gender, ethnicity and class have long been recognized as factors which can influence the behaviour and opinions of all actors in the courtroom.[18] It has also been recognized that the potency of immediate social and moral concerns within any society can also exert a significant influence upon the conduct of trials and how this is received and consumed. These trials can be heightened and extended in the hothouse atmosphere of a moral panic. In the twenty-first century, the legal system is, by comparison, responsive to issues that this range of unacceptable variables can produce. Indeed, in recent decades we have seen a transformation in how many procedures are conducted: all with the intention of levelling a perceived uneven playing field. This has addressed situations where both prosecution and defence cases face insurmountable difficulties in the successful presentation of evidence. Recognition of these issues was not so readily forthcoming in nineteenth-century Britain, however, and thus one aspect of this book that makes its contents distinctive is that it partly constitutes a history of places and experiences where dangerous anomalies were uncovered for the first time. It also tries to examine how these problems and anomalies were eventually addressed, albeit in piecemeal fashion and with varying degrees of success.

Unfair trials – Unfair issues

Gender is fundamental to the case discussed by Alyson Brown in the final chapter of this book. It was important in creating an archetype of the dangerous deviant young woman, with the threat enhanced by concerns about the moral welfare of both youth and girls in particular. Popular culture alternatively fed, and fed off, such concerns further adding to tensions both in and outside the courtroom. Yet beyond the 'trial by journalism' of this particular defendant, the court itself – and the judge in particular – may have been influenced by idealized rather than demonizing gender stereotypes. Whilst evidently convicted by the media, the judge in this particular case offered surprising levels of clemency to a woman who was nonetheless a convicted criminal.

Ethnicity and nationality appeared as determining aspects in two of the other cases in the volume, namely those discussed by Niamh Howlin and Conor Hanley in Chapters IV and V, respectively. In the context of a quasi-colonial situation in Ireland, the two cases discussed involved instances where legal mechanisms were tampered with in order to achieve certain political goals and explicitly avoid others. Most notably, this was evidenced in the decision to move the trials away from their native and original localities. Again it is worth suggesting that we may be encountering a considerable dark figure here, where the issue of nationality/ethnicity, and clashes around this, may have produced a considerable number of unfair trials for a variety of complex reasons. Ethnicity as a component of how individuals were treated by the courts is evident not only in the chapters by Howlin and Hanley, but also in that of Anne-Marie Kilday.

---

[18] See, for instance, S. D'Cruze, S. Walklate and S. Pegg (2006) *Murder: Social and Historical Approaches to Understanding Murder and Murderers* (Abingdon: Willan) and also C. Conley (2007) *Certain Other Countries: Homicide, Gender and National Identity in Late-Nineteenth Century England, Ireland, Scotland and Wales* (Columbus, OH: Ohio State University Press).

Indeed, Chapter VII is also useful for displaying just how tacit anti-Semitism could be as an unacknowledged monster prowling the courtroom.

Class appears in a number of the cases presented in this volume, both in muted forms and as constituting a significant part of arguments against obvious bias. It must, of course, seem an obvious question to consider how many lower class defendants were disadvantaged by courtroom procedures and the probing questions of highly educated and hostile counsel. We can see these issues arising in Chapter III by Helen Rutherford and Clare Sandford-Couch, and those by Niahm Howlin and Conor Hanley. This is obviously a further dark figure, yet the failure to potentially eliminate such issues is an important observation from one of the cases discussed in this book. The fact that the media and various forms of popular culture effectively filled in the relative silence of the defence, as though it could speak authoritatively upon the motivations and morals of the accused, adds further to the issues outlined here. Class was also intrinsic to David Nash's case study outlined in Chapter VIII, where the entire offence of blasphemy was deemed by the defendants to turn around this crucial concept. As was argued, a polite manner required an educated and refined skill in the deployment of language. This would, so it was reasoned, place the less well educated in the community at a disadvantage should they unfortunately find themselves in the dock. This suggests that the dimension of class was an important factor in influencing the conduct of many criminal trials.

Two of the cases outlined in this book (those by Lesley Hall in Chapter VI and David Nash in chapter VIII) also illuminate the issue of unwise prosecutions, initiated by authority figures who had made, with the benefit of hindsight, very poor choices. In both of these cases, the imperative to take action against sexually immoral and blasphemous publications, respectively, overrode the more cautious approaches that might otherwise have been adopted. If the intention was to curtail a social menace, it became obvious that the action against these was, to say the least, double-edged. If the intention had been to remove such menaces from view, this backfired spectacularly by giving them unforeseen publicity. In both instances, the protagonists in the cases admitted that this had been an unfortunate product of allowing said prosecutions to be brought and to proceed. This also illuminates a further legal history where discretion, and a desire to leave well alone, created a conception of the unwise trial, rather than an obviously unfair one. Such trials also awoke the opinions and primed the voices of libertarians and they were all too eager to paint such prosecutions as flawed and unfair. From there, it was a short step to depicting such prosecutions as indicative of legal, cultural and moral anachronism.

Scrutinizing fair and unfair trials means we are also given an insight into the varying levels of professionalism exhibited by the late nineteenth- and early twentieth-century police, legal profession and judicial authorities. Defendants and their counsel in the cases explored in this book are able to highlight problems with the wording of indictments. In the opening chapter by Heather Shore, this tied the court into acquitting a likely murderer. In other instances, such as the chapters by Niahm Howlin and Anne-Marie Kilday, the assembly and conduct of identity parades were shown to be riddled with inconsistencies and patent malpractice. In David Nash's chapter, the preparation of evidence, in the shape of testimony from police notebooks, could be shown to be the product of collusion and bias against the defence. Similarly, ascertaining the precise individual specimen copy of a blasphemous publication, purchased by an individual policeman, proved particularly problematic in the courtroom.

Although perhaps ultimately an imponderable, we can still speculate upon the consequences for defendants of the quality displayed by legal professionals in court. From the examples given in this book, it is possible to say that some counsel exhibit considerable degrees of professionalism, whilst from the historical record it appears that others may have been less diligent. It is perhaps worth noting that this may be a slightly distorted impression conveyed by the actual case notes and newspaper reporting of the individual cases. Such records will not provide an adequate picture of all the work that will have gone into an individual prosecution or defence case.

What can, in some instances, appear more obvious is when an individual counsel appears to have been hindered or hampered by the circumstances of the case or its conduct. Certainly this is evident in some cases explored in this volume. In at least one other example seen in this book, the conduct of the case may have been influenced by the employment of a particularly noteworthy, and arguably famous, defence counsel in creating a successful defence. Although it is difficult to be definitive about this, it seems likely that celebrity counsel were likely to have been influential in attracting extra attention and publicity and conceivably, when it was financially viable, they were employed for precisely this reason. In Chapter II by Katherine Watson, we also encounter the phenomenon of notoriety in the shape of celebrity forensic scientists who introduced a new dynamic to courtroom proceedings, transforming the nature of evidence in some trials. Whilst this again seems linked to the quest for justice to be modern, and to reflect and embrace innovation, the modern professional application of this was scarcely immediate. Indeed, in Anne-Marie Kilday's chapter, we also encounter a cluster of methods by which the notion of justice was compromised and circumvented. This was sometimes by design, but was also a consequence of vested interests, and covert policing and legal cultures. The evidence from this case indicates that they strove to operate in a partial and unfair manner against a defendant that had been identified as an outcast.

The structure of this volume

Readers who have encountered the work of the two editors before will have noticed that we are enthusiastic advocates of the micro history method of analysing and writing about the history of crime. Certainly this subject lends itself quite readily to this approach. In this instance, court cases quite obviously render themselves as viable case studies. Whereas in some of our previous work we assembled a range of material from disparate sources to construct a narrative and analyse its importance, this is obviously unnecessary in creating a case study from a court case. Much of this work, or at least the preliminary elements of it, has been substantially done for us. From here, there is considerable value that can be wrought from investigating court cases as case studies. However, we are also conscious that the power of the case study expands sometimes in response to the research findings uncovered, and the historiography that results from this. Thus, in this volume the majority of the chapters are individual case studies of specific court cases and incidents. Beyond this, the editors have expanded this definition to include two digressions from this format. The first of these relates to the eighth chapter in the volume and provides consideration of a number of cases that constituted a wider indictment of a whole offence rather than individual proceedings. This is seen as creating and nurturing a narrative of the unfair trial, aided and abetted by discriminatory and punitive laws that could be cast as anti-modern and against the tide of public opinion. The second of these digressions relates to the seventh chapter in the volume which acknowledges that unfair trials are capable of producing a backlash against the very mechanisms that expose them as unfair. This highlights the power of expected outcomes as well as the consternation when these do not occur. In the aftermath of a trial that begins to appear unfair, the agencies that promoted court room proceedings can close ranks and act against whistle-blowers anxious to expose inadequate or fraudulent procedure. As such this alerts us distinctly to the concept of the multiple or domino effect unfair trial. This can further multiply when efforts to exonerate an innocent but convicted defendant are coupled with efforts to persecute an innocent whistle-blower result in the escape of the guilty – a further 'unfair trial', at least when held up to philosophical standards of justice and its aims. Both of these chapters also illuminate how creating the narrative of an unfair trial and how to push this forward, or indeed seek to crush it, were a learning curve where cumulative knowledge of the law and its operation was a tool to accomplish ends.

As we suggest, a range of different cases can illuminate the whole panoply of ways in which a court case can be deemed fair or unfair. This can be for a variety of reasons and, to some extent, this book represents a composite history of the numerous influences that brought themselves to bear upon the legal and judicial system during the 'age of public criticism'. Thus, in many of the examples that follow, the authors have elaborated upon the issues raised by the case they have discussed. Frequently they are able to suggest how procedural anomalies were subsequently tackled or, how prevailing senses of injustice were eventually resolved. Sometimes this is through subsequent changes in legal procedure to close loopholes that created the unfair elements within specific trials. In other instances, the trial itself is revisited, in one case over a century after it had been concluded. Thus, in some respects this book also outlines a history whereby subsequent generations of legal professionals and authority figures not only undertake to improve and modernize legal and judicial mechanisms, but also strive to find closure in such instances where justice has not, in their view, been adequately served.

The first chapter, by Heather Shore, investigates the case of William Sheen, a man who, in 1827, almost certainly murdered his own child in cold blood. It seems evident that at no point did Sheen actively deny committing the murder. Yet, as the indictment against him was incorrectly worded and, through the procedural anomaly of *autrefois acquit* or double jeopardy, it became impossible for Sheen to be convicted. As Shore outlines, this was an unusual case in which an unfair trial worked to the advantage of a defendant. She also notes that this was a rare occasion when 'an ordinary plebeian Londoner' was able to take advantage of the labyrinths of the law and gain an acquittal. Nevertheless, this case did awaken an uproar amongst London's populace and Shore also shows how this society (both police and populace) continued to remember this miscarriage of justice over time.

The second chapter, by Katherine Watson, examines the case against William Palmer and how his encounters with the judicial system ended badly for him. Palmer appeared to have profited greatly from the deaths of three people, presumed to have been killed by poison, and this resulted in a substantial climate of suspicion being built up against him in the West Midlands locality where he resided. Before proceedings were held against him, Palmer's case demonstrates attempts by the judiciary (and Parliament) to address the prejudice he faced and thus the issues that might prevent a fair trial. This resulted in the passing of 'Palmer's Act', which permitted the case to be moved to London's Central Criminal Court. Whilst this was an act intended to restore the potential for justice to be served, those presiding over the case inadvertently opened up another area where their diligence would unravel. The eventual case against Palmer was potentially over-influenced by the innovative and 'novelty' nature of the forensic evidence offered against him. This last aspect highlights the potential power of new forms of evidence and how the authority they apparently express can be potentially overly persuasive, illusory and prejudicial.

The third chapter, by Helen Rutherford and Clare Sandford-Couch, concerns the trial of the nineteen-year-old youth George Vass, accused of murder in Newcastle in 1863. It was the contention of the defence that the trial and the potential attitude of the jury were both negatively influenced by the pre-trial publicity. In particular, the display of waxen images of Vass throughout the locality of Newcastle persuaded all that encountered them that Vass was obviously a murderer, long before he had been tried and convicted. Moreover, the Vass trial took place alongside the prosecution of a similar case in which the defendant was both found guilty and broke down creating a highly charged atmosphere, since he remained in court whilst Vass was tried. The judge then made remarks linking the two cases together as signifying the disorder that had prevailed on New Year's Eve and the hours just after. As a result, his conduct was potentially compared in court to that of another defendant. In time, both of these anomalies would be closed down by a legal system seeking to prevent the injustice of prejudicial pre-trial publicity.

Niamh Howlin's chapter is the first of two chapters that investigate the operation of the justice system in Ireland and what she calls its 'dysfunction'. Howlin's investigation involves a study of the three trials of Peter Barrett, a man accused of travelling from London to Galway with the intent to assassinate a local landowner in 1869. Against the backdrop of considerable animosity against 'landlordism', the Barrett trial unfolded in ways which produced a stark antipathy to the prosecution. This context influenced public opinion around the composition of the jury that would be empanelled to try him. This had been a longstanding issue in Ireland, where 'packing' such juries could be viewed as exhibiting the will of the ruling power and its local 'representatives'. In the end, Barrett underwent three trials before he attained a final acquittal. This narrative highlights the use of the judicial process as a species of local and national grievance pursued by other means. As such, it highlights the way in which political power and its manifestations can creep into the judicial process, whether through the manipulation of procedures or through the employment of prominent legal counsel who bring their own agenda to proceedings.

Howlin's chapter is followed by Conor Hanley's, which also examines an important trial that again was a consequence of Ireland's Land War. In 1882, five members of the

Joyce family were murdered by ten disguised men who entered a cottage in a remote part of County Mayo. These murders were to become notorious and they resulted in the arrest of a number of individuals implicated in the foul deed. Throughout what transpired, it seems evident that the Crown was determined to secure convictions. It used a number of procedural measures and also eventually transferred the case to Dublin. In the midst of this, the trial is portrayed as having engulfed one individual in the Crown case, Myles Joyce, who many believed was most likely innocent, an opinion formally confirmed over a century later. So successfully had the prosecution case been prepared that it swept up in its process an individual specifically exonerated by those who had admitted their guilt. Yet even here Joyce's fate was only sealed by the refusal of the Lord Lieutenant of Ireland to commute the sentence. The failure to do so, it is argued, was very likely an acute miscarriage of justice, and one only addressed although obviously unsatisfactorily within very recent times.

Lesley Hall's chapter investigates the case against George Bedborough, an instance which uncovers late nineteenth-century England's episodic and inconsistent approach to censorship. This issue was one that could entrap unfortunate individuals and make them become the temporary scapegoats of wider concerns. This was a possibility blatantly embodied in the erratic application of the 1857 Obscene Publications Act to real circumstances. This Act was applied without systematic purpose and was intensely reactive. As such, it was capable of proceeding against seriously intended scientific and other works, every bit as much as it could proceed against genuine pornography. Bedborough was ensnared by a police officer who purchased a copy of Havelock Ellis' *Sexual Inversion*. In truth, Bedborough and Ellis were both idealistic victims of the police and the government's attempts to clamp down on the Watford University Press. This was a shady publishing operation operated by a man subsequently unmasked as a swindler and one who made money from the pornographic potential of any work that might invite such an interpretation. Bedborough, mindful of recent action against other publishers, pleaded guilty to the charge of corrupting the morals of the Queen's subjects. This was an unfortunate outcome for him as he found himself alienated from the radical milieu he had devoted many years of his life to. Whilst subsequent police attention would move on to other targets, the fundamentals of the law's arbitrary application remained, at least temporarily, unresolved.

Anne-Marie Kilday's extended chapter is especially important in the quest to uncover how policing attitudes and methods can fuel unfair trials and miscarriages of justice, so that they acquire a malevolent and prolific life of their own. In this chapter, we discover how it is possible for a single miscarriage of justice to create additional unforeseen and unexpected miscarriages of justice – what we might call the domino effect of an unfair trial. The chapter's focus on the indictment of Oscar Slater for the murder of Marion Gilchrist in 1908 shows that the prosecution's case was profoundly flawed from the start. Indeed, as is noted, it became a byword for miscarriage of justice, at least to the extent that it preoccupied the attention of the renowned Scottish legal commentator William Roughead and others. This was scarcely all though, since when one individual policeman expressed his misgiving upon the direction and outcome of the case, his own treatment by his employer and colleagues exposed the unacceptable culture that existed within the Glasgow Constabulary. Detective-Lieutenant John

Thomson Trench, who questioned the professionalism and, more importantly, the motives behind the conduct of the police investigation, found himself targeted and stigmatized by the actions and words of his fellow officers and others in authority. Indeed it emerges as remarkable just how far the logic of protecting an authority from its own calumnies drove forward decisions and proceedings. Moreover, the creation of a manifestly unfair trial had the inevitable effect of creating a further miscarriage of justice. The culprit of an especially brutal murder remained at large and the public's faith in the effective functioning of their policing authority, and its ability to deliver the basic requirement of public safety, was severely shaken. This case reminds us that the pressures upon public policing, and the many faceted phenomenon of public expectation, could carry agendas forward and spectacularly see them run out of control and crash, with dire consequences for everyone involved.

Some themes about the law's apparent arbitrariness are illuminated in the next chapter in the volume by David Nash. This section of the work investigates how secularist campaigners could use past and present cases to easily indict the Common Law of Blasphemous Libel as inherently capable of producing a manifestly, perhaps even archetypal 'unfair trial'. The chapter shows how this narrative and trope grew during the nineteenth century under the careful and steady guidance of skilful writers and courtroom orators. The zenith of this is examined in a series of cases against three individuals: John William Gott, Thomas Stewart and Ernest Pack at the end of the Edwardian period and just after. These proceedings used past arguments about unfairness and the partial conduct of trials. Indeed, these defendants graphically illuminated how such prosecutions were the product of moral panics and the arbitrary reaction of policing agencies. As such, the work of blasphemers showed such laws and the trials for breaking them to be systematically unfair. Yet, the power of this narrative actively encouraged many to seek prosecution, so that forms of martyrdom before the law came to be viewed as the most effective way of discrediting and eventually ending them.

The final chapter in this collection seeks to subvert the conventional narrative of the court case as the source of an unfair trial. Alyson Brown's chapter is firmly rooted in material from the twentieth century. Arguably it shows the final and full flowering of the notion of public criticism and the directions in which this might potentially lead. The chapter investigates the case against Lillian Goldstein who acquired the soubriquet the 'Bob-Haired Bandit'. Brown argues that the media created this persona by fusing together a number of references which signified fears about the independent woman and her apparently inherent capacity for delinquency. Brown shows that this furore reached such intensity, that Goldstein's morals and lifestyle choices became the subject of ongoing newspaper debate. This occurred at such a pitch, and had such a broad reach, that it resembled a form of 'trial by journalism' which had run spectacularly out of control. Goldstein, although found 'guilty' by this unfair and overheated 'trial by journalism', was to encounter a different reception in the courtroom itself. Whilst convicted by the assize, the judge, conceivably reacting to the harsh treatment she had received at the hands of the press, treated her with a considerable degree of leniency.

In the end, the contents of this book illuminate, and problematize, the ideas and narratives associated with British Justice during a time of great change and uncertainty.

The cases demonstrate a catalogue of responses to what can go wrong, as much as its rational and satisfactory application. Geoffrey Robertson in the conclusion of his legal memoir *The Justice Game* argued that the legal system must be capable of providing the unexpected for it to be credible, and to reassure observers that outcomes are not predetermined.[19] His suggestion was meant to inspire confidence in the law and its search for fair and legitimate outcomes. Yet as this book clearly demonstrates, although the law is scarcely infallible, it can fail defendants, victims and society at large in spectacular manner. However, we should also remember that legal minds and other authorities, to their great credit, have responded and eventually turned their attention to exposing miscarriages of justice by suggesting ways by which they can be prevented and avoided.

---

[19] G. Robertson (1999) *The Justice Game* (London: Vintage), pp. ix–xiv.

1

'A Monstrous Innovation on the Laws': Murder and Double Jeopardy at the Old Bailey

Heather Shore
Manchester Metropolitan University

Introduction

On an evening in May 1827 in Whitechapel, Officer Ebenezer Dalton was called to a lodging in a house in St. Christopher Court, just around the corner from Lambeth Street Police Office. Dalton was greeted by a shocking sight:

> On entering the room I saw the child's head on the table, and a quantity of blood – I searched, and in the corner of the room was a bed, with the body of the child covered with a counterpane; there was a great quantity of blood on the floor, as well as on the table; the head appeared as if it had been cut off with some sharp instrument, which I looked for, but could not find.[1]

This was the first Act in a drama which would unfold at the Old Bailey courtroom over the early summer of 1827, with the initial trial taking place on the 31st of May and a second trial on the 12th of July. The outcome of these trials was that the accused, the father of the child, William Sheen, would be found not guilty for a murder of which he was very likely guilty. The evidence presented at the Old Bailey was largely circumstantial, and even taking into account the Common Law prohibitions against the testimony of spouses, there seems to have been little doubt from contemporaries that Sheen was the murderer.[2]

This case, like the others in this volume, can be seen as a failure of justice. However, unlike most miscarriages of justice, in this case justice worked in the favour

---

A longer and more detailed account of the life and activities of William Sheen and of his extended family can be found in H. Shore (2015) *London's Criminal Underworlds, c.1720–c.1930: A Social and Cultural History* (Basingstoke: Palgrave Macmillan), pp. 93–116.

[1] *Old Bailey Proceedings* (hereafter OBP), Trial of William Sheen, May 1827 (t18270531-14), evidence of Officer Ebenezer Dalton. All *OBP* references are taken from https://www.oldbaileyonline.org (accessed 1 October 2019) the trial (t) number can be used to locate the trial.
[2] C. Manchester (1979) 'Wives as Crown Witnesses', *Cambridge Law Journal*, 37, pp. 249–51.

of the accused: against justice for the victim, against the criminal justice system (the complexities of which created a loophole through which William Sheen gained his freedom). It also acted against the interests of the 'public', who suffered from Sheen being at large and able to pursue a criminal career over the following decades up to his death in 1851. By law, Sheen was not guilty of the crime of which he had been accused. However, Sheen didn't deny the murder although the evidence, whilst circumstantial, was compelling and the balance of probabilities tells us that not only did he commit the murder, but that the court knew this and were not able to do anything to affect the not guilty verdict. What follows is a story about a murder of a child which went unpunished. In part this was due to the machinations of the accused and his immediate family, but mainly it was because of the legal practice of *Autrefois Acquit* or double jeopardy. As Blackstone stated in the eighteenth century, 'The plea of *autrefois acquit*, or a former acquittal, is grounded on this universal maxim of the Common Law of England.'[3] Neither historical cases of double jeopardy or miscarriages of justice have received much attention from crime historians.[4] Certainly, these cases are relatively unusual. However, such cases can have a lasting effect on the development of case law.[5]

This chapter explores the working of the double-jeopardy rule through the case of William Sheen. Sheen's plea of *Autrefois Acquit* was based on a defect in the indictment, which arguably made the case a little more unusual, as we will see in the discussion below. However, what makes the case particularly distinct is the extraordinary set of events that led to the prosecution, and the aftermath of Sheen's acquittal. In this chapter, the ways an apparently ordinary plebeian Londoner (albeit a likely child murderer)[6] managed to exploit the criminal law will be examined. The first section of the chapter will focus on the murder and the manhunt for Sheen, drawing on contemporary press coverage and the first Old Bailey trial. The second section will concentrate on the prosecution, the trials of the 31st of May and 12th of July, and Sheen's plea of *Autrefois Acquit*, leading to the not guilty verdict, and the contemporary response to it. The section entitled 'After the Trials' will consider this verdict in the broader historical context of the double-jeopardy plea, and the place of Rex v. Sheen in Victorian case law. The final section will return to the aftermath of the trials of William Sheen.

---

[3] W. Blackstone's *Commentaries* (at pp. 335–6), cited in S. Broadbridge (2009) 'Double Jeopardy', House of Commons Standard Note: SN/HA/1082, p. 2 available at researchbriefings.files.parliament.uk/documents/SN01082/SN01082.pdf (accessed 2 August 2019).

[4] For miscarriages of justice, see F. Faust (1994) 'Hadley v. Baxendale: An Understandable Miscarriage of Justice', *Journal of Legal History*, 15, pp. 41–72; C. Hilliard (2017) *The Littlehampton Libels: A Miscarriage of Justice* (Oxford: Oxford University Press) and J. Rowbotham (2007) 'Miscarriage of Justice? Postcolonial Reflections on the "Trial" of the Maharajah of Baroda, 1875', *Liverpool Law Review*, 28, 3, pp. 377–403. For double jeopardy, see J. Hunter (1984) 'The Development of the Rule against Double Jeopardy', *Journal of Legal History*, 5, pp. 3–19 and mainly in the US context, J.A. Sigler (1963) 'A History of Double Jeopardy', *The American Journal of Legal History*, 7, 4, pp. 283–309.

[5] See the essays in C. Walker and K. Starmer (1999) (eds) *Miscarriages of Justice: A Review of Justice in Error* (Oxford: Oxford University Press).

[6] According to the 1841 census, Sheen was born in 1801; see the National Archives, Home Office papers (hereafter HO), Hundred: Ossulstone (Tower Division) Parish: Christ Church Spitalfields, Census Returns 1841, HO107/710, book 10.

The murder and arrest of William Sheen

William Sheen 'The Younger' was put on trial at the Old Bailey courtroom on the 31st of May 1827, for the murder his four-month-old child, Charles William Beadle.[6] According to reports, the murder had happened on the 10th of May, at the home of the accused, Christopher's Court, which was off Whitechapel's Lambeth Street. Members of his family lived close by. William (The Younger) and Lydia Beadle had had an illegitimate child in January of 1827. The child, named Charles William Beadle, had been born in the Poorhouse on Lombard Street and baptized in St. George the Martyr.[7] At the time of the birth and baptism, William and Lydia were not married, but were wed later on that year.[8] Newspaper reports noted that a baby had been found at the lodging house of John and Sarah Pomeroy.[9] The evidence of Joseph Corderoy, who had been with Sheen at the King of Prussia Public House (in Blue Anchor Yard), stated that Sheen had been drinking all afternoon. His wife, Lydia, had come to the King of Prussia to find him late afternoon, ' … he was in a very good humour; they went directly, and I went with them to their house'. Corderoy described the Sheens' lodging as a small upstairs room, furnished with a bed. He stayed there until 5.45 pm, and gave evidence that '… his boy was in her arms [his wife] alive and well'. Lydia called for the lodging house-keeper Sarah Pomeroy at 7.30 pm. On entering the room Sarah found the body of the baby, 'I saw a child's head on the table; it stood up, its neck being on the table'. The two women then went to Lambeth Street station, returning with the police officer, Ebenezer Dalton.[10] According to the Saturday edition of the *Morning Chronicle*, 'Yesterday morning the neighbourhood of Lambeth-street was crowded, in consequence of the horrid murder that was committed by William Sheen, upon his child, a little boy four months old. We regret to state, that the inhuman wretch has not yet been apprehended.'[11]

Newspaper reports described how Sheen had told his father that he'd been in a fight with some Irishmen, which had resulted in him stabbing one of them, presumably to explain his bloody appearance. This was confirmed in evidence given later by Sheen's father (William Sheen senior) at the first Old Bailey trial. Sheen senior described how they then went to Carnaby Market to see a friend, Joseph Pugh, from whom they borrowed some money and clean clothes. They also disposed of the clasp-knife which Sheen claimed to have used in his fight. Sheen then sought to avoid capture, by

---

[7] Lombard Street Poor House was located near the Mint in the parish of St. George the Martyr, Southwark. See G. Weight (1840) 'Statistics of St. George the Martyr, Southwark', *Journal of the Statistical Society of London*, 3, 1, pp. 50–71 at p. 53.
[8] See *OBP*, Trial of William Sheen, May 1827 (t18270531-14).
[9] For example, the *Morning Chronicle*, 14th May 1827, p. 3 and the *Morning Post*, 2nd June 1827, p. 1.
[10] Lambeth Police Court records only survive from 1877 (held at the London Metropolitan Archives, hereafter LMA). A coroner's inquest survives; see LMA, Middlesex Sessions' records, Coroner's Inquest, 12th May 1827, MJ/SPC, E 3309. The inquest was held at Whitechapel Workhouse on the 12th of May, *The Times*, 14th May 1827, p. 3.
[11] *Morning Chronicle*, 12th May 1827, p. 4.

leaving London to travel to family who lived in Radnorshire, Wales.[12] Pugh, who was interviewed by the magistrate at Lambeth street immediately after the events, claimed to have thought that Sheen (the younger) had been involved in a quarrel, ' … and that he was desirous of getting out of the way until he could make his peace with the parties with whom he had been engaged'.[13] According to the *Morning Post*, Pugh was a cow-keeper in Carnaby Market, and had known the prisoner from infancy, as they had been brought up together in Radnorshire, South Wales. He told the magistrate, Mr. Wyatt, that Sheen and his father came to him without hats or coats (Sheen had left his 'blood-stained coat' in his lodging room where the murder had taken place), ' … he therefore requested the loan of two coats and hats, and ten shillings, which would enable him to make all things right'.[14] As a result of this evidence a manhunt was raised, with the *Morning Post* noting, ' … all the officers are on the alert for the murderer, who is supposed to have bent his course towards Hertfordshire [probably Herefordshire]'.[15] Sheen headed to Wales, to the area of Radnorshire where he still had family.

The manhunt was led by Robert Davis, a Lambeth Street Officer. How frequently such manhunts took place in this period before the 1829 Metropolitan Police Act, and the 1842 establishment of a detective force, is not known. Whilst David Cox has noted how the Bow Street Runners had a remit beyond London and Middlesex, it is not clear how often officers other than those deployed from Bow Street were able to chase after a suspect like this and there is no evidence that Robert Davis was a Runner.[16] *The Newgate Calendar* gave a more detailed account.[17] In his evidence, Davis explained that he was directed by the magistrate to ' … procure the apprehension of the supposed offender'.[18] He then gave a detailed account of leaving on the Birmingham Coach, towards Herefordshire on the 18th of May, tracking various information and sightings of Sheen till he arrived at Kington, on the border of Herefordshire and Radnorshire. Here he waited for Sheen's arrival, taking care to conceal himself by assuming the smock dress of a countryman. After talking to locals in the public houses of Kington, where he asked questions undercover, he was given information that would lead him and a local constable named Yates, to Lane House in Llanbadenwaur [original spelling],[19] some seventeen miles away.[20] Here he arrested Sheen, who neither denied nor confessed to

---

[12] Davis's 'hunt' for Sheen is described in an account in the Newgate Calendar; see 'William Sheen: Tried for the Murder of His Son', available at http://www.exclassics.com/newgate/ng842.htm (accessed 12 September 2014).
[13] *Morning Chronicle*, 12th May 1827, p. 4.
[14] *Morning Post*, 12th May 1827, p. 3.
[15] Ibid.
[16] D.J. Cox (2010) *A Certain Share of Low Cunning: A History of the Bow Street Runners, 1792–1839* (Abingdon: Willan), pp. 144–56. See also, J.M. Beattie (2012) *The First English Detectives: The Bow Street Runners and the Policing of London, 1750–1840* (Oxford: Oxford University Press).
[17] It is not clear whether this was published in a second edition of the A. Knapp and W. Baldwin (1826) *The Newgate Calendar* (London: J. Robins) or Anonymous (1834) *The Annals of Crime and the Newgate Calendar* (London: Berger).
[18] 'William Sheen: Tried for the Murder of His Child'.
[19] Ibid. The farm/building in which Sheen was apprehended belonged to the Sheen extended family, and descendants of the Sheen family remain in this area (private email correspondence with Mark Midega-Faulknall, a descendant of one of Sheen's siblings).
[20] OBP, Trial of William Sheen, May 1827 (t18270531-14).

the murder. When asked by Mr Wyatt, the magistrate at Worship Street, where he was giving evidence, Davis stated:

> Sheen had made no confession to him directly, but that he heard him make one indirectly to the landlady of a public-house in Radnor, to whom he was known, and who asked him, 'How, in the name of God, came you to do such a cruel thing?' and he replied, 'It was not God, but the devil.'[21]

On the journey back from Radnorshire to London, there was little communication between Davis and Sheen, according to the former. The Old Bailey counsel, Mr Clarkson, asked whether any threat or promise was made to the prisoner (presumably to confess to the crime), but Davis noted merely that he heard Sheen say, 'Oh my poor mother, when she knows I am taken it will break her heart.' Contemporary accounts give a strong sense of the febrile atmosphere engendered by the manhunt, and the case was reported in both the London and provincial papers. The *Lancaster Gazetter*, for example, included a report from the Lambeth Street Office, which described the crowds waiting at the police office for Davis's return with the accused. Davis had sent a letter ahead, to say that he had Sheen in custody:

> At ten o'clock Davis had not arrived with his prisoner, and the Magistrates were about to Leave the office, when a coach drove up amid loud yelling and the execrations of the multitude: and in a few minutes Sheen was brought into the office. He is a good-looking man, and stood very firm, but there was a convulsive movement in his eye.[22]

The prosecution

First Trial

The trial opened on the 31st of May 1827. In the *Morning Post*, William Sheen is described as ' ... a good-looking young man, of florid complexion, and was respectfully dressed. When called upon to plead, he said he recollected nothing about it. He eventually pleaded *Not Guilty*.'[23] One of the key witnesses at the trial was his father, William Sheen senior. The *Morning Post* report noted, 'The witness appeared in a state of extreme agitation and wept bitterly.'[24] Sheen senior repeated much of the story that had already been told by the police officer Dalton and by the witness Joseph Pugh. In addition, he described his son's marriage to Lydia and the birth of his grandchild suggesting, ' ... he had been married about five weeks – I suppose his wife had had the child about two or three months before ... I did not know the name of the

---

[21] Ibid.
[22] *Lancaster Gazette*, 19th May 1827, p. 2.
[23] *Morning Post*, 2nd June 1827, p. 1.
[24] Ibid.

child till after it was dead'. Describing Lydia as a 'bad character', Sheen Senior showed little empathy for his daughter-in-law or the child.[25]

At some point in the proceedings a fustian coat, covered in blood and apparently belonging to Sheen, was submitted for evidence by the Lambeth Street officer Robert Davis. He explained how he had known the prisoner previously and had seen him wearing the coat. There is a lack of consistency between the Old Bailey proceedings and the press accounts, as to whether or not the coat was found at the scene of the crime.[26] However, it certainly caused a stir in the courtroom; a *Morning Chronicle* account from the 2nd of June noted, ' … its appearance excited universal horror in the court'.[27] Various other witnesses testified and were cross-examined by Clarkson, Sheen's defence counsel, who could ' … elicit nothing in favour of the prisoner'.[28] Towards the end of the witness testimony Sarah Pomeroy, the Sheens' landlady, was recalled and asked about her knowledge of the victim. It was at this point that the confusion around the child's name seems to have arisen. The original indictment had named the child Charles William Sheen. However, as a result of his illegitimate birth, his name at baptism was Charles William Beadle.[29] Moreover, Sheen was charged by the Coroner's Inquisition for the 'Wilful Murder of Charles William Beadle'. This confusion over the naming of the victim meant that Mr Clarkson (Sheen's defence counsel) called for a fresh indictment:

> The deceased child having been born out of wedlock had, in law, no name, consequently, if it had not by reputation acquired the name stated either in the indictment or inquisition, the case could not be supported, and that the certificate produced was not sufficiently shown to have been that of the deceased.[30]

At this stage there was clearly some debate between the judges and the counsel, not least as to what verdict should be brought. It was agreed that the confusion over the name of the infant could be ' … fatal to the indictment', but that Sheen would be subject to another indictment. The eventual decision was to find *Not Guilty* because of a legal technicality; an order to prefer a fresh indictment was made, Sheen was detained and the witnesses were bound over.[31]

---

[25] The *Morning Chronicle*, 2nd June 1827, did comment that Sheen senior was visibly upset: 'The poor father was exceedingly affected during the whole time he was under examination, and on quitting the Court he grasped his son's hand, and both burst into tears. The scene had a great effect upon the Court.'

[26] OBP, Trial of William Sheen, May 1827 (t18270531-14) and *Morning Chronicle*, 2nd June 1827, p. 4.

[27] *Morning Chronicle*, 2nd June 1827, p. 4.

[28] Sheen had originally been without any counsel. By this period, at least in cases of murder, it was the practice to be represented by a member of the Old Bailey Counsel, in this case William Clarkson. See A.N. May (2003) *The Bar and the Old Bailey, 1750–1850* (Chapel Hill, NC: The University of North Carolina Press), pp. 51–3.

[29] F.A. Carrington and J. Payne (1827) *Reports of Cases Argued and Ruled at Nisi Prius, in the Courts of King's Bench, Common Please, and Exchequer, Together with Cases Tried on the Circuits and at the Old Bailey* (London: S. Sweet and R. Pheney), p. 637 and W.O. Russell and C.S. Greaves (1843) *A Treatise on Crimes and Misdemeanours*, Vol. 1 (London: Saunders and Benning), pp. 832–4.

[30] OBP, Trial of William Sheen, May 1827 (t18270531-14).

[31] Ibid.

Second Trial and Autrefois Acquit

Unsurprisingly, there was some concern expressed in the press with regard to the potential outcome of the next trial. A report in *The Times*, for instance, feared that the accused would ' ... escape the hands of justice', and indeed the newspaper was already speculating that Sheen might plead *autre fois acquit*.[32] Such fears were not unjustified. The second trial took place on the 12th of July.[33] As the *Morning Chronicle* noted, 'The Court was crowded at a very early hour this morning, in consequence of its being generally understood that William Sheen would be tried for the murder of his child. The case still seemed to excite great interest.'[34] *The Standard* compared it to the 'Singular Analogous Case', of Lewis Houssart, who was prosecuted in 1724 for the murder of his wife Anne. In this case, there had been a similar problem with the spelling of the name of the accused (this time) on the indictment, and confusion between 'Lewis' and 'Louis'.[35]

Given this heated speculation about Sheen's case, the prosecution had worked hard to present the case in such a way as to meet any possible legal objections, by wording the count in thirteen different forms in the indictment: 'a male bastard child only', 'a male bastard child, called and known by the name of Charles William – William – Billy – Charles', 'a male child called and known by the name of William Sheen', 'a male child, whose name is unknown', and 'a male bastard child, whose name is unknown'.[36] Sheen's counsel Clarkson was out of town, but he had obviously received legal advice as to his position and to the process of autrefois acquit. After the indictment had been read, Sheen himself presented a written plea, in which he argued:

> That he has been before indicted, tried and acquitted, as well on that Indictment as on the Coroner's Inquest, at the last Session held in this place, for the murder of the same child as described in the present indictment; and that the same child was as well known by the name and description as contained in that Indictment and Inquest, as it is in the present Indictment.[37]

This was a plea of *Autrefois Acquit* (previously acquitted), and even though it had been written 'informally' and submitted on 'a small piece of paper', the court made the decision to allow time to submit a formal plea.[38] As a result, the case was adjourned to allow the more formal presentation of the plea. The trial resumed the next day (when Mr. Clarkson seems to have returned) and most of the evidence given in the trial was focused on the identity of the victim, with the discrepancy resting on whether the child was known as Beadle or Sheen. The prosecution produced evidence of the registry of birth for Charles William Beadle, son of Lydia Beadle, and evidence

---

[32] *The Times*, 7th June 1827.
[33] OBP, Trial of William Sheen, May 1827 (t18270531-14) and *Morning Chronicle*, 14th July 1827.
[34] *Morning Chronicle*, 14th July 1827, p. 1.
[35] *The Standard*, 11th July 1827, p. 3.
[36] OBP, Trial of William Sheen, May 1827 (t18270531-14) and *The Times*, 14th June 1827.
[37] *Morning Chronicle*, 14th July 1827.
[38] *The Times*, 13th July 1827 and *The Standard*, 11th July 1827.

from a Mrs Cable, a matron from Willis's poor-house where Lydia had given birth. As Justice Burrough put it to the Jury, 'The question for the jury to determine was, whether the child was known as Charles William Beedle [sic] as well as by the name of Sheen; if that was their opinion, then it was favourable to the prisoner.' Eventually, the jury found: ' ... that the child was as well known by the name of Charles William Beadle, as any other name'.[39] As a result this – and the fact that Sheen had previously been acquitted for the murder of both Charles William Beadle and Charles William Sheen – double jeopardy came into play and Sheen was discharged.[40] The prosecutor Sergeant Andrews had explained to the jury, ' ... that they were impanneled [sic] to decide a question which was one of the greatest novelties in the history of our law, and which he had never before heard of during the many years he had been in practice, and it showed that every endeavour had been made by the laws to protect human life' – in this case, Sheen's life.[41]

It was an extraordinary verdict and provoked considerable outrage. There is no evidence that the police suspected anyone else of the crime, and indeed the evidence, even though it was circumstantial, was damning. A surviving letter from the poet and novelist Emily Eden to her friend Miss Villiers noted that 'I am so disgusted with our foolish laws which could not hang, could not even punish, that William Sheen'.[42] A satirical commentary on the aftermath of the trials was published in *The Examiner*, 'A BALL has been given in Rosemary Lane in Honour of the Law of England, on the occasion of the acquittal of Sheen, who lately cut his child's head off.'[43] This referred to a party which was held in the house (in White's Yard, Rosemary Lane) of Sheen senior, which led to complaints by the neighbours.[44] As *The Examiner's* lengthy commentary noted:

> We see that the guilty escapes, and that such as man as SHEEN is let loose on society. Words are things indeed; and we may slay our fellow-creatures with impunity, provided there be some little confusion about their exact names. We are aware that in these remarks we have committed a great imprudence – we have not spoken of SHEEN with the caution of our contemporaries, as the alleged murderer, but have hinted that he actually did cut his child's head off, whatever may be the quality of that action. Thus according to law, we may have written a wicked and malignant libel on that worthy man .... if SHEEN did not cut the child's head off, some one else did, and why does not justice seek to discover the murderer? If it does not seek him, because it is satisfied that SHEEN and no other did cut the child's head off,

---

[39] *The Standard*, 14th July 1827 and *OBP*, Trial of William Sheen, May 1827 (t18270531-14) and (t18270712-36).
[40] The child was buried in St Mary's, Whitechapel. The burial can be found at LMA: Greater London Burial Index, City of London Burials 1754–1855, 'Sheen, Charles William, 4 m, Workhouse (Child's head removed from body by the father WILLIAM SHEEN)', 16th May 1827, P60.531 HAN.
[41] *Morning Chronicle*, 16th July 1827, p. 4.
[42] Letter from Miss Eden to Miss Villiers, from Bigod, Essex, July 1827 found in E. Eden (1919) *Miss Eden's Letters, Edited by her Great Niece, Violet Dickenson* (London: Macmillan), p. 137.
[43] *The Examiner*, 22nd July 1827, p. 2.
[44] *The Standard*, 17th July 1827 and Shore, *London's Criminal Underworlds*, p. 99.

how can we be punished for merely imputing to a man an action which have just seen in not punishable by the peculiar justice of the country.[45]

Arguably it was a specific legal climate that led to the confusion, and ultimately, to the miscarriage of justice that this case represents. During the early nineteenth century, the law was undergoing significant change. In particular, the reform of this era was characterized by restrictions on the death penalty, a significant ideological shift which Jeremy Horder has described as a 'strong body of support for liberal-progressive thinking about criminal law reform both inside and outside the House of Commons'.[46] This was reflected in the setting up of the 1819 Select Committee on Criminal Laws, which would make a number of recommendations which were acted on over the following decade or so.[47] The year before Sheen's trial had seen the passage of the Criminal Law Act (1826), which consolidated a large number of changes to criminal procedure. The decade had also seen the repeal of a number of capital sentences, and in particular the passage of the Judgment of Death Act in 1823, which gave judges the discretion to refrain from actually pronouncing sentence of death upon the great majority of the capital offenders whom they knew they were going to pardon.

Whilst the 1820s can be seen as a climate of reform, this didn't necessarily lead to a more liberal approach to those who were sentenced to death. As Simon Devereaux has demonstrated, there was a critical resurgence of the death penalty in the 1820s. This resurgence was not focused on murder (or on forgery, as it had been up to around 1821) but rather on burglary, robbery and theft in a dwelling. However, Devereaux points out that the revival of the death penalty 'was administered with more critical rigour and restraint than had prevailed on comparable occasions'.[48] The prevailing movement against capital punishment led to restraint by the authorities even in these years of revival. Behind this was the movement to reform the law, to remove the worst abuses of the discretionary system and to address the inadequacies of the criminal law. There were also increasing moves to ensure a fair trial, including the representation of poor prisoners. At the Old Bailey, the sheriffs of London and Middlesex could intervene in cases to provide counsel for prisoners who would otherwise have been unrepresented from at least the early 1820s. Sheen was one of the cases (allocated to William Clarkson), and indeed, according to David Bentley, this intervention by the sheriffs tended to be confined to murder cases.[49] What this tells us is that Sheen was tried in a period in which there was some anxiety about the criminal law, and in particular about the application of the death sentence. All this may have worked in Sheen's favour. Certainly, the evidence of the multiple versions of the indictment which were drawn up after the initial trial would suggest that the need to get it right and to be

---

[45] *The Examiner*, 22nd July 1827, p. 2.
[46] J. Horder (2012) *Homicide and the Politics of Law Reform* (Oxford: Oxford University Press), p. 10.
[47] Parliamentary Papers, *Select Committee on Criminal Laws Relating to Capital Punishment in Felonies: Report, Minutes of Evidence, Appendix*, 1819, 585, VIII 1 (SC 1819).
[48] S. Devereaux (2017) 'Execution and Pardon at the Old Bailey 1730–1837', *American Journal of Legal History*, 57, pp. 447–94, at p. 489.
[49] D. Bentley (1998) *English Criminal Justice in the Nineteenth Century* (London: Hambledon Press), p. 123, also p. 135 on *R v Sheen* (1827).

seen to have acted within the law was paramount. Ultimately, of course, this strategy failed, and Sheen was acquitted of the murder of his child.

After the trials

According to the contemporary edition of Burn's *Justice of the Peace and Parish Officer* Manual of 1831, *Autrefois Acquit* (more commonly known as 'double-jeopardy') was '… a plea by a person indicted of a treason or felony that he was heretofore acquitted of the same treason or felony, for one shall not be brought into danger of his life for the same offence more than once'.[50] Double jeopardy had been a basic principle of the English criminal justice system since the thirteenth century. In the seventeenth century, it was not attached to the trial until the jury had delivered their verdict. At this point new evidence might be presented.[51] It is important to recognize that in this earlier period, there was also no presumption of innocence and no right to remain silent. Defendants were expected to establish their innocence by disproving the evidence against them. By the early nineteenth century, however this was shifting, and treatises by both Jeremy Bentham and Cesare Beccaria had argued against established precedent and instead for a system where the innocence of the accused was the default position, and for guilt to be proven.[52] By 1827, Sheen benefitted from this system, where the court made sure a counsel was found to defend him and, despite the evidence (albeit some of which was circumstantial in character) and public feeling against Sheen, the Court followed procedure and had little option but to recognize Sheen's plea based on a defective indictment.

How common have such cases been historically? Infrequently seems to be the answer. Moreover, successful pleas of *Autrefois Acquit* are unusual, and indeed Sheen's case has often been invoked in treatises on law, since the early nineteenth century, as an example.[53] Rex v. Sheen would pass into case law and would feature in discussions of legal precedent over the course of the century. After the initial response to the verdict, a more academic discussion of the case would appear in legal texts. For example, in 1836 Sheen's case was referred to in the case of Rex v. Plant and Birchenough at the Chester Assizes, and in 1837, in the case of Rex v. Parry, Rea and Wright at the Oxford

---

[50] R. Burn (1831 edition) *The Justices of the Peace and Parish Officer* (London: S. Sweet), p. 296.
[51] J. Hostettler (2009) *A History of Criminal Justice in England and Wales* (Hook: Waterside Press), pp. 234–5.
[52] J. Bentham (1827 edition) *Rationale of Judicial Evidence as Applied to English Practice* [edited by J.S. Mill] (London: Hunt and Clarke) and C. Beccaria (1764), *Dei Delitti e Delle Pene [On Crimes and Punishments]* (London: R. Bell). For more on the presumption of innocence, see B.P. Smith (2005) 'The Presumption of Guilt and the English Law of Theft, 1750–1850', *Law and History Review*, 23, 1, pp. 133–71 and B.P. Smith (2005) 'Did the Presumption of Innocence Exist in Summary Proceedings', *Law and History Review*, 23, 1, pp. 191–9.
[53] J. Sprack (2011 edition) *A Practical Approach to Criminal Procedure* (Oxford: Oxford University Press), p. 287 and T. Sergeant and C.J. Lowber (1839) *Reports of Cases Argued and Determined in the English Courts of Common Law* (Philadelphia: Atwood and Culve), p. 299.

Circuit Assize.[54] In the former case, the prisoner Thomas Birchenough was charged with being present, aiding and abetting at the murder of the child of the accused, Louisa Plant. Whilst Plant was found guilty of murder, Birchenough was acquitted on the grounds that he was not present at the time of the murder. However, sufficient evidence proved that Birchenough had been with Plant when they brought the poison which killed the child, had cohabited with Plant and had been in the house when the murder took place. This resulted in a second indictment of Birchenough as accessory before the fact. It was at this point that his counsel, Mr. Cottingham, argued that because he had been acquitted of murder in the first count, it was not possible to then find him guilty as an accessory. He drew on Rex v. Sheen to argue his case, although as one of the other barristers pointed out, in that case the offences charged had been the same in both indictments.[55]

In the following decades, Rex v. Sheen would be similarly drawn on in legal handbooks, including handbooks on statute law and treatises on crimes – for example, in Carrington and Payne's *Report of Cases Argued and Ruled at Nisi Prius* (1833) and Archbold's *A Complete Practical Treatise on Criminal Procedure* (1860).[56] In the United States, the author Francis Wharton drew extensively on the Sheen case in his *Precedents of Indictments and Pleas, Adapted to the Use Both of the Courts of the United States and Those of All the Several States*, published in 1849.[57]

At the Old Bailey, cases of *Autrefois Acquit* were rare. Across the period of 1674 to 1913, for which we can search the digitized Old Bailey Proceedings, we find that twenty-five cases involved a reference to *autre fois acquit* (or *Autrefois Acquit*) including Sheen's case. Around half of them resulted in a not guilty verdict. All but four of the cases took place after 1827, presumably as a result of the growth of adversarial justice and defence counsel.[58] These cases involved a broad range of crimes, including not only the murder and manslaughter cases already mentioned, but also embezzlement, breaking the peace, conspiracy, fraud, animal theft, coining, rape and arson besides other offences. There are three murders and one manslaughter. Two of the men (Sheen and one other) charged with murder were found not guilty, and one was found guilty but for the lesser crime of manslaughter.[59] The individual prosecuted for manslaughter, Charles Henry Banks, an 'amateur' male midwife, had been found guilty of the manslaughter of a newborn child in 1911.[60] There is some suggestion that double jeopardy was used more

---

[54] F.A. Carrington and J. Payne (1837) *Reports of Cases Argued and Ruled at Nisi Prius, in the Courts of Kings Bench, Common Pleas, & Exchequer; Together with Cases Tried on the Circuits and in the Central Criminal Court* (London: S. Sweet), p. 578 and p. 845.

[55] Ibid.

[56] F.A. Carrington and J. Payne (1833) *Reports of Cases Argued and Ruled at Nisi Prius, in the Courts of King's Bench & Common Pleas, and on the Circuit* (London: S. Sweet), p. 153 and p. 339 and J.F. Archbold (1860) *A Complete Practical Treatise on Criminal Procedure, Pleading and Evidence, in Indictable Cases, Vol. 1* (London: Banks and Brothers), p. 364 and p. 403.

[57] F. Wharton (1849) *Precedents of Indictments and Pleas, Adapted to the Use Both of the Courts of the United States and Those of All the Several States* (London: J. Kay), p. 11 and pp. 659–60.

[58] Hostettler, *A History of Criminal Justice*, p. 167.

[59] See, *OBP*, Trial of David Roche, December 1775 (t17751206-25); *OBP*, Trial of William Sheen, May 1827 (t18270712-36); *OBP*, Trial of Antonio Salvi, October 1857 (t18571026-1125) and *OBP*, Trial of Charles Henry Banks, June 1911 (t19110627-56).

[60] *OBP*, Trial of Charles Henry Banks, June 1911 (t19110627-56).

commonly in offences involving financial deception of some form or another. Nine out of the twenty-five cases related to fraud, coining, forgery or embezzlement. In the 1912 case of twenty-two-year-old Frederick Arthur Golding, who was indicted on four counts (larceny, forgery, fraud, mail theft) relating to the theft, forging and uttering of a cheque, the defence counsel Mr McDonald attempted to raise the plea of *Autrefois Acquit*, 'submitting that prisoner had virtually been tried upon the same charge yesterday and acquitted by the jury'. However, the judge refused to accept the plea.[61] It may be that crimes of financial impropriety were more likely to involve multiple indictments and hence more opportunities for using the plea.

Finally, there are a number of examples of Sheen's case passing into popular evocations of the law. For example, in August 1827, at the Lambeth Street Police Court, a girl named Sarah Susannah Martha Davis applied for a warrant against her mother for 'treating her in the most barbarous manner'.[62] The accusation was taken seriously, and the mother was apprehended by an officer named Norris.[63] The girl, who was aged fourteen, was described as bearing very clear evidence of violence from the mother; it was noted that, ' ... she was in positive apprehension of her life, as her mother had been constantly declaring she would serve her as Sheen did his child'.[64] Interestingly the girl and mother lived in Rosemary Lane, so it is possible that they were acquainted with the Sheen family. In court, this prompted a discussion about Sheen's case. Norris noted how a dangerous idea existed amongst the people of White's-Yard (near Rosemary Lane, where Sheen senior lived), that an illegitimate child, or one with a number of names, could be murdered without any fear of punishment. Mr Wyatt (the sitting magistrate) responded, 'I fear that Sheen's acquittal will generate much immorality.'[65] In September 1827 a forty-one-year-old woman named Mary Wittenback was accused of murdering her husband, by poisoning him.[66] In the run-up to the trial, she had apparently drawn on Sheen's case to argue that there was a comparable problem with the indictment, 'Between the time of her committal to Newgate and that of her trial, she frequently adverted to the case of Sheen, and seemed to think that in her case there would be a discrepancy in the evidence with respect to the Christian name of her late husband'.[67] Whether or not Mary tried to use the plea at her trial isn't apparent from the Old Bailey account; she was found guilty at the Old Bailey and executed on the 17th of September 1827.[68] Finally, in September 1830, the *Poor Man's Guardian* published a column titled, 'Horrible Injustice of the Criminal Law', in which they pointed out that in the last seven years no less than seventeen people had been executed in England for sheep-stealing, while Sheen was acquitted of murder, not because there was any doubt that he'd cut his child's head off, but because of the faulty indictment: 'A miserable

---

[61] OBP, Trial of Frederick Arthur Golding, February 1912 (t19120227-22a).
[62] *The Standard*, 16th August 1827, p. 1.
[63] This may have been John Norris, a Bow Street officer who appears frequently giving evidence at the Old Bailey in the 1820s.
[64] *The Standard*, 16th August 1827, p. 1.
[65] Ibid.
[66] OBP, Trial of Mary Wittenback, September 1827 (t18270913-9).
[67] *Morning Post*, 20th September 1827, p. 4.
[68] *The Times*, 17th September 1827, p. 2.

technicality saves the paricide [sic], while the unfortunate man who steals a sheep (to which he is perhaps driven by sheer necessity) is hanged by the neck like a dog.'[69]

Aftermath

For William Sheen, and for his family, life after 1827 would be characterized by significant encounters with the police and the criminal justice system. Tentative evidence suggests that the Sheens already had a reputation for trouble prior to the murder. What is clear though is that the notoriety afforded to Sheen after this period both extended to his family (particularly his mother Ann) and resulted in his own criminality becoming rather more visible. As Sheen himself apparently complained in 1842, during an appearance in front of the Worship Street magistrate:

> Your policemen can all tell you that there's not a more peaceable man alive than I am, if they will only let me alone; but wherever I appear, they call out, 'There goes the murderer!' and I have not had a moment's peace or rest since the hour it happened. It would have been a mercy if they had hung me up at the time and put an end to me at once; my heart is broken. – [The prisoner here covered his face with his hands, and his muscular frame was apparently convulsed for some minutes].[70]

Sheen's protestations demonstrate a remarkable lack of remorse, given the evolution of his 'criminal career' in the decade or so since 1827. Between that year and 1847, William Sheen would appear at the magistrates' court, at the Middlesex Sessions, Clerkenwell and at the Old Bailey, as accused and witness. At various times, Ann Sheen, his brother John and his daughter would also appear as witnesses (and in Ann's case, the accused) in criminal trials. A more detailed account of the Sheens' activities over the 1830s and 1840s can be found elsewhere.[71] However, it's worth noting here that Sheen was more often discharged than found guilty. His appearances at the local Police Courts (at Lambeth Street or Worship Street) frequently related to violence, and often involved participants who were considered as equally guilty, resulting in a discharge, fine or being bound over to keep the peace. For example, in 1835 Sheen appeared at Lambeth Street for threatening the life of his father with a knife, which he said he would run into his body. Apparently, father and son had argued about the possession of one of their houses. The *Morning Chronicle* report noted:

> SHEEN AGAIN -. Yesterday, William Sheen, who been committed from this office some years since, on a charge of cutting off the head of his infant son, and who subsequently escaped that justice which his crime deserved, by a misnomer in the indictment.[72]

---

[69] *Poor Man's Guardian*, 29th September 1832, p. 6.
[70] *The Standard*, 16th September 1842.
[71] Shore, *London's Criminal Underworlds*, pp. 99–116.
[72] *Morning Chronicle*, 29th November 1834, p. 4.

Sheen then had gained a strange form of criminal celebrity, known variously as 'Sheen the infanticide' or the man who ' ... cut his child's head off'.[73] As we saw above, Sheen himself commented on his notoriety, and the family more broadly would be known as 'infamously notorious'.[74] Ruth Penfold-Mounce has suggested that 'notoriety' can be a resource, for those who crave 'well-knownness', arguing that in the case of some modern criminals, an 'underworld exhibitionist' status was developed.[75] In the case of William Sheen, his notoriety was not something he could escape from, although ultimately it did not dissuade him from criminal activity, nor did it seem to make that much difference to how the court dealt with him.

After being acquitted, discharged or bound over in the cases for which he was accused, in 1837 Sheen would finally fall foul of the law resulting in a conviction. This was in relation to a case involving accusations of running a disorderly house with young boys and girls. The case was brought by a voluntary organization, the London Society for the Protection of Young Females and the Prevention of Juvenile Prostitution, which had been founded in 1835 as part of the London City Mission. Its particular mission was to focus on the suppression of brothels and disorderly houses.[76] The case involved the abduction of a fourteen-year-old girl from Stepney named Maria Eagan. A report on 'Juvenile Prostitution', published in *The Champion* newspaper in March 1837, claimed that Maria had been ' ... decoyed to one of the numerous brothels in the neighbourhood'. A search had been carried out by her friends, which it was discovered, ' ... that she had been detained at a house in Wentworth-street, Whitechapel, – a brothel kept by a relative of the notorious Sheen, who some years since cut his child's head off'.[77] She was found by her uncle, who on searching the rooms where she had been kept, found twelve or fourteen girls who had been kept for the purpose of prostitution. As a result, the family ' ... applied to the London Society for the Prevention of Juvenile Prostitution for advice and protection'.[78] The Society worked with the local police to suppress Sheen's brothels. In the early morning of the 2nd of June, a party of Lambeth Street officers gained entry to Sheen's house, finding nine females and ten males ' ... lying indiscriminately and three-four, and five in a bed', who were then taken into custody.[79] Local police officers provided further evidence at the trial, stating that ' ... a number of juvenile thieves who infested many of the streets of the metropolis were harboured at the house of Sheen, and that the produce of their plunder passed through his hands'.[80]

---

[73] *The Examiner*, 22nd June 1834; *The Champion*, 2nd April 1837, p. 36 and *Reynold's Newspaper*, 27th October 1850, p. 8, for example.

[74] *Morning Chronicle*, 4th March 1840.

[75] R. Penfold-Mounce (2009) *Celebrity Culture and Crime: The Joy of Transgression* (Basingstoke: Palgrave Macmillan), p. 88.

[76] H. Shore (1999) *Artful Dodgers: Youth and Crime in Nineteenth Century London* (Woodbridge: Boydell), pp. 140–1. See also M.J.D. Roberts (2004) *Making English Morals: Voluntary Associations and Moral Reform in England, 1787–1886* (Cambridge: Cambridge University Press), p. 159.

[77] *The Champion*, 26th March 1837.

[78] *The Times*, 25th March 1837.

[79] *The Times*, 2nd June 1837.

[80] *Morning Chronicle*, 2nd June 1837.

Sheen was placed on remand in the New Prison, Clerkenwell. In a letter to the Lambeth Street magistrates from the 10th of June, Sheen attempted to plead his case:

I, William Sheen ... desirous (by God grace) of extricating myself from such abominable mode of living, do most humbly beg your worships to allow me to enter into my own recognizance, to abstain from such a course for the future, assuring you, gentlemen, I will have nothing more to do with lodging-house-keeping, but will, from henceforth, endeavour to get my living in a kindly upright way.[81]

He asked to be sent to his 'respectable' relations in Radnorshire who 'would be glad to receive me with open arms', so he could 'seek a refuge among my friends in the country, and endeavour to live a different life for the future'. He was encouraged by the prison chaplain David Ruell, who provided a supportive statement.[82] Sheen's pleas fell on deaf ears however, and his petition was not allowed. He stayed in New Prison until his trial.

The report of Sheen's trial at the Middlesex sessions noted that around twenty boys and ten girls had been found at the house, ' ... the boys were encouraged in picking pockets, and the wretched girls were made victims of the greatest depravity'.[83] Sheen was found guilty and sentenced to eighteen months' imprisonment with hard labour.[84] Richard Gregory, the treasurer of Spitalfields parish and a member of the society, would later brief a Police Select Committee reviewing this case. Describing the raid on Sheen's houses he noted: ' ... we took 18 boys and girls out of those houses, some of them very young, three weeks ago'.[85]

Whilst this would not be the last time Sheen encountered the criminal justice system, it was one of the only two occasions in which he received a sentence of imprisonment. The last would be in 1847, when he was sentenced to twelve months' imprisonment after being found guilty of an aggravated assault on his Common-Law wife, Mary Anne Sullivan.[86] This would be Sheen's final appearance in the criminal record. He died in December 1851, and his death was widely reported in the press. The *Northern Star* reported: 'DEATH OF SHEEN THE INFANTICIDE'.[87] Reports were also printed in *The Era*, *The Examiner*, the *Hampshire Telegraph and Sussex Chronicle*, the *Manchester Times*, the *Preston Guardian* and many other provincial newspapers.[88] To some extent, this may have resulted from the syndication of metropolitan news to

---

[81] *The Times*, 10th June 1837.
[82] Ibid.
[83] *Morning Chronicle*, 29th June 1837.
[84] *The Times*, 28th June 1837.
[85] Parliamentary Papers, *Select Committee on Metropolis Police Offices. Report, Minutes of Evidence, Appendix, Index*, 1837, 451, XII, p. 176. See also, *The Times*, 13th November 1838.
[86] Shore, *London's Criminal Underworlds*, pp. 112–13.
[87] *The Northern Star*, 27th December 1851.
[88] *The Era*, 21st December 1851; *The Examiner*, 27th December 1851; *Hampshire Telegraph and Sussex Chronicle*, 27th December 1851; *Manchester Times*, 27th December 1851; *Preston Guardian*, 27th December 1851 and *The Northern Star*, 27th December 1851. He was buried at St Mary's, Whitechapel; see LMA, Greater London Burial Index, City of London Burials 1754–1855, 24th December 1851, P60.531 HAN.

the provincial presses. However, it does seem likely that the reputation of Sheen had reached beyond London. Not surprisingly, the accounts of his death all referred back to the murder case of 1827, and most commented on his notoriety, both as a result of that case and in the following years.[89] As *The Standard* noted:

> The life so spared, however, has since been a most miserable one, and he has many times, even in the presence of the magistrates, expressed a wish that he had been hanged, for upon every slight occasion his neighbours taunted him with his great crime. He became utterly ferocious, although cowardly, and has been many times imprisoned for acts of violence, brothel keeping, and felonies.[90]

Conclusion

In a 2009 briefing note for the House of Commons, Sally Broadbridge explained the rule of double jeopardy, 'It is a general principle of English law that a person may not be tried twice for the same offence, whether he was acquitted on the first occasion (*Autrefois Acquit*) or convicted (*Autrefois Convict*)', which has been established as part of Common Law for many centuries.[91] Here Broadbridge was reflecting on the reversal of the principle during the early 2000s. The Stephen Lawrence case had been the initial cause for a reconsideration of the principle. In that notorious case, the murder suspects were arrested and charged with murder, but the charges were dropped in July 1993, as the Crown Prosecution Service cited insufficient evidence. A private prosecution was initiated by the Lawrence family in April 1994, which ran until April 1996, and resulted in the acquittal of Gary Dobson, Neil Acourt and Luke Knight (charges against Jamie Acourt and David Norris had been dropped earlier in the proceedings). After this trial, the Home Secretary ordered an enquiry into the events, to be headed by Sir William Macpherson. The Macpherson report of 1999 recommended that the double-jeopardy rule should be relaxed in murder cases, if new evidence became available. As the report noted:

> In the context of this case, whether the law which absolutely protects those who have been acquitted from any further prosecution for the same or a closely allied offence should prevail. If, even at this late stage, fresh and viable evidence should emerge against any of the three suspects who were acquitted, they could not be tried again however strong the evidence might be. We simply indicate that perhaps in modern conditions such absolute protection may sometimes lead to injustice. Full and appropriate safeguards would be essential. Fresh trials after acquittal

---

[89] *Manchester Times*, 27th December 1851.
[90] *The Standard*, 22nd December 1851, p. 1.
[91] Broadbridge, 'Double Jeopardy', p. 2.

would be exceptional. But we indicate that at least the issue deserves debate and reconsideration perhaps by the Law Commission, or by Parliament.[92]

This finding was broadly accepted in legal quarters, and in 2001 was given support by a Law Commission Report, 'Double Jeopardy and Prosecution Appeals'.[93] This report not only recognized the emergence of 'new evidence' or 'newly discovered facts', but also referred to the finding of a fundamental defect in first trials as a rationale for reversing the double-jeopardy rule.[94] The Criminal Justice Act of 2003 implemented the recommendations of both Macpherson and the Law Commissioners, with a new provision opening murder and other serious crimes to a second prosecution.[95] Gary Dobson and David Norris were arrested and charged in September 2010. Whilst Norris's charges had previously been dropped (in other words, he'd not been acquitted), Keir Starmer, the Director of Public Prosecution, applied for Dobson's original acquittal to be quashed, in light of new evidence. In January 2012, both Dobson and Norris were found guilty of Stephen Lawrence's murder.[96]

This landmark case demonstrates how an 800-year-old precedent required subsequent developments in modern law for it to be set aside in cases where new evidence could be identified. In the Lawrence case, new evidence was discovered (because of both scientific advances and the emergence of DNA techniques) which placed Gary Dobson in very close proximity to Stephen Lawrence both immediately before and after the murder.

Whilst the precedent had been historically intended to protect the accused, in a few cases, Sheen's being one of the most notable – the protection of the accused led to a fundamental miscarriage of justice. In 1827 there was no forensic test for blood. It would not be until 1901 that the Austrian biologist Karl Landsteiner discovered blood grouping, which would eventually allow forensic scientists to match bloodstains from the crime scene to the accused and victim.[97] There was a knife, which had been given to a Bow Street officer by a witness named Janet Pugh (wife of Joseph), but of course, there was no effective wound analysis. Whilst the knife was produced at the Inquest, there does not seem to have been any close investigation.[98] At the Sheen trial,

---

[92] W. Macpherson (1999) *The Stephen Lawrence Inquiry: Report of an Inquiry by Sir William Macpherson of Cluny*, February 1999, Cm 4262–1, point 7.46. https://assets.publishing.service.gov.uk/government/uploads/system/uploads/attachment_data/file/277111/4262.pdf (accessed 1 October 2019).

[93] The Law Commission (Law Com No. 267), *Double Jeopardy and Prosecution Appeals: Report on Two References under Section 3(1)(e) of the Law Commissions Act 1965* found at: https://s3-eu-west-2.amazonaws.com/lawcom-prod-storage-11jsxou24uy7q/uploads/2015/03/lc267__Double_Jeopardy_Report.pdf (accessed 2 August 2019).

[94] The Law Commission (Law Com No. 156), *Double Jeopardy: A Consultation Paper*, found at http://www.lawcom.gov.uk/app/uploads/2015/04/CP156.pdf (accessed 2 August 2019).

[95] See https://www.stephenlawrence.org.uk/wp-content/uploads/2019/03/Stephen-Lawrence-Timeline.pdf (accessed 2 August 2019).

[96] *The Times*, 4th January 2012, p. 1.

[97] W.J. Tilstone; K.A. Savage and L.A. Clark (2006) *Encyclopaedia of Forensic Science: An Encyclopaedia of History, Methods and Techniques* (London: ABC Clio), p. 10.

[98] LMA, Middlesex Sessions' records, Coroner's Inquest, 12 May 1827, MJ/SPC, E 3309. See also *The Times*, 14th May 1827, p. 3.

there was a more sustained discussion of the knife, with evidence from Dickenson, the Bow Street officer to whom the knife had been given, and the Whitechapel parish beadle, Thomas Smith. According to the evidence, Smith had examined the knife and the wounds on the victim's head and neck, before the Coroner, and concluded, ' … the head could be taken off with such as knife as this, according to my judgement'.[99] Undoubtedly, the trial contained evidence which by today's standards would have led to a guilty conviction. In the early nineteenth century however, the court only had the law to guide them. Ironically, in a period where the 'bloody code' was coming to an end and the criminal law was being rewritten and reformed, its representatives were trapped by the very law that they sought to refine in this period of change. As the satirists of the *Political Examiner* noted:

> A man who cuts babies' heads off cannot surely be too thankful to those servants of justice who show the circumstances under which such an action may be attended with no inconvenient consequences. Provided an individual takes the precaution to baptize his children by one name, and cause them to be known by another, he may cut their heads off with impunity whenever he has a mind. This is the law of England, and it is, in the language of the 'Soothing Syrup' advertisement, 'a real comfort to parents' – such as SHEEN.[100]

---

[99] OBP, Trial of William Sheen, May 1827 (t18270712-36).
[100] *Political Examiner*, 22nd July 1827, p. 1.

2

Legislating to Ensure 'Impartial' Justice: Palmer's Act of 1856

Katherine D. Watson
Oxford Brookes University

Introduction

On the morning of Wednesday the 14th of May 1856, a trial unparalleled in English legal history opened at London's Central Criminal Court. Its exceptional nature is revealed in the formal record of the trial, which first noted the presence of *four* judges. Then the indictment was read: 'Indicted at a session of oyer and terminer holden for County of Stafford. Ind[ictmen]t removed here under 19th Vict cap 16.' The charge itself was then set out: 'Staffordshire* William Palmer, wilful murder of John Parsons Cook. The like on a coroner's inquisition removed under some Act. Two coroner's inquisitions and one other indictment not tried.'[1]

This was the first-ever occasion on which an indictment found in a county outside the jurisdiction of the Central Criminal Court was tried before a London jury. The Attorney General, the lead prosecutor in the case, revealed the reason for this unprecedented event at the start of his four-hour opening address:

> The peculiar circumstances of this case have given it a profound and painful interest throughout the whole country. There is scarcely a man, perhaps, who has not come to some conclusion on the issue which you are now to decide. All the details have been seized on with eager avidity, and there is, perhaps, no one who is not more or less acquainted with those details. Standing here as a minister of justice, with no interest and no desire save that justice shall be done impartially, I feel it incumbent on me to warn you not to allow any preconceived opinion to operate on your judgment this day. Your duty – your bounden duty – is to try this case according to the evidence which shall be brought before you, and according to that alone. You must discard from your minds anything that you may have read or heard, or any opinion that you may have formed.[2]

---

[1] The National Archives (hereafter TNA), Central Criminal Court: Court Books, CRIM 6/8, 14th of May 1856, n. p. Quotations from Crown copyright documents held in TNA are acknowledged with thanks.
[2] Anon (1856) *Illustrated and Unabridged Edition of The Times Report of the Trial of William Palmer, for Poisoning John Parsons Cook, at Rugeley; from the Short-hand Notes Taken in the Central Criminal Court from Day to Day* (London: Ward & Lock), p. 6.

The 'peculiar circumstances' alluded to – William Palmer had been accused of committing three murders in the market town of Rugeley, and was suspected of others – gave rise to such fervent media interest and local feeling that Palmer and his solicitor realized there could be little hope of a fair trial at the Staffordshire assizes, where pre-trial publicity would preclude the selection of an unbiased jury. In recognition of this problem, Parliament rushed a new law onto the statute books: the Central Criminal Court Act 1856 (19 & 20 Vict c.16), originally known as the Trial of Offences Act and popularly known as Palmer's Act, allowed a crime committed outside London to be tried at the Central Criminal Court, rather than locally, if doing so appeared to be 'expedient to the ends of justice.'[3] Building on David Bentley's brief analysis of the role the case played in challenging pre-trial publicity,[4] this chapter investigates the genesis of the Act in more detail, to show why Palmer's trial proved to be both a forensic and a legal turning point.

The intense press coverage of the case was due in part to its uncommon toxicological characteristics: Palmer was alleged to have poisoned his gambling companion J.P. Cook with strychnine, a little-known substance which posed scientific difficulties that led eventually to a courtroom battle of apparently partisan expert witnesses.[5] While the tenor of this forensic clash was a major focus of interest both before and after the trial, it was also an inherent source of unfairness to Palmer, as he had to secure the testimony of a sufficient number of expert witnesses to refute the evidence of the most highly reputed toxicologist in England, Alfred Swaine Taylor (1806–1880), who served as an unofficial advisor to the Crown, helped to attract other experts of similar intellectual stature to the prosecution's cause, and wrote a long letter to the press about the case whilst Palmer was awaiting trial.[6] Nor was the press sensationalism fed solely by scientific controversy, for a series of associated accusations and incidents served to keep Palmer's story in the public eye. However, the voluminous case files in The National Archives reveal the existence of a further set of problematic issues intrinsic to the case. These range from the financial to the legal, particularly the decision as to which charge to focus on, and the related production of evidence, both of which were delayed to a degree that hindered the ability of Palmer's solicitor to marshal the necessary counter evidence. The key legal personnel also proved important: Palmer's

---

[3] An Act to empower the Court of Queen's Bench to order certain Offenders to be tried at the Central Criminal Court, 19 Vict c.16 s.1. See also H.D. Roome and R.E. Ross (1922) (eds) *Archbold's Pleading, Evidence and Practice in Criminal Cases, by Sir John Jervis*, 26th edition (London: Sweet and Maxwell), pp. 118–19.

[4] D. Bentley (1998) *English Criminal Justice in the Nineteenth Century* (London: Hambledon Press), p. 47.

[5] T. Golan (2004) *Laws of Med and Laws of Nature: The History of Scientific Expert Testimony in England and America* (Cambridge, MA: Harvard University Press), pp. 97–100; T. Ward (2005) 'A Mania for Suspicion: Poisoning, Science, and the Law' in J. Rowbotham and K. Stevenson (eds) *Criminal Conversations: Victorian Crimes, Social Panic, and Moral Outrage* (Columbus: Ohio State University Press), pp. 40–56 and I.A. Burney (2006) *Poison, Detection, and the Victorian Imagination* (Manchester: Manchester University Press). There had only been about fifteen recorded cases of strychnine poisoning prior to the Palmer trial (see Burney, *Poison, Detection, and the Victorian Imagination*, p. 140), of which only three had proved fatal (see Golan, *Laws of Med and Laws of Nature*, p. 98).

[6] A.S. Taylor and G. Owen Rees (1856) 'The Rugeley Suspected Secret Poisoning Cases', *The Lancet*, 67, 2nd February, pp. 134–5 reprinted in *The Cheshire Observer*, 9th February 1856, p. 4. See also Anon. (1856) 'Our Interview with Dr Alfred Taylor', *Illustrated Times*, 2nd February 1856, pp. 91–3. During the trial Taylor received a judicial rebuke for this (now utterly unacceptable) conduct: see *The Times Report*, p. 175.

team, though able, was not of the calibre needed to defend against a formidable prosecution quintet and an apparently hostile judge.

Following an overview of the case and the stages by which it was removed from Staffordshire to the Old Bailey, as the Central Criminal Court is known, this chapter covers new historical ground: it goes beyond the scientific disagreements and pre-trial reporting that have hitherto been suggested as key sources of bias in the Palmer case, to query its fairness as a legal process. However, notwithstanding a persuasive recent claim that the removal of Palmer's trial to London served to facilitate a 'show trial' where 'official resources and public opinion could be more effectively mustered against him',[7] there is little evidence to support an opposing view, that had the trial been held in Stafford 'no county jury would have convicted him'.[8] Thus, although it is by no means certain that Palmer's best hope of acquittal really did lie in London, the plain fact is that, in common with many trials for criminal poisoning, the weight of circumstantial evidence against him was likely to be convincing.[9]

Mysterious deaths at Rugeley: The Palmer case in brief

The main facts of the Palmer case have been recounted in several secondary sources,[10] and can also be found in digitized versions of the numerous verbatim accounts of the trial that were published in its immediate aftermath.[11] Online repositories of historical newspapers offer additional avenues for exploring the investigation, trial and public reception of Palmer's alleged crimes. In brief, William Palmer (the fourth son in a well-to-do Staffordshire family of five sons and two daughters) was a general practitioner who gave up medical practice to pursue his love of gambling and horseracing: by the

---

[7] R. Davenport-Hines (2009) 'Palmer, William [called the Rugeley Poisoner] (1824–1856), Poisoner and Physician', *Oxford Dictionary of National Biography*, https://doi.org/10.1093/ref:odnb/21222 (accessed 15 October 2019).
[8] G. Fletcher (1925) *The Life & Career of Dr William Palmer of Rugeley* (London: T. Fisher Unwin), p. 131. This view is attributed to the son of one of Palmer's counsel, writing in the 1920s.
[9] K.D. Watson (2006) 'Medical and Chemical Expertise in English Trials for Criminal Poisoning, 1750–1914', *Medical History*, 50, pp. 373–90 at p. 382 and Roome and Ross, *Archbold's Pleading*, pp. 357–9.
[10] In addition to the work of Burney, Golan and Ward cited in note 5 above, and that of Fletcher (see note 8), see also Anon (1856) *Illustrated Life and Career of William Palmer of Rugeley* (London: Ward and Lock); G. Lathom Browne and C.G. Stewart (1883) (eds) *Reports of Trials for Murder by Poisoning* (London: Stevens and Sons), pp. 85–232; L.A. Parry (1976 edition) *Some Famous Medical Trials* (Fairfield, NJ: Augustus M. Kelley), pp. 235–58; G. St Aubyn (1971) *Infamous Victorians: Palmer and Lamson, Two Notorious Poisoners* (London: Constable), pp. 3–152; T. Boyle (1989) *Black Swine in the Sewers of Hampstead: Beneath the Surface of Victorian Sensationalism* (New York: Viking), pp. 61–92.
[11] In addition to *The Times Report* cited in note 2 above, see also Anon (1856) *The Trial of William Palmer for the Alleged Rugeley Poisonings* (London: Henry Lea); Anon (1856) *The Queen v. Palmer. Verbatim report of the trial of William Palmer at the Central Criminal Court, Old Bailey, London, May 14, and following days, 1856, before Lord Campbell, Mr Justice Cresswell, and Mr Baron Alderson. Transcribed from the short-hand notes of Mr Angelo Bennett* (London: J. Allen); and G.H. Knott (1912) (ed.) *Trial of William Palmer* (Calcutta: Butterworth & Co. (India)). The trial report published online at *The Proceedings of the Old Bailey, 1674–1913*, www.oldbaileyonline.org, ref. t18560514-490, is incomplete: it does not include the opening addresses made by the prosecution and defence counsel, the closing speech for the prosecution, or the judge's summing up and sentencing.

early 1850s, he had acquired a stable of racehorses but had incurred significant debt and turned to moneylenders; he had begun to swindle his widowed mother by forging her signature on bills of credit. He had married, in 1848 at the age of twenty-three, the illegitimate daughter of an army officer; they had five children, only one of whom survived, before his wife died in 1854, insured for the enormous sum of £13,000. He then insured his older brother Walter Palmer, an alcoholic and 'all-round loafer',[12] for another £13,000 (having sought a total of £80,000 from six different companies) – but when Walter died soon after, the company refused to pay.[13] With hindsight, it became clear that theirs were not the first sudden deaths associated with Palmer: his mother-in-law died within a fortnight of arriving at his house for a visit early in 1849, and he acquired property by her death; in 1850 a racing companion to whom Palmer owed £800, Leonard Bladen, died in circumstances that were to be repeated in the case of John Parsons Cook; and an illegitimate child that Palmer fathered with his housemaid died suddenly after spending time in his company.[14]

Figure 2.1 William Palmer at 'The Oaks', 1854. With permission from the WS Society.[15]

[12] Fletcher, *Life & Career of Dr William Palmer*, p. 31.
[13] For a summary of the insurance on Anne and Walter Palmer's lives, see TNA, Treasury Solicitor and HM Procurator General Papers, Regina v William Palmer, Central Criminal Court, Tabular Statement of William Palmer's Insurances: Effected and Proposed, TS 11/433.
[14] Knott, *Trial of William Palmer*, pp. 16–17.
[15] Fletcher, *Life & Career of Dr William Palmer*, frontispiece; photograph taken from the copy held in the William Roughead Collection, Signet Library, Edinburgh. The Oaks Stakes is a thoroughbred flat race run annually since 1779 at Epsom Downs, Surrey.

The death that brought William Palmer to the attention of the authorities occurred in November 1855 when J.P. Cook died. Palmer was then in dire financial straits: he was unable to collect on the insurance policy on his brother's life as the company had launched an investigation (the state of Walter's health had been misrepresented to them), and there was ' … a court case pending against him and his mother for the recovery of money advanced on a forged bill of exchange'.[15] Palmer needed money, fast. Cook was a wealthy racing aficionado with whom Palmer co-owned some horses and attended race meetings. On the 13th of November Cook's mare, *Polestar*, won the Shrewsbury Handicap; he was to collect £1000 in London the following week on presentation of his betting book; two days later Palmer's horse, *Chicken*, was beaten and Palmer lost heavily. Cook became suddenly ill on the evening of the 13th of November in Palmer's company and again on the 16th of November after dining with him, and the following day 'took to his sick-bed', where he remained until his death in the early hours of the 21st of November, having taken pills administered by Palmer at 10.30 pm. Within two days Palmer's actions and the disappearance of Cook's betting book had raised the suspicions of William Vernon Stephens, Cook's stepfather, who contacted a solicitor in Rugeley (James Gardner), and pressed for a post-mortem examination and an inquest. The post-mortem was carried out on the 26th of November: Palmer was present and attempted to disrupt the proceedings, but samples were removed and taken to London for analysis by Alfred Swaine Taylor at Guy's Hospital.[17] The toxicological controversies that consequently emerged have been discussed in detail elsewhere and need not concern us here, but it is important to note that Taylor decided, upon learning of the pills given to Cook, that death was due to strychnine even though his analysis had not detected any in the body.[18]

Cook's mysterious and sudden demise raised questions about those of Palmer's wife and brother, and the Home Secretary ordered the exhumation of their bodies. Taylor attributed Anne Palmer's death to antimony, which was found in her body; and suspected Walter Palmer's death was due to prussic acid, although none was found in his body. By the end of January 1856, the nature of the case against William Palmer was well known and encompassed a mixture of legal fact (three inquest verdicts and verbatim reports of the inquest testimony printed in newspapers throughout the country) and moral indignation, with a strong suggestion that three deaths made for a difficult case to answer.[19] The key elements were succinctly summarized in *The Worcestershire Chronicle*:

> Wife, brother, children, mother-in-law, a couple of intimate friends, die suddenly, all but unaccountably, as regards natural causes, under his treatment – all but two of the dismal catalogue actually under his roof. He gains, through an insurance, by his wife's death. He attempts, by the same plan, to gain by his brother's death. The

---

[16] Burney, *Poison, Detection and the Victorian Imagination*, p. 118.
[17] For a detailed timeline of these events, see Knott, *Trial of William Palmer*, pp. 18–20.
[18] Burney, *Poison, Detection and the Victorian Imagination*, pp. 119–21 (quotation on p. 119).
[19] See, for example, *The Westmorland Gazette and Kendal Advertiser*, 26th January 1856, p. 8 reprinting an editorial from *The Times*.

insurance offices refuse transactions with him because of the suspicious nature of his proceeding. Of the bottles he keeps in his surgery few are at all full, and of those kept replenished, they are bottles marked 'poison'. He seduces his maid servant. He asks a postmaster to open letters. He asks the coroner to direct a favourable verdict. He induces a stable-help to attempt a fraud on an insurance-office. Lastly, he either induces his wife to a commit forgery, or benefits, silently, by that forgery committed.[20]

It was at this point that public discussion about Palmer's ability to get a fair trial began. An appendix at the end of this chapter summarizes the main facts of the case as they developed: each, following the death of Cook, was a point upon which the media pounced. Stories were printed in one part of the country and reprinted elsewhere a day or two later, as was typical of the Victorian press,[21] and this case became a *cause célèbre* among British newspaper readers: journalistic accounts merged investigation with human interest in what the *Illustrated Times* described as 'the crime of the age'.[22] At a time when serial murder by poison seemed frighteningly frequent,[23] the three accusations of murder, together with a catalogue of other mysterious deaths in Palmer's house, ignited a media storm. He was rarely out of the newspapers in the months between his committal to gaol in Stafford and the start of his trial in London.

The Trial of Offences Act

Public discussion of whether or not Palmer could expect to receive a fair trial began in early January 1856, following an article published in *The Globe* which claimed that:

> Certainly Palmer will have a fair trial. No 'discussion can injure him; to avoid allusion to his case would be the cant of forbearance; for the suspicious facts have themselves accumulated a weight of 'prejudice' which discussion can only qualify, not increase.[24]

The negative tone adopted here is unmistakeable, and the subsequent verdicts in the inquests on Palmer's wife and brother, together with the sale of his stable and earlier sale of his furniture and household possessions (during which a bundle of papers and an old diary were discovered in a desk and handed over to the police),[25] served only to heighten the public fascination. His appearance at the civil suit brought by a creditor

---

[20] *The Worcestershire Chronicle*, 30th January 1856, p. 4.
[21] A. Hobbs (2009) 'When the Provincial Press Was the National Press (c.1836–c.1900)', *International Journal of Regional and Local History*, 5, pp. 16–43.
[22] J.H. Wiener (2011) *The Americanization of the British Press, 1830s–1914* (Basingstoke: Palgrave Macmillan), pp. 73–4. and *Illustrated Times*, 2nd February 1856, pp. 1-2 – speaking of serial poisoning for money.
[23] K. Watson (2004) *Poisoned Lives: English Poisoners and Their Victims* (London: Hambledon and London) and V.M. Nagy (2014) 'Narratives in the Courtroom: Female Poisoners in Mid-Nineteenth Century England', *European Journal of Criminology*, 11, pp. 213–27.
[24] *The Globe*, 7th January 1856, p. 2.
[25] *Oxford Chronicle and Reading Gazette*, 12th January 1856, p. 6.

against his mother, on the 21st of January at Westminster Hall in London, led to another black mark against his name: Palmer, who did not seem to feel 'the perilous position in which he stood', caused a sensation when he admitted that he had asked his dead wife to forge his mother's signature on a bill of exchange.[26] By the 25th of January some newspapers had recognized that the local populace was hopelessly divided in opinion:

> There is excitement enough throughout the country upon the subject of Mr William Palmer and his proceedings at Rugeley, but, as may well be supposed, this excitement is at its height in the town of Rugeley itself and the immediate neighbourhood. The population is divided into Palmerites and Anti-Palmerites; – some persons are resolved that nothing shall convince them of Mr Palmer's guilt – others are equally fixed in their opinion of his culpability. It is the same thing at Stafford; the inhabitants of that town have prejudged the case, and it is therefore impossible that justice should be done there between the Crown and the prisoner. Under these circumstances, and presuming that on either side the only anxiety is to obtain a fair trial, would it not be advisable to remove the case to some other assize town on the same circuit, where a jury might be empanelled who would consider the weight of the evidence for the prosecution and the defence without favour or prejudice?[27]

The reports suggested that while 'a man's life must not be sacrificed to local prejudice', the Crown was entitled to have the indictments removed to another venue if it seemed 'the inhabitants of Stafford looked too favourably upon [Palmer's] case'.[28] In addition, the seriousness of the charges was believed to merit the oversight of one of the two highest judicial authorities in the land, the Lord Chief Justice of the Court of Queen's Bench or the Chief Justice of the Common Pleas, rather than one of the puisne (ordinary) judges who typically travelled the Oxford Circuit.[29] The obvious solution seemed to be to move the trial to another county on the same assize circuit.

However, Palmer had already decided that this would not suffice: on the following day, the 26th of January, he and his solicitor, John Smith of Birmingham, submitted affidavits to the Court of Queen's Bench, setting out the grounds on which they had come to believe that a fair trial could not be held anywhere in the Midlands. While Palmer focused on his innocence and lack of financial wherewithal to contest the testimony of A.S. Taylor, Smith referred more particularly to the widespread local prejudice caused by exaggerated and unfounded statements printed in local newspapers. It is worth reproducing these documents in full, as they formed the basis for the subsequent change to the law of England:[30]

---

[26] *Devizes and Wiltshire Gazette*, 24th January 1856, p. 2.
[27] *Evening Mail*, 25th January 1856, p. 6 and *The Times*, 25th January 1856, p. 7.
[28] Ibid.
[29] Staffordshire was one of the counties of the Oxford assize circuit, which included other Midland counties such as Shropshire; but not Warwickshire, which was part of the Midland Circuit.
[30] TNA, Treasury Solicitor and HM Procurator General Papers, Regina v William Palmer, Central Criminal Court, copies of affidavits by W. Palmer and J. Smith, 26th of January 1856, TS 11/433. These were published in full in *The Morning Advertiser*, 30th January 1856, p. 6.

Affidavit of William Palmer

I William Palmer late of Rugeley in the County of Stafford surgeon but now a prisoner confined in Her Majesty's Gaol at Stafford charged upon the coroner's inquisition with the wilful murder of the late John Parsons Cook make oath and say,

1. That for ten years I have been residing at Rugeley aforesaid occasionally practising as a surgeon.
2. The paper writing hereto annexed marked (A) is a copy of the warrant upon which I was arrested and am now detained in the [said] Gaol.
3. I am informed and believe that I cannot have a fair and impartial trial in the county of Stafford, or in fact elsewhere in the Midland Counties inasmuch as the prejudice against me is so great that I do not believe amongst an ordinary panel of jurymen any twelve men could be found unbiased and unprejudiced.
4. I say that in addition to the charge of murder of the said John Parsons Cook I am also charged on coroner's inquisitions with the murder of my late wife Ann Palmer and my late brother Walter Palmer all the said murders being alleged to have been committed by means of poison.
5. I am informed and verily believe that in and about the neighbourhood of Stafford (Rugeley being only nine miles distant from Stafford) I am also accused of having murdered several other persons which rumour is very generally believed to be true.
6. In each of the cases with which I am charged and upon which I am now in Gaol the same being charges of murder by poisoning Alfred Swaine Taylor of Guy's Hospital London doctor of medicine is the principal witness and in order to rebut the evidence given by him it will be necessary that I should have a sufficient number of scientific persons to give evidence upon my trial most of whom are resident in London.
7. I say the expense of such witnesses will as I am informed and believe be 1000 pounds or thereabouts if I am tried at Stafford.
8. I say of myself I have no funds wherewith to meet such expense and am consequently entirely dependent on my friends and relations and owing to my dependent position I fear I shall not be so well or properly defended unless I can be tried where the expence [sic] of such witnesses will be much less.
9. I am informed and verily believe that the Solicitor who is acting against me in the prosecution upon the charge of the wilful murder of my said late wife and said late brother has admitted to my solicitor that he does not believe it would be possible for me to have an impartial trial in the county of Stafford or its neighbourhood.
10. I say that I am innocent of having committed the said alleged murders or any or either of them.

Affidavit of John Smith

I John Smith of Birmingham in the county of Warwick attorney for William Palmer hereinafter mentioned make oath and say,

1. That the said William Palmer is and stands charged upon coroners inquisitions in the county of Stafford with three murders by poisoning, that is to say with the murder of Ann Palmer his late wife, Walter Palmer his late brother and one John Parsons Cook two of such murders being alleged to have been committed at Rugeley in the said county of Stafford and one of them at Stafford in the said county of Stafford.
2. That I appeared to watch the proceedings upon the inquisitions held on the bodies of Ann Palmer the wife of the said William Palmer and Walter Palmer the brother of the said William Palmer for and on behalf of the said William Palmer.
3. I say that by reason of my having so acted I am enabled to judge of the feeling of the inhabitants of Rugeley and the neighbourhood.
4. I say that upon the said inquisitions so held as aforesaid there were upwards of thirty newspapers represented by various reporters.
5. That the jury impanelled upon such inquisitions appeared to me to be greatly prejudiced against the said William Palmer.
6. I have been informed and believe that one of the jurymen who sat upon the said inquisitions assisted in getting up evidence against the said William Palmer.
7. That the evidence given upon the aforesaid inquisitions before the coroner has been published in the various newspapers published in Staffordshire Warwickshire and the neighbouring counties, and that numerous paragraphs have appeared in the newspapers unfavourable to the said William Palmer and in many instances assuming his guilt and that the effect has been that the bulk of the inhabitants of the counties of Stafford Warwick and other neighbouring counties are greatly prejudiced against the said William Palmer and eager for his conviction and punishment as I verily believe passing by the consideration of the question whether he can by evidence be proved to be guilty of the crimes with the commission of which he is charged and I verily believe that such prejudiced feeling has been raised to such an extent as to incapacitate the persons under its influence from fairly and properly doing the duty of jurors in the cases in which the said William Palmer is charged as aforesaid.
8. I say that many of the paragraphs which have so appeared in the said papers as aforesaid are false and have contained gross misrepresentations and have as I verily believe been written for the purpose of prejudging the case and abusing the public mind.
9. I believe amongst a very great number of persons in the county of Stafford Warwick and neighbouring counties the public generally are kept in a state of excitement and prejudice against the said William Palmer by the various articles which have from time to time appeared in the newspapers.
10. I do not believe that the said William Palmer could have a fair and impartial trial at Stafford Warwick of in any of the Midland counties owing to the prejudice which exists as before stated.
11. I say that Mr Deane the solicitor for the insurance offices and who conducted the inquiry before the coroner on behalf of the Crown in the cases of Ann (sic) Palmer and Walter Palmer informed me that he thought there was great prejudice in the minds of the inhabitants of Staffordshire, and surrounding counties, and he believed an impartial trial could not be had in the county of Stafford or any surrounding county.

Charles Wilkins, who had appeared for Sarah Palmer in the civil suit a week earlier, was counsel for William Palmer at the hearing held before the four judges of the Court of Queen's Bench, including the Lord Chief Justice, John Baron Campbell (1779–1861), beginning Campbell's close association with this case. The argument that Wilkins made was straightforward:

> It was shown by William Palmer and his solicitor, and even by the solicitor for the prosecution, that there was such an amount of excitement and prejudice in Staffordshire that it was impossible for the prisoner to have a fair trial if the inquisitions were not removed. … it would cost about [£1,000] to procure the attendance of witnesses of scientific skill to meet the case on the other side; whereas, if the trial were to take place in London, their attendance could be obtained at a comparatively small expense.[31]

Thus, Palmer's goal was a trial at the Central Criminal Court, considered the preeminent criminal court of England. It did not take the judges long to agree to remove the indictments and inquisitions into Queen's Bench from the Staffordshire assizes, and thence to the Old Bailey, but there was a technical difficulty: Queen's Bench had the power to try cases from anywhere in England (a trial at bar, an option the judges resisted), or to order their removal to any other county, but the jurisdiction of the Central Criminal Court was limited by statute to cases occurring within certain counties adjacent to the metropolis.[32] Thus, a new statute was required, one that would enable the judges to transmit from provincial counties to the Central Criminal Court serious criminal cases supposed to be exposed to local prejudices. Within days of the ruling, the Lord Chancellor introduced the necessary bill in the House of Lords, where it was championed by Lord Campbell, met with little resistance and soon passed to the House of Commons.[33] There, a handful of MPs argued against it in two debates, concerned that individuals charged with treason (clearly a reference to Ireland) might be forced to undergo trial in London, or that prisoners might be tried in London against their will. Two Staffordshire MPs denied that Palmer could not get a fair trial in the county, whereas an Irish MP felt certain there could be no fair trial for Palmer in Staffordshire. One by one, objections to the bill were withdrawn, as the Attorney General skilfully undermined them,[34] and the bill was passed without amendment on the 10th of March 1856. It received royal assent a month later. William Palmer had got his London trial.

---

[31] *Evening Mail*, 30th January 1856, p. 5.

[32] 4 & 5 Will IV c.36, An Act for establishing a New Court for the Trial of Offences committed in the Metropolis and Parts adjoining (Central Criminal Court Act, 1834) established the Old Bailey, renamed the Central Criminal Court, as the assize court for London, Middlesex and parts of Essex, Kent and Surrey. It also authorized this court to try offences committed on the high seas, but not elsewhere in England.

[33] *The Morning Advertiser*, 6th February 1856, p. 2 and *Aberdeen Press and Journal*, 6th February 1856, p. 5.

[34] *Hansard: House of Commons Debates*, 3 March 1856, Vol. 140, cc1768-70 and 10 March 1856, Vol. 140, cc2194-200.

A fair and impartial trial?

Palmer succeeded in having his case removed from Staffordshire, but distinct elements of unfairness remained in the prosecution, most especially in the preparation of the case, and potentially also in the trial itself. During the course of debate in the House of Commons, MPs had made two important observations: whereas in every other court Palmer would be tried by one judge, at the Old Bailey he would be tried by three judges; and, in relation to the even more important jury, an Oxfordshire MP had suggested that 'ninety-nine men out of every hundred, if asked the question, would rather stand before a county than an Old Bailey jury'.[35] With hindsight these appear prescient words, indeed. The jury had to rely on the judges in order to pick their way through the mass of evidence. Palmer's case 'was regarded as presenting so many unprecedented difficulties that three judges were appointed to try it':[36] Lord Campbell, Baron Alderson and Mr Justice Cresswell, two of whom, Campbell and Alderson, were later accused of unfair bias.[37] As we have seen, however, Lord Campbell did much to ensure that Palmer got his wish for an Old Bailey trial, and was clearly persuaded by the evidence presented by the prosecution, much of which relied on the efforts of the Attorney General (noted orator Sir Alexander Cockburn (1802–1880)), Alfred Swaine Taylor,[38] the detailed investigations of the Treasury Solicitor (Henry Reynolds) and the Rugeley solicitor James Gardner, and the preparations of four junior counsel – all of whom were notable legal figures in their own right and one of whom, John Huddleston, had previously acted for Samuel Cheshire (see Appendix), Palmer and his mother.

The immense amount of time and effort that the prosecution put into this case is suggested by the huge cost of the trial to the state: £7532.[39] By contrast, Palmer lost the services of his preferred barrister when Charles Wilkins became seriously ill; his replacement, William Shee, had never before defended in a murder trial and breached legal etiquette in proclaiming his belief in his client's innocence;[40] the expert witnesses for the defence were criticized and undermined both in and out of court; and it is likely that Palmer's family had only about £2000 to pay for his defence.[41]

Palmer was well defended but his team was always working under serious impediments: the constant flow of newspaper articles about the case, which circulated

---

[35] Ibid. One of the key legal differences between the Old Bailey and assize courts was that two judges sat upon trials in London, and three might do so. When Palmer's trial opened the three judges who were to preside were present, along with the Recorder of London.
[36] St Aubyn, *Infamous Victorians*, p. 39.
[37] Knott, *Trial of William Palmer*, p. 316.
[38] See TNA, Treasury Solicitor and HM Procurator General Papers, Regina v William Palmer, Central Criminal Court, TS 11/432 for Taylor's report and answers to queries from the prosecution about Anne Palmer's case, 3 April 1856 and in TS 11/431, a letter from A. S. Taylor to John Greenwood (Treasury), 9th of May 1856, recommending a possible witness.
[39] Judicial Statistics (1857), *Part I, England and Wales, Police – Criminal Proceedings – Prisons; Returns for the Year 1856* (London: HMSO), p. xv. This sum included costs in Staffordshire of £3504 and costs to the Crown Solicitor of £4028 12s. 7d. By contrast, the Dove case cost £1176 and other murders from £112 to £428. The average cost of a trial at the Old Bailey was 103s.
[40] Knott, *Trial of William Palmer*, p. 319 and Fletcher, *Life & Career of Dr William Palmer*, pp. 132–5
[41] *The Worcestershire Chronicle*, 30th January 1856, p. 4.

as freely in London as in Staffordshire; the need to prepare to defend three murder charges; and the complicated medico-scientific evidence that had to be countered with persuasive expert evidence. In March the trial of Palmer's close friend, Rugeley deputy postmaster Samuel Cheshire, brought renewed attention to Palmer's alleged suspicious actions, and further embedded Taylor in the prosecution: he appeared as a witness and explained how easy it was to open a letter deliberately.[42] Meanwhile, the death in Leeds of Harriet Dove, who was alleged to have been poisoned with strychnine by her husband,[43] provided the prosecution with renewed scientific focus.[44] When barrister George Knott edited the trial for publication in 1912 he believed that:

> had it not been for one or two definitely known cases of strychnia poisoning in the human subject, the prosecution would have failed, in spite of all the experiments on animals from which analogies as to Cook's symptoms were attempted to be drawn. There had been no trial for poisoning by strychnia before Palmer's. But it happened that while the Palmer case was pending Dr Dove, of Leeds, was accused of poisoning his wife by strychnia, and the symptoms of poison were more certainly ascertained. Yet Dr Nunneley, of Leeds, who made a report on this case, was called for the defence, not for the prosecution.[45]

The indictment for the murder of J.P. Cook was the main charge, but we should not forget that Palmer had been formally accused of two other murders and could be tried for both, although in the case of his brother a trial solely on a coroner's inquisition would be likely to fail. But clearly he had to be prepared, and on the 19th of April 1856 his solicitor wrote to the Treasury seeking clarification: 'Would you oblige me by saying whether it is the intention of the Crown to proceed with Walter Palmer's case? And also whether any further evidence is intended to be adduced in any of the cases other than that contained in the depositions?'[46] Three days later, he wrote again:

> I suppose the Crown will give some information respecting the additional evidence to be adduced on the trial of Wm Palmer, in order that he may be prepared to meet it. I should be glad to know what course the Crown intends adopting in reference to this point at your earliest convenience, as until I know briefs for defence cannot be delivered.[47]

---

[42] *The Derby Mercury*, 19th March 1856, p. 2.
[43] On the Dove case, see O. Davies (2005) *Murder, Magic, Madness: The Victorian Trials of Dove and the Wizard* (Harlow: Pearson Education) and Lathom Browne and Stewart, *Reports of Trials for Murder by Poisoning*, pp. 233–68.
[44] TNA, Treasury Solicitor and HM Procurator General Papers, Regina v William Palmer, Central Criminal Court, Dove's Case, TS 11/434/1370; at TS 11/434/1369, Additional evidence re strychnine and Medical Evidence in the case of Mrs Dove, Leeds 7 May 1856; at TS 11/433, Copy of Evidence on cases of poisoning by strychnine and at TS 11/431, Depositions in inquest on Harriet Dove, 4 March 1856.
[45] Knott, *Trial of William Palmer*, p. 2.
[46] TNA, Treasury Solicitor and HM Procurator General Papers, Regina v William Palmer, Central Criminal Court, Letter from John Smith to H.R. Reynolds, 19th April 1856, TS 11/434/1369.
[47] Ibid at TS 11/434/1369, Letter from John Smith to H.R. Reynolds, 22nd April 1856.

Smith was still awaiting a firm answer in early May, when in fact the prosecution had obtained important new scientific witnesses, including Professors Robert Christison and William Brande.[48] Smith wrote to Reynolds to complain that he had been informed of thirteen more witnesses at a late period, as he had been promised that any additional evidence would be furnished fourteen days before trial: 'It is impossible to get up the case properly unless the whole evidence is complete, as the facts stated in the new depositions cannot be enquired into, owing to distance and shortness of time. Need I mention that this is a case of life and death?'[49] The prosecution kept a list of the evidence sent to Smith in relation to the deaths of Cook and Anne Palmer, indicating that new issues were arising between the 1st and 12th of May, just two days before the trial began.[50] Smith was by then installed at Bacon's Hotel in London, so had the added inconvenience of working far from his client in Stafford Gaol and his office in Birmingham. The fact that the prosecution was nervous about its ability to prove both Palmer's motive and that Cook had died from strychnine is obvious: much of the new evidence concerned financial matters, Palmer's behaviour, the Dove case and other known deaths from strychnine. In early April the Attorney General had been asked to advise about 'whether too much detail on the question of motive may not tend to complicate and confuse the case on the part of the prosecution'.[51]

In 1925 George Fletcher, a doctor and magistrat who made a detailed study of the case, identified the key planks in the prosecution of William Palmer: (1) his poor financial circumstances, which spoke to motive; (2) the extensive and ultimately unrefuted circumstantial evidence against him, which occupied three-quarters of the trial and reinforced the argument that Palmer had means, motive and opportunity to poison Cook and then attempted to cover his tracks; (3) the medical evidence that Cook was poisoned by strychnine, for which the defence proposed a variety of hesitant alternatives. In short, Cook's symptoms – tetanic convulsions – were not in question, but their cause was. The seventeen medico-scientific witnesses for the Crown all agreed that death was from strychnine even though it was not detected by toxicological analysis, but their fifteen counterparts for the defence proposed half a dozen possible causes for the observed symptoms.[52] The prodigious mass of evidence, especially after the Dove inquest, as well as the need to defend against three different murder charges, proved a difficult, if not impossible task. And it seems clear that even had the prosecution for the murder of Cook failed, the Crown was ready to proceed against Palmer for the murder of his wife. Although he did not yet realize it, William Palmer was trapped in a vice from which there would be no escape.

---

[48] Ibid at TS 11/434/1369, Opinion of Professor Christison on the case of John Parsons Cook, copy, 21st April 1856; at TS 11/430, Opinion of Professor Christison in Anne Palmer's case, 23rd April 1856 and at TS 11/434/1370, Letter from W.H. Brande to H.R. Reynolds, 5th May 1856.
[49] Ibid at TS 11/434/1369, Letter from John Smith to H.R. Reynolds n.d. but probably after 7th of May 1856.
[50] Ibid at TS 11/434/1369, Listing of evidence sent to Smith re Cook and Anne Palmer, 1st May to 12th May 1856.
[51] Ibid at TS 11/433, Attorney General requested to advise as to course to be taken with regard to certain doubts, 3rd April 1856.
[52] Fletcher, *Life & Career of Dr William Palmer*, pp. 144–50, 161–76.

Conclusion

On the 27th of May 1856 one of the most memorable criminal trials in English legal history drew to a close when the Lord Chief Justice donned the black cap and told the defendant: 'William Palmer, after a long and impartial trial you have been convicted by a jury of your country of the crime of wilful murder. In that verdict my two learned brothers, who have so anxiously watched this trial, and myself entirely concur, and consider that verdict altogether satisfactory'.[53] But the verdict came as a surprise to Palmer and his solicitor, who avowed that 'but for the charge of Lord Campbell', the result 'might have been different'.[54] John Smith claimed that

> The jury had no alternative but to return a verdict of 'guilty', for his Lordship left the question to them as to whether the death of Cook was consistent with poisoning by strychnia, without putting the alternative as to whether the death of the late J. P. Cook might not be consistent with natural, although unknown causes.[55]

We do not have access to the jury's deliberations or evidence that they had any prior bias against Palmer, but the fact that one juror recused himself on the grounds of prejudice suggests that the decision to seek a trial in London because it was the seat of medical and scientific expertise might have failed for reasons in addition to those hitherto stressed in studies of this case, the unseemly 'battle of experts' and judicial bias. The more usual practice would have been to move the trial to another county, where jurors might well have been less willing to bring in a capital conviction, but it is understandable why Palmer felt this would be unwise, given the volume and tenor of the media reports about him. But the Victorian newspaper press was a national phenomenon, and what jurors read in Stafford, they also read in London. The jurors in Palmer's trial attended to their responsibility diligently, however: following the trial three of them submitted a memorial to the Treasury seeking financial compensation for the 'very serious pecuniary loss and inconvenience, not to say injury to health', that had arisen from their long confinement.[56] Their businesses had suffered whilst they were sequestered, but the

---

[53] Knott, *Trial of William Palmer*, p. 284.

[54] Thomas Palmer (1856) *A Letter to the Lord Chief Justice Campbell: Containing Remarks upon the Conduct of the Prosecution and the Judges, with Strictures on the Charge Delivered to the Jury, Illustrative of Its Dangerous Tendencies to the Long-Enjoyed Rights and Privileges of Englishmen* (London: T. Taylor), Appendix, p. vi, a copy of a letter to the Editor of *The Times*, 28th May 1856. Palmer remained remarkably calm throughout his trial and possibly thought he could not be convicted because if no poison was found in the body, there was no murder. This was the theory his defence team adopted, see Fletcher, *Life & Career of Dr William Palmer*, p. 173.

[55] Palmer, *A Letter to the Lord Chief Justice Campbell*, p. vi.

[56] TNA, Treasury Solicitor and HM Procurator General: Law Officers' and Counsel's Opinions, Regina v William Palmer, Application from certain of the jury on the trial of the above for remuneration for their services, 8 November 1856, TS 25/927. An analysis of this material appears in C. Watson (2019) 'Very Serious Pecuniary Loss and Inconvenience: A Jury's Plea', *Legal History Miscellany*, found at https://legalhistorymiscellany.com/2019/09/22/very-serious-pecuniary-loss-and-inconvenience-a-jurys-plea/ (accessed 15 October 2019).

law did not allow payments to jurors until 1949 and their polite request – the seeds of which had been planted by Lord Campbell[57] – was firmly refused.

Lingering doubts remain about Palmer's guilt. Did he murder Cook with strychnine, or with some other poison (brucine or morphine), or was he actually innocent?[58] But

Table 2.1 *Appendix:* Significant Events in the Prosecution of William Palmer

Date	Event
1824, 6 Aug	William Palmer born
1846, 10 Aug	Palmer qualifies MRCS
1847, 7 Oct	Palmer marries Anne Thornton; they soon move to Rugeley
1848, Oct	Birth of the Palmers' only surviving child, William Brookes Palmer
1849, 18 Jan	Death of Palmer's mother-in-law (age 50), twelve days after arriving at his house for a visit
1850, 13 May	Death of Leonard Bladen at Palmer's house in Rugeley; rumours of poisoning circulate locally[59]
1851–1854, Jan	Deaths of four Palmer infants (Elizabeth, Henry, Frank and John) from convulsions
1854, 29 Sep	Death of Anne Palmer (age 27)
1855	
13 Feb	Life insurance policy assigned from Walter Palmer to William Palmer
26 Jun	Eliza Tharm (housemaid) gives birth to Palmer's illegitimate son; the infant dies in convulsions five months later, after a visit from his father
16 Aug	Death of Walter Palmer (age 32)
20 Nov	Palmer purchases prussic acid, 6 grains of strychnine, and liquor of opium
21 Nov	Death of John Parsons Cook (age 28)
29 Nov	Inquest on J. P. Cook opened and adjourned
2 Dec	James Gardner writes to A. S. Taylor asking about the results of his examination of the contents of Cook's stomach
5 Dec	Samuel Cheshire, deputy postmaster of Rugeley, opens the reply from Taylor to Gardner and informs Palmer of the contents
15 Dec	Inquest on J. P. Cook returns a verdict of wilful murder against W. Palmer, who is arrested but, due to illness, not taken to Stafford Gaol until 17 Dec

Continued

[57] TNA, Treasury Solicitor and HM Procurator General: Law Officers' and Counsel's Opinions, Regina v William Palmer, Application from certain of the jury on the trial of the above for remuneration for their services, 8 November 1856, TS 25/927, pp. 2–3. See also Juries Act 1949 (12, 13 & 14 Geo VI c.27).
[58] For a summary of the main points suggestive of Palmer's innocence, see Reasons for Doubting the Safety of the Verdict, http://staffscc.net/wppalmer/?page_id=208 (accessed 29 September 2019); S. Bates (2014) *The Poisoner: The Life and Crimes of Victorian England's Most Notorious Doctor* (New York: Overlook Duckworth).
[59] Fletcher, *Life & Career of Dr William Palmer*, pp. 41–2.

Date	Event
22 Dec	Bodies of Anne Palmer and Walter Palmer exhumed and inquests opened
31 Dec	A friend of Leonard Bladen writes to the Chief Constable of Staffordshire to suggest that his death was suspicious and that Palmer profited from it
1856	
10 Jan	Samuel Cheshire charged with illegally opening a letter on 5 Dec 1855
12 Jan	Inquest on Anne Palmer returns a verdict of wilful murder against W. Palmer
14 Jan	Palmer's stable put up for auction, attracting a large crowd[60]
21 Jan	Palmer is in London to give evidence in Padwick v. Sarah Palmer, a civil action brought against his mother in relation to a bill he had forged
23 Jan	Inquest on Walter Palmer returns a verdict of wilful murder against W. Palmer
26 Jan	Writ of certiorari submitted by W. Palmer to the Court of Queen's Bench, asserting he could not receive a fair trial in Staffordshire or anywhere in the Midlands
26 Jan	Sworn affidavit by John Smith, Palmer's solicitor, claiming his client could not receive a fair trial in the Midlands[61]
29 Jan	Motion raised in Queen's Bench for a certiorari to allow Palmer's trial to be held in a county other than Staffordshire; the judges agree and issue a rule nisi[62]
31 Jan	The Court of Queen's Bench orders the removal of Palmer's trial from Stafford to the Central Criminal Court, London
1 Feb	The Home Secretary requests the Treasury Solicitor, Henry Revell Reynolds, to take charge of the several prosecutions of Palmer[63]
5 Feb	First reading of the Trial of Offenders Bill in the House of Lords[64]
11 Feb	The bill passes its second reading in the House of Lords[65]
12 Feb	W. H. Bodkin provides a formal opinion to the Treasury Solicitor as to the bills of indictment likely to be found by the Staffordshire grand jury: the murders of Cook and Anne Palmer
21 Feb	The amended bill is ordered for a third reading in the House of Lords[66]
25 Feb	The bill is sent to the House of Commons[67]

---

[60] *The Newry Examiner and Louth Advertiser*, 19th January 1856, p. 3.
[61] The copy in TNA states the 29th of January but a report of the hearing in Queen's Bench, held on the 29th of January, proves that Smith swore his affidavit on the 26th of January 1856.
[62] A rule nisi is a court order that will come into force at a future date unless a particular condition is met, whereupon the ruling becomes a decree (or rule) absolute and is binding. Typically, the condition is that an adversely affected party provide satisfactory evidence or argument that the decree should not take effect.
[63] TNA, Treasury Solicitor and HM Procurator General Papers, Regina v William Palmer, Central Criminal Court, Letter from H. Waddington to H.R. Reynolds, 1 February 1856, TS 11/434/1369.
[64] *The Morning Advertiser*, 6th February 1856, p. 2.
[65] This was widely reported in the Irish press, but not in English newspapers, according to searches of The British Newspaper Archive.
[66] *Berrow's Worcester Journal*, 23rd February 1856, p. 4.
[67] *The Times*, 29th February 1856, p. 9 and see also *Hansard: House of Commons Debates*, 25 February 1856, Vol. 140, c1311.

Date	Event
3 Mar	During a short debate on the bill, two Staffordshire MPs deny that Palmer could not obtain a fair trial in Stafford[68]
4 Mar	Inquest opens at Leeds on the body of Harriet Dove
10 Mar	After a short debate in the House of Commons, the Trial of Offences Bill is agreed[69]
14 Mar	The grand jury at Stafford assizes returns true bills for the murders of J. P. Cook and Anne Palmer; the bill in the case of Walter Palmer is ignored
14 Mar	Samuel Cheshire convicted at Stafford assizes of unlawfully opening a letter and sentenced to twelve months without hard labour
5 Apr	Letter from A. S. Taylor to H. R. Reynolds calls attention to misstatements published in the *Morning Advertiser*, a newspaper much read by 'the class of persons who are generally Old Bailey jurors'[70]
11 Apr	An Act to empower the Court of Queen's Bench to order certain Offenders to be tried at the Central Criminal Court (19 & 20 Vict c.16), receives royal assent and comes into effect the following day
16 Apr	Palmer ordered to show cause why the several indictments against him should not be tried at the Central Criminal Court
24 Apr	Rule absolute granted, appointing the trial date
14 May	Palmer's trial at the Central Criminal Court begins
14 May	Mr Mason, a juryman, informs the Court that 'he felt so strong a prejudice in the case that he did not feel competent to act', and is excused[71]
27 May	Conclusion of Palmer's trial: conviction and death sentence
c. 7 June	Publication of Thomas Palmer (1856), *A Letter to the Lord Chief Justice Campbell: Containing Remarks upon the Conduct of the Prosecution and the Judges, with Strictures on the Charge Delivered to the Jury, Illustrative of Its dangerous Tendencies to the Long-enjoyed Rights and Privileges of Englishmen* (London: T. Taylor)[72]
7 June	Thomas Wakley writes to the press to deny authorship of *The Cries of the Condemned, or Proofs of the Unfair Trial and (if executed) the Legal Murder of William Palmer, &c, by Thomas Wakley, Esq, Coroner*[73]
14 June	W. Palmer executed at Stafford (age 31)

---

[68] *Hansard: House of Commons Debates,* 3th March 1856, Vol. 140, cc1768-70.
[69] *Hansard: House of Commons Debates,* 10th March 1856, Vol. 140, cc2194-200. The word 'offenders' in the title had been changed to 'offences' by the second reading on the 3rd of March.
[70] TNA, Treasury Solicitor and HM Procurator General Papers, Regina v William Palmer, Central Criminal Court, Letter from A.S. Taylor to H.R. Reynolds, 5th April 1856, TS 11/434/1370.
[71] *Glasgow Sentinel,* 17th May 1856, p. 1.
[72] Most probably this was actually written by one of Palmer's junior defence counsel, Edward Kenealey: St Aubyn, *Infamous Victorians,* p. 41.
[73] *The Morning Post,* 9th June 1856, p. 4 and *The Times,* 9th June 1856, p. 9,

that was not the question that those who championed his cause focused on, or that this chapter has sought to illuminate. Contemporary observers believed Palmer did not have a fair trial because of judicial bias on the part of Lord Campbell and Baron Alderson, unfair advantages given to Taylor and other medico-scientific witnesses for the prosecution and virulent newspaper reportage. But issues of organization and finance also merit consideration. How fair is a trial when the prosecution can afford to spend the princely sum of £7500, produces thirteen new witnesses four days before trial and leaves the defence unsure as to what role one of the alleged murders might play? The constant production of new evidence worked against Palmer, but it also reveals weaknesses that the prosecution perceived in its own case as to the motive for and cause of death of John Parsons Cook. Ultimately, the question of whether or not William Palmer received a fair trial cannot be disentangled from the complicated medico-chemical, legal and financial issues so central to this unique case, or how they were managed by a judicial system hastily responding to new circumstances and contexts.

3

'All That They Had Heard, All That They Had Read, All That They Had Seen': Questions of Fairness and Justice in the Trial of George Vass

Helen Rutherford, Northumbria University and
Clare Sandford-Couch, Newcastle University

Introduction

On the 28th of February 1863, the *Newcastle Daily Journal* included a dramatic editorial comment:

> We publish the report of the trial of George Vass. We do not speak rashly; in a case of this kind it is our duty to deliberate, and to speak with hesitation, and with full knowledge of our responsibility. It cannot be supposed that we sympathise with the alleged acts of the accused man. We want justice to be done. Yet we regret to say that the trial, as it has been conducted, has not been characterised by the fairness and justice which ought to distinguish all our judicial procedures. The evidence of Mr. [sic] Rayne is, we understand, a stumbling block in the path of justice; and an important letter has been sent to us from a gentleman whose name was mentioned in the trial which, from the lateness of the hour of its arrival, we cannot publish. Before blood is shed, even in the name of justice, we must have the fullest consideration.[1]

The events that prompted this extraordinary paragraph began barely two hours into the New Year 1863 when an Irish woman, Margaret Docherty, was violently raped and beaten to death behind Newcastle's West Walls.[2] Three hours later a second brutal rape was reported in the town.[3] Although no strangers to rowdy behaviour, the people of

---

[1] *Newcastle Daily Journal*, 28 February 1863, p. 3.
[2] The spelling of her surname varies in contemporary documentation; 'Docherty' is the form most used in the newspaper accounts. For details about Margaret Docherty and her life, see C. Sandford-Couch and H. Rutherford (2018) 'From the Death of a Female Unknown to the Life of Margaret Dockerty: Rediscovering a Nineteenth Century Victim of Crime', *Law, Crime and History*, 8, 1, pp. 21–37.
[3] See The National Archives (TNA), Home Office and Prison Commission, Series 1, Newcastle upon Tyne Gaol: Calendar of Trials at Quarter Sessions and Assizes for the Town and County of Newcastle upon Tyne, PCOM 2/344.

Newcastle upon Tyne were unaccustomed to such violence. As the *Newcastle Guardian* commented, New Year festivities tended to be 'marked by no more serious crimes than the usual numerous cases of drunkenness and disorder'.[4] Within a few hours of the crimes being discovered, the alleged perpetrators of the two crimes were identified and arrested. George Vass, aged nineteen, was charged with the wilful murder of Margaret Docherty, and Patrick Manion, twenty-one, was charged with raping Jane Hall. Both men were subsequently tried, and found guilty, at the Newcastle Spring Assizes on the 27th of February 1863.

George Vass has the dubious distinction of being the last person executed in public in Newcastle. The sentence was carried out on the 14th of March 1863, seventy-two days after the body of his victim was found. The newspapers reported the crime and its aftermath in forensic detail. The tenor of the reporting was generally unsupportive of Vass and branded him as a murderer from the moment of his arrest. However, on the 28th of February, in the editorial quoted above, the *Newcastle Journal* hinted at several factors that called into question whether Vass received the 'fair' trial to which he was entitled under English law.[5]

A microhistorical approach is particularly suitable for the study of such criminal cases and the implications of their outcomes.[6] We wanted to explore, in detail, what may have led to concerns of fairness, when a cursory view of the facts suggested little doubt as to Vass' guilt. That there was no attempt to save Vass from the hangman's noose, indicating widespread popular agreement that the verdict was sound. In particular, we noted a plea by Vass's defence counsel to the trial jury, that they should 'dismiss from their minds all that they had heard, all that they had read, all that they had seen before coming to that court'.[7] In attempting to establish what may have provoked these concerns, we focus upon the reporting in the newspapers, together with other distinctive factors that appear potentially prejudicial to a 'fair' trial. The Vass case also affords a valuable opportunity to bring to wider attention a trial from the Northeast of England, a region relatively under-researched and under-represented in crime history scholarship.

Research for this chapter has relied upon newspaper reports as the chief source of information, not least because there is a lack of other sources. The Assize file includes information about the trial, depositions from the inquest and statements of witnesses in the Police Court, but despite a wide search we have been unable to find any other contemporary material.[8] There is an absence of ephemera: no local broadsides,

---

[4] *Newcastle Guardian*, 3 January 1863, p. 4.
[5] The changing meaning and uses of the notion of a 'fair trial' are discussed in I. Langford (2009) 'Fair Trial: The History of an Idea', *Journal of Human Rights*, 8, 1, pp. 37–52.
[6] This view is expressed for example in M.J. Wiener (1999) 'The Sad Story of George Hall: Adultery, Murder and the Politics of Mercy in Mid-Victorian England', *Social History*, 24, 2, pp. 174–95 at p. 174.
[7] *Newcastle Daily Journal*, 28 February 1863, p. 3 and *Newcastle Courant*, 6 March 1863, p. 2.
[8] TNA, Assizes: Northern and North-Eastern Circuit: Miscellanea, ASSI 47/47; TNA, Assizes: Northern and North-Eastern Circuits: Criminal Depositions and Case Papers, ASSI 45/74 and TNA, Assizes: Northern and North-Eastern Circuits: Indictment Files, ASSI 44/180 contain the available information. In addition to the National Archives, we have searched the Tyne and Wear Archives, Durham Archives, Northumberland Archives catalogues and found nothing of relevance.

pamphlets or published accounts, nor references to the execution in sources such as the *Newgate Calendar*. There are few references to Vass in popular compilations of executions such as the Hangman's Tales.[9] Although there can be problems relying upon newspapers as the primary source for research, in this case the newspaper accounts offer a wealth of material, including a rich account of the trial. A comparison of the depositions alongside the newspaper reports confirms that the reporting of witness evidence is accurate.

This chapter addresses the main points of contention arising in Vass's trial. As Langford noted, the mid-nineteenth century began to see a development in the understanding of what constituted a 'fair' trial, from referring not only to the right to due process, but to include 'the beginnings of what might be uses that imply a trial run to protect the rights of one party'.[10] Both meanings are reflected in the concerns expressed in the editorial of the *Newcastle Journal* and defence counsel's arguments in the Vass case. The chapter considers questions of fairness and justice not only in the light of prejudicial reporting, but also because of the presence of waxwork effigies of Vass displayed in Newcastle, both before and after the trial. It becomes necessary to examine the impact of the waxworks, and explore contemporary concerns relating to the conduct of the trial itself, not least the possibility that Vass may have had a defence, which, for quite unique reasons, might not have been fully considered by the jury.

Pre-trial – All that they had read – 'The cheap press of this town'

The role of reporting in the local and national press is central to the analysis of the Vass trial and whether there can be said to have been a miscarriage of justice. In the nineteenth century, the invention of the steam press and removal of punitive taxation on newspapers led to what Wiener described as 'an explosion' in the number of newspapers available in England.[11] Each had to fill pages with stories that would sell newspapers. As Rowbotham et al. noted, 'The popularity of legal news (particularly crime news) also helped shape the expansion of the press.'[12] There was an insatiable public appetite for accounts of sensational murders, and local, national and specialist newspapers catered for this.[13] Understandably, the 'West Walls murder', as the crime became known, was widely reported both locally and nationally. The interest of national newspapers in the Vass case was not unusual. *The Times* reported on virtually every assize session held and reports of murder trials sold particularly well: 'after 1840,

---

[9] It is not that the tradition of broadsides had ended in the North East by 1863. Some twelve years later, the execution of John William Anderson was the subject of a broadside ballad. See http://ballads.bodleian.ox.ac.uk/search/roud/V9451 (accessed 4 June 2019).

[10] Langford, 'Fair Trial', p. 47.

[11] M.J. Wiener (1999) 'Judges v. Jurors: Courtroom Tensions in Murder Trials and the Law of Criminal Responsibility in Nineteenth-Century England', *Law and History Review*, 17, 3, pp. 467–506 at p. 467 and p. 471.

[12] J. Rowbotham, K. Stevenson and S. Pegg (2014) *Crime News in Modern Britain: Press Reporting and Responsibility, 1820–2010* (London: Palgrave), p. 49.

[13] R.D. Altick (1970) *Victorian Studies in Scarlet* (London: J M Dent and Sons), p. 10.

no more than two or three per cent of murder trials, listed *in toto* in Home office files, failed to be noted in *The Times*.[14] Murder trials were uncommon in Newcastle, which ensured that the Vass case caught the public interest.[15] The police investigation; the coroner's inquest; the Police Court hearing; the trial; Vass's conduct in gaol, and finally his execution were reported as far away as Australia.[16]

The detailed reporting of the case prior to trial was of particular concern to Benjamin Brunton Blackwell, Vass's defence counsel. Contemporary newspaper reporting contained detailed accounts of the crime and, indeed, much of the resulting copy could be regarded as inflammatory. In court Blackwell emphasized that the crime had been put before the jury 'daily by the cheap press of this town, which had been teeming from time to time with recitals with regard to this terrible tragedy'; he noted that 'day after day [Vass] … had been pointed out as a murderer, and nothing less'. He asserted that editorials had been written 'in which the kind of life [Vass] had been leading had been recited'. Whilst flattering the jurors by stating that he knew that a Newcastle jury would give his client a fair hearing, he acknowledged that 'some of the jury must have read those recitals, and unfortunately, they could not help a "little prejudice" getting into their minds'.[17]

His concerns were justified. Even before the victim had been identified, *The Newcastle Guardian* named Vass as the murderer.[18] The problem of potentially prejudicial pre-trial publicity was recognized by all involved in the legal process, but as Bentley noted, 'newspapers had since the 1780s habitually reported evidence given at inquests and preliminary examinations of accused'.[19] This is evident in the reporting of the rape and murder of Margaret Docherty: both the *Newcastle Daily Chronicle and Northern Counties Advertiser* and the *Newcastle Journal* of the 3rd of January carried extensive coverage of the proceedings in the Police Court before the magistrates, and the inquest evidence was reported in detail. The *Newcastle Courant* and *Newcastle Guardian* of the 9th of January set out almost verbatim accounts of the witness statements. It would have been impossible for a reader of newspapers in Newcastle to avoid the coverage, regardless of which title they favoured.

The newspapers ensured that their readership was fully appraised of the character of the defendant. As Bentley has observed, 'if an accused committed for trial was known to be of bad character the public would be told'.[20] There was no doubt in the press that Vass, a man of 'bad character', was the culprit.[21] Newspaper comment on pending cases was a well-known problem for defence counsel, although proceedings for contempt

---

[14] Wiener, 'Judges v. Jurors', p. 468, note 2.
[15] Patrick Forbes' execution in 1850 had been the most recent.
[16] See, for example, *Goulburn Herald*, 16 May 1863, p. 4.
[17] The account of Mr Blackwell's defence argument on this point is taken from *The Newcastle Courant*, 6 March 1863.
[18] *The Newcastle Daily Chronicle and Northern Counties Advertiser* did the same; see 3 January 1863, p. 3.
[19] D. Bentley (1998) *English Criminal Justice in the Nineteenth Century* (London and Ohio: The Hambledon Press), p. 43.
[20] Ibid., p. 43.
[21] *The Newcastle Daily Journal*, 2 January 1863, p. 2.

were rare.²² It is evident from Blackwell's rather desperate attempts to flatter the jury into disregarding what they might have read that there was little that could be done to ameliorate such potentially prejudicial pre-trial publicity. The language used to report the case and its effect on readers of the newspapers are crucial to understand why Blackwell felt it necessary to address the jury on the issue of prejudice and implore them to 'dismiss from their minds ... all that they had read'.²³

All that they had seen – 'Come and look at the murderer George Vass'

The nature of pre-trial reporting, whilst sensationalist in its language, was to be expected. Contemporary murders were described in salacious detail, and the alleged perpetrators identified and reported as such long before the jury had reached its verdict. However, the Vass case featured an intriguing addition to the reporting of the crime and arguably a more persuasive source of prejudice. It was not just words that painted a portrait of a murderer. There was a much more tangible depiction of Vass, one accessible to even the illiterate in Newcastle, or any jurors who avoided the newspapers: his likeness, rendered in wax. The existence of waxworks raises a number of questions, none of which can be answered with certainty. What function were the waxworks intended to have? Who might have seen them? What might spectators of the waxworks have seen? What impact might they have had on the viewer? And what was their impact on the trial?

Vass's defence counsel was sufficiently concerned about the waxworks' potential as prejudicial pre-trial publicity to address the matter in court. Blackwell complained that waxworks exhibitions were 'publically placarded about the place, inviting the public to come and view Vass, the murderer of Mrs Docherty'.²⁴ Waxworks of Vass were also subsequently mentioned in evidence given to the Royal Commission on Capital Punishment in 1864 by the social reformer William Tallack.²⁵ Tallack was secretary to the Howard Association from 1866 to 1901 and a vocal activist for penal reform. In 1863, he was appointed as secretary to the Society for the Abolition of Capital Punishment, and in this capacity came to Newcastle. On the 30th of March 1863, he gave a lecture at the Friends' Meeting House titled 'Prisons, Convicts and Executions', and this must have been when he saw the waxworks. In his evidence to the Select Committee, he recalled seeing 'in two of the principal thoroughfares in Newcastle, two waxwork effigies with an inscription in front "A correct model of George Vass".' Vass was executed on the 16th of March, so Tallack's evidence indicates that exhibitions of

---

[22] Bentley, *English Criminal Justice*, p. 46, note 27 and p. 49, note 49.
[23] *The Newcastle Daily Journal*, 28 February 1863, p. 3.
[24] *The Newcastle Courant*, 6 March 1863, p. 2.
[25] (1866) *Report of the Capital Punishment Commission: Together with the Minutes of Evidence and Appendix; Presented to Both Houses of Parliament* (London: HMSO), para. 1331.

the effigy remained on display at least two weeks after the execution, giving them some form of post-mortem impact.

Whatever the effect of the waxworks on the members of the jury before the trial, they clearly made a strong impression on Tallack. The fact that he mentioned the Newcastle waxworks, and no others, in his evidence to the Select Committee might suggest that something about them was unusual. Why did they affect Tallack so profoundly? Unlike paintings or photographs, waxworks encourage 'in the round' viewing, making them potentially more realistic to a viewer than a two-dimensional image. Photographs were rare in 1863, and generally featured well-known people and places. The three-dimensional effect of a waxwork, possibly combined with suitable or authentic clothing items, would have a strong impact on the viewer, encouraging them to 'believe' in the reality of what they were seeing. Warner has suggested that viewers of waxwork images 'invest the stubborn, inanimate, horrible thing with life, with soul'.[26] For this to be the case, the image would need to be convincing. It is almost certain that a wax representation of Vass would have been life-size and this would increase its anthropological function, that is, representing, or standing in, for the actual person. This seems macabre, given that the waxwork outlived Vass himself.

There is no note of when these grisly mannequins were first displayed, nor precisely where. The waxworks were not advertised in the local newspapers. Blackwell's reference to placards suggests that some form of advertising was used to publicize them, perhaps a 'sandwich board' walked through the town. Tallack referred to the waxworks as 'displayed in leading thoroughfares in Newcastle', meaning that they would have been accessible to the local urban crowd and to casual visitors.[27] Location is obviously important when considering who might have seen the figures. The relatively low cost of attending waxwork displays made them attractive to individuals from many walks of life, although by the mid-nineteenth-century wax shows were often seen as a lower-class, popular entertainment.[28] However, entrance prices clearly anticipated visitors from all social classes; for example, in 1851 a waxworks show offered two entrance prices: 6d for ladies and gentlemen and 3d for working people, servants and children.[29]

Blackwell assumed that at least some members of the jury might have seen the waxworks, indicating their location was in a space likely to be visited by the class of person who served on a jury.[30] Although we have no evidence of a permanent exhibition, travelling waxwork shows regularly presented in Newcastle.[31] Most pertinently, we have discovered that there was a waxwork exhibition in a shop on Grainger Street

---

[26] M. Warner (2006) *Phantasmagoria* (Oxford: Oxford University Press), p. 55.

[27] (1866) *Royal Commission on Capital Punishment – Report of the Capital Punishment Commission: Together with the Minutes of Evidence and Appendix* (London: HMSO).

[28] P. Pilbeam (2003) *Madame Tussaud and the History of Waxworks* (New York: Hambledon and London), p. 234.

[29] *The Newcastle Daily Journal*, 11 October 1851, p. 1. It is possible that these prices were charged on different days, to cater for – and separate – particular audiences.

[30] In 1863 jurors were men, aged between twenty-one and sixty, who met a property qualification (Juries Act 1825).

[31] On the Springthorpe waxworks, see M. MacGilp (2014) 'Springthorpe: Waxworks, Views, Concerts, Marionettes', *Theatre Notebook*, 68, 1, pp. 2–18.

in January 1863, although there is no record of its contents.[32] Grainger Street is a main thoroughfare that leads to the town centre from the railway station, making it reasonable to surmise that this may have been the location of one of the Vass effigies.[33] Other references to waxworks in 1863 include an exhibition at a fair in the Spring held on Scotswood Road, another route into Newcastle.[34] A travelling exhibition would have included models not only of nationally (in)famous figures, but also would potentially appeal to local audiences by depicting people well known in that area. The population would have been greatly familiar with wax representations. As Pilbeam noted, 'before photography, wax models were the nearest most people got to knowing what the famous – and the infamous – looked like'.[35] The portrayal of criminals in some form of cultural ephemera in the nineteenth century is well documented; this included death masks, mass-produced figurines and even gingerbread effigies.[36] Full-sized waxworks were popular, often exhibited in dedicated museums, of which Madame Tussaud's is the most well known.[37] Tussaud's 1869 catalogue refers to a seemingly random mix of criminals, the notorious and more 'domestic' personalities.[38] Part of the attraction of Tussaud's Chamber of Horrors was that figures of notorious criminals were displayed whilst there was still contemporary interest in their case.[39]

Kornmeier suggested that part of the intention behind displaying famous felons was that their images could act as a deterrent in much the same way as images of leaders and royalty could inspire. In effect, it would act as an exemplum. However, 'the renown of the criminal was, in effect, created by the media: broadsheets and ballads, printed caricatures and newspapers that carried his name and the stories of his deeds into the public'.[40] Whether through such media or otherwise, Vass had some local renown: witnesses to the crime knew him by name, and the press reported that he had supporters. At the trial his defence counsel was cheered from the gallery, and there was a report that someone called his name as the lever was pulled on the scaffold.[41] It is possible that having his likeness on display in wax may in itself have enhanced the celebrity or notoriety of Vass created via other media, in and around Newcastle, prior

---

[32] *The Newcastle Daily Chronicle and Northern Counties Advertiser*, 31 January 1863, p. 7.
[33] Grainger Street was also the location of the tailor's shop where Margaret Docherty's husband was employed.
[34] *The Newcastle Daily Chronicle and Northern Counties Advertiser*, 7 April 1863, p. 2.
[35] P. Pilbeam (2002) 'Madame Tussaud and Her Waxworks', *History Today*, 52, 12, pp. 6–7.
[36] See D. Taylor (1998) *Crime Policing and Punishment in England, 1750-1914* (London: Palgrave), p. 136; J. Flanders (2011) *The Invention of Murder: How the Victorians Revelled in Death and Detection and Created Modern Crime* (London: Harper Press), pp. 4–68 and R. Crone (2012) *Violent Victorians: Popular Entertainment in Nineteenth Century London* (Manchester: Manchester University Press), pp. 80–116.
[37] Most histories of wax museums have focussed on Tussaud's, for example, L. Cottrell (1965) *Madame Tussaud* (London: Evans Brothers) and Pilbeam, *Madame Tussaud and the History of Waxworks*.
[38] Madame Tussaud & Sons' Exhibition (1869) *Catalogue Containing Biographical and Descriptive Sketches of the Distinguished Characters Which Compose the Unrivalled Exhibition and Historical Gallery of Madame Tussaud and Sons* (London: Printed for G. Cole), p.36.
[39] See P. Chapman (1984) *Madame Tussaud's Chamber of Horrors* (London: HarperCollins).
[40] U. Kornmeier (2008) 'The Famous and the Infamous: Waxworks as Retailers of Renown', *International Journal of Cultural Studies*, 11, 3, pp. 276–88, at 284.
[41] *The Newcastle Courant*, 6 March 1863, p. 2.

to and during his trial.⁴² Exhibiting in effigy a contemporary 'celebrity' figure (like Vass) would have been an attractive option for those running waxworks as popular commercial entertainment. Likenesses could be made relatively quickly and would not have been expensive because often only the head was modelled in wax and attached to a generic body. Waxworks were not anatomically correct and therefore clothing, hair and props were used to indicate gender and identity.⁴³ Real hair or teeth would be used to produce 'an uncanny figure in a liminal space between the organic and the inorganic, life and death'.⁴⁴ Actual clothes, or imitations, owned by the figures portrayed were used to make the waxworks as 'realistic' as possible. Tussaud's would buy a prisoner's clothes from the hangman; to enhance verisimilitude there was also a 'representation of a dock in which criminals are tried'.⁴⁵

The quest for realism is understandable, but how necessary was accuracy in representing a figure like Vass? MacGilp has suggested that a waxwork 'requires a certain input from the public: a suspension of disbelief and a willingness to engage in the life story or life events of the characters being represented'.⁴⁶ How many citizens in Newcastle would have known Vass by sight? He was apparently nondescript: a 'short, thick- set young man, of rather unprepossessing features'.⁴⁷ We know only that: 'his countenance ... is not positively ill-favoured. He [had] no beard, and his jet black hair was straightly parted and smoothed down.'⁴⁸ In fact, specific details about his appearance are scant because the newspaper reports generally focused on his demeanour. There appear to be no surviving engravings in the newspapers and no image in printed material. Possibly the waxwork represented a man who was not immediately recognizable to many; would particular items of clothing help to distinguish Vass from any other poor labourer in Newcastle? When arrested, he wore bloodstained clothes: did this feature? Was a label necessary? This might be the case, especially before the trial, when Vass would not have been widely recognized. However, there are what can be termed 'generative qualities in the act of looking', i.e. when looking we construct meaning behind the images themselves.⁴⁹ The descriptions by Blackwell and Tallack refer to some form of words accompanying the waxwork to identify it as George Vass and therefore we can assume that a reasonably credible representation, coupled with an identifying label, may well have been sufficient to satisfy those looking at the waxwork that what they saw was a likeness of 'George Vass'.

---

⁴² The relationship between fame, celebrity and waxwork images is discussed in Kornmeier (2008) 'Waxworks'.
⁴³ M.E. Bloom (2003) *Waxworks: A Cultural Obsession* (Minneapolis: University of Minnesota Press), p. 27.
⁴⁴ I. Junyk (2008) 'Spectacles of Virtue: Classicism, Waxworks and the Festivals of the French Revolution', *Early Popular Visual Culture*, 6, 3, pp. 281–304 at p. 285, note 8.
⁴⁵ Madame Tussaud & Sons' Exhibition, *Catalogue*, p. 36.
⁴⁶ MacGilp, 'Springthorpe', p. 2.
⁴⁷ *Morpeth Herald*, 10 January 1863, p. 6.
⁴⁸ *The Newcastle Daily Chronicle and Northern Counties Advertiser*, 3 January 1863, p. 3.
⁴⁹ Questions of spectatorship – how we look and think about or consume images – are the subject of much debate, and beyond the scope of this chapter.

The function of a label or sign carried by or attached to the waxwork of Vass deserves further consideration. Much could depend on what such labels said, and whether they were accompanied by text, outlining the crime, for example. As the intent was presumably popular entertainment, it is unlikely that they would have borne factually accurate references to the legal status of Vass pre-trial. Tallack referred to an inscription 'A correct model of George Vass' in his evidence to the Select Committee. Would these have been the same waxworks Vass's defence counsel indicated were on view in the town prior to the trial? If so, did the signs say more than this, as Blackwell intimated? Or was Vass by that time such a well-known figure in the city that no further identification of the man or his crime would be needed? Contemporary viewers may have made connections readily between figures in waxwork exhibitions and current events, including criminal trials. A label or sign may have been intended to encourage viewers or spectators to reflect on the horrific actions of the murderer whose wax representation stood before them. Doing so could perhaps reinforce a connection between the man and his crime, encouraging the viewer to identify the person with the act.

It is possible to take this further, to question whether merely seeing waxworks on display in publicly accessible areas pre-trial may have played a role in creating expectations of guilt. Might the image itself in some way form part of the accusation against Vass (along the lines of 'George Vass is rendered in wax; Criminals are rendered in wax; Ergo, George Vass is a criminal')?[50] Could the accompanying words 'George Vass' cause viewers to recall all that they had read or knew of the crime of which he was – at that stage – not yet convicted? Perceptions may be influenced by images in particular ways and the question arises whether potential jurors may be more (or even equally) influenced by visual media (e.g. images) than print media (e.g. newspaper articles). We cannot know the effect of the waxwork on a nineteenth-century jury; indeed, it appears there is relatively little research addressing how pictures or other images influence even modern-day jurors' verdicts.[51] However, it is at least arguable that an image 'in the round', like a waxwork, could have had more impact on jurors in its immediacy and accessibility than a two-dimensional image in print.

In 1863 – as now – there were tensions between pre-trial publicity and a fair trial.[52] In criminal cases, courts entrust the jury to make a decision based on the evidence presented to them and not on what they have gleaned outside of court. Much research has been carried out on the impact of prejudicial pre-trial publicity on modern-day

---

[50] On the developing field of visual criminology, see M. Brown and E. Carrabine (2017) 'Introducing Visual Criminology' in M. Brown and E. Carrabine (eds) *Routledge International Handbook of Visual Criminology* (Oxford and New York: Routledge), pp. 1–10.

[51] Interestingly, in 2017, the American Bar Association, drawing on studies showing that visual perception and visual communication have a distinct impact in a jury setting, released a guide, *Images with Impact: Design and Use of Winning Trial Visuals*, intended to 'help trial lawyers turn trial themes into effective visual images that juries are more likely to understand, believe and remember, which can contribute to winning the trial'.

[52] See Bentley, *English Criminal Justice*, pp. 43–9. On the historical development of criminal courts' approach to publicity and its impact on jurors, and difficulties in handling media prejudice, see D. Corker and M. Levi (1996) 'Pre-trial Publicity and Its Treatment in the English courts', *Criminal Law Review*, September, pp. 622–32.

jurors.[53] A US study found that such publicity, particularly negative information about a defendant's character, could influence initial judgements about guilt; this bias was only weakened, not eliminated, by the evidence presented at trial, leading the report's authors to conclude that pre-trial publicity may affect how jurors evaluate evidence presented at trial.[54] Defendants may be vilified before they have even appeared before a judge. Research has indicated that pre-trial publicity had a negative impact on juror perceptions of a defendant's criminality and produced an increased frequency of guilty verdicts.[55] A Ministry of Justice report, 'Are Juries Fair?' found that of the jurors questioned one-fifth would have found it hard to exclude pre-trial coverage from their minds during trial.[56] Would a jury in 1863 have responded differently? The risk – then as now – is that the objectivity required of jurors and other parties in the courtroom could be compromised by exposure to media coverage. The publication of images of Vass – whether in wax or otherwise – which may have referred to his crime, in the town in which his trial was due to take place, clearly had the potential to damage the defendant's character, or to lead jurors to assume guilt on the basis of that portrayal.

As objects of visual culture, waxworks of Vass are difficult to categorize, sitting somewhere between art, entertainment and reportage. Their impact upon the trial is similarly hard to assess. We can only imagine how the sight of a wax effigy with a placard stating 'the Murderer Vass' might have affected the members of the jury.[57] The presence of waxworks of Vass in the streets of Newcastle before the trial could be considered prejudicial; at the very least, such pre-trial behaviour seems inappropriate. Newcastle was a small town and the members of the trial jury would have been aware of waxworks so publically displayed. Legal professionals involved in the trial agreed on their likely effect. Blackwell, in his address to the jury, implored jurors not to be swayed.[58] Counsel for the prosecution, William Digby Seymour, described the existence of the waxworks as 'shocking'.[59] The judge suggested that the waxwork show was 'far worse' than any prejudice in the newspapers.[60] There is acknowledgement that

---

[53] The difficulties courts face over identifying whether pre-trial publicity was prejudicial to jury's treatment of evidence and verdict are explored in T.M. Honess, S. Barker, E. Charman and M. Levi (2002) 'Empirical and Legal Perspectives on the Impact of Pre-trial Publicity', *Criminal Law Review*, September, pp. 719–27. See also A. Ardill (2000) 'The Right to a Fair Trial: Prejudicial Pre-trial Media Publicity', *Alternative Law Journal*, 25, 1, pp. 3–9, which examines an accused's right to a fair trial after inadmissible and prejudicial material was published pre-trial.

[54] A.L. Otto, S. Penrod and H.R. Dexter (1994) 'The Biasing Impact of Pretrial Publicity on Juror Judgments', *Law and Human Behavior*, 18, 4, pp. 453–69.

[55] L. Hope, A. Memon and P. McGeorge (2004) 'Understanding Pre-trial Publicity Pre-decisional Distortion of Evidence by Mock Jurors', *Journal of Experimental Psychology: Applied*, 10, 2, pp. 111–19. See also C.L. Ruva and M.A. LeVasseur (2012) 'Behind Closed Doors: The Effect of Pre-trial Publicity on Jury Deliberations', *Psychology, Crime and Law*, 18, 5, pp. 431–52.

[56] C. Thomas (2010) *Are Juries Fair?*, Ministry of Justice Research Series 1-10 (London: Ministry of Justice).

[57] On the relationship between prejudicial pretrial publicity and jury decision-making, see J.M. Ellison and P.K. Brennan (2014) 'Prejudicial Pretrial Publicity', *The Encyclopedia of Criminology and Criminal Justice*, pp. 1–5 available online at http://onlinelibrary.wiley.com/doi/10.1002/9781118517383.wbeccj462 (accessed 3 June 2019).

[58] *The Newcastle Daily Chronicle and Northern Counties Advertiser*, 28 February 1863, p. 3.

[59] *The Newcastle Courant*, 6 March 1863, p. 2.

[60] *The Newcastle Daily Chronicle and Northern Counties Advertiser*, 28 February 1863, p. 3.

the mere presence of the waxworks could be prejudicial to a fair trial. It is not hard to argue that the waxworks of Vass formed part of the spectacle of the criminal justice process, in effect a facet of a 'pre-trial by media'.

The trial itself

Despite the consternation of the lawyers, the pre-trial publicity was, it would seem, not the main concern of the *Newcastle Journal*, when it suggested that the Vass trial 'as it has been conducted' had not been 'characterised by … fairness and justice'. What caused the *Newcastle Journal* to alarm its readership? Several aspects of the trial deserve closer consideration. In addition to the specific concerns raised in the *Newcastle Journal* editorial about the evidence of Dr Rayne, our research addresses the alternative construction of the events advanced on behalf of George Vass, and the infelicitous conjunction of Vass's trial with that of Patrick Manion.

Vass, as the law at the time prescribed, could not speak in his defence at his trial. His fate lay in the hands of his barrister Mr Blackwell. Vass was fortunate in having legal representation at all. Defendants in criminal cases were only allowed representation at the discretion of the judge until this was formalized in the Prisoner's Counsel Act 1836. Because of this legislation, defence counsel could examine and cross-examine witnesses, address the jury and offer observations about evidence. Technically the defence could also call witnesses; however, this right was relatively rarely used in criminal trials due to the inability of defendants to pay for legal representation who could secure witnesses and, as Bentley has noted, the poverty of potential witnesses who could not afford to give up time to attend court.[61] In fact, by 1860, as Bentley reports, in murder cases assignment of defence counsel had become an 'almost routine practice'. However, this was still at the discretion of the judge and the Assize judge in this case, Baron Martin, had a reputation for reluctance to assign counsel, even in murder trials.[62] That he did so, in the Vass case, makes it an exception to his more usual practice.

Blackwell was an experienced advocate who had attended court on the morning of the 28th of February to prosecute Patrick Manion for rape. Instead, he was assigned the unenviable task of defending Vass at only an hour's notice. Blackwell highlighted in his address to the jury the disadvantage of his late instruction. The effectiveness of such last-minute appointees has been questioned. Wiener contended that 'in the majority of murder trials, defense [sic] counsel, often engaged or assigned at the last moment, made little difference'.[63] Much depends of course on the definition of 'difference'. Blackwell fulfilled his dock brief to the best of his ability and carried out his, likely unpaid, role as defender of Vass with great skill and commitment. Blackwell had a very

---

[61] Bentley, *English Criminal Justice*, p. 154.
[62] Bentley cites examples of murder trials in 1857, 1858, 1859, 1861 and 1862, where Baron Martin had refused to assign counsel, see ibid., p. 112.
[63] Wiener, 'Judges v. Jurors', p. 474, note 22.

difficult task to perform and although his advocacy made no discernible difference to the eventual outcome, he carefully addressed each witness's testimony and each piece of evidence, suggesting alternative interpretations. The trial, which started at 10 am, did not finish until 7 pm. The judge told Vass that 'everything an advocate could say on your behalf was laid before the jury'.[64] This judicial praise was echoed at the close of the evidence when Blackwell's address to the jury was rewarded by 'applause from the mob in the gallery'.[65] What did he say, in advocating for Vass, to provoke such reaction?

In an English court of law, in 1863 as now, an accused person was innocent until proven guilty. The burden of proof was on the prosecution to prove guilt beyond reasonable doubt. If there was reasonable doubt, it had to be exercised in the defendant's favour. In this sense, Vass did not require a 'defence' so much as for his barrister to raise sufficient doubt in the jury's minds as to his guilt. Blackwell sought to achieve this. However, the swift nature of the jury deliberation and the final verdict suggests he was afforded no benefit of doubt from the jury, nor, arguably, was he considered innocent until proven guilty.

Blackwell's attempts to persuade the jury that there was reasonable doubt as to Vass's guilt required him to undermine what they had heard set out by counsel for the prosecution. He sought to do so, in part, by discrediting the witnesses, or their testimony.[66] His second strategy was even bolder: he attempted to raise doubt that there was a murder at all. Blackwell explained to the jury that they had two questions to answer: the first was to consider whether Margaret Docherty had been murdered; the second was to decide (if she had been) whether it had been proved, beyond all reasonable doubt, that Vass was the man who had committed that murder. Blackwell urged the jury to focus solely on the question of whether Vass had, with malice aforethought, murdered Margaret Docherty. The evidence of murder presented by the prosecution was circumstantial. Vass was seen dragging Margaret by the hair to the West Walls; he was observed attacking her, and when he was arrested, his clothes were bloodstained. Witnesses were aware of the brutality of the attack: one is recorded as shouting, 'Vass give over, you're killing the woman'.[67] However, no one testified to seeing how Margaret Docherty died.

Blackwell offered an alternative version of events, which, he hoped, would convince the jury that they could not be certain 'beyond reasonable doubt' that Vass intentionally killed Margaret Docherty. Vass admitted the rape, but his statement to the police, and the account of the witnesses, left a period of time when his victim lay unattended.[68] Blackwell sought to raise the possibility that the fatal injuries were inflicted not by Vass, but by a supervening act.

---

[64] The fact that Blackwell could mount a plausible defence indicates that someone else had been involved in gathering the information: we suspect that a solicitor, Mr John Alderton Bush, who had represented Vass in the Police Court, carried out the preparatory work.
[65] *The Newcastle Courant*, 6 March 1863, p. 2.
[66] For example, Blackwell described the actions of one witness as being to the 'discredit of humanity' – see ibid.
[67] TNA, Assizes: Northern and North-Eastern Circuits: Criminal Depositions and Case Papers, ASSI 45/74 – deposition of William Gillespie.
[68] He was not charged with rape.

This was not a fanciful suggestion, but one rooted in evidence tested at the trial. Dr Rayne, the police surgeon who had carried out the post-mortem examination, had deposed in his evidence at the inquest that he had not seen a body 'so fearfully mangled save by machinery'.[69] At the trial, Rayne testified that 'the bones of the upper portion of the face were smashed into innumerable pieces on each side' and that 'the liver was ruptured on both sides ... by direct violence'.[70] Police evidence at the trial suggested that the body was 'a mass of bruises and crushing'.[71] Witnesses testified that violence was used by Vass against Margaret Docherty, namely: blows to the face by his hand;[72] three blows to the ribs.[73] A young witness referred to Vass inflicting a kick, although this evidence was uncorroborated.[74] Another boy testified to seeing Vass lift his foot, but did not know whether he kicked her or not.[75] Blackwell suggested that the violence the witnesses testified to having seen, although dreadful, was insufficient to cause the terrible injuries recorded at the post-mortem examination. He argued instead that after she had been 'ravished' by Vass and struck by his hands, Margaret Docherty was left, alive, in the alleyway. He suggested that her fatal injuries had been caused by being run over by a carriage or cart. A policeman noted that Margaret's body was found lying 'on the carriageway with her head on the curbstone [sic]'.[76] The road behind the West Walls is narrow, but wide enough for small vehicles, and visibility would have been poor around 2 am on the 1st of January: Margaret Docherty was found 'beyond the bend where the lamp is situated'.[77] In Blackwell's words, 'Her death ... was in this way consistent with no murder having taken place at all'.[78]

The suggestion that the injuries suffered by Margaret Docherty were more likely to have been caused by a carriage wheel than a fist had apparently been advanced by a Dr Newton, who had examined the body in the presence of Rayne. Newton was not called at trial, but during cross-examination Blackwell used his comments, together with Rayne's reference to machinery, to attempt to place doubt in the minds of the jury that Vass had killed Margaret Docherty. Under direct questioning by Blackwell, Rayne denied having previously heard Newton express this opinion and in response to a question from the prosecution was adamant that 'the cart wheel could not have

---

[69] TNA, Assizes: Northern and North-Eastern Circuits: Criminal Depositions and Case Papers, ASSI 45/74 – deposition of Septimus Rayne (2 January 1863).
[70] *The Newcastle Courant*, 6 March 1863, p. 2.
[71] Opening address of Mr Seymour, ibid.
[72] See TNA, Assizes: Northern and North-Eastern Circuits: Criminal Depositions and Case Papers, ASSI 45/74. Witness John Buchan: '... he struck her several times over the face', and after questioning by Blackwell said, 'he struck her with his hand two or three times.' Similarly, witness William Gillespie: 'I saw him slap her on the face with his hand. It was only a lightish blow'; and witness Daniel Trainer: '... he hit her on the face.' See *The Newcastle Courant*, 6 March 1863, p. 2.
[73] Witness Henry Branscombe: '... he struck her three times in the ribs' – see *The Newcastle Courant*, 6 March 1863, p. 2.
[74] Witness Daniel Trainer: '... he kicked her two or three times' – see ibid.
[75] See the testimony at note 73 above.
[76] TNA, Assizes: Northern and North-Eastern Circuits: Criminal Depositions and Case Papers, ASSI 45/74 – deposition of PC Hepple.
[77] *The Newcastle Daily Chronicle and Northern Counties Advertiser*, 2 January 1863, p. 2.
[78] *The Newcastle Daily Chronicle and Northern Counties Advertiser*, 28 February 1863, p. 3.

caused the large aorta that rests on the vertebra to be ruptured through two of its coats'.[79] Blackwell suggested that Rayne had not accounted for the injuries to the back of Margaret Docherty's head, and in his closing speech for the defence relied on the alternative theory put forward by Newton, asserting that the injuries were 'just such as would have been occasioned by a wheel ... [and] ... by the hoofs of a horse attached to the vehicle'.[80]

This defence was sufficiently cogent to lead Baron Martin to recommend 'the address to [the jury's] careful consideration'.[81] The approach was 'all or nothing': there was no opportunity for mitigation. In the early nineteenth century, murder convictions had been largely reserved to cases where weapons were used (demonstrating the premeditation required by the legal definition of the offence of murder), but by the 1860s murder convictions were returned in cases of deaths caused by beating. Wiener offers an example, also from 1863, of a man tried for beating his wife to death, despite the attempted intervention of neighbours. Counsel in the case emphasized that the prisoner had used no weapon, only fists. The judge urged the jury to convict for murder in words which resonate with the Vass case: 'If a man used such brutal violence towards a woman ... and continued to do so, after having been warned and cautioned not to kill her, it was difficult to see that he could have meant anything else than to cause her death'.[82] The absence of a relationship between Vass and his victim may have inclined both judge and jury towards viewing his act as 'cold-blooded', and his lack of a weapon not leading to any mitigation. Thus, Blackwell sought to raise doubt: doubt that it was murder at all; and, if it was, doubt that Vass was the culprit. He was unsuccessful. Baron Martin conceded in his summing up to the jury that if a carriage had run over Margaret Docherty, it would not be murder, but commented that 'it seemed almost impossible that any reasonable doubt could exist in any mind as to a murder having been committed'.[83] Baron Martin accepted Blackwell's argument that there was no evidence that Vass's violence had caused the death but offered his own view that the evidence suggested instead that Vass had returned after the rape to commit 'that violence upon the woman that caused her death'.

It is probable that Dr Newton was the man referred to in the *Newcastle Journal* article as being the author of 'an important letter ... which, from the lateness of the hour of its arrival we cannot publish', having become concerned about the lack of weight attached to the alternative explanation for the fatal injuries.[84] Although this letter prompted the *Newcastle Journal*'s editorial drawing attention to the justice of the trial, inexplicably it did not subsequently publish the letter in full. The editorial in the *Newcastle Journal* is vehement in its language questioning the fairness of the trial

---

[79] *The Newcastle Daily Journal*, 28 February 1863, p. 3.
[80] *The Newcastle Daily Journal*, 28 February 1863, p. 3 and *Morpeth Herald*, 7 March 1863, p. 6.
[81] *The Newcastle Courant*, 6 March 1863, p. 2.
[82] R. v. Howes, *The Times*, 6 August 1863 and Wiener (1999) 'Judges v. Jurors', p. 494.
[83] *The Newcastle Daily Journal*, 28 February 1863, p. 3.
[84] Ibid.

(perhaps as some form of corrective to its own prior speculative and feverish reporting of the case). However, no other newspaper was inspired to carry similar reports or to follow up this intriguing reference, leaving the *Newcastle Journal* as a lone voice in presenting any form of counter-influence to those reports which seemed to presume Vass's guilt.

Blackwell was entitled to hope that there was sufficient doubt raised by his address to an intelligent Newcastle jury, in a town where the death penalty had last been used in 1850, to find Vass not guilty of wilful murder. In the ordinary course of events, there may have been. However, Blackwell had also to contend with events in court in addition to the trial of his client: the interwoven prosecution of Patrick Manion.

All that they had heard – 'He did not murder his victim, but you did'

The sequence of events in the Assize Court at the Newcastle Moot Hall on the 27th of February 1863 raises a number of further questions about whether Vass's trial was fair and just. The Vass case was the second matter on the list of cases to be tried by Baron Martin. The first was the trial of Patrick Manion.[85] It is impossible to consider Vass's case in isolation from that of Manion: the same jury heard the two cases concurrently. The fact that each case involved rape of a married woman made comparisons even more likely. In any event, the judge himself had drawn some form of conclusion from the two cases appearing together. When charging the Grand Jury on 26 February, Baron Martin highlighted the unusual nature of the Assize Calendar by emphasizing that it included 'crimes of a character that he had never experienced here before'.[86] He made clear he considered that Vass's crime, when taken together with 'another case in the calendar of a very shocking character indeed' (the Manion case), would 'argue very great immorality in Newcastle'.[87] It is likely that the trial jury would have read, or even heard, this address. The warning may have raised fears of a 'crime wave' or sense of increasing lawlessness in the town.

On the 27th of February, Vass entered the dock and pleaded not guilty. His case was then stood down whilst Blackwell took instructions. Vass remained in the courtroom whilst Manion was tried for the rape of Jane Hall. Defence counsel called witnesses to testify that Manion had an alibi for the time of the assault and suggested that the victim had incorrectly identified her assailant. Before the jury retired, Manion wept and cried, 'Gentlemen of the Jury, I beg mercy, I am not the man.'[88] The jury soon returned and found Manion guilty. Manion was not taken down immediately and was allowed to remain in court whilst Vass was tried. The court was full and the

---

[85] See TNA, Assizes: Northern and North-Eastern Circuit: Miscellanea, ASSI 47/47 for the minutes of the Newcastle Assizes 1863.
[86] *The Newcastle Daily Chronicle and Northern Counties Advertiser*, 27 February 1863, p. 3.
[87] *The Newcastle Daily Journal*, 27 February 1863, p. 3.
[88] *The Newcastle Courant*, 6 March 1863, p. 2.

atmosphere was highly charged. When the jury retired to consider their verdict in the Vass case, Manion was returned to the dock to be sentenced. In passing sentence of penal servitude for life on Manion, Baron Martin noted that he feared 'there was a great deal that took place in this town [on the morning of 1st January] that ought not to take place'.[89] Again, a connection between the two – unrelated – cases was made. Could the jury put from their minds the judge's words, and the guilty verdict they had returned on Manion as they decided Vass's fate? Might Blackwell's argument for Vass's defence have received a more sympathetic audience had the two cases not been tried side-by-side?

A further – but we think significant – point was the reported responses of the defendants to their respective trials. Manion's reaction to his sentence was dramatic: 'The prisoner fell down in the dock, exclaiming "Oh, my poor mother; I'll never see her more". This exclamation was followed by a voice from the gallery (supposed to be the mother of the prisoner). They both had to be carried out of the court.'[90] Did the jury hear, or witness, this reaction? Manion's outpouring of emotion would have merited comment when compared to Vass's reported stolidity and impassivity: 'during the whole trial he [Vass] manifested a perfect indifference to all that was going on. He even several times chatted and laughed with Manion ... whose demeanour presented a striking contrast.'[91] Might this apparent difference in response have influenced the jury, when they retired to consider their verdict on Vass?

When inevitable comparison was made between the concurrent cases – in the nature of the crimes, and the demeanour of the defendants – this would be to the detriment of Vass. Baron Martin highlighted the contrast in his words to Vass after donning the black cap:

> Upon that same morning two rapes were committed – you ravished this woman, and the man who was just removed ravished another. He did not murder his victim, but you did; and you thus have in this town on one and the same night two of the most atrocious offences recognized in the law committed on two women.[92]

There is no doubt that the judge distinguished the cases by emphasizing that Manion did not murder his victim. Although the point was not specifically raised by Blackwell (nor indeed by Manion's defence counsel), it remains distinctly possible that intertwining the two trials impacted upon the jury and so on the outcome of either, or even both, cases.

---

[89] Ibid.
[90] *Newcastle Guardian*, 28 February 1863, p. 8.
[91] Ibid.
[92] *The Newcastle Daily Journal*, 28 February 1863, p. 3.

Conclusion

> Of the guilt of a man convicted by an English jury, there can in ordinary cases be absolutely no doubt at all.[93]

To modern eyes, there was much in, and surrounding, the trial that led to the conviction of George Vass that is unusual, or appears potentially unfair, but inevitably our perception is coloured by contemporary law and practice in England and Wales. Most people are aware of legislation that guarantees a twenty-first century accused the right to a fair trial.[94] The pre-trial newspaper reports seem particularly prejudicial; however, even today, it is difficult to make general points about the modern treatment of contempt of court, as each case turns on its particular facts. Now – as in 1863 – the risk is that pre-trial publicity may prejudice, or even threaten, a juror's impartiality.[95] Contemporary courts in England and Wales are generally reluctant to halt a prosecution because of pre-trial publicity, although where the pre-trial publicity has been such that it is judged a fair trial is not possible, the proceedings may be stayed.[96]

Modern courtroom practice is also very different. We expect all those charged with serious offences to have the right to legal representation (although there is of course no requirement that a defendant must appoint a lawyer).[97] The current system of legal aid ensures that a defendant who wants legal assistance in a criminal case, but does not have the means to pay, will be provided with legal representation.[98] Facing a criminal

---

[93] J.F. Stephen (1860) 'Criminal Law and the Detection of Crime', *Cornhill Magazine*, II, pp. 697–708 at p.708.

[94] Under Article 6 of the European Convention on Human Rights and The Human Rights Act 1998.

[95] Section 1 of the Contempt of Court Act 1981 provides that it is a contempt to publish any matter which creates a substantial risk of serious prejudice or impediment to the course of justice in legal proceedings, irrespective of the intention behind the publication. For an accessible summary of current law and guidance on contempt of court, see https://www.cps.gov.uk/legal-guidance/contempt-court-reporting-restrictions-and-restrictions-public-access-hearings (accessed 28 May 2019). Problems remain in this area of law; for example, see the Law Commission (2012) 'Consultation Paper on Contempt of Court', No. 209, available at https://www.lawcom.gov.uk/project/contempt-of-court (accessed 28 May 2019).

[96] Under section 4(2) of the Contempt of Court Act 1981, courts can order that contemporary court reporting be postponed, where necessary to avoid a substantial risk of prejudice to those or other imminent or pending legal proceedings. If the defence argues that pre-trial publicity has amounted to an abuse of process, certain considerations as to how pre-trial publicity may affect a jury can be taken into account: see the discussion in a Scottish criminal case, Montgomery v H M Advocate and another; [2001] 2 W.L.R. 779.

[97] There is a right to legal representation under Common Law and under Article 6 of the European Convention on Human Rights. Despite the Prisoners' Counsel Act 1836, high fees often restricted the presence of defence counsel in criminal trials, until the Poor Prisoners Defence Act 1903 provided for defendants in criminal cases to gain financial assistance in an early form of 'legal aid'.

[98] Article 6 of the European Convention on Human Rights provides that if a defendant has insufficient means to pay for legal assistance, it should be given free when the interests of justice so require. The current system of legal aid has its roots in the Legal Aid and Advice Act 1949. Following much debate on access to criminal legal aid following changes which have arguably led (in magistrates courts at least) to an increasing number of unrepresented defendants, in December 2018, the Ministry of Justice announced a comprehensive review of criminal legal aid fee schemes: https://www.gov.uk/guidance/criminal-legal-aid-review (accessed 28 May 2019).

charge, a defendant has the right to adequate time and facilities for the preparation of their defence.[99] A defendant can now decide whether to give evidence in his or her own trial, and whether to answer questions.[100] The jury in such a case would be significantly more representative of society than a nineteenth-century jury. The number of people who qualify for jury service has dramatically increased.[101] In current court practice, twelve jurors from a pool of fifteen potential jurors are chosen at random by the court clerk to sit in an assigned trial, rather than hear all cases on a given day.[102]

Perhaps what is most striking, in the context of 1863, is that there was nothing unusual or 'wrong' in the handling of the Vass case. Neither the prejudicial pre-trial reporting nor the presence of the waxworks nor the treatment of a possible defence for Vass or even the concurrence of the trials of Vass and Manion were sufficiently unusual occurrences for the trial to be held to be unfair. Despite this, the 'fairness' of Vass's trial and the guilty verdict was questioned by defence counsel and one newspaper editorial at the time of the trial. Prompted by these contemporary doubts, we must examine whether this verdict was reached after a 'fair' trial, a key tenet of the English legal system.

In relation to the pre-trial labelling of Vass as a murderer, the existence of the waxworks in Newcastle did not lead the judge to conclude that a fair trial was impossible. As now, the problem was not the absence of law to control contempt, but the failure to enforce extant laws, whether against editors of newspapers who printed prejudicial material pre-trial, or proprietors of waxwork exhibitions.[103] Of course, an overriding factor in 1863 must have been that civil actions for contempt of court were usually brought by the victim of the prejudicial conduct and privately funded legal action was simply not possible for a defendant such as George Vass.[104] It is evident that little weight was given to Vass's possible defence by the trial jury, despite his barrister's valiant efforts.

In any event, Blackwell was prevented, by the law, from calling Vass in his own defence and thus he had to construct a defence as well as he could, by questioning the evidence presented by the prosecution and addressing the jury accordingly.[105] Standard nineteenth-century courtroom procedures were applied in the court: it was normal and expected that the same jury would sit and hear all the cases coming before the Assize judges that day. Theoretically, the position of a defendant should not have

---

[99] Article 6 of the European Convention on Human Rights.
[100] The Criminal Procedure Rules 2015.
[101] See the Juries Act 1974, available as amended at: http://www.legislation.gov.uk/ukpga/1974/23/contents (accessed 28 May 2019).
[102] The Criminal Procedure Rules 2015.
[103] M. Hewitt (2017) 'The Law and the Press' in J. Shattock (ed.) *Journalism and the Periodical Press in Nineteenth Century Britain* (Cambridge: Cambridge University Press), pp. 147–64 at p. 162.
[104] Bentley, *English Criminal Justice*, p. 49.
[105] The Criminal Evidence Act 1898 allowed for the first time that a defendant could be a witness in their own trial. Section 1 provided that 'every person charged with an offence ... shall be a competent witness for the defence at every stage of the proceedings'. As this right was only exercisable 'upon his own application', a defendant could not be compelled to appear as a witness.

been prejudiced merely because someone else was tried alongside him. It was usual procedure to hear as many cases as possible each day, in the most efficient manner, given that the time for the Assizes was limited. The jury was drawn from a small pool of men who met age and property ownership criteria. Most, if not all, members of the jury would have experience of serving on juries and could be relied upon to undertake their role responsibly. It was practical expediency to swear just enough jurymen to deal with the court calendar for the week. Blackwell did his best: he highlighted the pre-trial prejudice of the newspapers and drew the attention of the court to the waxworks, and implored the jury to 'dismiss from their minds all that they had heard, all that they had read, all that they had seen before coming to that court'. However, the jury had little doubt of Vass' guilt, returning their verdict after only eighteen minutes.

In isolation, the court processes and procedures were unremarkable on the day of the Vass trial. However, what was different on the 27th of February 1863, and what might raise questions about the fairness of the trial, was the coincidence of several factors, and exceptional nature of the case being heard. Questions of unfairness in the verdict on Vass arose from the circumstances engendered by the Assize calendar, specifically the intersections between the two trials heard that day: one of rape and one of rape and murder. This conjunction may have led (at least in part) to the jury failing to give Vass the benefit of the 'reasonable doubt' demonstrated by Blackwell, based upon the medical evidence as to the cause of Margaret Docherty's injuries.

The judge noted that the cases were unusual and not what he expected to see in Newcastle. Local newspapers (and the proprietors of local waxwork exhibitions) would never have encountered such a controversial case as that of George Vass, nor would the jury have faced anything similar. Yet, despite its exceptional nature, the case attracted no subsequent notoriety. The verdict was not questioned by the public or the 'usual' channels (such as abolitionists or the Society of Friends). Concerns about fair process did not extend as far as prompting petitions for mitigation of the sentence.[106] As the *Newcastle Guardian* noted: 'Even those who are opposed to *all* capital punishments were silent ... [there was no attempt] on any ground, to save his life'.[107] The *Newcastle Chronicle* confirmed that there was no public appetite for a memorial (petition) to the Home Secretary.[108] In fact, there is no evidence of any discussion about George Vass's guilt in the 150 years following his execution.

It is at least debatable that, were he to be tried today, the prejudicial pre-trial reporting, or the presence of waxworks, or the scant treatment of a possible defence, or even the nature of the judge's summing up and directions to the jury in the trial of

---

[106] Although Vass's name appears in the *Return of Appeals on Behalf of Persons Convicted of Capital Offences to Home Secretary, for Exercise of Royal Prerogative of Pardon or Mitigation of Sentence, 1861–80*, there is no evidence that a petition existed. A petition may have been assumed when the Return was compiled because this usually happened in capital cases. See *Parliamentary* Papers, 1881, HC 437, LXXVI, 391.
[107] *Newcastle Guardian*, 21 March 1863, p. 3.
[108] *The Newcastle Daily Chronicle and Northern Counties Advertiser*, 14 March 1863, p. 5.

George Vass, would be sufficient grounds for appeal against conviction. Even in the context of the time, doubts were expressed about the fairness of aspects of the trial. The concern of defence counsel and the *Newcastle Journal* had some substance. At the very least, the nature of the pre-trial publicity and the presence of waxwork effigies were inappropriate. When viewed alongside the possibility that the fatal injuries to Margaret Docherty were caused by a cart, the shadow cast by the knitting together of the two New Year cases, and the statement by Baron Martin at the commencement of the Assizes, there are indeed grounds to question whether the conviction for murder was: 'characterised by the fairness and justice which ought to distinguish all our judicial procedures'.[109]

---

[109] *The Newcastle Daily Journal*, 28 February 1863, p. 2.

4

The Trials of Peter Barrett: A Microhistory of Dysfunction in the Irish Criminal Justice System

Niamh Howlin
University College Dublin

Introduction

In 1869 an assassination attempt was made on Captain Thomas Eyre Lambert. Lambert, a prominent Galway landowner, was returning home to Castle Lambert from his brother, Giles's residence at neighbouring Moor Park.[1] Lambert spotted a man lurking beneath some lime trees near the entrance to his house, and was fired at a number of times. He was eventually felled by a shot to the forehead. He staggered to the door of his house, and later recalled: ' ... [w]hen I reached the hall door I knocked violently, my butler opened the door and I fell into his arms.'[2] He soon sent for his brother. Given a description of the assailant, Giles hastened to the Athenry constabulary station, a mile or two away, and relayed the information to acting constable John Griffith.[3]

Sub-constable Edward Hayden was quickly dispatched in plain-clothes to take the midnight train to Oranmore, ten miles away, to try to apprehend the suspect.[4] He returned around 5 am the following morning with Peter Barrett in custody, having spotted him sleeping in his train compartment. On being asked a few questions by sub-constable Hayden, his answers were 'both evasive and contradictory',[5] and he was arrested. Barrett appeared to match the description given by Lambert: 'I described the assassin as a man of slight figure dressed in dark clothes sharp features with not much hair on his face darkish complexion.'[6] Furthermore, Lambert said he told his brother that 'if Peter Barrett was in the country he was the man'.[7] Lambert, as will be seen, had reason to suspect that Barrett might have had a motive for the assault.

---

[1] *The Galway Express,* 17th July 1869.
[2] National Archives of Ireland (NAI), *Queen v Barrett,* Copy of Information of Thomas Eyre Lambert, 12 July 1869, CCS/1870/197, Box 1.
[3] Ibid., Copy of information of Acting Constable John Griffith, 12 July 1869, CCS/1870/197, Box 1.
[4] Ibid.
[5] Ibid., Copy of Information of Sub-Constable Edward Hayden, 12 July 1869, CCS/1870/197, Box 1.
[6] Ibid., Copy of Information of Thomas Eyre Lambert, 12 July 1869, CCS/1870/197, Box 1.
[7] Ibid.

Barrett was committed for trial at the next assize in August. On its face, this had the appearance of a relatively straightforward case destined for a quick resolution. However, this was not to be. What ensued were three trials, a change of venue to Dublin, allegations of jury intimidation, extensive press coverage around the UK, enormous expense and, ultimately, an acquittal. This chapter analyses the trials of Peter Barrett in 1869 and 1870 in the context of a moral panic. It assesses whether they could be deemed fair or unfair, and examines the role of press reporting in the case.

Context

The shooting of Captain Lambert in Galway was one of forty-three reported cases of firing at the person for the year 1869 in Ireland,[8] sixteen of which were classified as agrarian cases. This may not seem like a high number of instances, but forty-three cases represented a sharp increase compared to the previous three years, which had averaged at around twenty-two cases per annum, of which two were agrarian.[9] There was also, in 1869, a significant rise in the number of homicide and other offences against the person.

What was the reason for these increasing levels of violence? In a nutshell – land. Land reform had become an increasingly pressing issue in Ireland, with Gladstone's Liberal party having been elected in November 1868 on promises to address the 'Irish question'.[10] The disestablishment of the Church of Ireland was firmly on the agenda[11] and landlord-tenant relations were increasingly strained in the late 1860s. Fenianism had been in the ascendant since a failed uprising in March 1867, and one of Gladstone's first acts in March 1869 was to free almost fifty Fenian convicts.[12] The scale of the amnesty was disappointing to many of Gladstone's Irish supporters, and the Amnesty Association,[13] headed by barrister Isaac Butt (of whom more later), began to campaign with public meetings in the autumn of 1869.[14] The issues of amnesty and tenant rights went hand-in-hand. As Comerford puts it,

---

[8] Parliamentary Papers (forthcoming), *Return of Outrages Reported to Constabulary Office in Ireland, 1869*, C. 60.

[9] Ibid., pp. 24–7.

[10] See R.V. Comerford (2010) 'Gladstone's First Irish Enterprise, 1864–70' in W.E. Vaughan (ed.) *A New History of Ireland: Volume V–Ireland under the Union 1801–70* (Oxford: Oxford University Press), pp. 431–51.

[11] See K. Robbins (forthcoming) 'The Disestablishment of the Church of Ireland' in K. Costello and N. Howlin (eds) *Law and Religion in Ireland, 1695–1950* (Basingstoke: Palgrave).

[12] Comerford, 'Gladstone's First Irish Enterprise', p. 445.

[13] See B. Jenkins (2008) *The Fenian Problem: Insurgency and Terrorism in a Liberal State 1858–1874* (Montreal: McGill-Queen's University Press), pp. 278–80. Jenkins notes on p. 278, that '[r]are was the weekend throughout the autumn of 1869 that did not witness multiple amnesty rallies'.

[14] Ibid., pp. 446–7.

The Irish tenants and their friends expected land legislation from Gladstone as firmly as they expected disestablishment. Many of them did not wait for the legislation ... The result was a wave of agrarian unrest.[15]

Once disestablishment legislation had been successfully passed,[16] attention focused squarely on the land question in the summer of 1869. In November 1869 the Chief Secretary Chichester Fortescue proposed that the 'Ulster custom' of security of tenure[17] be protected by law. Gladstone's Land Bill was laid before the House of Commons in February 1870,[18] and was passed into law in August 1870.[19] The Act legalized the Ulster custom, and afforded greater security of tenure to some tenants, as well as a right to compensation where improvements had been made to their holdings.[20]

It was against this backdrop of unrest among tenants and unease among landlords that the shooting of Lambert had taken place. The authorities took the attempted assassination seriously, and were determined to secure a conviction. As one newspaper opined, the fact that Lambert was a landlord and Barrett's father his recently evicted tenant led the authorities to conclude that this case was part of the tenant right movement. The *Dublin Weekly Nation* described such reasoning as one which 'only those conversant with the state of social relations in Ireland [could] understand'.[21]

Who was Peter Barrett?

By all accounts, Peter Barrett was a handsome and respectable young man. He was described in the *Freeman's Journal* as 'about twenty-five years of age, tall, [with] dark brown hair'.[22] The *Galway Vindicator*, a liberal-independent newspaper, expressed sympathy 'for the position in which young Barrett is placed, as he is a person of very respectable appearance.'[23] Barrett lived in lodgings in London, where he worked as a letter-carrier in the General Post Office. This was a position secured for him by Captain Lambert's brother, Richard. The popular perception of Barrett was reflected in a ballad written around the time of his eventual release: 'But Barrett was respected well/In London and in Ireland O/Young and old and rich and poor/His conduct all admired O.'[24]

---

[15] Ibid., pp. 447–8.
[16] Irish Church Act 1869 (32 & 33 Vic., c. 42).
[17] Under the 'Ulster custom', tenants who paid their rent could expect reasonable security of tenure; by contrast, tenants in other parts of the country did not enjoy such security.
[18] *Hansard: House of Lords Debates*, 3rd series, Vol. 199, Col. 333 (15 February 1870).
[19] Landlord and Tenant (Ireland) Act 1870 (33 & 34 Vic., c. 46).
[20] A. Jackson (1999) *Ireland 1798-1998* (Oxford: Blackwell), p. 107.
[21] *Dublin Weekly Nation*, 2nd October 1869.
[22] *The Freeman's Journal*, 29th September 1869. In his opening statement at Barrett's first trial in Galway, the Attorney General described him as 'a person of respectable character'. Ibid., 30th September 1869.
[23] *The Galway Vindicator*, 11th August 1869.
[24] National Library of Ireland (NLI), 'Lines Written on the Liberation of Barrett', Ms. LO 4051/112.

Peter was the oldest son of Pat Barrett, a 'respectable' and 'snug farmer',[25] later described by Justice Keogh as 'worthy and excellent'.[26] Pat was a fairly formidable figure, described as 'a man of gigantic stature ... over six feet one inch, and made in proportion, and about seventeen stone weight'.[27] He was a tenant of Captain Lambert, occupying a seventy-seven-acre farm and a 'handsome slated cottage'[28] in a place later known as 'Barrett Hill'. Pat Barrett had been forced to surrender his lease in the early summer of 1869, apparently over a dispute relating to covenants in Barrett's lease[29] to repair and to rotate his crops.[30] An alternative version of events, which has been handed down through folk histories, was that the cause of the eviction was jealousy. The Barrett family's smart cottage was said to be superior to the house of Thomas Lambert's brother Tom, who was also a tenant on the estate, and this was a cause of some embarrassment.[31] Other accounts of the case point to a religious dispute between the two families, relating to the use of a burial ground. In either case, it seems that there was more to the Barrett-Lambert animosity than was acknowledged in the court proceedings.

Thomas Eyre Lambert had taken possession of the Lambert estate on the death of his father, Walter Lambert, in 1867.[32] In accounts of the Barrett trial, descriptions of Lambert and his standing in the community vary. The *Galway Vindicator* wrote before the first trial that 'the name of Lambert is one much respected in our county'.[33] It referred specifically to Captain Lambert's deceased father, Walter Lambert, as ' ... one of our best landlords, and deservedly beloved by his tenantry'.[34] Respect for the Lambert family did not universally extend to the current generation, and, as will be seen, there were intimations of Captain Lambert's poor local standing during the Barrett trials. Cork MP McCarthy Downing, for example, described Thomas Eyre Lambert as 'one of the most unpopular men in Galway'.[35]

Pre-trial proceedings

In August, Peter Barrett was committed for trial at the next assizes, and it was reported that 'many of the lower classes of the people testified their warm sympathy with the

---

[25] *The Galway Express*, 21st July 1869.
[26] Parliamentary Papers, *Shorthand Writers' Notes of Judgment of Mr Justice Keogh on Trial of Galway County Election Petition; Minutes of Evidence, Appendix, Index.* 1872 HC 241 xlvviii 17, 71, 14.
[27] *The Galway Express*, 21 July 1869. He was politically active, and in an 1872 bye-election supported Captain Nolan. He was said to have insulted and intimidated voters, and was imprisoned for contempt of court – see Parliamentary Papers, *Shorthand Writers' Notes*, v. 193, pp. 254–5 and pp. 371–5.
[28] *The Galway Vindicator*, 25th May 1870.
[29] *Freeman's Journal*, 30th September 1869.
[30] *The Galway Vindicator*, 25th May 1870.
[31] See, for example, *The Flag of Ireland*, 2nd July 1870.
[32] Walter Lambert had been a high-profile figure locally, serving as a Justice of the Peace and High Sheriff. F. O'Regan (1999) *The Lamberts of Athenry* (Athenry: Lambert Project Society), p. 176.
[33] *The Galway Vindicator*, 11th August 1869.
[34] Ibid.
[35] *Hansard: House of Lords Debates*, 3rd series, Vol. 200, Col. 429 (22 March 1870).

prisoner by cheering him in the streets'.[36] Instead of having Barrett tried at the assizes, however, the Lord Lieutenant issued a special commission for Galway.[37] This meant that the judges would make an additional visit to Galway outside of the scheduled assizes. The *Galway Vindicator* was critical of the use of the special commission, describing it as ' … a disgrace to our peaceable county',[38] and criticizing the expense involved. It was claimed that Barrett ' … should have ordinary jurors and not the landlords and magistrates of the county'. A letter to the paper stated that:

> 'to try Barrett by such a jury, as will, in all likelihood be empanelled at the special commission, would be to expose trial by jury of one's peers to all distrust which forms the disintegrating element in the present relations between landlord and tenant.'[39]

Two days later, the paper further entreated the government to ' … let the accused be tried by ordinary tribunal and avoid the excitement which necessarily must be created by a special commission'.[40] It was unusual to issue a special commission where there was just a single prisoner to be tried, as was highlighted by the *Flag of Ireland*: 'A Special Commission for the trial of one man not charged with a capital offence looks more like a Governmental attempt at intimidation, rather than a desire to administer impartial justice.'[41] Despite such misgivings, the sub-sheriff of Galway, Richard Carter, was served with notice of the special commission on the 4th of September.[42]

At the opening of the commission, Chief Justice Whiteside referred to the otherwise 'relatively tranquil' state of county Galway, and ' … the danger of its being affected by the contagion of a bad example'.[43] In his address to the grand jury at the opening of the special commission, the Chief Justice remarked that ' … [t]he spirit which invades one class of the community will extend to the destruction of the rights and liberties of others'.[44] This sort of rhetoric, also found in some newspaper accounts of the trial, hints at the unease developing among members of the landed classes in Ireland in 1869. It also reflects what were probably Whiteside's own views of the developing situation in Ireland.[45] The grand jury found a true bill against Barrett and he was then arraigned for trial.[46]

---

[36] *The Galway Express*, 7th August 1869.
[37] *Dublin Evening Mail*, 20th August 1869.
[38] *The Galway Vindicator*, 23rd August 1869.
[39] Ibid.
[40] *The Galway Vindicator*, 25th August 1869.
[41] *Flag of Ireland*, 2nd October 1869.
[42] *Dublin Evening Mail*, 6th September 1869.
[43] *The Freeman's Journal*, 29th September 1869.
[44] Ibid.
[45] As a devout Anglican, he vehemently opposed the disestablishment of the Church of Ireland. P. Maume, 'James Whiteside', *Dictionary of Irish Biography*, available at www.dib.cambridge.org (accessed 1 February 2018).
[46] It was later asserted that one of the Grand Jurors who had delivered the true bill, Robert Bodkin, ' … one of the most influential men in the county of Galway' had later said that 'he did not believe any jury would believe the evidence of said Thomas Eyre Lambert the prosecutor in this case', see NAI, *Queen v Barrett*, Affidavit of John Kirwan, 2 December 1869, CCS/1870/197, Box 1. Kirwan was also a grand juror and a special juror, though he had not been involved in Barrett's trial.

First trial

Shortly before the first trial was due to commence, *The Galway Express* mused that it would undoubtedly ' ... cause a great sensation',[47] due to the increasing centrality of the land question. It hinted that someone like Barrett should have the sympathy of 'the peasant and middle-class section of the community'.[48] Whatever their sympathies, Barrett's trial certainly attracted significant press attention, as well as ' ... considerable interest from the upper, as well as from the middle and lower classes', according to the *Freeman's Journal*.[49] It is worth noting that the proprietor of the *Freeman's Journal*, Sir John Gray, MP, was a strong proponent of tenant right, and the organizer of a series of well-attended public meetings in 1869 and 1870 on the question of land reform.[50] Reporting on Barrett's case may have been subsumed by the general pro-tenant, anti-landlord position of his paper.

A public subscription was raised in order to fund Barrett's defence,[51] and a fundraising concert was organized by a temperance society.[52] This was initially proposed to his father, Pat Barrett, in August, with the hope of employing eminent Queen's Counsel Isaac Butt, or someone of a similar calibre. Barrett's solicitor objected to this manner of funding the defence, and recommended that Barrett apply to the government for his legal fees,[53] as was the usual practice in Ireland. Before the opening of the special commission, it was reported that a memorial ' ... bearing the names of several of the most influential shopkeepers and traders of Galway' had been forwarded to Denis Caulfield Heron QC, asking him to defend Barrett.[54] Heron was an extremely high-profile barrister who had previously served as law advisor to the Lord Lieutenant and as professor of jurisprudence at Queen's College, Galway. He had been involved in defending a number of the Fenian prisoners in 1867.[55] Also defending Barrett was Hugh MacDermot, a junior barrister on the Connaught circuit, instructed by Henry Concannon and Henry White. They faced the sessional Crown Solicitor, P.J. O'Loughlin, Attorney-General Edward Sullivan MP, Solicitor-General Charles Barry, Mr West QC and Mr Jordan.

Chief Justice Whiteside and Justice Keogh presided over the trial. Galway courthouse was crowded on the first day, with a number of 'ladies and gentlemen' having gained access before the courthouse officially opened.[56] At the outset, Barrett's counsel challenged the array of the jury panel. This was a challenge to the manner in which the panel of jurors had been constituted, rather than a challenge to a particular

---

[47] *The Galway Express*, 26th September 1869.
[48] Ibid.
[49] *Freeman's Journal*, 29th September 1869.
[50] Jackson, *Ireland*, p. 107.
[51] *Irish Times*, 28th September 1869.
[52] *Pall Mall Gazette*, 4th September 1869.
[53] Ibid.
[54] *Dublin Evening Mail*, 23rd September 1869.
[55] B. Hourican, 'Denis Caulfield Heron', *Dictionary of Irish Biography*, available at www.dib.cambridge.org (accessed 1 February 2018).
[56] *Freeman's Journal*, 29th September 1869.

juror. Two jurors were appointed to try the issue, as was the usual practice. Heron claimed that the jury panel had not been impartially returned and was not the same as the panel returned for the assize.[57] Noting several differences between the two, Heron pointed out that while there were thirty-one landlords on the assize panel, on this panel there were seventy-seven landlords, as well as twenty-nine magistrates. The landlords' names had been placed at the top of the panel, which made it more likely that they would be sworn onto the jury. Unlike in civil cases, where the names of jurors were randomly drawn by ballot, in criminal trials the jurors were called in the order in which they appeared on the panel. Coupled with the common practice of putting the names of the highest-ranking men at the start of the panel, this unsurprisingly led to allegations of jury packing. In this instance, the panel was specially drafted for the special commission, so it appeared inevitable that Barrett would be tried by a jury of landlords for shooting at a landlord. Sullivan, the attorney general, refused to consent to the jurors being balloted for. The triers, on the direction of the Chief Justice, found that the jury panel had been impartially arrayed by the sheriff.[58] Twelve jurors were duly sworn, with the prisoner exercising his right to peremptorily challenge several potential jurors.[59]

In his opening statement, Attorney General Sullivan was at pains to create some distance between Peter Barrett and his father's dispute with Captain Lambert.[60] He also emphasized that it had been eighteen months since Peter had last lived locally. The purpose of this appears to have been to add weight to Captain Lambert's statement that he believed that had Barrett been in the country, he would have named him as his attacker more definitely. The prosecution case rested mainly on Captain Lambert's identification of Barrett. His testimony reflected the information he had sworn in the aftermath of the trial, referred to at the start of this chapter. The rest of the evidence was circumstantial, going to show that Barrett had taken sick leave from his work, purchased a pistol in London and had been seen in the vicinity of Athenry after the attack. The identification of Barrett also seemed in a large part to be based on the type of hat he wore – Lambert described it as a flat hat, while other witnesses referred to a tall hat, or implied that Barrett might have had with him two hats.

Michael Kelly, variously described as a butler or a servant boy, testified that he had seen a person dressed in black near Castle Lambert on the evening in question. He had ' ... whistled to him to go off the grass', and soon afterwards heard shots fired.[61] He could not, however, identify the man as Barrett. Giles Lambert testified that he had been summoned by his brother and had travelled to Athenry police barracks.[62] Sub-constable Hayden then picked up the narrative, describing his journey to Oranmore

---

[57] Ibid.
[58] Ibid.
[59] The jurors names were Redmond S. Burke (foreman), James A. Jackson, John M.A. Lewis, Charles M. Blake, John Fahey, Anthony Lynch, Yelverton Leonard, Lawrence Mullen, James F. Egan, Owen Lynch, Stephen J. McDonagh and Martin T. Conlahan.
[60] *The Freeman's Journal*, 30th September 1869.
[61] Ibid.
[62] Ibid.

and his apprehension of Barrett.[63] Two passengers on the train corroborated Hayden's testimony, but only one of them could positively identify Barrett.[64] The other witness, Martin McDonnell, stated that the man on the train had two hats, one tall and one flat.[65] Mariott Wilson, a railway porter at Athenry station, testified to having spoken briefly with Barrett around ten o'clock on the night in question. He also heard him enquire about buying a ticket all the way to London.[66] This was corroborated by the stationmaster, James Carberry. Constable Griffith told the court about sub-constable Hayden bringing Peter Barrett back to the Athenry barracks, where he was recorded as having in his possession a tall hat.

A significant crown witness was Thomas Wolloms, from Tottenham Court Road in London. Wolloms was a seller of surgical instruments and firearms. He testified that on the 9th of July a man he identified as Peter Barrett came into his shop to look at some firearms. The man had told him he needed a revolver for taking care of a house for a family, and rented a small, cheap revolver for 25 shillings. A document was drawn up and it was signed 'P Barrett'. Wolloms testified that the pistol was 'more a toy pistol which might make a noise in a home and alarm the police than anything else'.[67]

The next witness was Mrs Stirling, in whose house Peter Barrett lodged in London. She had last seen him on the morning of Saturday the 10th of July, when he said he was going to visit a cousin for a day or two. He had been wearing a low crowned hat.[68] George Clarke, chief inspector of detectives at Scotland Yard, testified that he had visited Mrs Stirling's house at Valsover Street and found a box of Barrett's possessions, which included the bill relating to the pistol and a black hat.[69] Dr Edward Leonard then gave dramatic testimony about attending Captain Lambert on the night of the attack. He presented to the court the bullet he had extracted from Lambert's temple.

It was noteworthy that all of the prosecution witnesses who had dealings with Barrett described him as respectable. As his own barrister pointed out, Barrett was far from a 'wretched peasant' whose 'family had been cast out on the roadside'. It would seem that Heron QC sought to distance Barrett from the narrative of the poor, angry tenant who was driven by desperation to attack his landlord. He asked the jury to consider the likelihood that a young man of previously ' … irreproachable character should all at once become a murderer like Cain'.[70]

The strategy devised by the defence was that this was a case of mistaken identity, and that Peter Barrett was not the man responsible for the attack. However, they proffered no alternative explanation as to why Barrett was in the country. Heron in his opening address to the jury referred in somewhat vague terms to a 'band of private assassins

---

[63] Ibid.
[64] Ibid. Evidence of Martin McDonnell and William Cotton.
[65] Ibid.
[66] Ibid.
[67] Ibid.
[68] Ibid.
[69] Ibid. William Manly of the London Post Office testified the Barrett had been certified for sick leave from the 9th until the 14th of July. This was corroborated by Dr Lancelot Hare, who had examined Barrett's apparently sore knee.
[70] Ibid.

who now keep Ireland in terror'.[71] He sought to cast doubt on the prosecution's case by suggesting that other men had been lurking around the grounds of Castle Lambert on the day in question, and furthermore that the distances between various places where supposed sightings of Barrett had taken place rendered it impossible that he was at Castle Lambert at the relevant time. Heron QC, when cross-examining Lambert, sought to imply that Lambert had disputes with a number of other tenants, any of whom may have been his attacker. He highlighted a recent case in which one of Lambert's tenants, Shaughnessy, had brought an action against Lambert for false imprisonment after Lambert, in his capacity as JP, had issued a warrant for his arrest and subsequently refused him bail. Lambert had accused Shaughnessy of removing sheep stock from the land. The civil jury, however, had found in favour of Shaughnessy and awarded 80 pounds in damages. This dispute was referred to several times in the reporting of the Barrett trials, usually in the context of demonstrating the low regard with which the residents of Galway regarded Captain Lambert. It was generally viewed as having been an embarrassment for him, and called into question his integrity and judgement. This would prove crucial, as the prosecution rested on the veracity of Lambert's witness testimony. The defence also pointed out inconsistencies as to the crown witnesses' statements of the time of the attack. Heron asked why Captain Lambert would have called out to his attacker asking who he was, when Peter Barrett was well known to him. He questioned the identification of Barrett by his hat, which was of a fairly common design at the time.

Curiously, one of the servants at Castle Lambert, Bridget Browne, had sworn a deposition but had not been produced as a crown witness. The defence therefore called her as their witness. She had been alone in Castle Lambert on the 11th of July, as the rest of the household attended church services. She testified that several times that afternoon, starting at 1 pm, there was a double knock at the hall-door of the house, but when she went to the door there was nobody there. On the third occurrence of the knock, she saw through the hall window the dark-trousered legs of a man running away. Despite testifying for the defence, Bridget continued in the employment of Captain Lambert.[72]

Other witnesses testified to having seen Barrett, or someone resembling him, at times and places which did not accord with the prosecution evidence. Timothy Keenan, who knew Barrett, testified to having seen him at Athenry railway hotel between 9.30 and 10 o' clock that night. Michael Cannon, who also knew Barrett, testified to having seen him around 9 o' clock on the road near Athenry railway station.[73] This was corroborated by another witness who was with him.[74]

Bridget Murray who lived about two miles from Castle Lambert said that on the day in question a man called to her house around 3 pm and she gave him some bread and

---

[71] Ibid.
[72] Bridget Browne's upkeep at Castle Lambert was paid by the Crown for the duration of the trials. It will be seen that Lambert subsequently sought to pay her passage to the United States, which was one way of dealing with her unhelpful testimony. NAI, *Queen v Barrett*, Affidavit of James Blake Concannon, 13 December 1869, CCS/1870/197, Box 1.
[73] *The Freeman's Journal*, 30th September 1869.
[74] Ibid., 1st October 1869.

milk and refused payment. She saw him walking towards Castle Lambert. She said on re-examination that the man was not Barrett and had told her he was from Tipperary.[75] Thomas Conlan, a tenant on the Lambert estate who lived about a mile and a half from the house, testified that he saw a tall man walking in a lane near the house between 3 and 4 that afternoon.

In his closing statement, McDermott reminded the jury of the presumption of innocence and urged them to decide on the evidence alone. He referred to the ongoing outrages around the country which could blind the jury's judgement of an individual case. He tried to discredit the evidence of Captain Lambert who, he said, ' ... had not sufficient opportunity in the terrible excitement of the moment to see the man who fired at him'. His speech was met with ' ... loud applause in the court, which was instantly suppressed'.[76] Members of the jury (who had been quite active in questioning witnesses in this case[77]) then requested that Captain Lambert be recalled. The Chief Justice hesitated, considering this to be an unusual development, but allowed it. Captain Lambert was closely questioned as to what he had said, and in what order, to the man he had spotted lurking beneath the trees, at what stage he had set his dog on him, and whether he had recognized him as Peter Barrett. Lambert swore that he had indeed recognized the man as Barrett. The jury deliberated for seven hours and failed to reach a verdict,[78] and were discharged.

Reaction

It was reported in the *Freeman's Journal* that nine jurors had been in favour of an acquittal and three for a conviction.[79] The immediate public reaction to this in Galway was described as 'dissatisfaction' that Barrett had not been acquitted. This was said to have been 'expressed in a rather violent manner immediately after the adjournment of the special commission'.[80] The courtroom itself was packed, and outside the building was ' ... an immense crowd of people of the humbler classes' awaiting the outcome of the trial.[81] Local and national newspapers reported that ' ... a common rumour got afloat through town that eleven to one were for liberating the prisoner'.[82] It was later claimed in the House of Commons that

> ... [w]hile the jury were in deliberation in the room one of them threw up the window and flung down to the excited mob outside a slip of paper containing the names of the jurors who were favourable to conviction.[83]

---

[75] Ibid.
[76] Ibid.
[77] See N. Howlin (2014) 'Irish Jurors: Passive Observers or Active Participants?', *Journal of Legal History*, 35, 2, pp. 143–71.
[78] Ibid.
[79] *The Freeman's Journal*, 2nd October 1869.
[80] Ibid.
[81] Ibid.
[82] *The Galway Express*, 2nd October 1869. See also *The Freeman's Journal*, 2nd October 1869.
[83] *Hansard: House of Lords Debates*, 3rd series, Vol. 200, Col. 441 (22 March 1870, Lord John Manners).

The prosecution claimed that ' ... even before the jurors were discharged by the Court, the name of one of those who were in favour of a conviction (Jackson) became known to the people in and around the Court',[84] and that a crowd of locals pursued him through the town.[85] The *Galway Express* reported, somewhat sensationally, that the mob had attempted ' ... the summary execution of a refractory juryman'. Jackson was ' ... hooted and groaned' at, and ' ... attacked with bricks and stones, and one old woman seemed so bitter that she brought out a sod of turf and rolled it in the mud before throwing it at him'.[86] Jackson was assisted by a priest well-known to him, Father Dooley, and two other Galway residents, who escorted him, along with the acting sergeant, down the street to the barracks. Just as they reached the barracks a stone, presumably thrown at Mr Jackson, hit a soldier in the face. Jackson was later escorted by fifty armed police to Black's hotel. The mob apparently continued to shout and throw stones, one of which hit the carriage of the two judges who were passing the crowd on their way to Salthill. Several persons who had thrown stones were arrested, and the police maintained their presence at Black's hotel, where some of the jurors were staying.[87]

The cheers for the defence counsel and the dissatisfaction publicly expressed when Barrett was not acquitted, demonstrated where the majority of public sympathy in Galway lay. The respective reputations of Lambert and Barrett played a significant part. In particular, Barrett's personal characteristics (his respectability and good looks) contrasted with Lambert's slightly tarnished reputation and his unclear and at times inconsistent recollections of the attack. However, beyond the Galway community, where the parties and their families were not so well known, views about the case may have differed. This possibility seems to have led the prosecution to consider where Barrett's next trial ought to take place.

A change of venue

Although traditionally criminal trials were to be conducted in the county where the alleged offence had taken place, it was possible in some instances to have the venue moved to a different county. This was usually done where it was considered unlikely that a fair and impartial trial could take place in the original county, because of, for example, the intimidation of jurors or witnesses, or because of the standing or influence of an accused person or victim.[88]

The crown decided that in this instance it would be desirable that the second trial of Barrett take place somewhere other than Galway. This was not without controversy. A

---

[84] *R v Barrett* (1870) Ir Rep 4 CL 285, 286. The Attorney General believed that such happenings had 'no precedent in the history of Irish trials'. *The Freeman's Journal*, 17th January 1870.
[85] See also the *Irish Times*, 2nd October 1869.
[86] *Galway Express*, 2nd October 1869.
[87] *The Freeman's Journal*, 2nd October 1869.
[88] For example, many such instances were discussed by a parliamentary committee in the 1850s: Parliamentary Papers, *Report from the Select Committee on Outrages (Ireland)*, HC 1852 (438) xiv, 1.

memorandum sent by the chief crown solicitor, William Lane Joynt, to solicitor Lewis Clare stated: 'I fancy that there will be fierce opposition … Pray keep a close watch on the case.'[89] Attorney General Sullivan sought a writ of *certiorari* removing the trial to the Queen's Bench, so that a motion for a change of venue could then be made.[90] The *certiorari* was granted, and handed in to the adjourned special commission two days later in Galway.[91] Sullivan referred to the attack on Mr Jackson, and ' … indecent and lawless scenes of outrage'.[92] It would seem that perceptions of the 'scenes of outrage' around Galway varied. The *Galway Vindicator*, a liberal newspaper, described the precautions taken by the authorities in relation to security around Barrett as 'extraordinary': 'A company of twenty-four men were day and night guarding the prison, which we emphatically assert was absolutely unnecessary.'[93] It certainly appears, from the affidavits discussed below, that such measures represented an over-reaction by an administration made nervous and tense by the increase in agrarian violence around this time.

Barrett was then transferred to custody in Dublin, and the attorney general applied for a change of venue in January 1870.[94] The motion for a change of venue was largely based on the alleged intimidation of jurors at the first trial.[95] In support of the motion, a number of affidavits were sworn by the resident magistrates and the Galway Crown Solicitor, from one of the jurors, and from several members of the constabulary. According to those affidavits, around the time of the attempted assassination, several serious outrages had been perpetrated around the county, and there existed amongst the peasantry 'a strong sympathy in favour of many of the parties arrested for such offences, and a disinclination to aid the Government in detecting the criminals'.[96]

It was also claimed in the affidavits that during the first trial, the people of Galway ' … manifested, in the most marked manner, their sympathy for the accused; that several of the jurors were threatened, and thereby intimidated and prevented from attending the assizes'.[97] These claims were corroborated by reports from the conservative *Galway Express*, which described how '[a]n organised mob, with the avowed determination to obstruct the course of justice by every possible means, took possession of our streets.'[98] The claims in this newspaper ought to be read alongside the knowledge that

---

[89] NAI, *Queen v Barrett*, Memorandum, 12 October 1869, CCS/1870/197, Box 3.
[90] *The Freeman's Journal*, 12th October 1869.
[91] Ibid., 15th October 1869.
[92] Sullivan also made somewhat mysterious references to another, 'unprecedented' outrage, ' … which in the presence of your lordships I do not wish to more particularly refer to than to say that of its true character there can be no doubt, as very soon will be made apparent.'
[93] *The Galway Vindicator*, 16th October 1869.
[94] See the *Irish Times*, 15th January 1870, for an account of the motion for a change of venue.
[95] As the 1870s and 1880s progressed, motions for changes of venue became increasingly frequent, particularly in cases of an agrarian nature. See N. Howlin (2017) *Juries in Ireland: Laypersons and Law in the Long Nineteenth Century* (Dublin: Four Courts Press), pp. 161–5. A parliamentary committee on Irish jury laws devoted significant attention to this issue in 1881: *Report from the Select Committee of the House of Lords on Irish Jury Laws*, HC 1881 (430) xi, 1.
[96] *The Galway Express*, 26th September 1869.
[97] *R v Barrett* (1870) Ir Rep 4 CL 285, 286.
[98] *The Galway Express*, 2nd October 1869.

it was self-described as 'the only Protestant organ in Galway',[99] and was likely to have a pro-landlord bias.

Barrett denied all claims of juror intimidation and insisted that 'no where can there be so fair and impartial a trial as in the County of Galway'.[100] He swore that there was no 'intimidation practiced by my friends or by any person on my behalf or at all'. A number of the special jurors who had tried Barrett denied having been in any way influenced or intimidated.[101] For example, one man swore that he was ' ... not in the slightest degree influenced' in his decision'.[102] Another, who described himself as ' ... a special juror with £2,000 a year landed property', swore that he was in no terror or dred [sic] whatever'.[103] In total, seven of the twelve jurors swore that they had not been intimidated or terrorized.[104] It would also appear that the crowds of supporters for Barrett who were seen on the streets during the trial were mainly women, who were attracted by his youth and good looks. Similarly, many of those sitting in the courtroom were 'respectable' ladies, similarly attracted. The 'mob' which had followed and attacked Jackson was sworn by many to have consisted entirely of women and children. Several witnesses swore that there was not a man among them, and that the threat posed to Jackson was not to be taken seriously.[105] Others claimed that no stones had been thrown at Jackson, and that the missiles were merely sods of turf or mud. A Roman Catholic Priest, Martin Murphy, also swore an affidavit to the effect that there was no intimidation of the Galway special jurors, and no risk of a partial trial.

Lest it be considered that all of these affidavits were sworn by Barrett's supporters to downplay the extent of the threat in Galway, it is worth pointing out that one of the prosecution witnesses backed up this version of events. Mary Anne Starling, Barrett's landlady from London, swore that she walked openly through the town every day without 'the slightest insult'. She said that it was 'well known' around the town that she had travelled from England to give evidence against Barrett. Nevertheless, she did not feel threatened, either in a general sense or more particularly by the crowd of women and children at the court house each day.[106]

Against the application for a change of venue, it was also claimed that since the trial, Captain Lambert had encouraged one of the witnesses, Bridget Browne, to emigrate to America, and that he had done other acts which would 'affect injuriously the evidence against the prisoner at a second trial'.[107] It was also suggested that a fair trial could not be had in Dublin, because of a sign posted by Lambert at his Dublin club, where

---

[99] M-L. Legg (1999) *Newspapers and Nationalism: The Irish Provincial Press 1850–1892* (Dublin: Four Courts Press), p. 195.
[100] NAI, *Queen v Barrett*, Affidavit of Peter Barrett, 3 December 1869, CCS/1870/197, Box 1.
[101] Ibid., Affidavit of Stephen J. McDonagh, 4 December 1869, CCS/1870/197, Box 1.
[102] Ibid., Affidavit of Martin Colohan, 6 December 1869, CCS/1870/197, Box 1.
[103] Ibid., Affidavit of John Michael Aylward Lewis, 12 Dec1869, CCS/1870/197, Box 1.
[104] These were John Michael Aylward Lewis, Anthony Lynch, Owen Lynch, Lawrence Mullen, John Fahy, Edward Rochford and James J Egan.
[105] For example, NAI, *Queen v Barrett*, Affidavit of Edward Rochford, 3 October 1869, CCS/1870/197.
[106] Affidavit of Mary Anne Starling, 1 December 1869, CCS/1870/197, Box 1.
[107] *R v Barrett* (1870) Ir Rep 4 CL 285, 287.

many potential special jurors were likely to see it.[108] The sign in the United Service Club was as follows: 'Captain Lambert being about to leave Ireland in consequence of the late attempt on his life at Castle Lambert in the County of Galway, is anxious to sell a wagonette (reversible) a horse now 7 years old and harness, all in perfect order, the horse has been driven by a lady. Price £120.'[109] It was alleged that this notice had been the subject of gossip in all of the Dublin clubs, and was likely to influence special jurors.[110]

Despite the various affidavits to the effect that there was no culture of intimidation of the jurors, Chief Justice Whiteside granted the motion for the change of venue. He emphasized the importance of protecting the institution of trial by jury. Jurors, he said, suffered considerable inconvenience, and ' ... must not be allowed to suffer additional persecution at the hands of lawless mobs'.[111] These lawless mobs would appear to have been manufactured from fear at the possibility of a tenant uprising. It is worth reflecting that the Chief Justice's judgement in this instance may have been clouded by the fact that his own carriage had been struck by a stone or a sod of turf in the rowdy aftermath of the trial.

The impact of granting of the motion to change the venue to Dublin was not as potentially unfair in this case compared with the Maamtrasna case, discussed by Conor Hanly in Chapter V; a language barrier, for example, was not an issue for Peter Barrett. As against that, however, there were in this case less compelling reasons to change the venue. It was a less serious offence, and there was not the same confusing tangle of family relationships between the victims, complainants and accused; the country was in a less tumultuous state and there were not as many people involved. The main motivation appears to have been to secure a conviction, away from the effects of Barrett's and Lamberts' family reputations.

Second trial

The case was set to be tried again in February 1870, in the Court of Queen's Bench before a special jury of the county of Dublin. In the interlude since the first trial, there had been some changes in personnel on the legal teams. Edward Sullivan had taken up the post of Master of the Rolls in Ireland and Charles Barry had been appointed Attorney General for Ireland in his place. Denis Caulfield Heron had been returned as a Liberal MP for Tipperary, so this time Barrett was represented in court by Isaac Butt QC, who had developed a reputation as ' ... a friend of the tenants, by means of propaganda on the land question'.[112] Butt's profile was considerable in early 1870. Like Heron, he had defended the Fenian prisoners, and he had recently been appointed

---

[108] NAI, *Queen v Barrett*, Affidavit of James Blake Concannon, 13 December 1869, CCS/1870/197, Box 1.
[109] Ibid., The Queen v Peter Barrett – Copy Notice posted in Club, CCS/1870/197, Box 2.
[110] Ibid., Affidavit of James Blake Concannon, 13 December 1869, CCS/1870/197, Box 1.
[111] *R v Barrett* (1870) Ir Rep 4 CL 285, 287.
[112] Comerford, 'Gladstone's First Irish Enterprise', p. 447.

president of the Amnesty Association, which sought amnesty for Fenians imprisoned after the 1867 uprising. The landlord-tenant angle of Barrett's case probably suited Butt's political agenda at the time, and press reporting on the second and third trials certainly emphasized this aspect of the case.[113]

The second trial at the court of Queen's Bench in Dublin was well-attended by the public,[114] and several security measures were taken; Barrett was escorted to the court by a party of mounted police; he was guarded by three warders while in court; police officers were stationed around the passages in the court building and a barricade was erected at the door of the court of Queen's Bench.[115] Public attendance appears to have outstripped attendance by potential jurors. A number of the jurors did not answer to their names, and Chief Justice Whiteside indicated that fines on absent jurors would be strictly enforced.[116] About 61 of the 128 jurors summoned answered on the first call, and 9 more answered when fines were threatened. This was not an unusually low turnout of jurors – usually around half of the jurors summoned actually presented themselves for service and answered when their names were called.[117] Butt, for the accused, objected that the panel contained more than sixty names, without any precept having been issued to authorize this. It was, however, quite common for large numbers of jurors to be summoned,[118] particularly where it was anticipated that there would be a low turnout, or in what was considered to be a serious criminal case or a state trial.

Butt unsuccessfully challenged the array of the jury panel. He also claimed that the jurors' names ought to be balloted for,[119] rather than being called in the order in which they appeared on the panel. It will be recalled that this had been the cause of a challenge to the array in the first trial. Legislation provided for jurors' names to be drawn at random from a box in civil actions, but at the time of Barrett's trials this had not yet been made mandatory for criminal cases. Both parties would have to consent to balloting in this way, and the Attorney General in this instance declined to consent. When the panel was called over, the Crown ordered a number of jurors to stand aside.[120] The power to order jurors to stand aside was a controversial power enjoyed by

---

[113] Butt was probably also relieved that Barrett's legal fees were to be defrayed by the government. Despite his high profile, Butt existed in a continual state of poverty or near-poverty, and had served a period in debtors' prison following his defence of the Fenians in 1867. P. Bull, 'Isaac Butt', *Dictionary of Irish Biography*, available at www.dib.cambridge.org (accessed 1 February 2018). Correspondence with William Lane Joynt, the Crown and treasury solicitor, indicates that Butt was anxious that his fees were paid: e.g. *Butt to Joynt*, 1 July 1870; *Butt to Joynt*, 13 July 1870, *Butt to Joynt* 29 July 1870. A memo dated 30 July 1870 indicates that Butt's fees were to be increased – see NAI, *Queen v Barrett*, CCS/1870/197, Box 1.

[114] The *Warder and Dublin Evening Mail*, 19th February 1870 and *Irish Times*, 19th February 1870.

[115] *Tuam Herald*, 19th February 1870.

[116] It was common for jurors to be called on threat of fines where attendance was particularly poor, although such fines were not always strictly enforced – see Howlin, *Juries in Ireland*, pp. 111–15.

[117] See ibid., pp. 105–6.

[118] Ibid., p. 102.

[119] Ibid., pp. 117–18.

[120] According to *The Evening Freeman*, 17th February 1870, there were twelve men ordered to stand aside, while the *Daily Telegraph*, 19th February 1870, reported that there were eight. The *Warder and Dublin Evening Mail*, 19th February 1870, listed eight names, including two Justices of the Peace.

the crown.[121] Unlike an accused person's right to challenge jurors peremptorily, there was no limit to the number of jurors who could be objected to in this way. Barrett meanwhile challenged twenty jurors in total.[122]

The jury was reported to be composed largely of Catholics.[123] Like the Galway jury, they frequently questioned the witnesses and played quite an active role in the trial.[124] They also recalled one of the witnesses in order to further question him. This was Wolloms, the proprietor of the shop from which Barrett had obtained his pistol. On being questioned, he stated that he could not say with any certainty whether the bullet extracted from Lambert's skull came from the pistol which he had sold to Barrett. The bullet was so flattened and misshapen that he could not identify it.[125] Butt QC observed that the bullet extracted from Lambert was ' … evidently a bullet which struck on the skull with considerable force', and asked the jury to consider whether this was 'consistent with it being fired from a toy pistol at twelve yards'.[126]

In this and in other regards, Butt appears to have thrown considerable doubt on the prosecution case. The identification of Barrett the day after the attack was portrayed as prejudicial, as he was brought to Lambert manacled and accompanied by police officers, with no attempt made to include similarly built men, as in a line-up. Butt also argued that the sightings of Barrett before and after the alleged attack rendered it impossible that he was the perpetrator.[127] He also questioned the reliability of Captain Lambert as a witness, pointing out that he had deliberately mis-stated the time of the attack in his original deposition.[128] 'Equivocation,' said Butt, ' … was characteristic of his entire evidence.'[129]

Lambert's testimony was similar to that given at the first trial, and it was noted in the *Cork Examiner* that his identification of Barrett ' … was not shaken on cross-examination'.[130] However, Butt skilfully poked holes in Lambert's story, and the *Galway Vindicator* noted that Lambert had 'somewhat varied his evidence since the first trial'.[131] Comments which had been made in Galway[132] to the effect that Lambert's story was not to be believed appear to have been borne out by his testimony in Dublin. Butt cross-examined him closely as to the nature and shape of the lime trees under which Barrett had apparently lurked on the night of the attack. Lambert swore

---

[121] See R.B. Blake (2004) '"A Delusion, a Mockery, and a Snare": Array Challenges and Jury Selection in England and Ireland, 1800–1850', *Canadian Journal of History*, 39, 1, pp. 2–26.

[122] The *Warder and Dublin Evening Mail*, 19th February 1870.

[123] *The Evening Freeman,* 21st February 1870. Their names were James Barrett, John Buckley, Arthur Galway, John Denis, James Drury, William Gardiner, Andrew William Ferguson, Edward Lea, Robert Tedcastle, Daniel Sullivan, Horatio Wallace and Patrick Kenney, see *Warder and Dublin Evening Mail*, 19th February 1870.

[124] For example, *The Evening Freeman,* 19th February 1870.

[125] *The Galway Vindicator,* 23rd February 1870.

[126] Ibid.

[127] *Irish Times,* 19th February 1870.

[128] Ibid.

[129] Ibid.

[130] *The Cork Examiner,* 19th February 1870.

[131] *The Galway Vindicator,* 19th February 1870.

[132] See above notes 70–76.

that there was dense foliage, but not so as to obscure his view of Barrett's face. Giles Lambert, however, stated on cross-examination that the foliage from the trees was likely to obscure the face of a man standing under them.[133] Crucially, it appeared that Captain Lambert had made changes to the crime scene in the aftermath of the shooting – under close questioning from Butt, he admitted that he had had the lime trees moved since the attack. This meant that the map of the estate, which was being used at the trial, was inaccurate.[134] It also meant that there was no way to be sure whether the tree branches would actually obscure an intruder from view. This threw serious doubt over the witness identification evidence, an unreliable form of evidence even at the best of times.

At the end of the third day of the trial, the jurors retired at around half past five to deliberate. Almost three hours later, they came back to the box, and informed the judge that they were unable to agree on a verdict. He sent them back to the jury-room, although one juror complained that he would 'catch his death' if forced to remain in the chilly jury-room much longer.[135] When asked two hours later whether there was any possibility of reaching agreement, one juror evoked laughter from the court, replying: ' ... not in the slightest, my lord, if you keep us until this day twelve months'.[136] Eventually, when midnight approached they were discharged without a verdict.[137]

The Chief Justice expressed his disappointment with this outcome.[138] The crowds which had gathered outside the courthouse (and which had remained there until almost midnight) ' ... cheered Mr Butt vociferously'.[139] Barrett was returned to Kilmainham gaol. The *Dublin Daily Express* considered the inability of the jury to agree on a verdict as a 'failure of justice'.[140] The *Freeman's Journal* reported that ten of the jurors had been in favour of a conviction,[141] while the *Dublin Daily Express* reported that eight had been for a conviction, two for an acquittal and two were undecided.[142] Either way, it is clear that a clear majority on the jury wanted to convict Barrett, but the law only allowed for unanimous verdicts.[143] The case was discussed in the House of Commons, with Gladstone on the defensive, stating that the outcome of the Barrett trials was due to 'special circumstances', rather than an outright failure in the administration of justice.[144]

---

[133] *Irish Times*, 19th February 1870.
[134] The *Warder and Dublin Evening Mail*, 19th February 1870.
[135] *Dublin Evening Mail*, 21st February 1870. This was a common complaint; a few years later, the Dublin Jurors' Association was established in order to address complaints about poor juror facilities in the city. See *Freeman's Journal*, 31 January 1875.
[136] Ibid., 21st February 1870.
[137] *The Galway Express,* 19th and 26th February 1870.
[138] *Dublin Daily Express*, 21st February 1870.
[139] Ibid.
[140] Ibid.
[141] *The Freeman's Journal,* 21st February 1870.
[142] *Dublin Daily Express*, 21st February 1870. The *Irish Times* reported that the jurors were eleven to one for a conviction – see *Irish Times*, 21st February 1870.
[143] Majority verdict was not introduced until the twentieth century.
[144] *Hansard: House of Lords Debates*, 3rd series, Vol. 199, Col. 876 (28 February 1870).

The Crown was embarrassed at this second failure to secure a conviction in a case which, at the outset, had appeared straightforward. There was some speculation that Barrett would not be tried for a third time, particularly given the considerable expenses incurred during the first two trials.[145] Yet there was support from some quarters for trying Barrett again. The *Belfast Newsletter,* for example, ran an editorial stating that if Barrett were guilty, 'he ought not to escape punishment.'[146] An editorial in the *Derry Journal* stated that this second abortive trial 'suggests very ugly conclusions, so far as appertains to the practical workings of our jury system.'[147] It speculated that ' ... [t]he immunity with which agrarian murderers have been allowed to escape of late, may probably induce the crown to make a third attempt to obtain a conviction against Barrett'.[148] Indeed, the crown did make such an attempt, and Barrett was set to be tried again in the summer.[149] While not unheard of,[150] it was unusual for a defendant to be tried multiple times like this. Why were the authorities so determined to successfully prosecute Barrett? They seem to have been convinced of his guilt, based on the circumstantial evidence but this was not sufficient for proof beyond a reasonable doubt. The authorities undoubtedly viewed this as a landlord and tenant case and were determined to make an example of Barrett.[151] However, the prosecution case grew weaker with each successive trial, as will be seen.

Third trial

Barrett was tried for a third time in June 1870 in Dublin at the court of Queen's Bench,[152] this time before Justice Fitzgerald. It was considered necessary to have policemen stationed around the courthouse to prevent overcrowding and possible violence.[153] At first, there was some difficulty in securing a jury, as only forty-six of the 120 men called responded. Justice Fitzgerald warned that he would have no difficulty in levying fines

---

[145] *Clare Journal and Ennis Advertiser,* 21st February 1870; *Pall Mall Gazette,* 21st February 1870 and *Irish Times,* 21st February 1870.

[146] *Belfast Newsletter,* 21st February 1870.

[147] *The Derry Journal,* 23rd February 1870.

[148] Ibid.

[149] In May 1870, shortly before Barrett's third trial was due to commence in Dublin, a letter from Captain Lambert was published in a number of Irish newspapers. It outlined his version of the dispute over Pat Barrett's lease, and described how he had taken civil action against Barrett. This may have been misguided, as it had the potential to prejudice the third trial, but it does not appear to have attracted significant attention – see *The Galway Vindicator,* 25th May 1870.

[150] See, for example, D.S. Johnson (1985) 'The Trials of Sam Gray: Monaghan Politics and Nineteenth Century Irish Criminal Procedure', *Irish Jurist – New Series,* 20, pp. 109–34 at p. 109.

[151] This prosecutorial zeal was later mirrored (albeit with tragic consequences) in the Maamtrasna trials of 1882.

[152] Again, the case was tried by a special jury.

[153] *The Galway Express,* 25th June 1870.

of £50 on those who failed to answer,[154] and a further eighteen jurors materialized.[155] About twenty-four jurors were fined in total.[156] Of the sixty-four jurors who answered to their names, the crown ordered nineteen to stand aside, and the prisoner challenged twenty-three. By the time the panel was exhausted only ten jurors had been sworn. Justice Fitzgerald ordered that the names be called over again on 100 pound fines, which he emphasized that he would strictly enforce.[157] No additional jurors answered, so those who had been directed to stand aside were called again. The Attorney General suggested that the trial might be postponed until the following day because of the low juror turnout but Justice Fitzgerald wanted to move things along,[158] and so the trial commenced.

Whilst the authorities were determined to secure a conviction in this case, they do not appear to have gone so far as to effectively pack the jury. An unsigned note found among the Barrett files indicates that there was once more a majority of Catholics on the jury. The note, presumably from one member of the legal team to another, stated, somewhat baldly: ' ... if you packed the jury, it is clear you packed it *the other way*'. It is accompanied by a list of the jurors, with either 'Catholic' or 'Protestant' written beside each name.[159] Only Robert Neil and Samuel Wall were described as 'Protestant'.[160] Allegations of jury packing were common in Ireland during periods of political turmoil but, as has been demonstrated elsewhere,[161] such claims were often exaggerated.

In his opening statement, the Attorney General referred to the fact that the case had been tried before and asked the jurors to 'dismiss from your minds all you have ever heard and all you have ever read in reference to this trial'.[162] By this stage, even the complainant, Captain Lambert, had lost the appetite for prosecution. When he came forward to testify, he asked the court whether the case could be abandoned: 'I have come forward twice to prosecute, and I wish the matter to be dropped.'[163] Justice Fitzgerald pointed out that he had no power to make such an order, and the examination of the witness proceeded. Butt's cross-examination makes it clearer why

---

[154] He said he would impose the fines, '... and let the jurors try, as best they could, to get out of the matter afterwards' – see *The Galway Express*, 25th June 1870.

[155] (1870) *The Queen against Peter Barrett: Report of the Third Trial of Peter Barrett for Shooting at with Intent to Murder Captain Thomas Eyre Lambert on Sunday the 11th of July 1869* (Dublin: Alexander Thom), p. 2.

[156] As at the second trial, Butt asked that the jurors' names be drawn by ballot, although he had no expectation that the court would acquiesce to this, remarking: 'Your lordship will, of course, take the course the Chief Justice took at the last trial. It is a mere matter of form.' See ibid., p. 3.

[157] Ibid., p. 11. It was later reported that the fines, which had risen to £150, were reduced to £50 by Fitzgerald J., and were levied on thirty jurors who had failed to attend for the third trial – see *Freeman's Journal*, 16th July 1870.

[158] *The Queen against Peter Barrett*, p. 12.

[159] The jurors for this trial were James P. Corcoran [foreman] Robert Neill, William McDonnell, High O'Rourke, Francis P. Malins, Gregory Murphy, Joseph Croker, Samuel Wall, James Duffy, Walter Tyrell, William Meagher, Patrick Joseph Fogarty. Meagher and Fogarty had originally been asked by the Crown to stand aside.

[160] NAI, *Queen v Barrett*, List of Jury Members, CCS/1870/197, Box 2.

[161] Howlin, *Juries in Ireland*, chapter 10.

[162] Ibid., p. 13.

[163] Ibid., p. 26.

Lambert had wanted the case to be dropped. He had emerged from the second trial looking less than heroic, after it transpired that he had moved some of the lime trees where the attack took place, and whose position was crucial to the issue of identifying the assailant. Lambert was quite vague and uncertain when being cross-examined about the time at which he had been shot.[164] He testified that he had said between 9 and 10 when giving his deposition as he did not want to be too specific, in case this could be used by the defence to concoct an alibi; he ' ... did not think it expedient that the prisoner's legal advisors should know everything'. However, he testified in court that he had been shot at 9.15 pm.

He was also cross-examined in relation to the lime trees outside his house. He testified that the first shot fired had gone into the tree branches.[165] This seemed to be the first time in the entire proceedings that he had mentioned this. When asked about whether the low-hanging branches might have obscured his view of Barrett's face, he told the court that on the day following the attack, he had asked either his brother or brother-in-law to stand in the same position under the tree, in order to determine if he could identify him, and he could.[166] He had not said a word about this at the previous trial. Butt also questioned him about the cutting down of the lime trees, implying that this had been done with an improper motive.[167] Lambert's protests that the trees had been moved at the behest of his wife rang somewhat hollow. Butt referred back to Giles Lambert's testimony at the second trial, to the effect that the branches on the lime trees would obscure the face of anyone standing under them. He implied that Thomas had been angry with Giles for this testimony, and had spoken harshly to him about it.[168] This may or may not have been true, but helped to diminish Captain Lambert's reliability. It would be a reasonable assessment to say that Butt's cross-examination of Lambert threw considerable doubt on his evidence.

By the time all witnesses had been examined and counsel's speeches had concluded it was after 6 pm. Proceedings were adjourned until the next day so that the jurors could have refreshment.[169] At some point, it must have become known to the prosecution which way the jurors were voting, as a note found among the Barrett files states that 'Wall, Neill, Williams are for a conviction but are timid men and will give in'.[170] It is possible that this became known overnight when the jurors were staying at the hotel; security in such situations could be lax.[171] When they returned to court the following morning, Justice Fitzgerald advised the jurors ' ... if you entertain rational doubt of his guilt, you can and you ought to acquit him. But rational doubt is not that wild

---

[164] Ibid., pp. 36–40.
[165] Ibid., p. 40.
[166] Ibid., pp. 41–2.
[167] Ibid., pp. 42–3.
[168] Ibid., p. 42.
[169] Ibid., p. 152. Once the jurors withdrew to consider their verdict, they would be denied refreshment or a fire in their room; thus it made sense to wait until the following day to deliver the charge.
[170] NAI, *Queen v Barrett*, List of Jurors' Names, CCS/1870/197, Box 2.
[171] For example, at the 1882 trial of Francis Hynes, the jurors stayed overnight in a hotel and were seen in the hotel billiard room mixing with persons who were not on the jury – see *Dublin Commission Court (Francis Hynes)*, HC 1882 (408) lv, 167, 5.

conjecture, or wild suspicion, or wild doubt, that people of weak mind may entertain, but that real doubt that you would entertain on any occasion.'[172] His charge to the jury took almost three hours; the jurors spent less time than that deliberating, before delivering an acquittal. Peter Barrett was then finally discharged from custody.[173]

Reaction

Public reaction to the trials and acquittal can be illustrated by a popular ballad circulated soon after Barrett's acquittal, with the chorus: 'Thank Heaven, Butt and the jury too/The news is great and glorious O,/Their evidence was knocked to rags/ Young Barrett is victorious O.'[174] The *Flag of Ireland* described the scenes at Dublin's Four Courts when the verdict was delivered: 'A motley collection of human beings, of all classes and both sexes, thronged every available spot, yelling, shouting and applauding.'[175] The acquittal, however it might have been viewed by the authorities, was welcomed by the inhabitants of Galway; ' ... [t]he town here this afternoon was in the greatest ecstasies on receipt of information relative to the acquittal of Barrett. At every corner, crowds were congratulating each other with agreeable news.'[176] The *Galway Vindicator* reported that church bells were rung in Galway city.[177] Support for Barrett was also evident in Dublin. A bonfire was lit in celebration by some of those who had waited near the court buildings in Dublin, and a number of young men were arrested for rowdy and drunken behaviour. Butt was also heartily congratulated as he made his way through the city.[178] On Monday morning, Barrett was driven through Dublin city with his parents. When they stopped off at a photographic studio with Butt to have their pictures taken, a large crowd of well-wishers gathered.[179] On his return to Galway, he was warmly greeted by supporters, including Captain Richard Lambert, another of Captain Lambert's brothers, 'who shook him heartily by the hands'.[180] A fund was established for the benefit of Peter Barrett and his family.[181]

Overall, public attitudes towards Barrett following his acquittal, certainly as expressed in the press, were positive. The *Northern Star*, for example, remarked that 'right [had] triumphed over might'.[182] The *Freeman's Journal* rued that 'Peter Barrett, now free and innocent in the sight of the law, is a ruined man. The honourable and respectable office he held is filled by another, and there is little probability of his ever

---

[172] *The Queen against Peter Barrett*, p. 185.
[173] Ibid., p. 186. In April 1871 he emigrated to the United States – see *The Evening Freeman* 4 April 1871. He married and ultimately settled there – see O'Regan (1999) *The Lamberts of Athenry*, p. 205.
[174] NLI, 'Lines written on the Liberation of Barrett'.
[175] *The Flag of Ireland*, 2nd July 1870.
[176] *The Galway Express*, 2nd July 1870.
[177] *The Galway Vindicator*, 19th July 1870.
[178] *The Irishman*, 2nd July 1870.
[179] *The Irish Canadian*, 20th July 1870.
[180] *The Freeman's Journal*, 1st July 1870.
[181] See, for example, ibid., 1st, 4th and 12th July 1870.
[182] *The Northern Star*, reprinted in the *Irish Canadian*, 20th July 1870.

again being employed in the department from which the cruel and unjust charge brought against him drove him as one with Cain's brand upon his brow.'[183] The *Irishman* published an editorial approving the acquittal of 'the trice-tried and sorely persecuted Peter Barrett'.[184]

Speaking some years later before a parliamentary committee examining Irish jury laws, Justice Lawson condemned the trial and similar cases, and claimed that it would be better to ignore the offence in question than to have justice receive such a public affront.[185] Why had popular support ended up so firmly behind Barrett? Initially, his personal characteristics appear to have been an important factor. As time went on, an impression took hold that he was being persecuted by the authorities, and this seems to have swayed much public opinion in his favour. The distortion of legal proceedings, while not a stated aim of Government policy, nevertheless seems to be a consequence of perhaps an over-cautious, reactionary policy to prosecute crimes perceived to be a threat to social order – as indeed violence against landlords must have been deemed. Unfortunately, the over-zealous pursuit of Barrett seems merely to have had the effect of engendering widespread sympathy for him in the popular press, and beyond the working classes and tenants.

One effect of the Barrett trials was the significant expense incurred by the Crown. Many of the surviving documents from the trials relate to accounts and expenses. Legal teams, witnesses and jurors all had to be paid for, as well as the expenses paid to sheriffs and other officials. Jurors were well-accommodated during the trials. For example, at the first trial, the jurors were accommodated in Black's hotel in Galway.[186] Jurors at the second and third trials in Dublin were put up in a Dublin hotel (probably the Gresham or the International). At the second trial in Dublin, Chief Justice Whiteside remarked that he hoped that the jurors 'would not be the worse for it in the morning'[187] – this may be a reference to his belief that the jurors would be drinking and carousing until a late hour. Based on the practice in other trials,[188] it is probable that all of the jurors' hotel expenses were paid, including food and liquid refreshments. Details of the expenses incurred accommodating the jurors at the third trial show that £27 was spent on keeping the jurors for three days, with an additional £3 for the bailiffs and police who supervised them, and £3 for car hire to transport them to and from the hotel.[189]

Witness expenses also had to be paid, and as some of the witnesses had travelled from London, these were not insignificant. When it became clear that there was to be a second trial, and that the London witnesses would have to travel once more,

---

[183] *The Freeman's Journal*, 9th July 1870.
[184] *The Irishman*, 2nd July 1870.
[185] *Report from the Select Committee of the House of Lords on the Operation of the Irish Jury Laws as Regards Trial by Jury in Criminal Cases, with the Proceedings, Evidence, Appendix and Index, 1881*, par. 4054, H.L. 1881 (430), xi, 1.
[186] *The Freeman's Journal*, 30th September 1869.
[187] Ibid., 18th February 1870.
[188] For example *R v Hynes, Dublin Commission Court (Francis Hynes)*, HC 1882 (408) lv, 167.
[189] NAI, *Queen v Barrett*, Sheriff's Account. *Account of Expenses Incurred by the Sub-Sheriff of the County of Dublin for Keep of Jury during Trial of Defendant for a Period of Three Days*, 24 August 1870, CCS/1870/197, Box 2. This appears to be similar to the expenses incurred at the second trial.

not all of them were happy about this. Walloms, the shopkeeper, for example, seemed to be extremely reluctant to travel again.[190] He wrote to Thomas O'Farrell, the crown solicitor: 'It is perfectly useless your wasting your time and words either threatening me with consequences or coaxing me with fine promises, neither will succeed.'[191] He demanded to be fully compensated for his time and expense, initially claiming 30 pounds.[192] This rose to forty[193] and then to 100 pounds,[194] and he then threatened to act as a defence witness if his demands were not met.[195] The authorities took a relatively dim view of this, and refused to pay him the 100 pounds. After some grandstanding, Wolloms eventually travelled to Dublin for the second trial in February. Having been subpoenaed, it may have simply been too risky not to appear and testify. He also testified at the third trial in June. The Galway witnesses also had to travel twice down to Dublin, incurring travel and accommodation expenses. Both the prosecution and the defence witnesses were paid for by the crown. Most received 3 or 4 pounds.[196] Captain Lambert proved to be the most expensive witness of all. As well as the security provided to him by the Royal Irish Constabulary, he submitted expense claims amounting to hundreds of pounds.[197]

Another expense incurred by the trials related to cartography. Several maps were drawn up for the purpose of illustrating the relative distances between various locations referred to in witness testimony. When it emerged that these maps may not have been entirely accurate, new maps had to be drawn up.[198] Legal fees were, unsurprisingly, another significant expense. It was common practice in Ireland at the time for the state to cover a prisoner's legal costs in serious criminal prosecutions.[199] Before the first trial, Under-Secretary J.H. Burke wrote to Concannon, Barrett's solicitor, to relay the Attorney General's opinion that,

> as the prisoner's attorney you ought to be allowed your proper fees in regard to his trial and that the prisoner ought to be permitted to select any counsel he may wish to name on the Connaught circuit to aid in his defence; that the crown solicitor ought to supply you with copies of all informations and that all the foregoing expenses ought to be defrayed by the crown.

---

[190] NAI, *Queen v Barrett*, Wolloms to O'Farrell, 10 September 1869; Wolloms to O'Farrell, 11 September 1869 and Wolloms to O'Farrell, 14 September 1869, CCS/1870/197, Box 1.
[191] Ibid., *Wolloms to O'Farrell*, 14 September 1869, CCS/1870/197, Box 1.
[192] Ibid.
[193] Ibid., Wolloms to O'Farrell, 22 November 1869, CCS/1870/197, Box 1.
[194] Ibid., Crown Solicitor to Attorney General, 16 November 1869, CCS/1870/197, Box 1.
[195] Ibid., Henderson to O'Farrell, 7 December 1869, CCS/1870/197, Box 1.
[196] Ibid., Names of Witnesses to Be Subpoenaed and Amount of Viaticum Paid to Each, 13 June 1870, CCS/1870/197, Box 2.
[197] He claimed £742 2 s. in total. See ibid., Thomas Lambert's Account 1870, CCS/1870/197, Box 2.
[198] Ibid., John Coghlan to William Lane Joynt, 26 January 1870; J. Nagle to William Lane Joynt, 14 June 1870, CCS/1870/197, Box 1. See also ibid., Maps Made by Mr Fitzgerald, 23 June 1870, CCS/1870/197, Box 2.
[199] For example, this was also done at the Maamtrasna trials, discussed by Conor Hanly in Chapter v of this book.

Burke also wrote that it was 'reasonable' that the cost of employing the attorney and counsel 'should not be borne by the prisoner'.[200] This was common enough practice at the time, and the prisoner was entitled to choose his own counsel. The advocacy of Isaac Butt QC came at a significant price – for example, at the third trial his fees were set at '£31, 10 shillings for the first day and £5, 5 shillings a day for each day in court'.[201]

It was estimated that the cost of the first two trials was around £15,000.[202] If this is to be taken as broadly accurate, the final figure for the three trials may have exceeded £20,000. This represents an extraordinary expenditure by the Crown in pursuit of an elusive conviction, and to almost no avail.

Conclusion

The trials of Peter Barrett, described by one newspaper at the time as ' ... one of the curiosities of legal history'[203] were widely reported in national and regional papers in Ireland, England, Wales and Scotland.[204] They also received some coverage in North America.[205] During other periods of the nineteenth century, a non-fatal attack such as this may have been relatively unremarkable. But coming at this precise moment, when the 'Irish question' was to the fore, the Liberals were in power, and agrarian violence was just beginning to increase, its significance became heightened.

The Barrett affair was, objectively speaking, a relatively mundane case; there had been no loss of life, no destruction of property and no severe or long-lasting injury to the victim. However, it took place against a dramatic backdrop of church disestablishment, land agitation, law reform and the prominence of the 'Irish question' in parliament. As the case became bound up with the landlord and tenant question, it is impossible to view the trials in a political vacuum. For example, Gladstone's Land Bill was published just before Barrett's second trial in February 1870. In March 1870, shortly after the second trial, a Peace Preservation Bill for Ireland was debated in the House of Commons. Chief Secretary Chichester Fortescue specifically mentioned the attack on Lambert and the trials of Barrett when describing the rise in agrarian outrages over the previous eighteen months or so.[206] He argued that the recent wave of both violent and non-violent agrarian criminality required a firm response. This led to the passing of the Peace Preservation (Ireland) Act 1870, a coercive measure which allowed, amongst other things, for the suspension of *habeas corpus*.[207] It was

---

[200] NAI, *Queen v Barrett*, Copy of letter from Under-Secretary JH Burke to JB Concanon, Esq, 10 September 1869, CCS 1870/197, Box 1. It was also noted that 'the expenses of any witnesses which the prisoner may adduce cannot be so defrayed'.
[201] Ibid., Memorandum by the Attorney General, 30 July 1870, CCS/1870/197, Box 2.
[202] *Clare Journal and Ennis Advertiser*, 21st February 1870.
[203] *Flag of Ireland*, 2nd October 1869.
[204] The case also made its way into the law reports: *R v. Barrett* (1870) Ir Rep 4 CL 285.
[205] *The Irish Canadian*, 20th July 1870 and the *Daily Alta California*, 26th July 1870.
[206] *Hansard: House of Lords Debates*, 3rd series, Vol. 200, Col 81–83 (17 March 1870).
[207] See J. Gantt (2010) *Irish Terrorism in the Atlantic Community, 1865–1922* (Basingstoke: Palgrave), pp. 73–4.

shortly after Barrett's acquittal that Gladstone's Land Act was passed, in August 1870. As Comerford points out, it marked 'the interference of parliament with previously sacrosanct property rights'. Although a significant step towards protecting the rights of tenants, it ultimately did not go far enough, and its passing did not represent closure on this chapter of Irish politics and law reform.

How had press reporting impacted on the case? The trials of Barrett were widely reported, with the public interest and press reporting increasing as the proceedings dragged on. For the most part, while the case was ongoing, reporting on the trials tended to be limited to factual accounts of the court proceedings. Some newspapers such as the nationalist *Dublin Weekly Nation* and the *Flag of Ireland* openly expressed support for Barrett,[208] but most waited until his final acquittal before openly making strong statements in Barrett's favour.

It is likely that the jurors at the third trial had read about it by that stage. It is difficult to assess whether this may have prejudiced them for or against Barrett, but the fact that at least one major national paper (the *Freeman's Journal*) took a pro-tenant stance (and appeared to be supportive of Barrett) may have been a relevant factor. The Catholic majority on the final jury may have had an influence, but it must be remembered that these were city jurors – special jurors at that – with little in common socially or economically with the son of a Connemara farmer.

The failure to secure a conviction in this case cannot be blamed on press reporting. It seems rather that the crown lost on the basis of weak evidence, the quality of the defence's legal representation, the sympathetic characteristics of the accused and the perception of the case as a David and Goliath-esque battle. It says a lot about depictions of criminality that Barrett's charm, handsome looks and respectability were so frequently referred to in both the press and the legal proceedings. The more he was pursued, the more sympathy he gained, while Lambert increasingly came across as shifty, unreliable and perhaps bearing a grudge against the Barretts.

Had Barrett's case arisen at another time in Irish politics, it probably would not have gained such notoriety in the press; nor, it is suggested, would the authorities have pursued Barrett with such determination. As to whether Barrett's trials can be regarded as fair or unfair, arguably there is an inherent unfairness in trying the same person three times for the same offence. However, other than applying for a change of venue on what can be described as rather shaky grounds, there is no evidence of corrupt or unfair practices by the crown, such as might be seen in cases like Maamtrasna. The Barrett trials might better be characterized as heavy-handed, than unfair.

---

[208] *Dublin Weekly Nation*, 2nd and 9th October 1869.

5

The Maamtrasna Murders: The Trial of Myles Joyce

Conor Hanly
National University of Ireland, Galway

Introduction

In 1882, five members of the Joyce family were brutally murdered in a rural part of western Ireland. Utilizing all its legal powers and privileges, the Crown secured convictions against three men who were sentenced to death, and another five men changed their pleas to guilty and ultimately were sentenced to imprisonment for twenty years. A controversy developed shortly afterwards and continues to this day concerning one of the executed men, Myles Joyce, who was and is widely regarded as being innocent of the charges. This chapter considers the principal procedural issues that arose during the Maamtrasna trials, and shows that the Crown's actions were entirely within contemporary trial procedures. This does not mean that the trial and execution of Myles Joyce was necessarily fair, however; the aggregation of the Crown's tactics, combined with a poor defence and a slanted judicial summary, together with information that came to the attention of the executive authority prior to Myles Joyce's execution, suggests that an innocent man may indeed have been executed.

Overview of the case and the controversy

On the 17th of August 1882, a group of men entered a house in Maamtrasna in rural County Galway (now County Mayo) and murdered four people: John Joyce, his wife Bridget, his mother Margaret and his daughter Margaret (known as Peggy).[1] Two boys, Patsy aged about ten and Michael aged seventeen, were left seriously injured: Michael later died of his injuries. A police officer spoke with both boys who told him that the men responsible had blackened or disguised faces. A magistrate took statements from

---

[1] The most convenient account of the Maamtrasna murders and the resulting trials, and the one from which this chapter draws, is J. Waldron (1992) *Maamtrasna: The Murders and the Mystery* (Dublin: Edmund Burke). The most recent account is set out in M. Kelleher (2018) *The Maamtrasna Murders* (Dublin: UCD Press).

both boys. Two days after the killings, three men – Anthony Joyce, his brother John and John's son – gave sworn statements to the police that they had followed the perpetrators for some three miles to the Joyce house and saw them enter the house. These witnesses identified ten men as part of the group: Anthony Philbin, Thomas Casey, Myles Joyce, Martin Joyce, Paudeen Joyce, Tom Joyce, Patrick Casey, John Casey, Michael Casey and Patrick Joyce. The police arrested and charged these men with the Maamtrasna murders, to be tried in Dublin before a Special Commission[2] and a special jury.[3]

The trials began on the 13th of November 1882; the Attorney General and two other Queen's Counsel represented the Crown, while one Queen's Counsel and a junior counsel represented the defendants. The defendants were tried serially and individually for the murder of one specifically named victim. The Crown's case centred on the statements from the three Joyces and the testimony of two of the ten men – Anthony Philbin and Thomas Casey – who had agreed to give evidence against the others, thereby becoming 'approvers'. The Crown dropped all charges against these approvers. In the first trial, the Crown also called Patsy Joyce but dismissed him having determined that he was unable to give sworn testimony. After two-day trials, Patrick Joyce and Patrick Casey were convicted of the murders of John Joyce and Bridget Joyce, respectively. Both men were sentenced to death. Myles Joyce was the third man tried, for the murder of Peggy Joyce. The defence sought a postponement of his trial in case the jurors might have been inflamed by the evidence in the first two trials, but the application was refused. Myles Joyce was also convicted and sentenced to death. The juries that convicted the three condemned men had spent a combined total of twenty-six minutes in their deliberations. The Lord Lieutenant refused clemency, and all three men were executed at Galway Gaol on the 15th of December 1882, with Myles Joyce protesting his innocence.[4] Under pressure from their solicitor and their parish priest, the fourth defendant to be tried (Michael Casey) and the other four defendants changed their pleas to guilty, and were formally sentenced to death. These death sentences were commuted to life imprisonment; Michael Casey died in prison, while the others served twenty years before being released in October 1902.

The immediate reaction to the trials and convictions appears to have been satisfaction, and even the Irish nationalist press seemed to accept the verdicts. *United*

---

[2] Murders were usually tried at the Assizes which traditionally sat twice a year in the counties, and six times a year in Dublin. The judges presiding over these trials did so on foot of royal commissions. Outside of the regular sittings, the Crown could issue a special commission ' … as often as the exigency of the times may require it, for the trial and punishment of certain offenders or offences therein particularly mentioned'. See E. Hayes (1843 edition) *Crimes and Punishments, or a Digest of the Criminal Statute Law of Ireland* (Dublin: Hodges and Smith), p. 601.

[3] Most criminal matters were decided by common juries drawn from lists prepared annually of men who met property ownership criteria set by legislation. Special juries were drawn from a more select group of men who owned more valuable property. See N. Howlin (2009) 'Controlling Jury Composition in Nineteenth-Century Ireland', *Journal of Legal History*, 30, 3, pp. 227–61 at p. 227. The use of a special jury in criminal matters was unusual, but the Prevention of Crimes (Ireland) Act 1882 empowered either the Attorney General or the defendant to demand one.

[4] Myles Joyce's execution was botched, and he died slowly from strangulation rather than immediately from a fractured neck. See the coroners' jury verdict found at the National Archives of Ireland (hereafter NAI), CRF/1902/J13/18/7. See also Chief Secretary Papers, *Inquiry into the Execution of Myles Joyce*, NAI/CSORP/1883/189. The report of this inquiry is dated 2nd January 1882, but this is clearly an error, and should read 1883.

Ireland, a Parnellite newspaper,[5] wrote in the aftermath of Myles Joyce's conviction, that the ' ... public are satisfied that a disgusting butchery has been avenged upon convincing evidence by juries comparatively fairly chosen'.[6] Similarly, *The Connaught Tribune* noted the 'strong evidence' of guilt against the condemned men, and suggested that convictions were a foregone conclusion before any jury.[7] This satisfaction began to evaporate within a short time, however.[8] The night before their executions, Pat Joyce and Pat Casey made independent statements to the Prison Chaplain accepting their own guilt but exonerating Myles Joyce.[9] These statements were presented to the Lord Lieutenant, Earl Spencer, by the defence solicitor as part of the unsuccessful plea for clemency. Most dramatically, in August 1884, Thomas Casey, one of the approvers, publicly recanted his testimony at a Mass before the Archbishop of Tuam.[10] Casey told the congregation that he had borne false witness against Myles Joyce and the imprisoned defendants both to save his own life, and because the Crown solicitor, George Bolton, had offered him £300. Bolton was by then mired in scandal: he had been dismissed from his position as Crown solicitor for committing embezzlement and for a sexual relationship with a servant girl. Nevertheless, he denied that improper pressure had been brought to bear on Casey. A resident magistrate and the governor of the prison, who had both been present when Casey agreed to turn Queen's evidence, supported Bolton's statement. The three men alleged that Casey was part of a campaign against the administration of the law.

Also in 1884, the imprisoned defendant Michael Casey wrote a letter stating that Myles Joyce had been innocent,[11] and Tim Harrington, a nationalist MP, published a book arguing that the Crown had perverted the course of justice and that Myles Joyce had been innocent of the charges.[12] In his book, Harrington pointed out various discrepancies in the evidence given by the Crown's witnesses, and also that Anthony Joyce, the primary 'independent' witness, in fact had a grudge against Myles Joyce.

---

[5] 'Parnellite' refers to supporters of Charles Stewart Parnell, the leader of the Irish Parliamentary Party, the principal Irish nationalist political party that pushed for Home Rule in Ireland. Parnell became an MP at Westminster in 1875, and soon demonstrated his mastery of political procedure. By the middle of the nineteenth century, he held the balance of power in Westminster, and Gladstone's Liberals formally adopted a policy of Home Rule for Ireland. Parnell, often referred to as the '... uncrowned king of Ireland', was toppled in 1890 once his adulterous affair with Kitty O'Shea was revealed. See P. Bew (1991) *Charles Stewart Parnell* (Dublin: Gill and Macmillan).

[6] *United Ireland*, 25th November 1882, cited in Waldron, *Maamtrasna*, p. 132. George Trevelyan, Chief Secretary for Ireland, subsequently stated in a House of Commons debate that this '... admission, considering the quarter from which it comes, is higher praise than the conduct of any criminal trial in my day in Ireland ever received before'. *Hansard: House of Commons Debates*, 24 October 1884, col. 225.

[7] *The Connaught Tribune*, 18th November 1882, cited in Waldron, *Maamtrasna Murders*, p. 132.

[8] By the end of 1882, for example, *United Ireland*, wrote that '... [b]oth as to the tribunal and as to the evidence, the proceedings against these men bear an indelible taint of foul play' – see *United Ireland*, 23 December 1882, cited in Waldron, *Maamtrasna*, p. 156.

[9] These statements are reproduced in Waldron (1992) *Maamtrasna* at pp. 142–4.

[10] For an account of this incident, see ibid., Chapter 11.

[11] Casey's letter is reproduced in ibid at pp. 227–8. Casey insisted that he had not taken part in the killings, and that his presence at the scene had been coerced. Interestingly, Casey also stated that Pat Joyce was innocent, which contradicts Joyce's own statement.

[12] T.C. Harrington (1884) *The Maamtrasna Massacre: Impeachment of the Trials* (Dublin: Nation Office).

In October 1884, Parliament debated Harrington's motion for an official enquiry into Myles Joyce's execution and the imprisonment of the five surviving Maamtrasna defendants. The debate continued across five days and involved luminaries from all parties, including the Prime Minister, William Gladstone. Perhaps surprisingly, the Tory Party – not usually friendly to Irish nationalism – sided with Harrington and the nationalists, but ultimately the government defeated the motion by a considerable majority. Officially, the verdicts stood, but to this day, the trial and execution of Myles Joyce is considered by many to be a gross miscarriage of justice.[13]

The context of the killings

Nineteenth-century Ireland was a violent place: Johnson shows that the homicide and assault rates in late nineteenth-century Ireland were considerably higher than in other western European countries.[14] Some of this violence arose from two long-running intermittent and overlapping conflicts.[15] The first was between tenants and landlords and their agents. Tenant farmers in most of the country lived in wretched conditions, and had only a tenuous grip on the land they worked.[16] Throughout the eighteenth and nineteenth centuries, these farmers agitated to improve their situation. This agitation was often violent, especially towards those that ignored prior warnings: Cronin notes that such persons ' … were badly beaten, had their ears cropped and their backs lacerated by wool combs, or were buried up to their necks in thorn-filled trenches'.[17] By the end of the eighteenth century, murder became more common.[18] The agrarian effort culminated in the so-called Land War that erupted between 1879 and 1882. Led by the Land League, large numbers of tenant farmers withheld their rent payments, resulting in increased eviction attempts by landlords, which often turned violent. The Land League led boycotts against landlords, their agents and their property, and against anyone who took over farms from which farmers had been evicted. There were also frequent incidents of intimidation by secret societies involving physical attacks, and destruction of property and livestock.[19]

---

[13] See, for example, *Irish Independent*, 9th July 2015 and *Irish Times*, 20th May 2016.
[14] D. Johnson (1996) 'Trial by Jury in Ireland 1860–1914', *Journal of Legal History*, 17, 3, pp. 270–93, especially Tables 3 and 4.
[15] Finnane points out that ' … taking the volume of arrests, prosecutions and punishments in Ireland, agrarian unrest, even at its height, was never of major significance in the working of the criminal justice system'. See M. Finnane (2006) 'Irish Crime without the Outrage' in N.M. Dawson (ed.) *Reflections on Law and History* (Dublin: Irish legal History Society), pp. 203–22 at p. 207.
[16] Kelleher cites several contemporary sources that illustrate these conditions, see Kelleher, *Maamtrasna Murders*, pp.16–18.
[17] M. Cronin (2012) *Agrarian Protest in Ireland 1750–1960* (Dublin: Economic and Social History Society of Ireland), p. 8.
[18] Ibid.
[19] See G.E. Christianson (1972) 'Secret Societies and Agrarian Violence in Ireland, 1790–1840', *Agricultural History*, 46, 2, pp. 369–84.

The second conflict was political. Secret nationalist organizations launched three full-scale rebellions during the nineteenth century: the United Irishmen (1803), the Young Irelanders (1848) and the Irish Republican Brotherhood (known as the Fenians) (1867–1868). Outside of these rebellions, political unrest continued intermittently throughout the century. The most spectacular and notorious event was the Phoenix Park murders in May 1882: a group called the Invincibles assassinated Lord Frederick Cavendish, Chief Secretary for Ireland, and Thomas Henry Burke, the Permanent Under-Secretary and the most senior member of the Irish civil service.[20]

The executive authorities in Dublin, headed by the Lord Lieutenant, had considerable resources with which to meet these challenges. The Royal Irish Constabulary (RIC), formed in 1822, had some 11,000 members by the end of the nineteenth century. The constabulary could be supplemented by the British Army, whose numbers in Ireland reached 25,000 at particularly violent times during the nineteenth century.[21] Unlike England, a centralized system of public prosecution developed in Ireland with Crown solicitors in each county controlled from Dublin Castle.[22] These solicitors employed a variety of prosecutorial techniques such as jury packing to counter the perceived bias of potential jurors. The Crown's prosecutorial powers were strengthened by the enactment of emergency powers statutes known collectively as the Coercion Acts.[23] The Protection of Persons and Property (Ireland) Act 1881, for example, allowed the Lord Lieutenant to order imprisonment without trial.[24] The Prevention of Crime (Ireland) Act 1882,[25] enacted in the aftermath of the Phoenix Park murders, allowed the Attorney General to order the transfer of a trial to Dublin, the use of special juries and the establishment of a non-jury trial court.[26]

Crown view of the case

The Crown approach to the Maamtrasna case was coloured by the backdrop against which the killings occurred. The RIC assumed the Maamtrasna killings to be an agrarian crime:

---

[20] See S. Molony (2006) *The Phoenix Park Murders: Conspiracy, Betrayal and Retribution* (Cork: Mercier Press) and J.L. Hammond (1938) *Gladstone and the Irish Nation* (London: Longmans), Chapter 16.

[21] W.J. Smyth (2017) 'Conflict, Reaction and Control in Nineteenth-Century Ireland: The Archaeology of Revolution' in J. Crowley et al. (eds) *Atlas of the Irish Revolution* (Cork: Cork University Press), pp. 21–55 at pp. 21–2.

[22] See, for example, the evidence of John Napier, former Attorney General for Ireland, Parliamentary Papers, *Select Committee on Public Prosecutors – Report*, 1854–55, 481, at Q.1818.

[23] During the currency of the Union (1801–922), Westminster enacted over one hundred Coercion Acts applicable to Ireland – see L. Donohue (2003) 'Civil Liberties, Terrorism and Liberal Democracy: Lessons from the United Kingdom' in A. Howitt and R. Pangi (eds) *Countering Terrorism: Dimensions of Preparedness* (Cambridge, MA: MIT Press), pp. 411–46 at p. 421.

[24] 44 & 45 Vict, c.4, s.1. Under this legislation, most of the leaders of the Land League, including Parnell, were imprisoned until 1882.

[25] 45 & 46 Vict, c.25.

[26] This court was never implemented, largely due to opposition from the Irish judiciary.

It is supposed that John Joyce belonged to a secret society, and incurred the displeasure of the members by threatening to give information in revenge for being accused of stealing sheep.[27]

Given the backdrop described above and the nature of the crime – an extremely violent set of murders that took place at night in an area of the country that had seen a great deal of agrarian violence – the Crown's view was not unreasonable. But that view affected the manner with which the case was dealt. In particular, the Crown invoked its powers under the 1882 emergency legislation to transfer the trial to Dublin, which put the defence at an immediate disadvantage. This official view was effectively unchallengeable in court as judges tended to defer to the view of the Crown authorities. In the earlier case of *R v. Phelan and Phelan*, for example, the defendant was charged with a murder that the Crown characterized as agrarian in nature.[28] Justice Fitzgerald deferred to the official view:

> It has been said that this was not a crime of an agrarian character. That is a matter as to which the Court must be guided by the opinions of experienced men who are acquainted with the local circumstances. Here we have the Crown solicitor and the sub-inspector of constabulary stating that as a result of their inquiries that the crime was of an agrarian character, the murdered man being the son of a man who was described as a not over merciful landlord.[29]

Thus, the Maamtrasna court almost certainly would have rejected any defence attempt to challenge the Crown's assessment of the incident.

Transfer of the trial

The Maamtrasna trials took place in the Green Street Courthouse in Dublin. This was unusual; in Ireland, as in England and most of the Common Law world, criminal trials usually took place in the locality in which the offence was alleged to have occurred. As noted above, however, the Prevention of Crime (Ireland) Act, 1882 entitled the Attorney General to direct the removal of a trial to another county if he certified that in his opinion such removal was expedient in the interests of justice.[30] This removal of power was not peculiar to Ireland; the Central Criminal Court Act

---

[27] NAI, *Return of Outrages Specially Reported to the Constabulary Office: Homicides Reported in 1882*, CSO/ICR/2/1882/8, p. 8. See also NAI, Transcript of Proceedings, CRF/1902/J13/29, p. 155 where the Attorney General explains that Myles Joyce and the other men were ' … acting under some secret organisation'.
[28] (1881) Cox CC 579.
[29] Ibid. The Crown solicitor in question was George Bolton, the Maamtrasna prosecutor.
[30] 45 & 46 Vict, c.25, s.6(1). This section required the Attorney General to formally petition the High Court, but on provision of the appropriate certification, the Attorney General was 'entitled as of right' to the order.

1856, for example, permitted trials to be removed from provincial courts in England to the Old Bailey in London.[31]

Notwithstanding its legal basis, moving the trial to Dublin had unfortunate consequences for the defence. A jury composed of Dubliners would be unlikely to have much understanding of conditions in the rural west. As Waldron notes, Myles Joyce and the other defendants essentially were on trial in a foreign land.[32] This lack of understanding was exacerbated by the inability of the jury to view the scene of the crime.[33] Travelling from Dublin to a remote part of the west would have been impractical: it took the local coroner almost a whole day to travel the twenty-three miles from Oughterard to Maamtrasna.[34] This practical difficulty was compounded by the Crown's decision to charge the defendants serially rather than together[35] – it was clearly impracticable to delay each trial by a week to allow the jury to view the scene. A more practical solution would have been to transfer the trials back to Galway, and the defence requested that this be done before the first trial. The trial judge, Justice Barry, refused the application – probably correctly. The 1882 Act gave the Attorney General what amounted to an absolute right to select the trial venue. Had Justice Barry granted the defence motion, he would have effectively undone one of the key points of the Act. The Dublin juries, therefore, would have to rely for their geographical understanding on witness testimony and on the detailed map prepared by an engineer.[36]

Approver evidence

The Crown's case was built on two pillars: the evidence of the three Joyce witnesses, and that of the defendant approvers Anthony Philbin and Thomas Casey who testified against their fellow defendants. Blackstone described approvement thus:

> A person, indicted of treason or felony, and arraigned for the same, doth confess the fact before plea pleaded; and appeals or accuses other, his accomplices, of the same crime, in order to obtain his pardon.[37]

Traditionally, the approvers' pardon was contingent upon a conviction; if the accomplices were acquitted, the approver would stand convicted by his own confession

---

[31] 19 & 20 Vict, c.16, s.1.
[32] Waldron, *Maamtrasna*, p. 108.
[33] The Juries Procedure (Ireland) Act 1876, 39 & 40 Vict, c.78, s.11 allowed a trial judge to adjourn a trial to allow for this to happen.
[34] See Waldron, *Maamtrasna*, p. 33.
[35] Given the Crown's theory of the crime – a joint unlawful enterprise – charging each defendant individually seems odd. The Attorney General stated that this was done to ensure fairness to each defendant; see the second reference at note 28 above.
[36] This map is reproduced on the back sleeve of Waldron's book, and in colour on the back sleeve of Kelleher's book.
[37] W. Blackstone (1769) *Commentaries on the Laws of England – Volume IV* (Chicago: University of Chicago Press), p. 324.

and would be executed.[38] By the nineteenth century, however, approvers could usually expect the Crown's mercy, notwithstanding the acquittal of their accomplices.[39] By confessing their involvement in the Maamtrasna killings, Philbin and Casey saw the charges against them dropped in advance of the trial hearings.

The value of an approver to a Crown prosecution is obvious: the approver was a part of the criminal enterprise and therefore was in a position to give detailed evidence as to what happened. But the approver also had an incentive both to minimize his own involvement in the enterprise and to deflect attention on to others. Blackstone noted, '[M]ore mischief hath arisen to good men by these kind of approvements, upon false and malicious accusations of desperate villains, than benefit to the public by the discovery of real offenders.'[40] Because of this, approver evidence became comparatively rare in English courts by the seventeenth century.[41] In Ireland, however, the courts continued to accept this kind of evidence throughout the nineteenth century. Nevertheless, a judge sitting in the Dublin Commission, Justice Torrens, noted that it was a ' … wise and salutary rule that, unless the evidence of an approver be corroborated by a faithworthy witness, although it is evidence to go to a jury, an intelligent jury will be slow to convict without such corroboration.'[42] Furthermore, a court had discretion to exclude an approver's testimony (especially if the approver was the principal offender), and more than one approver in a single case was generally frowned upon.[43] Finally, in *R v. Glennon, Toole and Magrath*, Chief Justice Doherty indicated that the approver's evidence should be heard first, before that of other witnesses who might provide corroboration.[44]

In the Maamtrasna case, there are some issues with the admission of Philbin and Casey's evidence. The court permitted the Crown to call the approvers after the Joyces, thereby inverting the usual order of witnesses. In *Glennon, Toole and Magrath*, Chief Justice Doherty noted that having the approver testify first allowed the defence to cross-examine the corroborating witnesses after the approver evidence had been concluded.[45] The Chief Justice did not indicate whether such an inversion would invalidate an approver's evidence; probably, this would be a matter for the trial judge's

---

[38] Ibid., p. 325.
[39] Hayes, *Crimes and Punishments*, p. 5.
[40] Blackstone, *Commentaries on the Laws of England – Volume IV*, p. 329. The nineteenth-century judiciary made similar comments: see *R v. Farlar* (1837) 8 C & P 106 (Lord Abinger commenting that ' … when a man is fixed, and knows that his own guilt is detected, he purchases impunity by falsely accusing others') and *R v. Green* (1825) 1 Craw & Dix CC 158 (Justice Jebb stating that ' … the temptation to save his own life is so strong, that [the approver] can seldom be trusted').
[41] M. Hale (1736) *History of the Pleas of the Crown – Volume II* (London: E. Rider), pp. 226–7.
[42] *R v. Dunne* (1852) 5 Cox CC 507. The same judge expressed particular concern about the approver appearing to be guiltier than the defendant, who was a young boy. A quarter of a century earlier, an Irish court had indicated that an approver's testimony should be disregarded unless some corroboration existed. *R v. Sheehan* (1826) Jebb CC 54.
[43] See W.E. Vaughan (2009) *Murder Trials in Ireland, 1836–1914* (Dublin: Irish Legal History Society), pp. 200–1 [citing T.A. Purcell (1848) *A Summary of the General Principles of Pleading and Evidence, in Criminal Cases in Ireland* (Dublin: Grant and Bolton) at pp. 354–5]. Note that Edmund Hayes, another contemporary commentator, suggested that the admissibility of an approver's evidence should be left to the discretion of the Crown counsel – see Hayes, *Crimes and Punishments*, p. 6.
[44] (1840) 1 Cr. & Dix. 359.
[45] Ibid.

discretion. Nevertheless, by allowing the approvers to give evidence after the Joyces, the benefit identified by Chief Justice Doherty was denied to the Maamtrasna defendants. A further issue arises in respect of Casey's evidence, especially: in their post-trial statements, Pat Joyce, Pat Casey and Michael Casey all indicated that Thomas Casey was one of the men who had actually committed the Maamtrasna killings. If true, his guilt would have been greater than that of many of the defendants, thereby raising the moral issue that troubled Justice Torrens in the *Dunne* case: protecting the main offender while using his testimony to convict and hang a lesser offender.

There is no question, however, that Irish law allowed for the admission of approver evidence. In his charge to the jury, the trial judge, Justice Barry, alluded to the ' ... humane practice of the law of this country ... that a jury are advised by the presiding judge ... not to convict on the testimony of any number of approvers [in the absence of corroboration]'.[46] And the defence counsel specifically reminded the jury of the part played by the approvers' in the killings: 'Such a pair as was never seen, they are the originators of this transaction, they are the persons who first seem to have the intention of doing something that night'.[47] There is no way, however, to know how much impact the approvers' testimony had on the jury's decision to convict Pat Joyce, Pat Casey and Myles Joyce.

Language in court

The Maamtrasna trials were held in Dublin before an English-speaking jury, an English-speaking judge and English-speaking officials. The defendants, however, came from an Irish-speaking part of Ireland; Kelleher describes Myles Joyce as a ' ... monoglot Irish speaker'.[48] One of the abiding images of the trial of Myles Joyce was painted by Tim Harrington, MP, who told Parliament that the

> Judge, who tried [Myles Joyce], was to him as much a foreigner as if he were a Turk trying the case in Constantinople. The very crier of the Court, and the counsel who represented him, were foreigners to him; and the whole trial, as far as he was concerned, was an empty show and a farce.[49]

Similarly, James Joyce later wrote of a ' ... dumbfounded old man ... deaf and dumb before his judge'.[50] A trial in which the defendant cannot understand the evidence against him is surely the epitome of unfairness.

---

[46] NAI, Transcript of Proceedings, CRF/1902/J13/29, p. 205.
[47] See Waldron, *Maamtrasna*, p. 77.
[48] Kelleher, *Maamtrasna Murders*, p. xix. Kelleher gives the following breakdown of the Maamtrasna defendants' linguistic abilities: Patrick Joyce, Patrick Casey, Thomas Casey and Anthony Philbin spoke English and Irish; Tom Joyce may have had some competence in English; John Casey, Michael Casey, Myles Joyce, Martin Joyce and Paudeen Joyce spoke only Irish – see ibid.
[49] *Hansard: House of Commons Debates*, 13 August 1883, col. 283 and 294–5.
[50] J. Joyce (1959) 'Ireland at the Bar' in E. Mason and R. Ellmann (eds) *The Critical Writings of James Joyce* (London: Faber & Faber), pp. 197–200 at p. 198 (translation from the Italian published as 'L'Irlanda all Sbarra' in *Il Piccolo della Sera*, Trieste, 16 September 1907).

By statute,[51] the language of the courts in Ireland was English, but Irish speakers could give their evidence in Irish through an interpreter.[52] The Maamtrasna court appointed an RIC officer – Constable Evans – to act as an ad hoc interpreter. Notwithstanding the obvious conflict of interest in a serving police officer acting for the court in this role, it appears that Evans did a good job.[53] The Crown's case was built on two pillars: the evidence of the two approvers and the evidence of the three independent witnesses. The two approvers gave their evidence in English. No translation was provided to Myles Joyce, but until 1915 there was no legal requirement to do so if the defendant was represented by counsel.[54] The theory appears to have been that what a man's counsel knew, the man was deemed also to know.[55] Be that as it may the nationalist *Freeman's Journal* reported that Joyce indicated, via Constable Evans, that he understood the evidence given in English: 'The interpreter asked the prisoner in Irish if he understood the evidence that was being given in English, and informed the court that the prisoner replied in the affirmative.'[56] This is remarkable as all the accounts suggest that Myles spoke only Irish[57] Phelan speculates that perhaps there was a misunderstanding between Joyce and Evans: the latter spoke Ulster Irish while the former spoke Connemara Irish.[58] Kelleher goes further and suggests that Joyce's ' ... answer in the affirmative (that he did understand the interpreter's speech in Irish) was taken to mean that he understood evidence given in English.'[59] But this interpretation does not conform to the *Freeman's Journal*'s account. Whatever Joyce's intended meaning, from the trial court's perspective, this exchange justified not providing the interpreter services that were available to other Maamtrasna defendants.

As for the evidence of the three independent witnesses – who gave the Crown's primary evidence – being Irish speakers, they gave their evidence in Irish through the medium of Constable Evans. As an Irish speaker, Myles Joyce would have had the same linguistic advantage in respect of this key evidence as has been attributed to the Crown in respect of the approvers' evidence and the proceedings overall. Furthermore, as Myles's trial was the third to be heard, all of the evidence to be given was already known to the defence. It is arguable, therefore, that the actual impact of linguistic matters on the outcome of the trial was less than is sometimes suggested.

[51] Administration of Justice (Language) Act 1737, 11 Geo. 2, c.6.
[52] *R v. Burke* (1858) 8 Cox CC 44.
[53] Evans received several compliments for his translation efforts from the court. For a summary of these compliments, see M. Phelan (2013), *Irish Language Court Interpreting, 1801–1922*, unpublished Ph.D dissertation, Dublin City University, p. 88 (M. Phelan (2019), *Irish speakers, Interpreters and the Courts, 1754–1921*, (Dublin: Four Courts Press)).
[54] In *R v. Lee Kun* [1916] 1 KB 337, the King's Bench ruled that the safer and better practice was to ensure that the evidence against a defendant would be translated unless defence counsel specifically indicated that doing so was unnecessary.
[55] Ibid.
[56] *Freeman's Journal*, 20th November 1882, at p. 2.
[57] See Kelleher, *Maamtrasna Murders*, p.xix. Joyce's own Queen's counsel, George Malley, referred to his client as '... this wretched Irish-speaking creature, who has never had the advantage of education, who is unable to understand the language in which his accusers will give their evidence, or the language in which the counsel will arraign him, or your lordship's address to the jury'. See NAI, Transcript of Proceedings, CRF/1902/J13/29, p. 149.
[58] Phelan, *Irish Language Court Interpreting*, p. 91.
[59] Kelleher, *Maamtrasna Murders*, p.119.

Jury packing

As noted earlier, a central nationalist accusation was that the Crown packed the Maamtrasna trial juries with reliable jurors. Using its so-called stand-by power, the Crown was entitled essentially to skip any number of jurors whose names had been called in the ballot without showing cause, unless the entire panel had been gone through before twelve jurors had been empanelled. If this happened, each of the jurors thus skipped would be revisited in turn, and the Crown would have to either accept the juror or show cause why he should be removed. Going through the entire panel was rare so the Crown effectively had an unlimited power of peremptory challenge.[60] That the Crown utilized its power in the selection of the four Maamtrasna juries is beyond doubt, as the following table shows:

Thus, even disregarding the thirteen jurors who were stood by because of their earlier service, the Crown skipped half the jurors whose names were called.

The suggestion of unfair jury packing received a boost through the chance discovery of the brief for Peter O'Brien, one of the Crown's counsels. The brief contained the jury panel on which the letter 'C' had been marked against the names of many of the jurors. To nationalists, this was proof that the Crown had actively sought the removal of Catholic jurors from the Maamtrasna juries. Yet even the nationalist press

Table 5.1 Crown challenges to the appointment of jurors in the trials of P & M Joyce and P & M Casey

Defendant	Total No. of Jurors Called	No. of Jurors Stood By (Crown)	No. of Jurors Peremptorily Challenged (Defence)
Patrick Joyce	68	37	19
Patrick Casey	56	27[61]	17
Myles Joyce	55	27	16
Michael Casey	70	41[62]	18[63]
Totals	249	132	69

[60] Johnson, 'Trial by Jury in Ireland 1860–1914', pp. 270–93. Similarly, George Bolton, the Maamtrasna prosecutor, told a House of Lords Committee that such a situation had never happened to him. See Parliamentary Papers, *Select Committee on Irish Jury Laws – Report*, 1881, 430 at Q.3956.

[61] This figure includes eleven jurors who had served on the first trial. The Attorney General stated that in the second and third trials he would stand by any juror who had served in the earlier trials. There is no indication that this courtesy was necessary in the third trial. In the fourth trial, the Attorney General was willing to stand by jurors from the third trial only because of a shortage of jurors. In total, six jurors who had served on the first jury were called to serve on the fourth. The defence unsuccessfully challenged four of them – the Attorney General stood by one, the defence peremptorily challenged two, and the fourth was sworn. The other two jurors from the first jury requested excusal; one was peremptorily challenged and the other was stood by (and excused by the court from further service on the grounds of ill health).

[62] This figure includes two jurors who had served on the first Maamtrasna jury and were stood by.

[63] This figure includes three jurors from the first trial; the defence had unsuccessfully challenged two of them, and the third had requested to be excused. The defence peremptorily challenged all three.

acknowledged that half of the men on the first Maamtrasna jury were Catholic,[64] and skipping jurors on the basis of their religion would have been contrary to formal standing instructions on the use of the stand-by power.[65] O'Brien himself claimed that the letter 'C' simply indicated the jurors to be challenged, a claim that seems likely to be true. O'Brien had earned the nickname 'Peter the Packer', having ' ... built up a reputation for winning cases by the simple if controversial expedient of challenging all jurors whom he considered unreliable'.[66] Given the Crown's almost unlimited stand-by power and O'Brien's reputed packing ability, it seems unlikely that any Catholics would have made it on to the Maamtrasna juries had the Crown really wished to exclude them.

So, there is no question that the Crown used its stand-by power to pack the Maamtrasna juries with jurors that it considered reliable, although probably not on the basis of religion. While such tactics were unusual in England,[67] they were used more frequently in Ireland, and were not used secretively. Several Crown solicitors told parliamentary committees that the stand-by power was entirely necessary to counter bias among potential jurors. For example, George Bolton, the Maamtrasna prosecutor and the Crown solicitor for Tipperary, gave evidence to a House of Lords Committee in 1881. He referred to an assize session in Clonmel earlier that year, at which he and the local RIC Inspector concluded that out of 167 names on the jury panel, only 12

> would try a case fairly, and give fair weight to the evidence ....[A]s to the rest we were thoroughly satisfied there was not a man on the panel but would acquit under any circumstances, no matter what the evidence was.[68]

He went on to say that it was ' ... thoroughly useless to expect a conviction in Tipperary'.[69] He concluded that the stand-by power was 'absolutely necessary'.[70] Given

---

[64] Waldron, *Maamtrasna Murders*, p.132 (citing a comment in *United Ireland* that at least five, and perhaps six, of the jurors empanelled in the first trial were Catholic).
[65] Parliamentary Papers, *A Copy of the Instructions Given to the Respective Crown Solicitors on Each Circuit, Respecting the Challenging of Jurors in Crown Cases*, 1842, 171 at 1. Guidelines issued by Attorney General Robert Warren in 1868 provided that a juror should be stood by only if the Crown solicitor had reason to believe that the juror might be ' ... hindered from giving an impartial verdict by favour towards the accused, fear of the consequence s to their persons, property, or trade, or any other motive, although same may not amount to a legal ground of challenge, or may not admit of legal proof'. Set out in Parliamentary Papers, *Select Committee on Juries (Ireland), First, Second and Special Reports*, 1873, 283 at Q.1746-47 (evidence of Constantine Molloy, barrister).
[66] L.P. Curtis (1963) *Coercion and Conciliation in Ireland 1880-1892: A Study in Conservative Unionism* (Princeton, NJ: Princeton University Press), p. 192.
[67] Sir James Fitzjames Stephen wrote that in his career he could remember only one or two trials in which the Crown had stood by a large number of jurors – see J.F. Stephen (1883) *History of the Criminal Law of England – Volume I* (London: Macmillan and Co.), p. 303. See also N. Howlin (2008) 'Merchants and Esquires: Special Juries in Dublin 1725-1833' in G. O'Brien and F. O'Kane (eds) *Georgian Dublin* (Dublin: Four Courts Press), pp. 97-109 at p. 107 and Howlin, 'Controlling Jury Composition', pp. 227-61.
[68] Parliamentary Papers, *House of Lords Select Committee on Jury Laws – Report*, 1881, 430 at Q.3865.
[69] Ibid at Q.3869. Note that many of the cases Bolton discussed in his evidence were neither agrarian nor political in nature.
[70] Ibid at Q.3952.

the poor conviction rate in Ireland relative to England,[71] Bolton might have had a point: Johnson suggests that tactics such as jury packing were probably necessary to achieve even this low number of convictions.[72]

The defence also utilized its powers to the full in an attempt to pack the juries in its favour. In a felony trial, a defendant was entitled to challenge up to twenty jurors peremptorily,[73] in addition to an unlimited number of challenges for cause. In the four Maamtrasna trials, the defence challenged a total of sixty-nine jurors – nearly 90 per cent of the total number permitted to them. The difference, of course, is that while the defence's ability to influence the composition of a jury was limited to twenty challenges, the Crown's power to do so was limited only by the number of jurors who formed the jury panel. As Daniel Crilly noted in 1887, as long as a sufficient number of jurors had been summoned, the defence would exhaust its peremptory powers long before the Crown reached its limit.[74] Thus, through an entirely lawful selection process, a 'Castle jury' generally could be ensured.[75]

Inadmissibility of the Joyce Boys' statements

First-hand eyewitness accounts of what happened in John Joyce's house were available as the two young Joyce boys – Michael, aged seventeen, and Patsy, aged about ten – survived the attacks and gave statements to a magistrate. These statements contained information about the attackers' appearance that might have been useful to the defence in undermining the evidence of the independent witnesses. Tim Harrington, MP, argued that this information, ' … if clearly established, puts an end completely to the evidence at trial, and stamps it as a fraud and a murderous perjury'.[76] Yet none of the trial juries ever heard the boys' statements.

Michael died shortly after making his statement, and the only way that his statement could have been admitted was as a dying declaration. Such a statement obviously could not be tested under cross-examination, but was admissible if

> made in extremity, when the party is at the point of death, and when every hope of this world is gone; when every motive to falsehood is silenced, and the mind is induced by the most powerful considerations to speak the truth.[77]

---

[71] Johnson shows that both the conviction rate and the imprisonment rate were markedly lower in Ireland than in England – see Johnson, 'Trial by Jury in Ireland', pp. 274–6.
[72] Ibid., p. 286.
[73] Criminal Law (Ireland) Act 1828, 9 Geo. 4, c.54, s.9.
[74] D. Crilly (1887) *Jury Packing in Ireland, as Illustrated by the Prosecution of J. Dillon* (Oxford: Oxford University Press), p. 34. Crilly was one of several parliamentarians charged with conspiracy to incite non-payment of rents, and wrote this pamphlet describing his experiences.
[75] This phrase invokes Dublin Castle, the seat of executive power in Ireland.
[76] Harrington, *The Maamtrasna Massacre*, p. 38.
[77] *R v. Leach* (1789) 1 Leach 500, 502.

Two requirements, however, limited the admissibility of statements from deceased witnesses, and both were relevant to Michael's statement. First, the statement had to have been made ' ... under a clear impression that [the deponent] was in a dying state'.[78] In most cases, such an impression had to be clear from the statement itself: in *R v. Reaney and Reddish*, for example, the deponent stated, 'I have made this statement believing I shall not recover.'[79] Michael made no such declaration; the closest he came was that 'I am very sick. I cannot raise myself up ... I have no pain at all.'[80] It is unlikely that this comment would have been sufficient to establish Michael's statement as a dying declaration, and therefore the statement probably would have been deemed inadmissible.

Even if Michael's statement was judged to have met the first requirement, the second was fatal to its admissibility. A dying declaration was admissible only ' ... where the death of the deceased is the subject of the charge, and the circumstances of the death the subject of the dying declaration'.[81] Had the Crown charged the defendants with the murder of all the victims, Michael's statement would have met this requirement as he was one of the victims. Such a charge would have made sense given the Crown's theory of the case – that all the defendants were engaged in a criminal enterprise the purpose of which was to kill the members of the Joyce family. In modern terms, this is known as the doctrine of joint enterprise. But the Crown chose instead to charge each of the defendants with the murder of one specific victim; Michael's death was due to be the subject of the fifth trial. This prosecutorial arrangement meant that as Michael's death was not the subject of Myles Joyce's trial, Michael's statement was inadmissible in Myles' case. It is conceivable that the Crown chose to prosecute each defendant for a specific victim's death in order to limit the admissibility of Michael's declaration – as noted above, the prosecutorial arrangement does not sit easily with the Crown's theory of the crime. The Crown's true intention is unknown, however; as the declaration was probably inadmissible anyway, it seems more likely that the second limitation was merely a useful by-product.

Patsy also made a statement in which he specifically stated his belief that he was dying.[82] The rules on dying declarations were irrelevant to his case, however, as he survived, and therefore was in a position to testify personally. The Crown called Patsy as a witness but the Attorney General determined that he did not understand the nature of an oath and therefore could not give sworn testimony.[83] While technically correct, however, the Crown could easily have arranged for Patsy to receive some moral instruction on the nature of an oath so as to allow him to testify – as Harrington pointed out, ' ... this boy had been in the hands of the Crown officials for three months

---

[78] *R v. Mooney* (1851) 5 Cox CC 318 (per Pigot LCB at the Dublin Commission).
[79] (1857) 7 Cox CC 209.
[80] See Waldron, *Maamtrasna*, p. 211.
[81] *R v. Mead* (1824) 2 Barn & Cress 605, 608.
[82] Waldron, *Maamtrasna*, p. 211.
[83] NAI, Transcript of Proceedings, CRF/1902/J13/29, p. 49. Patsy indicated that while he knew what a lie was, he did not know his catechism or what would happen to him if he told a lie, and also stated that he had not said his prayers. On this basis, the Attorney General concluded that there was ' ... no use of asking him any other questions'.

and surely even [the Crown solicitor] might have told him that Hell was intended for the wicked'.[84] It may be that the Crown did not want him to testify – George Bolton, the Crown solicitor, had deemed his evidence to be worthless.[85] So why call him at all?

Waldron suggests that calling Patsy was a masterly tactical decision on Bolton's part:[86] the jurors would have been unaware of how easily Patsy could have been rehabilitated as a witness, but by calling him anyway the Crown gave the impression that it wanted Patsy as a witness. This in turn might have suggested to observers (and to the jurors) that Patsy's evidence, if only it could have been admitted, would have bolstered the Crown's case. Furthermore, calling Patsy showed that the Crown was calling all available witnesses, and therefore was not engaged in any cover-up. Again, the Crown's intentions are unknown, but Waldron's suggestion would explain the Crown's rather desultory efforts to establish Patsy's understanding of an oath. What is less easy to explain is the defence's failure to take steps to rehabilitate Patsy as a witness: the content of his statement to the magistrate had been reported in the *Freeman's Journal* in its coverage of the coroner's inquest, so the defence lawyers should have been aware of this evidence and its potential importance. They could have arranged for Patsy to receive the necessary instruction from a priest in the run-up to the trials, or indeed, after the trials had begun. Yet there is no evidence that they made any such attempt, a failure that surely constitutes a serious dereliction of their duty to their clients.

Conclusion

The dominant view of the Maamtrasna trials in Ireland – then and now – is of a gross injustice perpetrated by the Crown, and that Myles Joyce was an innocent man. The trials raised multiple questions of nineteenth-century Irish criminal procedure; limitations of space required that this chapter focus on only the principal trial issues. This focus demonstrates that the Crown acted within its powers and privileges: the Prevention of Crime (Ireland) Act 1882 permitted the Attorney General to transfer the trial to Dublin; the Crown's efforts to pack the juries were entirely permissible under Irish law and practice at the time; and the exclusion of the Joyce boys' evidence was within the laws of evidence. Even the language issue has been overstated by nationalists: half of the Crown's evidence was given in Irish, and according to the *Freeman's Journal*, Myles Joyce indicated that he understood the other half. And the Crown's view of the case was not unreasonable given the context in which the killings occurred.

Furthermore, many of the practices that the Crown used in the Maamtrasna prosecutions remain a part of modern criminal trial procedure. Moving a trial to prevent anticipated unfairness among local jurors was permitted in England,[87] and continues to be permissible under Irish law.[88] Emergency powers, which involve the

---

[84] Harrington, *The Maamtrasna Massacre*, p. 42.
[85] Ibid.
[86] Waldron, *Maamtrasna*, p. 73.
[87] The Central Criminal Court Act 1856, 19 & 20 Vict, c.16.
[88] See, for example, Court and Court Officers Act 1995, s.32 (allowing for the transfer of trials from a county Circuit Court to the Dublin Circuit Court).

suspension of ordinary trial procedures, are permissible under the Irish Constitution,[89] and modern Irish law allows for trials before a non-jury court in cases involving subversives or organized crime.[90] It remains the case in both English and Irish law that a dying declaration is admissible only in respect of a trial for the homicide of the declarant, and that the declarant must have made the declaration under a settled expectation of death.[91] Accomplice (i.e. approver) testimony is also permitted under modern Irish law, providing juries are warned of the dangers of accepting such evidence without corroboration.[92] Even jury packing – surely the most objectionable aspect of the Maamtrasna trials – continued after Irish independence, despite longstanding nationalist complaints about the practice.[93] Only with the enactment of the Juries Act in 1976 did this practice come to an end in Ireland.[94]

So the Crown did nothing unlawful in its attempts to secure convictions against the Maamtrasna defendants. Yet the fact that the Crown's actions were lawful does not necessarily make them fair. The Crown did not have to transfer the trial to Dublin or pack the jury – these were tactical *choices* rather than actions mandated by law. Michael Joyce's statement was excluded by law, but this arose at least in part from the Crown's *choice* not to charge the defendants with the murder of all the deceased members of the Joyce family. And Patsy's evidence could have been presented to the jury had the Crown *chosen* to arrange for a minimal level of moral instruction, thereby allowing him to give sworn testimony. Each of the Crown's choices fits within the law and practice of the time, and is defensible individually from a narrow legal perspective. The cumulative effect of these choices, however, was to hamstring the defence: the cases were decided by juries with no knowledge or understanding of local conditions and no opportunity to view the scene of the crime; the juries were packed with men the Crown thought reliable; evidence that might have undermined the Crown's central evidence was not put before the jury. In effect, the decks were stacked against the defendants to such a degree that the chances of an acquittal were almost non-existent.

Given the brutality of the Maamtrasna killings, one can have some sympathy for the Crown trying to bring the perpetrators to justice, and on its face, the Crown's case was strong. Furthermore, many of the Maamtrasna defendants undoubtedly were guilty. Patrick Joyce and Patrick Casey, the other two men executed, accepted their guilt. Michael Casey accepted that he had been part of the group but denied killing anyone (a distinction with no legal significance because of the effect of the joint enterprise doctrine). There seems little doubt that Thomas Casey, one of the approvers, was

---

[89] See Article 28.3.3° of the Irish Constitution (Bunreacht na hÉireann).

[90] The Special Criminal Court, established under the Offences Against the State Act 1939, is composed of three judges and sits without a jury. It is worth noting that with the enactment of the Prevention of Crime (Ireland) Act 1882, 45 & 46 Vict, c.25, the Crown had the option of establishing a similar court in Ireland, but the operative provisions were never implemented.

[91] See D. McGrath (2005) *Evidence* (Dublin: Thompson Round Hall), paras. 5.166–5.178.

[92] Ibid., at Chapter 4.C (paras.4.18–4.109).

[93] See C. Hanly (2016) 'The 1916 Proclamation and Jury Trial in the Irish Free State', *Dublin University Law Journal*, 39, 2, pp. 373–404 at pp. 387–9.

[94] Note that an expert Irish judicial committee endorsed the stand-by power as late as 1966. See ibid., at p. 389.

guilty; indeed, Patrick Joyce and Patrick Casey specifically named Thomas Casey as one of the killers. Whether Anthony Philbin was involved is unclear: as an approver, he accepted his own guilt, but Patrick Joyce and Patrick Casey both stated that he was not present at the scene of the murders. The other four men pleaded guilty in order to avoid execution, but on receiving the mandatory death sentence they immediately professed their innocence, a stance supported by the Joyce and Casey statements. There is no way now to objectively assess whether they were in fact guilty. However, it is not unusual even today for defendants to plead guilty to avoid a heavier sentence, and that such a plea is not usually taken to indicate innocence.

But there are substantial reasons to doubt Myles Joyce's guilt – discrepancies in the evidence given by the independent witnesses; the fact that one of those witnesses bore a grudge against Joyce; the other two condemned men accepted their own guilt but specifically exonerated Joyce, as did Michael Casey. Yet so successfully had the Crown used its trial powers that Joyce had no real prospect of securing an acquittal notwithstanding his probable innocence. This, surely, comes close to the very definition of an unfair trial. Furthermore, Earl Spencer, the Lord Lieutenant, as the Crown's representative in Ireland, had the power to show mercy on account of these factors. The defence made representations to Spencer, who had access to all the trial information, the excluded statements from the Joyce boys, along with the statements from Patrick Joyce and Patrick Casey exonerating Myles. Spencer ultimately decided, however, that the law should take its course. Undoubtedly, this was his right: the power of mercy was a prerogative of the Crown rather than an entitlement of the accused. Nevertheless, there was ample justification for Spencer to issue a pardon or a commutation, and his failure to do so contributes to the sense of injustice at Myles Joyce's execution.

Postscript

On the advice of the Irish Government, the president of Ireland signed a formal posthumous pardon in respect of Myles Joyce on 3 April 2018.[95]

---

[95] See *Irish Times*, 4th April 2018. The Government had made its wishes known the previous week: see Press Release from the Department of Justice and Equality, 28 March, available at www.justice.ie.

6

The Bedborough Case, 1898: 'A Curious Gonfalon Round Which to Fight'

Lesley A. Hall
Wellcome Library

Introduction

One might imagine that publishing the first serious scientific study in English on homosexuality a mere two years after the high-profile trial of Oscar Wilde, leading to his incarceration in Reading Gaol, would have inevitably resulted in furore and censorship. The timing of the publication of *Sexual Inversion* as the first volume of Havelock Ellis's multi-volume *Studies in the Psychology of Sex* seems quite incredibly badly chosen, though, in other ways, very apposite. At least one commentator specifically cited the Wilde case as a reason why the subject needed to be illuminated by the light of science.

> For the exercise of sexual perversion, only a few months ago, a gentleman was sent, under tragic auspices, to collect material for a 'Ballad of Reading Gaol' ... If one man is punished for sexual perversion, and another man is punished for circulating a book showing how to eliminate sexual perversion – for the best way to eliminate it is to impart a scientific knowledge of the nosological principles upon which it is based – can inconsistency and fatuity further go?[1]

The case, in fact, exemplified the haphazard operation of the laws of censorship: less a deliberate than an opportunistic prosecution of works deemed to be obscene, with no real working definition of what constituted obscenity, a vagueness which meant that serious studies such as Ellis's could be deemed as actionable as any outright commercial work of pornography. The law in question was the Obscene Publications Act (Lord Campbell Act) of 1857, giving magistrates powers to issue search warrants to the police on the receipt of sworn information about suspect operations. This was not, Campbell gave assurances, meant to affect serious works. However, Lord Cockburn's judgement

---

[1] Anonymous (1898) 'Prosecution of George Bedborough', *The Agnostic Journal*, 11 June, p. 380.

in Regina v. Hicklin, 1868, made the test of obscenity the tendency ' … to deprave and corrupt those whose minds are open to such immoral influences and into whose hands a publication of this sort might fall': a ruling greatly extending the opportunities for interested parties to pursue censorship campaigns. The force of the law fell on the publisher or seller of the book rather than its author, who was not necessarily given any chance to defend its *bona fides* in court, while the actual defendants were seldom highly motivated in making a principled stand.[2] It was George Bedborough, Secretary of the Legitimation League, who had been persuaded to sell a copy of the book to a police officer, who was the defendant in this case.

This prosecution has been discussed in several biographies and studies of Ellis and it had a significant impact upon him so early in his project on the study of sex.[3] However, the wider resonance of the case has been less discussed and this chapter considers the more general reception of the prosecution and its significance. The *Sexual Inversion* prosecution was somewhat of an outlier for the period: most prosecutions for publishing and selling works likely to corrupt the morals of Her Majesty's subjects were brought at the initiative of social purity organizations, which had become particularly aggressive in pursuing this aspect of reforming the morals of society during the final decades of the nineteenth century. Many of the works they pursued were pornographic, Leeds doctor Henry Allbutt was struck off the Medical Register in 1887 for producing a cheap pamphlet of health advice, *The Wife's Handbook*, including information on contraception, following a campaign by the Leeds Vigilance Association.[4] In 1888, at the instigation of the National Vigilance Association, the elderly publisher Henry Vizetelly was prosecuted, fined and eventually imprisoned for publishing English editions of the novels of Zola and other French Realist authors.[5]

Ellis and his publisher had had no intention to emulate Charles Bradlaugh and Annie Besant by doing for the study of sex what they had done twenty years earlier when they published American doctor Charles Knowlton's work on birth control *Fruits of Philosophy*, and defended their right to do so in court as a test case.[6] Once

---

[2] E. Bristow (1977) *Vice and Vigilance: Purity Movements in Britain since 1700* (Dublin: Gee & Macmillan), pp. 46–9; M.J.D. Roberts (1985) 'Morals, Art, and the Law: The Passing of the Obscene Publications Act, 1857', *Victorian Studies*, 28, pp. 609–29.

[3] I. Goldberg (1926) *Havelock Ellis: A Biographical and Critical Survey* (New York: Simon and Schuster), pp. 151–68; H. Peterson (1929) *Havelock Ellis: Philosopher of Love* (London: George Allen and Unwin), pp. 237–62; A. Calder-Marshall (1959) *Havelock Ellis: A Biography* (London: Rupert Hart-Davis), pp. 157–72; V. Brome (1979) *Havelock Ellis, Philosopher of Sex: A Biography* (London: Routledge and Kegan Paul), pp. 101–8; P.E. Stepansky (1980) 'A Footnote to the History of Homosexuality in Britain: Havelock Ellis and the Bedborough Trial of 1898' in E.R. Wallace and L.C. Pressley (eds) *Essays in the History of Psychiatry: A Tenth Anniversary Supplementary Volume to the Psychiatric Forum Columbia* (Columbia, SC: WM. S. Hall), pp. 72–102; P. Grosskurth (1980) *Havelock Ellis: A Biography* (London: Allen Lane), pp. 191–204 and C. Nottingham (1999) *The Pursuit of Serenity: Havelock Ellis and the New Politics* (Amsterdam: Amsterdam University Press), pp. 209–10.

[4] P. Fryer (1965) *The Birth Controllers* (London: Secker & Warburg), pp. 169–72 and Anonymous (1889) 'H.A. Allbutt v. the General Medical Council', *British Medical Journal*, II, p. 88.

[5] Bristow, *Vice and Vigilance*, pp. 207–8.

[6] S. Chandrasekhar (1981) *'A Dirty Filthy Book': The Writings of Charles Bradlaugh and Annie Besant on Reproductive Physiology and Birth Control, and an Account of the Bradlaugh-Besant Trial* (Berkeley, CA: University of California Press).

the *Sexual Inversion* case was under way, some defenders of the book, or at least of the right of such books to be published, seem to have considered it a similar moment: *The Malthusian*, indeed, described it as 'A Sequel to the Bradlaugh-Besant Prosecutions'.[7] Their hopes were to be thwarted. Ellis had entertained no intention of seeking martyrdom or challenging the law: he had published his work in as unobtrusive a way as possible, eschewing wide advertisement and only sending review copies to serious medical, scientific and legal journals. In his pamphlet on the case he declared, in defiance of those who thought he should have made more of a protest:

> The pursuit of the martyr's crown is not favourable to the critical and dispassionate investigation of complicated problems. A student of nature, of men, of books, may dispense with wealth or position; he cannot dispense with quietness and serenity. I insist on doing my own work in my own way, and cannot accept conditions which make this virtually impossible.[8]

The troubled road to publication and prosecution

Havelock Ellis (1858–1939) was the author of the seven-volume *Studies in the Psychology of Sex* and the major British figure in the development of sexology in the later nineteenth and early twentieth centuries. He was a medical doctor, having obtained the humble Licentiate of the Society of Apothecaries as a necessary prerequisite to what he believed to be his life's vocation, the study of sex, but did not practise. By the end of his life his pioneering efforts had become widely recognized, and shortly before his death he received the accolade of election to the elite Fellowship of the Royal College of Physicians. By 1898 he was a known and respected literary figure and editor of the *Contemporary Science Series*.

Sexual activity between men in England was penalized under the Offenses Against the Person Act 1861, which had removed the previous capital penalty but still imposed severe sentences for sodomy and attempted sodomy. In 1885 the Criminal Law Amendment Act had introduced the notorious 'Labouchère Amendment', criminalizing (but with a lesser sentence) 'gross indecency' in public or private between males. This was regarded as a 'blackmailer's charter' (although blackmail for homosexual activity was already prevalent) and not repealed until 1967. It was under this clause that Oscar Wilde was tried and imprisoned in 1895. Homosexuality thus became more visible because of the increasing number of prosecutions. Concern was manifested by those suffering under the law as it stood and those who sympathized with them. These included Ellis, who, though not himself homosexual, was married to the predominantly lesbian Edith Lees and a close friend of Edward Carpenter (as 'out' a homosexual as it was possible to be in the 1890s) and his circle.

---

[7] Anonymous (1898) 'The Bedborough Case (A Sequel to the Bradlaugh-Besant Prosecutions)', *The Malthusian*, XXII, 8, p. 62.

[8] Havelock Ellis (1898) *A Note on the Bedborough Trial* (London: University Press Ltd), p. 16.

Bringing the volume *Sexual Inversion* into print and availability in Britain had involved a troubled course. Ellis had not originally intended it as the first volume of his *Studies*, but in 1892 the writer and literary critic John Addington Symonds, himself an 'invert' who had privately published and discreetly circulated two pamphlets on the subject of homosexuality, *A Problem in Greek Ethics* and *A Problem in Modern Ethics*, approached Ellis, via their mutual friend the decadent poet Arthur Symons, to suggest contributing a study of homosexuality to the *Contemporary Science Series*. This led to what seemed a mutually advantageous collaboration: Ellis could bring medical and scientific knowledge and status, Symonds his collection of case histories and familiarity with the historical aspects. However, Symonds, who had long suffered from tuberculosis, died early in 1893 before the volume was complete, leaving the final stages in Ellis's hands.

A German edition was published under both names in 1896, but British medical and scientific publishers were reluctant to take on the venture. A dubious character called de Villiers (one among many pseudonyms) undertook to publish *Sexual Inversion* in Britain through his imprint, the University Press, Watford (where there was no university) and it appeared, under both authors' names, early in 1897. At this juncture Symonds's executor Horatio Brown, previously supportive, under pressure from Symonds's family and friends bought up and had destroyed the entire first printing. He also prevailed upon Ellis to remove Symonds's name and all material attributed to him, and to undertake considerable rewriting to obliterate any possible association of Symonds with the work. This substantially revised edition appeared in November 1897 under Ellis's name alone. A miasma of confusion and muddle had already begun to accrete about the enterprise.

Ellis was by no means entirely naïve concerning the dubious nature of the University Press. His friend F.H. Perry-Coste had initially put him in touch with G. Astor Singer, allegedly a man of wealth living abroad setting up this small publishing house and associated magazine, whose London agent, and editor of the *University Magazine*, was his brother-in-law, Dr Roland de Villiers. Ellis's comments in letters to Perry-Coste expressed considerable scepticism that these personages were separate individuals.[9] However, Ellis was not sufficiently concerned about the *bona fides* of the operation to eschew publishing with them: perhaps he had grown tired of the struggle to find a publisher. Perhaps he actually believed that Singer/de Villiers was a wealthy eccentric genuinely interested in publishing works unlikely to be of interest to mainstream publishers, rather than, as subsequently turned out, a major dealer in pornography.

Watford University Press also published *The Adult*, the journal of the Legitimation League, a small society initially formed to advocate the removal of the legal disabilities on illegitimacy, which then moved on to promote other radical reforms in sexual mores. Its editor, George Bedborough, sold the journal, along with other publications including *Sexual Inversion*, out of his front room: as Ellis pointed out

---

[9] British Library, Department of Manuscripts, Havelock Ellis Papers, 'Havelock Ellis to F.H. Perry-Coste, 1897–1899', Additional Manuscripts, 70524.

The sale of the book was effected in a private house, with closed doors, and … neither the book in question nor any other books were exposed for sale, or announced for sale, in the window or elsewhere. No commercial transaction could conveniently be effected with less publicity.[10]

However, the Legitimation League was at that time under surveillance by the Metropolitan Police, in particular Inspector John Sweeney. Scotland Yard was interested in the League because, supposedly, ' … many Anarchists in London were regularly attending the League's meetings' to proselytize, since its freedom of discussion provided a 'decoying ground'. Also, Sweeney averred, the League ' … seemed rather to encourage illicit unions', and the abolition of marriage would form ' … a stepping-stone to the abolition of all laws'.[11] He contrived to get on good terms with Bedborough and other leading members of the League while attending their meetings incognito.

Early in 1898 he became aware of Ellis's work ' … dealing with certain abnormalities which the law of England has decided wisely enough cannot be discussed in books sold to the general public' and that Bedborough undertook an agency selling this at his home, which was also the office of the League, 16 John Street, Bedford Row, Holborn, London. Sweeney was delegated to discover whether Bedborough had other objectionable works for sale.[12] While these enquiries were going on, there was a complaint to the Metropolitan Police from the parents of a young man in Liverpool who had been sent a copy of *Sexual Inversion* in error. Sweeney applied for a warrant for Bedborough's arrest,

convinced that we should at one blow kill a growing evil in the shape of a vigorous campaign of free love and Anarchism, and at the same time, discover the means by which the country was being flooded with books of the 'Psychology' type.[13]

Sweeney boasted of sounding Bedborough's character as an individual who would not fight out this case to the end, although it was several months before this became completely apparent. He depicted Bedborough as a patsy: '… the victim of one of the most unscrupulous villains of modern times' (de Villiers), '… taken advantage of by a nice little gang of Secularists, Socialists, Anarchists, Free-lovers and others anxious to obtain a little cheap notoriety by defending Ellis's book on principle'.[14] Sweeney claimed that his careful handling of this 'delicate case' had prevented:

---

[10] Ellis, *Bedborough Trial*, p. 5.
[11] F. Richards (1904) (ed.) *At Scotland Yard: Being the Record of Twenty-Seven Years' Service of John Sweeney, late Detective-Inspector, Criminal Investigation Department Scotland Yard* (London: Grant Richards), pp. 178–9.
[12] Richards, *At Scotland Yard*, p. 185.
[13] Ibid., p. 186
[14] Ibid., pp. 187–8.

The growth of a Frankenstein monster wrecking the marriage laws of our country, and perhaps carrying off the general respect for all law; or, on the other hand, of raising about the ears of the authorities a shriek of popular objection to our interference with the rights of free speech.[15]

A tortuous progress through courtrooms

On the 31st of May 1898, Sweeney, along with several colleagues, went to John Street with a warrant for Bedborough's arrest on a charge of publishing and selling an indecent libel, and uttering the books with the intention of corrupting the morals of Her Majesty's subjects. Bedborough, who had previously encountered Sweeney as a sympathizer if not a friend, was somewhat confused. Unfamiliar with police court proceedings, he nonetheless refused to say anything until represented by a solicitor. Books and papers from the League's offices were taken into police possession, while Bedborough was taken to Bow Street Police Court, and remanded for seven days.[16] His solicitor, Mr Wyatt Digby, applied for bail on the 3rd of June, and Sir John Bridge agreed to take two sureties of £500. This was an inordinately high amount: Ellis commented, 'Dangerous criminals against the person are often easily admitted to bail in very small sums. This is a tribute to the awe which surrounds ideas.'[17] Bedborough was liberated on the understanding that he would sell no more books before the next hearing.[18] Ellis had immediately, with the publisher's consent, suspended the sale of the book.[19]

The League, and *Sexual Inversion*, immediately gained far more publicity than they had hitherto commanded. Following this first hearing the case was reported fairly widely in the London and provincial press, though mostly not in any great detail, alongside other police court cases. Mostly these reports were headlined 'Bow Street' or 'Charge against a Publisher', but the *South Wales Echo* drew attention to 'Free Lovers in Court'[20] and the *Dundee Evening Telegraph* to 'Studies in the Psychology of Sex: Publisher Arrested'.[21]

The case went through several hearings at Bow Street. On the 7th of June, when Ellis himself and several members of the Free Press Defence Committee which had rapidly been set up were present, it was agreed, since defence counsel, Mr Avory, had only been briefed half an hour previously, that only formal evidence should be heard, with opening deferred until the next hearing. However, the prosecution wished to call a witness who had been summoned from Liverpool: Frederick William Hardesty, a

---

[15] Ibid., pp. 189–90.
[16] London Metropolitan Archives, Bow Street Court Register: Court of Summary Jurisdiction 31 May 1898: No 38 PS/BOW/A1/6; *The Morning Post*, 1st June 1898, Issue 39309, p. 2 and *The Standard*, 1st June 1898, Issue 23065, p. 2.
[17] Ellis, *Bedborough Trial*, p. 6.
[18] *The Standard*, 3rd June 1898, Issue 23067, p. 6.
[19] Ellis, *Bedborough Trial*, p. 12.
[20] *South Wales Echo*, 8th June 1898, p. 9.
[21] *The Evening Telegraph* (Dundee), 1st June 1898, p. 2.

clerk aged eighteen, who had ordered the book *The Blight of Respectability* advertised in *The University Magazine* and been sent *Sexual Inversion* in error. Avory objected that this had nothing to do with Bedborough but Wontner, prosecuting, said that he would prove a close connection. Inspector Sweeney mentioned that in searching the defendant's bedroom two scrapbooks containing 'objectionable photographs' had been discovered, though no evidence that these were being offered for sale. Bedborough was again remanded on bail.[22]

At the next hearing, on the 13th of June, Mr Danckwertz, prosecuting, began to read passages from the book, over objections from Mr Avory. Before he began, the magistrate, Sir John Bridge, said,

> 'We are now about to hear that which no decent woman ought to hear, and if there is any woman in the Court with any decency at all in her she will at once go out. She, of course, has a right to stay if she wishes; but I feel sure no decent woman will stay in Court while these things are being read.' There were several women sitting on the front seat reserved for the public, but no-one moved. Sir John then added that he wished to conduct the case in such a way that the morals of no person would be injured. He felt sure that the persons who had remained in Court after what he had said were not persons of ordinary intellect. Had they been so, they would not have remained to hear a case like the present one.[23]

After the request for women to leave the court,

> Everyone's attention now turned to the women, but the only movement they made was to lean forward in their seats in order to hear more distinctly what prosecuting counsel was about the read. Sir John Bridge looked sternly yet sorrowfully at them, but they eyed him calmly through their glasses.[24]

This was followed by the evidence of Detective-Sergeant Croxton that on the 17th of May he had purchased a copy of *Sexual Inversion* from a sixteen-year-old female servant at the League's premises in John Street, who sounded entirely too knowing about the work.[25]

This implicit invocation of the 'wives and servants', who were notoriously to feature over sixty years later in the trial of Penguin Books for publishing the unexpurgated version of D.H. Lawrence's *Lady Chatterley's Lover*,[26] did not go unprotested. *The New Age* saw this in the light of a general principle:

---

[22] *The Globe*, 7th June 1898, p. 5.
[23] *The Morning Post* 14th June 1898, Issue 39320, p. 3.
[24] *Reynolds's Newspaper*, 19th June 1898, Issue 2497, n.p. and *The Mid Cumberland and North Westmorland Herald*, 18th June 1898, p. 6.
[25] *The Morning Post* 14th June 1898, Issue 39320, p. 3.
[26] C.H. Rolph (1961) (ed.) *The Trial of Lady Chatterley: Regina v. Penguin Books Ltd: The Transcript of the Trial* (Harmondsworth: Penguin), p. 17 – Mr Mervyn Griffith-Jones, prosecuting, opening speech to the jury: 'Is it a book that you would even wish your wife or your servants to read?'

> When a charge relating to the sexual problem is brought before them, [magistrates] absurdly assume that women should clear out of the court, while men should remain.... We should like to see all cases of this kind tried by a mixed jury of men and women.[27]

Mary Reed wrote to the *Saturday Review* expressing considerable exception to Sir John Bridge's ' ... invidious comments ... upon those women who remained in Court to hear the evidence': these were, she protested, matters 'of the gravest importance to the mothers of the race'.[28] Edward Carpenter similarly described these ladies ' ... as good as insulted by the magistrate': ' ... who more fit to understand and consider these problems than the mothers or future mothers of our children?'[29]

When the hearing resumed on the 21st of June,

> a few women were in attendance. They looked slightly anxious when Sir John Bridge entered the court, but, on finding that they were not to be again reminded of what a decent woman would do in such circumstances, they settled themselves down to hear the case.[30]

Avory said that he realized that the case would have to go before a jury, and that he was prepared to maintain that the works in question, in particular *Sexual Inversion*, were not obscene. On being pressed on this point by Sir John Bridge, Avory declared that it was a scientific work and the practices mentioned were not, as the prosecution had stated, advocated by the author. Bail was granted.[31]

On the 9th of August, Avory went before a Divisional Court of the Queen's Bench to move the issue of a writ of certiorari, removing the case from the Central Criminal Court into the Court of Queen's Bench. He argued that the case ought to be tried before a High Court Judge and a special jury since it raised an important question in the law of obscene libel. (The Bradlaugh/Besant trial had taken place in the Court of Queen's Bench, creating a certain precedent.) Avory said that the work was published at 10 shillings and ' ... but for the ill-advised prosecution would never have fallen into the hands of persons except those who were interested in the scientific investigation dealt with'. He emphasized Ellis's medical and scientific credentials and that the book was intended to suggest remedies for the matters with which it dealt. Anyone, he suggested, could take extracts from a medical book and bring a prosecution against the author. The application was refused.[32]

This was considered extraordinary by the secularist campaigner G.W. Foote, speaking at a meeting of the Free Press Defence Committee on the 15th of August: 'The jury of the Old Bailey were quite unfit to decide upon questions referring to the liberty

---

[27] *The New Age*, 23rd June 1898, VII, 195, p. 164.
[28] *Saturday Review*, 16th July 1898, p. 80.
[29] Ibid., 5th November 1898, p. 610.
[30] *Evening Standard*, 22nd June 1898, p. 9.
[31] *St James's Gazette*, 22nd June 1898, p. 10.
[32] *Daily News*, 10th August 1898, Issue 16341, n.p.

of the press. They were composed of publicans and shopkeepers, without any scientific training. The judges were no friends of liberty.'[33] A sympathetic article in the *Sketch*, 'Is He An Obscene Writer?', made a similar complaint that 'the question, which is one bristling with difficult technicalities, will be fought out before a Common Jury, which is perhaps one of the most incompetent tribunals for such issues', but this appeared, alas, rather in arrears, on the 2nd of November, two days after the verdict at the Old Bailey had been pronounced.[34]

On the 14th of September the Grand Jury returned a true bill that Bedborough:

> being a person of a wicked and depraved mind and disposition, and unlawfully and wickedly devising, contriving, and intending, to vitiate the morals of the liege subjects of our said Lady the Queen ... unlawfully, wickedly, maliciously, scandalously and wilfully did publish, sell, and utter, and cause and procure to be published, sold and uttered, a certain lewd, wicked, bawdy, scandalous and obscene libel, in the form of a book entitled *Studies in the Psychology of Sex: Vol. I. Sexual Inversion*, by Havelock Ellis.[35]

Avory applied to the presiding judge at the Central Criminal Court for an adjournment of the case until the October Sessions, which was granted. This gave him a further six weeks to prepare his case.[36] This was not necessarily an advantage, given the outcome.

Ten days before the trial was due to take place, it was discovered that Bedborough had made a deal, with the connivance of his solicitor, Wyatt Digby, the defence counsel, Avory, not being involved. The prosecution had offered a compromise: if Bedborough would plead guilty to the first three counts of his indictment, involving *Sexual Inversion*, an issue of *The Adult* and a lecture, the other eight involved would not be pressed, and he would simply be bound over on his own recognizance to keep the peace. Bedborough, summoned to a special meeting of the Free Press Defence Committee, declared that he had ' ... fought because there was no alternative, not as an enthusiast, but as a stoic', and as ' ... a way of escape had opened ... he should avail himself of it'. He was, he pointed out, ' ... not primarily responsible for the publications included in the first three counts'.[37]

This account, in which Bedborough had been solicited to a deal, was contradicted by the tale given by prosecuting counsel at the Old Bailey on the 31st of October. It was stated that it was supposed when bringing the prosecution that Bedborough was the 'chief offender' and 'prime mover' in 'the publication and sale of this disgusting book' and 'the circulation of this specious literature'. But Bedborough, on his own initiative, had gone to Scotland Yard and communicated to the authorities that he had ' ... taken no principal part in this terrible traffic, but that his part was entirely subordinate'. The

---

[33] *The Malthusian*, September 1898, XXII, 9, pp. 66–7.
[34] *The Sketch*, 2nd November 1898, p. 76.
[35] Cited in Houston Peterson (1928) *Havelock Ellis: Philosopher of Love* (London: Allen and Unwin), pp. 247–8.
[36] *The Adult*, October 1898, II, 9, p. 253.
[37] Ibid., December 1898, II, 11, pp. 339–41.

person in control, for whom he had been sub-agent, was de Villiers, who had absconded and for whose arrest a warrant was out. While this did not 'very materially reduce the quality of the prisoner's guilt', given his undertaking to sever himself entirely from the Legitimation League and its publications, the prosecution recommended leniency and Bedborough was bound over in the sum of £100.[38]

The Recorder, pronouncing judgement, declared that Bedborough had acted wisely, ' … for it would have been impossible for you to have contended with any possibility of being able to persuade anybody that this book, this lecture, and this magazine were not filthy and obscene works'. He was willing to believe that he might 'at the first outset, perhaps, have been gulled' into a belief that this was 'a scientific work', when, according to the Recorder:

> It is impossible for anyone with a head on his shoulders to open the book without seeing that it is a pretence and a sham and that it is merely entered into for the purpose of selling this filthy publication.[39]

Thus Bedborough got off more or less scot-free, if no longer *persona grata* in his previous circles, *Sexual Inversion* was condemned from the bench as 'this filthy work', and there was considerable suspicion that Wyatt Digby had been playing fast and loose with the funding raised for the defence (indeed, on the 16th of June 1899, he was struck off the rolls of solicitors for misappropriation of funds in this case[40]). It was not a glorious moment.

'[A] shriek of popular objection'?

Most of the press reporting consisted of bald accounts of the various court proceedings, which, although not front-page news, did disseminate the existence of the Legitimation League and the publication of *Sexual Inversion* well beyond those circles within which such knowledge might previously have circulated. It was alleged, by de Villiers/Singer, that as a result:

> [D]emand for Dr Havelock Ellis's book increased very considerably …. Among those anxious to acquire the book were many students at Oxford and Cambridge, boys at Eton, Rugby and Harrow, even girls at boarding schools, all of whom would never have heard of its existence if the great publicity given to the police-court proceedings by the entire press in Great Britain had not called their attention to this medical work.[41]

---

[38] *Reynolds's Newspaper*, 6th November 1898, Issue 2517, n.p.
[39] Ibid.
[40] *The Morning Post*, 17th June 1899, Issue 39636, p. 4.
[41] G. Astor Singer, M.A. pseud. [i.e. George Ferdinand Springmuhl von Weissenfeld] (1899) *Judicial Scandals and Errors* (London: The University Press), p. 52.

This possibly rather exaggerated the reach of the reporting.

A Free Press Defence Committee was set up with great expedition to ensure that the case would be effectively defended in the courtroom: Chris Nottingham aptly describes this as a 'Who's Who of progressive London'.[42] However, although it included strong representation from writers, artists, intellectuals, journalists and champions of press freedom, it was significantly lacking in any members of the medical profession prepared to subscribe their names to the cause alongside G.B. Shaw, H.M. Hyndman, Henry Salt, Frank Harris, Walter Crane, Mrs Despard, George Moore, Mona Caird, Edith Lanchester, G.J. Holyoake and others.[43]

The matter was taken up in radical, secularist and freethought organs as well as some weekly literary periodicals, since it was regarded as manifesting a dangerous attack on the freedom of the press and the right to discuss controversial topics. However, in spite of the antipathy to the prosecution, there was considerable ambivalence towards *Sexual Inversion* and the Legitimation League. Ellis enjoyed a significant amount of existing cultural capital: his volume of essays, *Affirmations*, was receiving positive reviews in the literary press concurrently with *Sexual Inversion* creeping under the radar. But while deploring the prosecution, and expressing their high opinions of Ellis himself, several writers claimed not to have read the book. They also felt it obligatory to dissociate themselves from any sympathy with 'free love', while defending the right to debate the subject. *The New Age*, unusually, without exactly declaring itself for Free Love, did consider the League composed of ' … honest men and women … horrified at the gross immorality which disgraces our present-day society … determined to try to modify or put a stop to it', and that the prosecution might have given the League beneficial publicity.[44]

The Adult, under the editorship of Henry Seymour, who had stepped up in place of Bedborough upon his arrest, put forward 'a strong opinion that the prosecution of Mr Bedborough is aimed at the suppression of all discussion of the vexed problem of marriage'. Seymour, not himself a member of the League nor an advocate of 'Free-love', believed that these subjects should be discussed and that *The Adult* should continue to be published.[45] This view that the Legitimation League was the real target was similarly embodied in the initial circular issued by the Free Press Defence Committee: 'It is surmised that the attack upon the book in question is merely an insidious attempt to crush the Legitimation League, the active spirit of which Mr Bedborough has undoubtedly been.'[46] Its stance on the question of *Sexual Inversion* was

> It is written in a spirit of scientific detachment. It throws light upon certain abnormalities, with a view to their rectification; it is unpleasant in the way that a treatise on cancer is unpleasant.[47]

---

[42] Nottingham, *Pursuit of Serenity*, p. 209.
[43] *The Adult*, August 1898, II, 7, pp. 189–91.
[44] *The New Age*, 23rd June 1898, VII, 195, p. 164.
[45] *The Adult*, July 1898, II, 6, p. 160.
[46] Ibid., July 1898, II, 6, p. 159.
[47] Ibid., August 1898, II, 7, p. 189.

The radical *Reynolds's Newspaper*, in its 'Notes and Gossip' column, led off with the opinion that:

> A distinguished philosopher and scientific man of world-wide reputation, Mr. Havelock Ellis, writes a semi-medical work on 'The Psychology of Sex,' the price of which stays its sale to the multitude. Among the agents for its distribution is Mr. George Bedborough, Secretary of the Legitimation League. He is arrested, his offices are ransacked by the police, and the work confiscated.[48]

This was attributed to Mr Robert Anderson of the Political Detective Department, who, failing to find 'dynamiters and Anarchists', turned to 'suppression of the moral dynamiters'.[49]

It is curious that *Reynolds's* waxed so passionate in defence of Ellis's work, when a few months before they had published a scathing notice of Edward Carpenter's pamphlet *An Unknown People* (a version of his essay on Homogenic Love): 'it deals with … those beings of either sex whose perverted longings demand that they be classified among the world's monstrosities.'[50] But opposition to censorship and police interference with the freedom of the press trumped distaste. G.W. Foote of *The Freethinker* conceded that the subject of *Sexual Inversion* was 'unpleasant' but addressed in a 'scientific spirit', and 'maladies of every kind must be treated frankly if they are to be remedied'. While he did not hold with the views of the Legitimation League on marriage, he did not believe that their opinions should be suppressed and that it was certainly not for the police to do so.[51] The *Literary Guide and Rationalist Review* (in which advertisements for the publications of the University Press Watford, including *Sexual Inversion*, had appeared over several months) considered the prosecution ' … a colossal blunder' and a 'wanton insult' to Ellis. Although they had not examined the incriminated book, from the list of contents, and knowledge of Ellis's other writings, they suggested 'we decline to believe that his study in the psychology of sex is an obscene publication'. '[T]his grave attack on the liberty of the press' should be 'unflinchingly resisted by every section of advanced thinkers'.[52]

The Agnostic Journal, while considering that the volume's circulation should *not* be restricted to 'Medical Men, Lawyers and Teachers', also doubted that it was ever likely to command much in the way of a popular sale. It would disappoint anyone looking for the 'prurient and pornographic':

> It is not seductive, but repulsive, as a treatise dealing with nosology and deformity must necessarily be …. Anyone who reads it must do so impelled by a sense of duty rather than seduced by a sense of pleasure. Everywhere is the cold, dry light

---

[48] *Reynolds's Newspaper*, 5th June 1898, Issue 2495, n.p.
[49] Ibid.
[50] Ibid., 3rd April 1898, p. 2.
[51] *The Freethinker*, 12th June 1898, p. 374.
[52] Anonymous (1898) 'Random Jottings', *Literary Guide and Rationalist Review – New Series*, 25, 1st July, p. 105.

of scientific method; you could cull as much pruriency and erotics out of Elliott's treatise on Algebra. Repulsive in its subject, and circumscribed in its scope, it is a curious gonfalon round which to fight the battle of a Free Press.[53]

They later characterized the case as one in which Bedborough was not being prosecuted 'as a "Free Love" evangelist' but for selling a copy of a 'hard, dry, repellent scientific work, which certainly has no more to do with "Free Love" than it has with the Binomial Theorem'.[54]

Although much of this protest came from a radical fringe, there was a swingeing attack on the prosecution in the more mainstream literary and cultural journal *Saturday Review* by Frank Harris. Declaring that 'We have not the advantage of an exact knowledge of the particular book in question', and that ' ... we have no wish to pronounce the book fit for decent persons to read', the author of the article went on to argue

> if this particular volume is at all similar to the works of the standard authorities upon sexual inversion it must abound in descriptions of facts at least as disgusting as the facts of delirium tremens. But we suspect that the object to them is not that they are disgusting, but that they relate to the functions of sex.[55]

Averring that most people found description of bodily organs and functions repellent, and even more so when proceeding to disorders of function, ' ... who doubts the importance of a widely diffused general knowledge of human anatomy and physiology? One exception is made by law and by ignorant opinion.'[56] Correspondents expressed sympathy with these views.

Most commentary, therefore, about the case was moderately favourable, although running counter to Ellis's own aims. His defenders leant heavily upon the 'unpleasant' nature of the subject and the therapeutic efficacy of the work as a study in pathology rather than, as what he had expressed as his intention in a letter to Edward Carpenter:

> sympathetic recognition for sexual inversion as a psychic abnormality which may be regarded as the highest ideal, & to clear away many vulgar errors – preparing the way, if possible, for a change in the law.[57]

One of the most (relatively) sympathetic responses came, rather surprisingly, from the campaigning journalist and purity campaigner W.T. Stead, most famous for his

---

[53] ' W.S.R.' (1898) 'The Prosecuted Volume', *The Agnostic Journal*, 18th June, p. 391.
[54] Anonymous (1898) Response to 'Letter to the Editor: Free Love in England', *The Agnostic Journal*, 9th July 1898, pp. 29–30.
[55] *Saturday Review*, 25th June 1898, 85, 2226, pp. 836–7: although this article was unsigned, G. W. Foote attributed it to Frank Harris, see *The Malthusian*, September 1898, XXII, 9, pp. 66–7. Harris was a member of the Free Press Defence Committee.
[56] Ibid.
[57] British Library, Department of Manuscripts, Havelock Ellis Papers, 'Havelock Ellis to Edward Carpenter, 17 December 1892: Copy', Additional Manuscripts 70536.

'Maiden Tribute of Modern Babylon' articles in the *Pall Mall Gazette* which had led to the passing of the 1885 Criminal Law Amendment Act. He actually admitted to having read the book, and could not believe that anyone who did so 'with an impartial mind could come to the conclusion that it was published with the intention of corrupting the morals of Her Majesty's subjects'. Rather, it embodied a ' ... painstaking desire to ascertain the scientific truth concerning certain obscure problems which lie at the base of grave questions of criminal jurisprudence'. Ellis's enquiry went, Stead perceived,

> to the very root of the theory upon which one section of the Criminal Law Amendment Act is based, and if the conclusions at which he arrives are sound, the principle of that legislation is unsound, and will have to be modified.[58]

Although he framed this as a question of 'disordered minds', he did acknowledge the desirability of legal reform. Admitting the subject to be 'unpleasant', he added ' ... the mischief accruing from the publicity occasioned by the prosecution immensely outweighs whatever gain it might be imagined could accrue from a successful prosecution'.[59]

It was also argued that while the police were attacking Ellis's 'dry' scientific work, ' ... really indecent literature was circulated with perfect impunity'.[60] A lengthy diatribe in *Reynolds's Newspaper* set up Ellis's work 'written by a distinguished scientist and sociologist, with a view to the better understanding and cure of the sexual extravagances which are rife', as entirely distinct from

> the hundreds of works published in *editions de luxe* at huge prices which may be bought at almost any respectable shop. Not a bookseller in the West End but will sell you volumes which, if exposed for sale in Holywell Street, would ensure the prompt conviction of the shopkeeper and very likely twelve months imprisonment ....

> The Treasury is always particularly careful to wink at the proceedings of these purveyors for rich men's vices. They are contented now and again to prosecute and imprison the publishers of cheap editions of Zola's novels and of scientific works.[61]

On a rather different note, the following week the 'Up to Date' column snarkily reported that there was no truth in the rumour that after the Bedborough prosecution was concluded ' ... the authorities intend ... to take proceedings against the publishers of the Old Testament'.[62] *The Reformer* contended that 'the young are much more likely to be injured by the sporting news and the unpleasant details of breach of

---

[58] W.T. Stead (1898) 'The Police and the Press: Scotland Yard Censorship', *The Review of Reviews*, XVIII, August, p. 162.
[59] Ibid.
[60] *The Malthusian*, September 1898, XXII, 9, pp. 66–7.
[61] *Reynolds's Newspaper*, 12th June 1898, Issue 2496, n.p.
[62] Ibid., 19th June, 1898, Issue 2497, n.p.

promise cases and divorce proceedings' so extensively reported in the press, adding condemnation of ' ... suggestive scripture lessons' and 'erotic classics' as taught in schools.[63] J.M. Robertson in the same issue argued, 'There was no thought at the time of the Wilde trial of saving the young and unthinking from reading the newspaper reports ... of all the nauseous details of that miserable case.'[64]

The most hostile press comment came *after* the verdict at the Old Bailey, in a leader in the influential *Daily Chronicle*. In spite of Ellis's personal intervention with H.W. Massingham, the editor, this strongly celebrated the outcome and seconded the judge's statements concerning *Sexual Inversion*: 'The plea of guilty avoided that washing of dirty linen in public which is one of the mischiefs of police proceedings against improper literature.' They would not name the author or the book:

> We give weight and credit to the protests of the writer as to his scientific *intentions* .... But for our part we cannot take the view that the book has any scientific value whatever .... The book in question is a highly morbid production. We think it worthless as science, even if the science it professes to advance were worth studying.[65]

Conceding that ' ... we do not see any internal evidence that the book was really written with an evil intent', and that they had a due regard for the freedom of the press, nonetheless 'for the protection of the young and the unthinking, a law there must be.'[66]

The *Saturday Review* considered the collapse of the case a ' ... monstrous miscarriage of justice'. Counsel had been prepared to defend *Sexual Inversion* and ' ... evidence of the most conclusive kind was in readiness, with eminent men of science testifying that Mr Havelock Ellis's was a perfectly proper scientific discussion of a serious subject'.[67] John M. Robertson wrote in *The Reformer*:

> The whole episode really beggars comment. England, there is reason to believe, suffers more than any other of the leading civilised nations from the form of vice handled in Mr Ellis's book. Mr Ellis's book is the first attempt by an English author to put in the hands of doctors, teachers, and others, the knowledge requisite for a sane, corrective treatment of the trouble, against which there is no other sort of provision save an occasional prosecution duly reported in the daily newspapers for the stimulation of the morbid curiosity of the 'young and unthinking'.[68]

This effectively combined the notion of the therapeutic intent of Ellis's work with the theme of the immoral tendencies of press reporting.

---

[63] *The Reformer*, 15th November 1898, II, 21, pp. 226–7.
[64] Ibid., 15th November 1898, II, 21, pp. 228–30.
[65] *Daily Chronicle*, 1st November 1898, Issue 11439, p. 6.
[66] Ibid.
[67] *Saturday Review*, 5th November 1898, p. 594.
[68] *The Reformer*, 15th November 1898, II, 21, pp. 228–30.

The medical press had remained remarkably silent during the course of the prosecution. While *Sexual Inversion* had received positive notices in some specialist medical journals on its first appearance, excerpted in Ellis's pamphlet on the case,[69] the two major British medical journals, *The Lancet* and the *British Medical Journal*, maintained a policy of discreet silence while the prosecution was ongoing. Only after the case was concluded, did *The Lancet* concede that ' ... the subject of sexual inversion has its proper claims for discussion', and even that *Sexual Inversion* was written in a ' ... purely dispassionate and scientific style'. They did not altogether concur with Ellis's views, but that was not their reason for not reviewing the book: they had been deterred by ' ... the circumstances attendant upon its issue': it had not been published ' ... as a scientific book [for] a scientific audience'. While

> A book written solely in a spirit of scientific enquiry into a subject which, though odious in itself, has yet to be faced cannot possibly be included under the head of indecent literature. But such a book may become indecent if offered for sale to the general public with a wrong motive.[70]

The moral they drew was ' ... be careful about the publisher'.[71]

The *British Medical Journal*, while invoking terms such as 'disagreeable', and 'unpleasant' to characterize the subject matter, nonetheless considered that it had been dealt with in a scientific manner, that the book had not been advertised or exposed for sale and there was nothing to ' ... pander to the prurient mind'. It was ' ... one of those unpleasant matters with which members of the medical profession should have some acquaintance'.[72]

The *Journal of Mental Science* was also ambivalent in its response to the verdict:

> Mr. Ellis's well-known reputation as a criminal anthropologist will be a sufficient guarantee of his motives in writing the work in question, but it is certainly most unfortunate that a man who must plead guilty of the sale of an indecent lecture and an indecent journal should have the opportunity of claiming a scientific study as part of his peccant matter.[73]

However, like *The Lancet*, they cavilled at the mode of publication, because

> unsavoury ... details which, however harmless they may seem to us who are accustomed to the vagaries of insane passion, will, if they fall into the hands of the vulgar, be treated as a mere bundle of very dirty stories, and as such are liable to become part of the stock-in-trade of the pornographic bookseller and his wretched clientele. We are sorry for Mr. Ellis, especially as he was unable to defend himself,

---

[69] Ellis, *Bedborough Trial*, Appendix B, pp. 25–6.
[70] *The Lancet*, 19th November 1898, pp. 1344–5.
[71] Ibid.
[72] *British Medical Journal*, 5th November 1898, p. 1466.
[73] Anonymous (1898) 'The Bedborough Case', *Journal of Mental Science*, 44, 184, pp. 122–3.

the charge being only against the vendor of various works; but we are of opinion that he should have exercised more care with regard to the mode of production and sale of his volume in its English form.[74]

There was a double bind in operation: it was agreed to be a subject falling within the remit of the medical man, but one that had to be very carefully ring-fenced for that audience. Even though Ellis had included a proviso that the book was only for sale to a suitably restricted readership, the fact that it was not issued by a recognized medical or scientific publisher told heavily against it, particularly the claim to a spurious academic and scholarly respectability, a point brought up during the prosecution at the Old Bailey:

Mr Matthews ... [H]e, the defendant, acted as sub-agent for that press ....
The Recorder: What is it called?
Mr Matthews: The Watford University Press, my lord.
The Recorder: It has nothing to do with any university at all, I suppose?
Mr Matthews: No, my lord, it is a mere title.
The Recorder: It is a very high-sounding title, which may take in a great many people.
Mr Matthews: No doubt, my lord, and we may take it to be so.[75]

However, as Ellis pointed out in a very measured response to *The Lancet*

None of the medical publishers whom I approached cared to take up a work on sexual inversion, one or two adding that they would have done so with pleasure had it not been their privilege to live in England.[76]

Conclusion

While the Free Press Defence Committee might have been thinking of the Bradlaugh and Besant case, it is likely that Bedborough himself was troubled by the thought of the elderly publisher Henry Vizetelly, imprisoned in 1888 for publishing the works of Zola and other French novelists at popular prices, even after omitting the most objectionable passages. It is also possible that by the time the case came into the Old Bailey, the attention of the police had shifted from possibly chimerical anarchists to the actual many-pseudonymed criminal Singer/de Villiers, and that the compromise achieved had been in return for Bedborough communicating to the police any knowledge he had of this elusive character.

---

[74] Ibid.
[75] Cited in Peterson, *Havelock Ellis*, p. 252.
[76] *The Lancet*, 26th November 1898, p. 1437.

In his memoirs, Sweeney gave a colourful account of George Ferdinand Springmuhl von Weissenfeld, his numerous aliases, female associates and history of scams and swindles. Sweeney indicated the authorities had come to believe that de Villiers was the real publisher during the course of the case and taken belated and unsuccessful steps to arrest him. A raid on the press at Watford some months after the trial found thousands of volumes of Ellis's work, which were destroyed. It was not until 1902 that the police finally laid hands on this slippery customer, residing in Cambridge under the name of Dr Sinclair Roland, in a house replete with secret hidey holes and passages. He dropped dead shortly after arrest, according to the coroner from apoplexy, or was it, as Sweeney alleged, an undetectable poison of which de Villiers had previously boasted?[77] On the 30th of January 1902, his wife and other associates were charged at Bow Street 'with conspiring to print, sell, and publish obscene books, pictures, and pamphlets'.[78] The University Press, Watford, compulsorily wound up shortly afterwards, had been dealing in works 'relating to the psychology and pathology of sex', advertised through catalogues.[79] Arthur Calder-Marshall in his biography of Ellis claimed that de Villiers's 'interest in the *Studies* was the money which he could make from its sale as a pornographic work'.[80] This seems a not unwarranted assumption.

There was no particularly concerted campaign of censorship as an outcome of the prosecution of *Sexual Inversion* but the existing cautious self-censorship by publishers and authors may have increased, which is a good deal harder to track down than state action. In 1907 the English translation of German sexologist Iwan Bloch's *The Sexual Life of Our Times* was condemned to be destroyed at Bow Street, but in spite of the translator M. Eden Paul's desire to 'fight the matter up to the "House of Fossils"' (i.e. the House of Lords), Ellis predicted in a letter to Carpenter that a compromise with sales limited to doctors would be reached.[81] The case did not garner much press interest. The fact that the publisher, Rebman, were a reputable firm associated with works of medicine and science was probably a significant factor in the appearance of a British edition with such a restriction in 1908.[82]

Edward Carpenter avoided prosecution for disseminating his views on *The Intermediate Sex*, published in 1908, and virulently reviewed in the *British Medical Journal*.[83] Even the obsessive campaign against him by anti-socialist and homophobe M.D. O'Brien failed to resonate much beyond Sheffield and vicinity, where Carpenter had a strong basis of support,[84] although Carpenter and his partner, George Merrill,

---

[77] Richards, *At Scotland Yard*, pp. 191–7.
[78] *The Times*, 31st January 1902, Issue 36679, p. 2.
[79] Ibid., 21st March 1902, Issue 36721, p. 10.
[80] Calder-Marshall, *Havelock Ellis*, p. 171.
[81] Sheffield City Archives, Papers of Edward Carpenter, 'Havelock Ellis to Edward Carpenter, 17 May 1907', MSS357/14.
[82] I. Bloch (1908) *The Sexual Life of Our Time in Its Relations to Modern Civilization – Translated from the Sixth German Edition by M. Eden Paul* (London: Rebman).
[83] *British Medical Journal*, 26th June 1909, pp. 1546–7.
[84] S. Brady (2005) *Masculinity and Male Homosexuality in Britain, 1861–1913* (Basingstoke: Palgrave Macmillan), pp. 44–9 and Sheila Rowbotham (2008) *Edward Carpenter: A Life of Liberty and Love* (London: Verso), pp. 285–8.

were placed under observation by the Derbyshire Police. This agitation led the Home Office to consider whether Carpenter's works contained grounds for prosecution and whether action should be taken. While admitting that O'Brien was a 'crank', nonetheless Home Office officials read and made extensive notes on Carpenter's works, which they considered 'did a good deal of harm'. However, they were opposed to

> calling public attention to Mr Carpenter and his works ... any public discussion of this subject greatly exceeds any mischief which is possible to the readers of books, who would not buy them unless they were in search of what they contain.[85]

Possibly this conclusion was influenced by the amount of attention the prosecution of *Sexual Inversion* had received.

It is hard to contend that the publication of *Sexual Inversion*, even with the publicity given it by this prosecution, opened up a discussion in Britain about homosexuality and the reform of the law. At best, it opened up a discussion as to whether the topic *should* be discussed, at least by doctors and scientists if not the general public. It might be argued that even that was an advance: Sean Brady has pointed out the resistance of the authorities to any attempts to clarify or investigate crimes of sex between men during the later decades of the nineteenth century and the evasion of any public debate on the subject.[86] What the prosecution and the consequent publicity did perhaps provide was the knowledge that such a study existed to those who might have been desperately seeking such a thing.

The Legitimation League's journal *The Adult* ceased publication in 1899 and so apparently did the League's activities. George Bedborough perhaps might have considered himself ill-done-by: he had escaped imprisonment, but he had done so at the expense of pleading guilty to a charge of corrupting the morals of the Queen's subjects, and by so doing had alienated himself from the circles in which he had previously been a leading figure. Whether a dangerous anarchist campaign had been thwarted remains an exercise for the imagination: the anarchist journal *Freedom* does not appear to have parsed the case as specifically directed towards their own cause, while exhorting readers to give what they could to the defence fund: '... here is a man attacked because he wishes to have the sex question discussed in all its phases ... love of liberty as opposed to statute law and ignorant conventionality in any direction, whether conscious or not, certainly makes for Anarchism'.[87]

Looking back several decades later with the serenity of hindsight, and the gratification of international recognition of his endeavours, in his posthumously published autobiography *My Life*, Ellis remarked

> Law and the Press ... between them ... thought that they had dismissed me and my book from the world ... My 'filthy' and 'worthless' and 'morbid' book has been

---

[85] The National Archives (TNA), Home Office: Registered Papers, Supplementary: Indecent Publications: Homogenic Love, 1909–1910, HO/144/1043/183473.
[86] Brady, *Masculinity and Male Homosexuality*, pp. 85–112.
[87] *Freedom: Supplement*, July 1898, p. 43.

translated into all the great living languages to reach people who could not say what a Recorder is, nor read the *Daily Chronicle* if they ever saw it.[88]

Ellis displayed a significant degree of schadenfreude in writing

> I had modestly chosen to issue my book in the quietest way I could find, almost privately. Order and Respectability killed, not the book, but the method of publication … and I immediately turned to the United States and placed my *Studies* in the hands of an active medical publishing house with a high reputation and an army of travellers. By the method which Order and Respectability closed to me my books would perhaps have sold by the dozen; by the method Order and Respectability forced me to adopt they have sold … in an ever-increasing circle around the world.[89]

When even his defenders could only frame his plea for tolerance of the inverted in terms heavy with revulsion and at best invoking the desirability of remedies for societal pathology, his rather zen refusal to pursue a 'martyr's crown' in preference to 'critical and dispassionate investigation of complicated problems'[90] seems prescient. Indeed, owing to the peculiarities of the English obscenity law, it is not entirely clear what recourse he had: a similar fate befell Radclyffe Hall's novel *The Well of Loneliness*, thirty years later, published with a preface by Ellis himself praising its evocation of the inner life of the 'female invert'. Hall, and the gallery of expert witnesses who had rallied to the book's defence had no chance to give evidence, as it was the publisher, Jonathan Cape, who was in the dock, and the presiding magistrate at Bow Street refused to hear them, judging the book 'vile', 'unnatural' and 'filthy'.[91]

---

[88] H. Ellis (1939) *My Life* (London: William Heinemann Ltd), p. 310.
[89] Ellis, *My Life*, p. 311.
[90] Ellis, *A Note on the Bedborough Trial*, p. 16.
[91] L. Doan (2001) *Fashioning Sapphism: The Origins of a Modern English Lesbian Culture* (New York: Columbia University Press), pp. 1–30. and A. Travis (2000) *Bound and Gagged: A Secret History of Obscenity in Britain* (London: Profile Books, 2000), pp. 45–73.

7

'Circumstances of Unexplained Savagery': The Gilchrist Murder Case and Its Legacy, 1908–1927

Anne-Marie Kilday
Oxford Brookes University

Introduction

When the well-known Scottish lawyer and amateur criminologist William Roughead (1870–1952) was describing the murder of an elderly woman in her own home in Glasgow in the winter of 1908, he said the crime was conducted 'in circumstances of unexplained savagery'.[1] Although Roughead was referring to the vicious methodology deployed by the perpetrator in this particular assault, the phrase he used described not only the homicidal episode that took place, but also the deplorable treatment of the individual accused of her murder *and* the scandalous persecution of the leading detective investigating the case. Indeed, the murder of Marion Gilchrist on the 21st of December 1908 fits seamlessly into this volume as it effectively ignited not one, but arguably *three* 'miscarriages' of justice.

First, there were the unquestionably problematic prosecution and subsequent conviction of Oscar Slater, the purported killer of Miss Gilchrist.[2] His trial in 1909 has become infamous in the annals of Scottish and indeed British legal history and is widely accepted as the quintessential example of a miscarriage of justice for a wide variety of reasons which will be examined below. Second, there were the blatant and relentless attempts by the Scottish authorities to stigmatize and discredit Detective-Lieutenant John Thomson Trench, who dared to suggest that the police investigation into the murder (to which he himself had been a crucial contributor) was fundamentally flawed. The staggering lengths that the Scottish authorities went to in order to silence one of their own, which will be exposed in the course of this chapter, reveal the extent to which Trench was indisputably a victim of 'rough justice' from within, just as Oscar Slater had been so from without. Then finally, and most importantly, if Oscar Slater did not murder Marion Gilchrist, as Detective-Lieutenant John Thomson Trench and indeed many others past and present have argued, then the savage, brutal and

---

[1] W. Roughead (1950 edition) (ed.) *Trial of Oscar Slater* (Edinburgh: William Hodge and Co.), p. xiv.
[2] Oscar Slater's real name was Oscar Joseph Leschziner and he was born in Germany, to Jewish parents, on the 8th of January 1872. See ibid., p. xviii.

seemingly gratuitous killer of this vulnerable, eighty-three-year-old woman, has never been identified, caught nor punished. Of the various legacies that emerged from this case, beyond its immediate historical context, this is surely the greatest 'injustice' of all. By bringing the threads of this complicated case together for the first time, through exhaustive and multi-faceted research, this chapter sheds new light on an infamous criminal trial to reveal not only how far the Scottish authorities were prepared to go to protect their supremacy in matters of law and order, but also how successful they were in these endeavours during the first third of the twentieth century.

The murder of Marion Gilchrist

Miss Marion Gilchrist was a frugal, security-conscious, eighty-three-year-old spinster who lived alone in her apartment at 15 Queen's Terrace in the centre of Glasgow. Whilst she was not inordinately wealthy, Miss Gilchrist did like to portray herself as someone with status who had a taste for the refined things in life, and as a result all the photographs that exist of her in life (such as the one below) depict her in lavish clothes adorned with fine jewellery of various sorts.[3]

Figure 7.1 Photograph of Marion Gilchrist (undated).[4]

---

[3] It is clear from various sources that whilst she lived comfortably, the wealth of Miss Marion Gilchrist had been greatly exaggerated by the press – see, for instance, National Records of Scotland (NRS), Justiciary Court, Process Papers, Inventory of Possessions, JC34/1/32/9 valued at £1875 6s 3d (which equates to approximately £158k in today's money) as well as the commentary provided in NRS, Justiciary Court, Precognition Papers, Memorandum Regarding the Case of the Death of Marion Gilchrist, AD21/17/7.

[4] Signet Library, Edinburgh (SL), William Roughead Collection, R+343.1.S1.15/v2528.

Marion Gilchrist was extremely careful with her possessions. She had a safe in the parlour of her home which stood upon a wooden stand which ' … would probably take two men to lift'.[5] She had double locks secured on all the doors. She hid her jewellery amongst her clothes in her wardrobe and never in plain sight. Frequently she asked friends to look after her belongings so that nothing of value could be stolen from her directly.[6] Marion Gilchrist had taken precautions regarding her own personal safety too. She had arranged with the family who lived beneath her, that if she ever got into any difficulty whilst her maid was out or absent, she would knock on the floor to let them know that she needed their assistance. This arrangement became established after an incident in 1904 or 1905 when Miss Gilchrist came to their door late one night, saying that she needed protection from a male intruder in her house. Yet when her neighbour, Arthur Adams, went to investigate Miss Gilchrist's apartment, he could find no one there and no evidence of anyone having been there. Gilchrist asked Adams if one of his sisters could stay in the upper flat overnight for her peace of mind, but the women were too frightened to do so, and it was then that Adams came upon the idea of the knocking personal alarm system. As he said to his neighbour, reassuringly ' … just give three knocks on the floor and I'll be up like a shot.'[7]

At around 7 pm, on the evening of the 21st of December 1908, Marion Gilchrist's servant of a little more than three years, twenty-one-year-old Helen Lambie went out to buy a newspaper, as she normally did. Not long after this, Arthur Adams ' … heard a noise from above, and then a very heavy fall, and three sharp knocks', so he went to Miss Gilchrist's flat to investigate, believing that she was in distress. Yet, when he went upstairs and rang Gilchrist's doorbell, no-one answered. He testified later in court that he ' … could hear a noise as if someone was chopping sticks' but as he could not enter the apartment, he went back downstairs to his own flat. The strange noises from above continued however, to the extent that in his view ' … the ceiling was like to crack' and so his sister persuaded him to go back upstairs to the Gilchrist residence. On this subsequent occasion, Arthur Adams met Helen Lambie returning from her errand. She proceeded to unlock the door (using two keys) and after entering the apartment, she went towards the kitchen. A man then suddenly emerged from the bedroom and calmly left the apartment, walking past both Arthur Adams and Helen Lambie, before bolting down the stairs and fleeing the building entirely.[8] During a quick search of the premises in an attempt to locate Miss Gilchrist, Adams and Lambie discovered a body on the floor of the dining room which had been covered with a skin rug and so they called for the police.

Figure 7.2 is a photograph of that room at 15 Queen's Terrace, Glasgow, in the immediate aftermath of the murder of Marion Gilchrist. One of the first individuals to

---

[5] NRS, Justiciary Court, Precognition Papers, Testimony of Helen Lambie, AD21/5.
[6] See, for instance, NRS, Justiciary Court, Precognition Papers, Testimony of Dr Robert Perry, AD21/5 who took possession of some of Miss Gilchrist's jewellery for a while at her request in 1902. Dr Perry was Miss Gilchrist's GP at that time and he made a detailed inventory of the items he stored for her in his home.
[7] NRS, Justiciary Court, Precognition Papers, Testimony of Arthur Montague Adams, AD21/5.
[8] Ibid and also NRS, Justiciary Court, Precognition Papers, Testimony of Helen Lambie, AD21/5.

arrive at the scene was William Douglas, superintendent of police based in the Western Office in Glasgow. He recounted: 'I went into the dining room and saw the body of Miss Gilchrist lying on the hearthrug and I noticed that her head had been badly battered.' As well as noticing various 'pools' and 'streams' of blood near the body of the victim, the officer also saw ' … part of the deceased's brains on the rug between the body and the fender of the fireplace'. Douglas noted that he found no weapon with which he believed the crime could have been committed.[9] Professor John Glaister and Dr Hugh Galt then observed the body *in situ* after removing the skin rug which had more or less covered the victim's remains. They agreed with Superintendent Douglas that her head and face 'had been very much smashed', and indeed the esteemed forensic scientist and police surgeon Glaister exclaimed ' … it was one of the most brutally smashed heads I have ever seen in my experience'.[10]

Figure 7.2 Crime Scene Photograph, Glasgow – 1908.[11]

[9] NRS, Justiciary Court, Precognition Papers, Testimony of William Douglas, Superintendent of Police, Western Office, Glasgow, AD21/5. Corroborated by NRS, Justiciary Court, Precognition Papers, Testimony of John Pyper, Detective Inspector, Western District of Glasgow Police, AD21/5.
[10] NRS, Justiciary Court, Precognition Papers, Testimony of John Glaister, Professor of Forensic Medicine, Glasgow University and Testimony of physician and surgeon Dr Hugh Galt, AD21/5.
[11] NRS, Justiciary Court, Precognition Papers, Crime Scene Photograph, AD21/5. Note that the white cushion in the picture, identified by the author's addition of a yellow (in the original) arrow, marks the spot where the victim's body lay.

According to Glaister and Galt's Crime Scene Medical Report:

> There were wounds on the right side of the victim's cheek extending from the mouth, wounds of the right forehead, and of the right side of the head. There was a deep hole on the left side between the eye socket and the left ear. The left eyeball was entirely amissing, having either been driven into the cavity of the brain or having been gouged out. The right eye was partially torn out of its socket by the deep fractures of the right side of the brow. There was much blood on and among the hair of the head. On the carpet rug beneath the head on both sides was a considerable amount of clotted blood, and fluid blood had soaked into the substance of the rug. Between the head and the fender of the fireplace a piece of brain tissue weighing about three quarters of an ounce, as well as smaller pieces, and several pieces of bone covered with blood, were found.[12]

The medical men concluded from the blood splatter and associated evidence that the victim had been attacked where she had been found ' ... and that the injuries had been produced by very forcible application of some instrument'. It was noted too that the victim's gold plate of artificial upper teeth had been knocked out and was found near the fireplace.[13] Certainly, from all of this evidence, William Roughead's description of the assault on Miss Gilchrist as a 'savage' attack was wholly accurate. The body was formally identified as being Miss Marion Gilchrist and was subsequently removed to the mortuary of Glasgow Royal Infirmary for further investigation.[14]

After a detailed post-mortem examination of Miss Marion Gilchrist, the coroners' report testified to the extent of the horrific injuries that this elderly woman had endured. As is partly evident in Figure 7.3, the victim had received multiple lacerative wounds to her face, head and neck and innumerable fractures to the bones in her face, jaw and skull. An internal examination also revealed the victims' brain to be 'greatly torn and disorganised with several pieces amissing'.[15] Significantly, it was further discovered that in the chest of the victim, ' ... the breast-bone had been fractured completely through its entire thickness about its middle' and on the right side, ' ... her third, fourth, fifth and sixth ribs were all fractured, some multiple times, whilst on the left side, the fourth rib was broken'.[16] These findings suggested to Professor Glaister and Dr Galt that the killer may well have knelt on top of the victim's chest in order to initially subdue her and then once in this dominant position, they then chose to inflict the various wounds to her face and head.[17]

---

[12] NRS, Justiciary Court, Process Papers, Crime Scene Medical Report, JC34/1/32/4. See also *The Scotsman*, 5th May 1909.
[13] Ibid.
[14] Roughead, *Trial of Oscar Slater*, pp. 108–9.
[15] NRS, Justiciary Court, Process Papers, Coroners' Report, JC34/1/32/5.
[16] Ibid.
[17] Ibid.

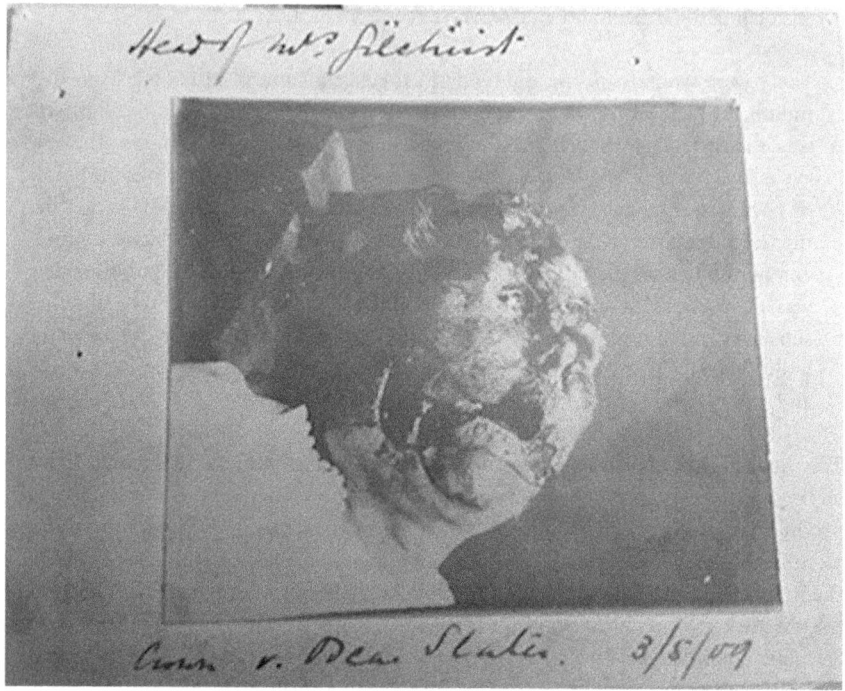

Figure 7.3 Mortuary Photograph of Miss Marion Gilchrist – 1908.[18]

After detailing the nature and extent of the injuries, the two medical men then tried to determine what kind of weapon could have been used to inflict them. This part of their investigation was complicated by the fact that no obvious murder weapon had been left behind by the killer and because so many of the wounds were described as being 'irregularly formed' or 'spindle-shaped' and followed no consistent pattern of impression.[19] Whilst Glaister and Galt could not be specific about the likely murder weapon used, and indeed offered no speculation, they concluded that Marion Gilchrist died from the extensive wounds and fractures she had received, together with the associated shock and bleeding that must have transpired.[20] In their view, all that could be said was that her injuries were consistent with those produced by '... forcible contact with a wide, heavy, blunt weapon, and that the violence applied was perpetrated with considerable force'.[21]

In the immediate aftermath of Marion Gilchrist's murder, police attention focussed on trying to identify the man who was seen by Arthur Adams and Helen Lambie leaving Miss Gilchrist's apartment. Neighbour Arthur Adams, for his part, said he only

---

[18] NRS, Justiciary Court, Precognition Papers, Mortuary Photograph of Miss Marion Gilchrist, AD21/18/13.
[19] NRS, Justiciary Court, Process Papers, Coroners' Report, JC34/1/32/5.
[20] Ibid.
[21] Ibid.

got a 'passing view' of the man and told the authorities that in any case, he did not have his spectacles on at the time.[22] Helen Lambie's initial, rather limited observation, was that whilst she only saw the side of the man's face, she could discern that he was between twenty-five and thirty years of age, five feet eight or nine inches tall, of slim build with dark hair and clean shaven.[23] After a £200 reward for aiding the police with their investigation was advertised, officers were also approached by fifteen-year-old Mary Barrowman who told them that a man in a hurry had 'knocked-up against her' in West Princes Street not long after 7 pm on the night of the murder, very near to the victim's residence. She confidently reported that she could offer a good description of the man, despite saying that he had a hat pulled down over his face 'further down than is generally worn by a man'.[24]

Evidently, the police did not have a whole lot to go on, from these generic and unhelpful descriptions. However, when Superintendent Douglas entered the spare bedroom in the Gilchrist apartment in the wake of the murder, he discovered the contents of the room were in some disarray with boxes and papers strewn about the floor. When he quizzed Helen Lambie about whether anything was obviously awry, she reported that a diamond crescent brooch that usually lay in a toilet dish on her mistress's dressing-table was now missing.[25] Now the authorities had an evident motive for the murder of Miss Gilchrist – jewellery theft. This notion became rapidly cemented in their minds just a few days later when Allan McLean, a cycle dealer in Glasgow contacted them after reading about the murder. He reported that a man whom he believed fitted the description of the would-be assailant had offered a pawn ticket for a diamond brooch to a friend of his.[26] When the police discovered that the man with the pawn ticket, Oscar Slater, not only had a criminal record and several aliases, but had also recently fled the city with a lady-friend (who wasn't his wife[27]) bound first for Liverpool and then New York, they believed these circumstances beyond coincidence and that they had the iniquitous culprit firmly in their sights.[28]

---

[22] NRS, Justiciary Court, Precognition Papers, Testimony of Arthur Montague Adams, AD21/5.
[23] NRS, Justiciary Court, Precognition Papers, Testimony of Helen Lambie, AD21/5. See also Roughead, *Trial of Oscar Slater*, p. xv.
[24] NRS, Justiciary Court, Precognition Papers, Testimony of Mary Barrowman, AD21/5.
[25] NRS, Justiciary Court, Precognition Papers, Testimony of William Douglas, Superintendent of Police, Western Office, Glasgow, AD21/5.
[26] NRS, Justiciary Court, Precognition Papers, Testimony of Allan McLean, cycle dealer in Glasgow, AD21/5.
[27] Oscar Slater married Marie (or Mary) Curtis in Glasgow on the 12th of July 1901. Mrs Marie Slater was someone well known to the police and she had been indicted for theft on two occasions and was described as having '… lived an immoral life.' She and Oscar Slater parted company, when he started an affair with Andrée Junio Antione, known 'professionally' as Madame Junio. By the time of Oscar Slater's trial, in 1909, Mrs Slater had not seen her husband for two and a half years. It was Andrée Junio Antione, who was accompanying him to Liverpool and then New York. See Glasgow University Archives (GUA), Records of the Department of Forensic Medicine and Science (FM), Case Files 1906-1969 – Oscar Slater, 2B/5/5.
[28] Roughead, *Trial of Oscar Slater*, p. xvi. See also NRS, Justiciary Court, Precognition Papers, Testimony of Gordon Henderson, Master of the Motor Club, Glasgow, AD21/5 who had been approached by Oscar Slater on the eve of his departure from Glasgow desperately anxious for cash.

Oscar Slater was extradited from the United States to stand trial for the murder of Miss Marion Gilchrist at the High Court in Edinburgh. Upon his arrest, he was found to be in possession of a small tin-tack hammer and this, together with a select array of his clothing, was all shipped back to Scotland, forensically examined and taken into custody as evidence for the prosecution.[29] The judicial hearing began on the 3rd of May 1909 and Oscar Slater was charged that 'he did assault the said Marion Gilchrist, and did beat her with a hammer or other blunt instrument and fracture her skull, and did murder her'.[30] After hearing evidence for four days, Mr Alexander Ure, the Lord Advocate, summed up the prosecution's case, describing the murder of Miss Gilchrist as ' … a dastardly outrage … an act of savagery which happily finds few parallels in the annals of crime'.[31] Choosing to concentrate on the immoral character of Oscar Slater, rather than the evidence submitted, the lawyer argued that the accused ' … was capable of this atrocious crime' and was a man ' … who had the whole knowledge necessary to enable him to commit the crime with success'.[32] With little counter-evidence offered by Mr A.L. McClure in defence, and a scathing description of the accused from the trial judge in his summation, it is unsurprising that the jury only took fifty-five minutes to convict Oscar Slater of all the charges against him, albeit only by a majority verdict.[33] The judge, Charles, Lord Guthrie (1849–1920) ordered Slater to be taken back to prison in Glasgow to remain imprisoned until the 27th of May 1909. He also ordered that on that same day, Oscar Slater was to be executed within the walls of the prison between eight and ten in the morning and subsequently buried there too.[34] Slater recalled that when he heard the final judgement in court,

> I felt some force take me in its grip and hold me as a man intoxicated. I felt as though I had suddenly surrendered to the influence of a hypnotist. Truly I was for a few moments hypnotised. I had lost all my faculties. I was a man of stone.[35]

The flawed prosecution of Oscar Slater

A close examination of the voluminous primary source documentation related to this case reveals significant shortcomings regarding the evidence which led to the arrest, prosecution and conviction of Oscar Slater. The first of these concerns the diamond crescent brooch, taken from Marion Gilchrist's house and linked to Oscar Slater via the pawn ticket. This had been the breakthrough that the authorities were hoping for and it led them to Oscar Slater as the chief suspect in the Gilchrist murder. Subsequent police

---

[29] See Roughead, *Trial of Oscar Slater*, p. xxi.
[30] NRS, Justiciary Court, Process Papers, Indictment, JC34/1/32/2/2.
[31] NRS, Justiciary Court, Precognition Papers, Summation for the Prosecution, AD21/6.
[32] Ibid.
[33] NRS, Justiciary Court, Precognition Papers, Summation for the Defence, AD21/6; NRS, Justiciary Court, Precognition Papers, Judge's Summation, AD21/6 and NRS, Justiciary Court, Process Papers, Verdict, JC9/7. See also *Edinburgh Evening News*, 6th May 1909 and *The Scotsman*, 7th May 1909.
[34] NRS, Justiciary Court, Process Papers, Sentence, JC9/7.
[35] *The Sunday Mail*, 20th November 1927.

investigations showed that he had been engaged in the jewellery trade in the past and was planning further ventures in the future.[36] However, there were two problems with this piece of evidence. First, as William Sorley, a jeweller in Glasgow later testified at Slater's trial, the Gilchrist brooch had just a single row of diamonds in it, whereas the one pawned by Oscar Slater contained three rows of gemstones.[37] Secondly, it is evident that Oscar Slater's pawn ticket was for a brooch that had been in pawn since the 18th of November 1908, several weeks before the Gilchrist murder.[38] Clearly the two brooches were different, and this cornerstone of the initial case against Oscar Slater was a patent red herring.

According to William Roughead, it seemed incontrovertible that the timing of Oscar Slater leaving Glasgow (in the wake of offering a pawn ticket for a diamond crescent brooch) and the timing of the Gilchrist murder were sufficient to raise suspicion amongst the authorities; after all, Slater was a man known to them and a convicted criminal.[39] However, just as with the missing brooch, the police appear to have been too quick to jump to conclusions and too short-sighted in their endeavours, instead of linking the evidence from a crime to a potential suspect as is the norm in thorough, multi-agency criminal investigations, they were all too willing to operate in reverse. It is clear that Oscar Slater's so-called flight from justice was nothing of the sort. Indeed, plenty of evidence points to Slater having made well-formed plans to leave Scotland for the United States at least three weeks ahead of his departure. He had made these arrangements publicly and had openly told several friends and various business acquaintances of his intentions.[40] None of his actions were covert or had been done in haste as had been portrayed by the authorities and by the prosecution. For instance, the Lord Advocate stated at the trial that Oscar Slater fled Glasgow on Christmas night, because his name and his description appeared in the newspapers.[41] This was scandalously inaccurate. The evening of the 25th of December was when Allan McLean first told police about the pawn ticket for the brooch and it wasn't until

---

[36] See, for instance, a business card found in Oscar Slater's possession which states: 'Oscar Slater, Dealer in Diamonds and Precious Stones. 33 Soho Square, Oxford Street, W.' found in NRS, Justiciary Court, Process Papers, JC34/1/32/11. That Slater had undertaken this kind of endeavour in the past was corroborated by the testimony provided at the trial by one of his oldest friends, see NRS, Justiciary Court, Precognition Papers, Testimony of Max Rattman, AD21/5 and also P. Hunt (1951) *Oscar Slater: The Great Suspect* (London: Carroll & Nicholson), p. 52. That Oscar Slater planned to return to the jewellery trade at some point in the future was corroborated by a letter from an American colleague of his, one D.R. Jacobs, dated the 28th of December 1908, see NRS Justiciary Court, Process Papers, JC34/1/32/11.

[37] NRS, Justiciary Court, Precognition Papers, Testimony of William Sorley, AD21/5.

[38] See Roughead, *Trial of Oscar Slater*, p. xvii.

[39] Ibid., p. xxiii. See also the evidence at notes 26 and 28 above. In addition, a telegram was sent by the Glasgow Police to their London equivalents on the 26th December 1908, noting that in the wake of the Gilchrist murder, a convicted criminal called Oscar Slater was noted to have 'hurriedly' left Glasgow without good reason. He was thus, in their view, a man of interest to their inquiries. See GUA FM Case Files 1906-1969 – Oscar Slater, 2B/5/2/58.

[40] See a letter from Oscar Slater to the Post Office Savings Bank dated 20th November 1908 (using the alias Adolph Anderson) saying he would like to cash in his deposit book and investment stock as he was leaving for America – NRS, Justiciary Court, Process Papers, JC34/1/32/27. For other examples see Roughead, *Trial of Oscar Slater*, p. xxiii and p. xlix.

[41] Roughead, *Trial of Oscar Slater*, p. xxiv.

Oscar Slater was half way across the Atlantic on a boat to New York – several days after this – that his description was first made public!

The next problematic element of the case against Oscar Slater was the constant reference to him being a convicted criminal and a man of ill-repute. His ongoing bad behaviour and association with the criminal fraternity rendered him capable – in the minds of the authorities at least – of the murder of Marion Gilchrist. Certainly, it is clear, from a variety of different sources, that Oscar Slater, by his own admission, had lived ' … an unsteady life'.[42] Slater adopted multiple aliases to facilitate his illicit lifestyle, and aside from the Gilchrist murder he had been arrested on at least three separate occasions. On the 10th of April 1896 Slater had been accused of the malicious wounding of fellow Jew Isaac Levy at the North London Sessions.[43] Slater was acquitted, but three years later, the Edinburgh Police Court did convict him of disorderly conduct (fighting when drunk) and he was sentenced to a fine of £1 or imprisonment for seven days.[44] Oscar Slater was described by the arresting officer in this case as a man who ' … had the reputation of being a low class foreign bully'.[45] It is unclear whether the officer used the word 'bully' in this context to mean a tyrant or the more colloquial term for a pimp. Certainly Oscar Slater could fit either definition of this word. Whilst in Edinburgh, he was known to the authorities as the pimp of a prostitute called Annie Hansen[46] and as one Detective Officer from the City Police testified:

> [Slater]… was a notorious gambler and was a drunken, dissolute fellow. He was of a vicious disposition and was constantly quarrelling and fighting with his associates over their gambling transactions. In these fights he used his feet more than his fists. The woman Hansen often had bruises about her face which she told me had been caused by Slater's illusage.[47]

The final incident on Oscar Slater's criminal record, prior to the murder of Miss Marion Gilchrist, occurred in 1900. Testimony from Sergeant James Stuart of Edinburgh's City Police revealed that he was on duty in April of that year and decided to pay a visit to Oscar Slater as ' … he had a bad reputation in the city' and he wanted to keep an eye

---

[42] This is a quote taken from a petition that Oscar Slater sends to the Secretary of State for Scotland on the 12th of November 1910 asking for his release – see NRS, Justiciary Court, Criminal Case File 1909–1921: Oscar Slater, Peterhead Prison Records, HH16/110.

[43] See London Metropolitan Archives, Calendar of Prisoners and North London Sessions, ILS/B/45/001 and especially London Metropolitan Archives, Quarter and General Sessions held at North London (10th April 1890), LJ/SR/155.

[44] NRS, Justiciary Court, Papers relating to the Trial of Oscar Slater, AD21/19/16.

[45] NRS, Justiciary Court, Precognition Papers, Testimony of William Moodie, Detective Lieutenant in Edinburgh's City Police, AD21/5. [Author's addition in parenthesis.]

[46] For the arrests and convictions relation to Annie Hansen (such as 24th March 1900 for breach of the peace and the assault of a police officer) and 15th May 1900 (for loitering for the purposes of prostitution) see NRS, Justiciary Court, Papers relating to the Trial of Oscar Slater, AD21/19/16.

[47] NRS, Justiciary Court, Precognition Papers, Testimony of John Mowatt, Detective Officer in Edinburgh's City Police, AD21/5. [Author's addition in parenthesis.]

on him.⁴⁸ Stuart accordingly visited Slater and after making his enquiries, he was just about to leave, when Slater said to him: 'You buggar! I'll shoot you yet!' Whilst Sergeant Stuart confirmed that Oscar Slater was not armed at the time he made this statement, he was nonetheless arrested for threatening a police officer.⁴⁹ All this evidence gives some credence to the authorities' suspicion of his potential involvement in the demise of Marion Gilchrist, when set alongside observations made about his activities following her murder. However, we need to remember that Slater had never been embroiled or indeed convicted of any criminal activity more significant than a misdemeanour in the past. Thus, once the authorities became aware of the erroneous evidence regarding the brooch and Slater's apparent 'flight from justice', we might expect that they would overlook him as a suspect and seek another. Yet they seemed more determined than ever to ensure that Oscar Slater remained the chief (and only) suspect in this case. This was primarily through the promotion of evidence identifying Slater as being at or near the crime scene not only on the 21st of December 1908 – the night Marion Gilchrist was brutally slain in her own home – but on previous occasions too, as the killer seemingly planned the crime and his subsequent escape.

In order to extradite Oscar Slater from the United States to stand trial, the three key witnesses – Arthur Adams, Helen Lambie and Mary Barrowman – each had to positively identify him as the man they saw leaving the Gilchrist apartment. To ensure that this happened, the authorities did several things which were highly questionable and evidently prejudicial. First, they showed each witness a photograph of the suspect prior to the identity parade. Second, the sworn statements of each of the witnesses were taken multiple times to derive greater consistency between them.⁵⁰ Third, they allowed Lambie and Barrowman to share a cabin on the twelve-day sea voyage to New York without any form of supervision.⁵¹ Perhaps most remarkably of all, prior to the hearing, when Slater was brought to court by two officials and Deputy US Marshal, Mr John W.M. Pinckley, Slater was made to walk past the three witnesses en route to the courtroom. Pinckley later recalled how Slater was handcuffed to him in plain sight and that when they walked past the assembled group, Mr Charles Fox, one of the UK government officials pointed to Slater and asked the three witnesses 'Is that the man?'⁵² One might expect from these endeavours that the identification

---

⁴⁸ NRS, Justiciary Court, Precognition Papers, Testimony of James Stuart, Sergeant in Edinburgh's City Police, AD21/5.
⁴⁹ Ibid. See also G. Dilnot (1925) 'The Man with the Twisted Nose', *Detective Magazine*, April edition, pp. 1057–65 at p. 1057 found in NRS, Justiciary Court, Criminal Case File 1927–1976: Oscar Slater, HH16/112/58 and K. Baston (2012) 'Oscar Slater: Presumed Guilty', *Signet Magazine*, 2, pp. 13–16 at p. 13.
⁵⁰ All three witnesses testified to having been shown a photograph of Oscar Slater prior to the hearing. Helen Lambie said her declaration had been taken ' … more [times] than I can tell you' and Mary Barrowman claimed she had been interviewed every day for two weeks to try to get her statement right – see NRS, Justiciary Court, Precognition Papers, Extradition Application Hearing, Testimony of Arthur Montague Adams, Testimony of Helen Lambie and Testimony of Mary Barrowman, AD21/5. See also Roughead, *Trial of Oscar Slater*, pp. xviii–xix and Hunt, *Oscar Slater*, p. 62.
⁵¹ Roughead, *Trial of Oscar Slater*, p. xix.
⁵² Ibid. See also Hunt, *Oscar Slater*, p. 46.

of Oscar Slater would have been relatively straightforward for Adams, Lambie and Barrowman, but this was not in fact the case.

Arthur Adams was asked whether there was anyone in court who he could identify as the man he saw leaving Miss Gilchrist's apartment. He replied, 'I couldn't say positively.' When pushed, all he would add was 'I say he resembles him in appearance'.[53] Mary Barrowman was asked the same question and gave a similar response, saying 'that man here is very like him' whilst pointing to Oscar Slater.[54] Helen Lambie, in her turn, was asked whether the man from the night of her mistress's murder was present in the courtroom. Cryptically, Lambie replied, 'One is very suspicious if anything.' The question to the witness was repeated and eventually she said, 'I couldn't tell his face; I never saw his face.' Helen Lambie said that it was the man's walk that was his most distinguishing feature. 'He didn't walk straight,' she said ' … he was sort of shaking himself a little.' When asked whether she had seen any man walk in this fashion since arriving in America, she reluctantly (and after a great deal of persuasion) pointed to Oscar Slater.[55] What is all the more remarkable about Helen Lambie's testimony is that by the time she had crossed the Atlantic once more and came to testify against Oscar Slater at the High Court in Edinburgh, she had entirely changed her view on her ability to identify him as the suspect in this case. For on the second day of the murder trial, Lambie told the packed courtroom, 'I did see his face!' When challenged by the defence as to why she had not mentioned this before, with the passing of many months since her testimony in New York, Lambie defiantly exclaimed, 'I am saying it now!' The defence chose not to press her any further on this matter.[56]

By the time the trial at the High Court had been initiated against Oscar Slater, some twelve witnesses had come forward to testify that they had each seen an individual who appeared to be staking out the Gilchrist residence in the weeks before the murder. All twelve positively identified Oscar Slater from a line-up as being the man who came to be known as 'The Watcher'.[57] The cumulative effect of this testimony was significant to the prosecution's case. However, the evidence submitted was not without its problems. For one thing, prior to attending the line-up, all of the witnesses had been given a photograph of Oscar Slater as the suspect in custody. Then secondly, the actual identification parade itself was considered by Slater's defence team to be 'unsatisfactory' as the other eleven individuals standing in line were Scottish and none of them looked even vaguely like Oscar Slater.[58] This was considered 'inappropriate' when it was known

---

[53] NRS, Justiciary Court, Precognition Papers, Extradition Application Hearing, Testimony of Arthur Montague Adams, AD21/5.

[54] NRS, Justiciary Court, Precognition Papers, Extradition Application Hearing, Testimony of Mary Barrowman, AD21/5.

[55] NRS, Justiciary Court, Precognition Papers, Extradition Application Hearing, Testimony of Helen Lambie, AD21/5.

[56] NRS, Justiciary Court, Precognition Papers, Testimony of Helen Lambie, AD21/5.

[57] See, for instance, NRS, Justiciary Court, Precognition Papers, Testimony of Francis Brien, Constable in the Glasgow Police and Testimony of Mrs Margaret Dickson (or McHaffie) who lived opposite the victim's house at 16 West Princes Street, AD21/5. See also *The Scotsman*, 4th May 1909.

[58] NRS, Justiciary Court, Precognition Papers, Testimony of John Thomson Trench, Detective Officer, Central District of Glasgow Police, AD21/5. See also Roughead, *Trial of Oscar Slater*, pp. xxi–xxii.

that Slater was a German Jew and thus likely to be ' ... of foreign appearance'. When the police were asked in court whether Oscar Slater should have been placed in a line-up with individuals who looked more or less like him, one officer under examination said, 'It might be the fairest way, but it is not the practice in Glasgow'.[59]

It was clear in 1909 and remains clear now that the crux of the prosecution's case against Oscar Slater related to his identification by so many witnesses. However, this evidence was flawed and unreliable, as it was based purely on vague personal impressions. As William Roughead later concluded, 'The three crucial witnesses had but a fleeting glance at the man; and all witnesses before they identified Slater had seen his photograph and read his description, so there were present in that case every circumstances that increased the elements of uncertainty and liability to error.'[60]

One of the most controversial pieces of prosecution evidence in the trial of Oscar Slater related to the physical evidence which purportedly linked him to the crime and the scene of the Gilchrist murder. The first medical professional who saw the victim's body *in situ* – Dr John Adams – was not called upon to testify in court. According to William Roughead, this was contrary to standard judicial procedure and indeed he remarked that it would be hard for anyone to ' ... recall a case of homicide in which the Crown had gone to the jury without producing the doctor who first saw the body after death'.[61] Perhaps the reason the prosecution dispensed with Dr Adams's testimony was because he had significant doubts about the murder weapon said to have been used. Adams thought it wholly unlikely that Oscar Slater's tin-tack hammer could have inflicted the wounds upon the victim shown above in Figure 7.3. It was too small, too lightweight and made different shaped impressions from those shown in the mortuary photograph. Rather, Dr Adams ' ... expressed a most decided opinion that the injuries were inflicted with the leg of a chair'.[62] Despite there being no conclusive evidence of blood on the hammer, or indeed on any of Slater's confiscated clothing,[63] Professor John Glaister and Dr Hugh Galt, who did testify in court, were of the view that the hammer *could* have been the murder weapon if it had been used forty to sixty times on the victim, although they admitted that due to the nature and severity of the wounds, they would have expected a much 'heavier' weapon to have been utilized.[64] It seems

---

[59] Ibid.
[60] Roughead, *Trial of Oscar Slater*, p. l.
[61] Ibid., p. xliii.
[62] Ibid. The suggestion that the leg of a chair could have been the murder weapon was later disputed by David Dick who was a witness for the Crown and was one of the few individuals to see the crime scene first hand. Dick wrote to William Roughead on the 23rd of February 1910 saying that Dr Adams was wrong in his judgement as there was no blood on the seat of the chair in question and as the weapon used had been sufficiently sharp enough to cut a piece out of the coal scuttle next to the fireplace. In his view, a chair leg could not have caused that specific kind of damage. For further detail, see SL, William Roughead Collection, R+343.1.S1.15/v2528/19.
[63] See the report compiled by Professor Harvey Littlejohn dated 11th March 1909 – NRS Justiciary Court, Process Papers, Forensic Report, JC34/1/32/6. An auger found in the back court at 15 Queen's Terrace by Alexander Rankin was also examined as a potential murder weapon and ruled out; see NRS, Justiciary Court, Precognition Papers, Testimony of Alexander Rankin, Inspector in the Western District of Glasgow Police, AD21/5.
[64] Roughead, *Trial of Oscar Slater*, p. xxv.

inexplicable that the imprecise and inconclusive testimony provided by these two medical experts was not scrutinized further by Oscar Slater's defence team.

There were a few other examples where crucial testimony was offered but not highlighted, challenged or explored by the courtroom lawyers. For instance, Frederick Nichols, a hairdresser in Glasgow, testified that he shaved Oscar Slater (a regular client of his) on Christmas Day 1908 (four days after the murder) and Slater not only had a close-cut moustache about a quarter of an inch long, but he also had about two weeks growth of dark facial hair at that time.[65] Yet, all three of the key witnesses in this case – Arthur Adams, Helen Lambie and Mary Barrowman – had each testified that the man they saw leave Miss Gilchrist's residence was clean shaven. Why was this discrepancy not questioned? Likewise there was the question of Oscar Slater's alibi. Whilst it might seem reasonable not to give a great deal of credence to the testimony of Catherine Schmalz, Slater's domestic servant, or Andrée Junio Antione, his lover, who said he was at home eating his supper at the time of the murder,[66] there were multiple independent witnesses who could attest to having seen a 'calm' Oscar Slater at various points and in various places that evening.[67] Cumulatively, their testimony wholly undermined and dismantled that of several Crown witnesses who pointed to seeing Slater fleeing the scene of the crime.[68] Yet, these details were not explored, their significance was played down and some key pre-trial precognition evidence was ignored altogether by both the prosecution and the defence.[69] Furthermore, if we consider that the prosecution called sixty witnesses to the High Court to testify against Oscar Slater, whilst the defence called just fifteen who testified to his good character rather than offering evidence of his innocence, then we can start to establish why the majority of the jury reached the verdict they did.

Although initially there had been an unfavourable public attitude to Slater, in the immediate aftermath of the trial doubts started to emerge as to his guilt and the appropriateness of a capital sentence in the face of this uncertainty. As William Roughead describes, 'The atmosphere of excitement, rumour, and suspicion inseparable from a sensational murder case began to clear; and people realised that the weak links in the evidential chain by which the conviction had been secured were neither few nor far between.'[70] Almost immediately, a series of petitions, campaigns and appeals which challenged both the original verdict and the sentence were either formally

---

[65] NRS, Justiciary Court, Precognition Papers, Testimony of Frederick Nichols, AD21/5.
[66] NRS, Justiciary Court, Precognition Papers, Testimony of Catherine Schmalz and Testimony of Andrée Junio Antione, AD21/5.
[67] See, for instance, the testimony of Duncan MacBrayne available at NRS, Justiciary Court, Criminal Case File 1914–1948: Oscar Slater, HH16/111. See also *The Scotsman*, 6th May 1909.
[68] The evidence referred to at note 66 above was in complete opposition to testimony that the prosecution held to be central to their case namely NRS, Justiciary Court, Precognition Papers, Testimony of Annie Armour, AD21/5.
[69] See, for instance, the testimony of Agnes Brown, who was not called to court to give evidence at the trial but whose pre-trial precognition completely undermined the testimony of key witness Mary Barrowman with regards to how Oscar Slater was dressed when leaving the crime scene – see NRS, Justiciary Court, Criminal Case File 1914–1948: Oscar Slater, HH16/111.
[70] Roughead, *Trial of Oscar Slater*, p. xxvi.

lodged or publicly articulated.[71] The Secretary of State for Scotland, John Sinclair, Lord Pentland (1860–1925) asked the judge in the case to provide his views on the verdict the jury had reached. The judge, Lord Guthrie stated that in his view the evidence was legally sufficient to entitle the jury to convict the accused, considering the verdict to be correct. However, he thought that the sentence should be commuted given the divided opinion of the jury.[72] Similar views were expressed in letters supporting Slater's reprieve which were sent to the Secretary of State for Scotland from the Society for the Abolition of Capital Punishment and from ordinary members of the public such as one S. McIlwraith dated the 19th of May 1909 which plainly said, 'The man [Slater] MAY be guilty, but he certainly has not proved to be.'[73] One of Oscar Slater's lawyers, Ewing Spiers, also submitted a public petition for his client's reprieve ' … due to the strength of public opinion regarding his innocence' and managed to accumulate over 20,000 signatories (many of whom were lawyers).[74] Cumulatively, all of these views seemed effective as on the 25th of May 1909, a royal warrant ordered that the capital sentence against Oscar Slater be commuted to penal servitude for life. This decree came just two days before Slater's execution was scheduled.[75]

The campaigns related to the Oscar Slater case did not conclude with this reprieve, however. Over the next nineteen years, there were various formal and informal attempts made to quash the original conviction using some, but not all of the evidential problems and procedural flaws. The first of these came in 1912 with the publication of Sir Arthur Conan Doyle's work *The Case of Oscar Slater* which the author sent, along with a letter, to the Secretary of State for Scotland. Conan Doyle (1859–1930) stated in his missive dated the 7th of September: 'There is a general uneasiness as to the facts of this man's trial and condemnation.'[76] In particular, he emphasized the falsehoods in the speech given in court by the Lord Advocate and how divided the jury had been in their decision. Just over three months later, Sir Edward Marshall Hall, MP for Liverpool East Toxteth (1858–1927) and an eminent English barrister, challenged the

---

[71] It is worth noting that there were also a series of evidently anti-Semitic submissions to the Secretary of State for Scotland arguing that Slater should not benefit from any sort of reprieve – see, for instance, NRS, Justiciary Court, Criminal Case File 1909: Oscar Slater, Letter to *The Scotsman*, 26th May 1909, HH16/109/2. For further discussion of the anti-Semitic elements of this case and the context in which it occurred see B. Braber (2003) 'The Trial of Oscar Slater (1909) and Anti-Jewish Prejudices in Edwardian Glasgow', *History*, 88, 290, pp. 262–79. For evidence of it in the newspapers in the aftermath of 'The Secret Inquiry', see, for instance, *The Perthshire Advertiser*, 1st April 1914, p. 4 and 18th April 1915, p. 6.
[72] NRS, Justiciary Court, Criminal Case File 1909: Oscar Slater, Judge Guthrie's Case Review, 13th May 1909, HH16/109.
[73] See NRS, Justiciary Court, Criminal Case File 1909: Oscar Slater, Petition for Clemency from the Society for the Abolition of Capital Punishment, 12th May 1909, HH16/109 and NRS, Justiciary Court, Criminal Case File 1909: Oscar Slater, Letter from S. McIlwraith to the Secretary of State for Scotland, 19th May 1909, HH16/109/04. [Author's addition in parenthesis.]
[74] NRS, Justiciary Court, Criminal Case File 1909: Oscar Slater, Petition for Clemency by Ewing Spiers, 19th May 1909, HH16/109/7.
[75] NRS, Justiciary Court, Criminal Case File 1909: Oscar Slater, Remission from Capital Sentence, 25th May 1909, HH16/109 and NRS, Justiciary Court, Minute Book, JC9/7.
[76] NRS, Justiciary Court, Criminal Case File 1909–1921: Oscar Slater, Letter from Sir Arthur Conan Doyle to the Secretary of State for Scotland, 7th September 1912, HH16/110. See also A. Conan Doyle (1912) *The Case of Oscar Slater* (New York: Hodder & Stoughton).

then Secretary of State for Scotland, Thomas McKinnon Wood (1855–1927) in the Houses of Parliament about aspects of the Slater case, using Conan Doyle's criticisms as his main reference point. Hall asked his colleague if he would state what steps he proposed to take to address the problematic issues related to the verdict. McKinnon Wood replied that he proposed to take none.[77]

By 1914, however, McKinnon Wood had changed his view and had appointed Mr Gardner Millar, Sheriff of Lanarkshire, as commissioner of an enquiry he ordered into the case. McKinnon Wood's volte-face had been prompted by David Cook, a solicitor from Glasgow, who in March of that year had presented the Secretary of State for Scotland serious allegations about how the initial investigation and subsequent prosecution of Oscar Slater had been handled. In particular, Cook focussed on the construction of the 'flight from justice' narrative, the problematic nature of the details of Mary Barrowman's testimony and more crucially perhaps, the suggestion that one of the three key witnesses had named another person (other than Slater) as the individual seen leaving the Gilchrist apartment on the night of the murder.[78] This latter proposition had come from Detective-Lieutenant John Thomson Trench, one of the lead detectives investigating the murder, and thus could not be ignored. The content and ramifications of this allegation will be dealt with in more detail in the subsequent section of this chapter.

The review of the Oscar Slater case began on the 23rd of April 1914 and quickly became known, unofficially at least, as 'The Secret Inquiry'.[79] This was for several reasons. First of all the proceedings were to be held in private at the County Buildings in Glasgow, with the only individuals present being the Commissioner, his clerk and the witnesses giving testimony. Secondly, the testimony provided was not to be given under oath and the Commissioner had the freedom to edit the statements made and to redact certain passages of evidence if he thought that was appropriate. Thirdly, Oscar Slater was to have no representation present at the enquiry and finally, it was decreed that the conduct of the trial was not to form any part of the re-examination of the case. Thus, as William Roughead sarcastically put it, ' … compared with the restrictions by which this quest for truth was handicapped, the task set by Pharaoh to the captive Israelites was fair and reasonable'.[80] Given all this, there was no great surprise when David Cook received a letter from the Secretary of State for Scotland on the 16th of June 1914, saying he had ' … fully and carefully considered the information obtained by the Sheriff in the course of an exhaustive investigation, and is satisfied that no case is established which would justify him in advising any interference with Slater's sentence'.[81]

---

[77] HC Deb 10th December 1912, Vol. 45, Col 244, from https://hansard.parliament.uk (accessed 11 July 2019).
[78] See Roughead, *Trial of Oscar Slater*, pp. xxix–xxx.
[79] NRS, Justiciary Court, Criminal Case File 1914–1948: Oscar Slater, Evidence heard at the Inquiry held by the Sheriff of Lanarkshire, 23rd–25th of April 1914, HH16/111.
[80] Ibid. Roughead's sarcasm was picked up by the press who produced cartoons emphasizing the 'secretive' nature of the enquiry – see SL, William Roughead Collection, R+343.1.S1.15/v2527, *The People's Journal*, 2nd May 1914.
[81] NRS, Justiciary Court, Criminal Case File 1909–1921: Oscar Slater, Letter from the Secretary of State for Scotland to Mr David Cook, 16th June 1914, HH16/110. The white paper from the enquiry was published on the 27th of June 1914 – see Roughead, *Trial of Oscar Slater*, p. xxiv.

The outbreak of the First World War likely put paid to any further efforts to solicit a reprieve for Oscar Slater until 1925 when Sir Arthur Conan Doyle wrote (at the direct behest of the prisoner) to the new Secretary of State for Scotland, Sir John Gilmour (1876–1940), asking for Slater to be released, given that had now served fifteen years of his sentence.[82] His pleas fell on deaf ears, but momentum was starting to build once more. A series of newspaper articles, editorial comments and also a book by William Park, all published between March 1926 and November 1927, sensationally offered new impetus to the campaign for Slater's release. On the 28th of March 1926, *Empire News* produced an article naming a new witness in the case: Minnie Hepburn. Mrs Hepburn had been near the crime scene on the night of the Gilchrist murder and had seen a man running from the residence. She had not come forward to offer testimony before now, because her husband hadn't wanted her to get involved, but she felt that she could no longer keep silent. Her description of the man she saw was diametrically opposed to that of Oscar Slater and to the testimony of the other key witnesses in the case.[83] In July of 1927, William Park's work *The Truth about Oscar Slater* was published. In this, the author claimed that Slater was the victim of an appalling miscarriage of justice and craved that pressure be put on the Secretary of State for Scotland to reopen the case.[84] Park's clarion call was given impetus by a further *Empire News* article published on the 23rd of October 1927 where Helen Lambie (now Helen Gillon) offered an entirely different version of her original statement to the police. Astonishingly, she now admitted that the man she saw leaving the apartment ' … did not seem strange to me' as he ' … was in the habit of visiting my mistress' and that she had told Detective-Lieutenant Trench who that individual was, saying he was a friend of Miss Gilchrist. She further revealed that she had been unable to pick Oscar Slater out of a line-up in New York, but had been told to 'keep trying' by the authorities until she got it right and so she chose to pick out the only man of foreign appearance in the room.[85]

(James) Ramsay MacDonald (1866–1937), leader of the Labour Party, had read these latest press revelations and wrote to the Secretary of State for Scotland, Sir John Gilmour twice in October of 1927, saying that he had been ' … considerably disturbed' by what he had come across.[86] He further acknowledged the existence of ' … some most unpleasant evidence' which involved the police and the real culprit. He stated that it was clear to him that 'The Scottish legal authorities and the police strove for

---

[82] Roughead, *Trial of Oscar Slater*, p. xxxv. For more on the lengthy campaign by Sir Arthur Conan Doyle to exonerate Oscar Slater, see M. Fox (2018) *Conan Doyle for the Defence: A Sensational Murder, the Quest for Justice and the World's Greatest Detective Writer* (London: Profile Books) and *Empire News*, 13th November 1927.

[83] NRS, Justiciary Court, Criminal Case File 1914–1948: Oscar Slater, *Empire News*, 28th March 1926, HH16/111.

[84] W. Park (1927) *The Truth about Oscar Slater (With the Prisoner's Own Story)* (London: The Psychic Press), p. 5.

[85] NRS, Justiciary Court, Criminal Case File 1914–1948: Oscar Slater, *Empire News*, 23rd October 1927, HH16/111. See also Hunt, *Oscar Slater*, p. 195.

[86] NRS, Justiciary Court, Criminal Case File 1914–1948: Oscar Slater, Letter from Ramsay MacDonald to the Secretary of State for Scotland, 27th October 1927, HH16/111.

his [Slater's] conviction by influencing witnesses and withholding evidence'.[87] If this correspondence did not convince Sir John Gilmour to intervene, then a further dramatic revelation by key prosecution witness Mary Barrowman in a *Daily News* article of the 5th of November 1927, may have been decisive in this respect. In this piece, Barrowman said that she only ever wanted to say to the authorities that Oscar Slater was ' … very like the man' who she encountered on the street outside the Gilchrist residence, but acknowledged that she had been 'bullied' by the procurator fiscal to say ' … he *was* the man.'[88]

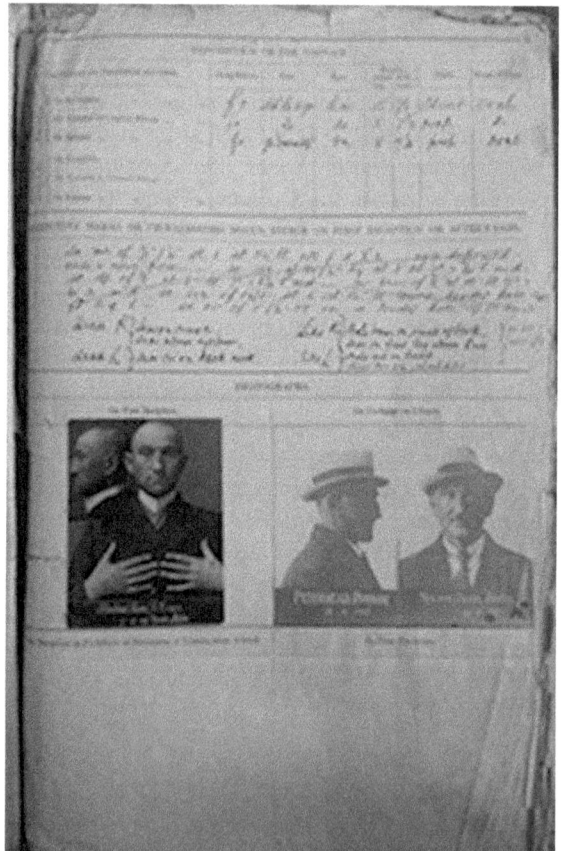

Figure 7.4 Photographs of Oscar Slater – 1909 and 1927.[89]

[87] NRS, Justiciary Court, Criminal Case File 1914–1948: Oscar Slater, Letter from Ramsay MacDonald to the Secretary of State for Scotland, 24th October 1927, HH16/111. [Author's addition in parenthesis.]
[88] NRS, Justiciary Court, Criminal Case File 1914–1948: Oscar Slater, *Daily News*, 5th November 1927, HH16/111.
[89] NRS, Justiciary Court, Prisoner Record 1909–1927: Oscar Slater, HH15/20/1.

On the 10th of November the Secretary of State for Scotland dramatically ordered that Oscar Slater be released on licence. This was granted four days later.[90] By this point in time, Slater had served eighteen-and-a-half years of his life sentence in Peterhead Prison. Figure 7.4 shows the contrast in the appearance of Oscar Slater upon his arrest and then at his subsequent release. He later said in a serialization of his story published by *The Sunday Mail* on the 20th of November 1927 that his experience in prison had been ' ... a vale of grief, suffering and tribulation through which an unconsciously cruel and relentless fate compelled me to tread'. He had become ' ... a man destined to oblivion'. Indeed, Oscar Slater seemed genuinely bewildered by his release from prison after so many years. He said in the same newspaper article: 'I am still dazed. I feel I want to sleep ever so much. I am a stranger to your world.'[91]

On the 15th of November 1927, Sir John Gilmour, Secretary of State for Scotland, announced that there would be another enquiry into the Oscar Slater case, and all questions on the matter should be remitted to the newly established Scottish Court of Appeal under the provisions of section 16 of the 1926 Criminal Appeal (Scotland) Act. To facilitate this, Parliament first had to pass legislation allowing the retrospective effect of the Act, rather than restricting it to individual sentences after the new legislation had come into force (from 31st October 1926).[92] After an extensive investigation, Slater's legal team submitted a petition of appeal on 2nd March 1928, which was latterly referred to the High Court of Justiciary for its consideration. In the end eleven grounds for appeal were submitted, many of which related to the procedural malpractices, evidential weaknesses and judicial misdirections. The legal team made plain that they considered Hellen Gillon (née Lambie) to be integral to determining the truth of what happened on the night that Miss Marion Gilchrist was murdered, and they requested that she be located and impelled to testify.[93]

The appeal hearing began on 8th June 1928 before five appeal court judges. Despite the protestations of the defence team, the court ruled that the parameters of the appeal would be restricted and ' ... only new evidence could be allowed'.[94] Any information previously debated upon in the original trial could not now be considered, even if it was now erroneous, altered or corrected. The court also decreed that only evidence that had been formally submitted to the authorities could be considered. Anecdotal commentary, statements published by the press, reported casual conversations or amateur sleuthing around the case were not permissible as evidence. Furthermore, they determined that Oscar Slater himself would not be allowed to testify, as he had

---

[90] NRS, Justiciary Court, Criminal Case File 1927–1976: Oscar Slater, Licence for Oscar Slater's Release, 14th November 1927, HH16/112. See also *Sunday Chronicle*, 18th November 1927.
[91] NRS, Justiciary Court, Prisoner Record 1909–1928: Oscar Slater, HH15/20/3.
[92] Roughead (1950 edition) (ed.) *Trial of Oscar Slater*, pp. xxxix–xl. See also *Daily News*, 18th November 1927.
[93] For the details submitted in the petition, see NRS, Justiciary Records, Trial of Oscar Slater (Murder), AD21/14/7/2 and AD21/14/7/3.
[94] NRS, Justiciary Court, Criminal Case File 1927–1976: Oscar Slater, Transcript of Appeal Hearing, June–July 1928, HH16/112.

not done so in the original trial.[95] Slater was so incensed by this decision, that on the 13th of June 1928, he withdrew his appeal in its entirety to the utter amazement and consternation of his legal team.[96] This decision was quickly reversed however, and the appeal recommenced in earnest on the 9th of July 1928 when it was announced by the court that Hellen Gillon (née Lambie) had steadfastly refused to give evidence at the hearing and that there was no legal or judicial mechanism to compel her to do so, despite the widely held belief that she was ' ... an untruthful and insolent witness' who was ' ... false and unscrupulous'.[97]

Given the appeal court's parameters, many of arguments posited in the original petition by Oscar Slater's legal team had become effectively redundant. Consequently, there were essentially just three grounds for appeal now being considered:

(1) Mis-statements of fact, including prejudicial suggestions of the gravest kind, made by the Lord Advocate in the course of the trial, and in particular his speech to the jury;
(2) The withholding of evidence by the Crown favourable to the prisoner; and
(3) Issues with the judge's charge to the jury with reference to the attack on character, certain inadequacies in that charge as to questions of fact, and misdirections in law both positive and negative.[98]

As is clear, many of the fundamental flaws and scandalous errors associated with the prosecution of Oscar Slater were ignored, in favour of elucidation of the supposed biases articulated by both the Lord Advocate *and* Judge Guthrie during the closing stages of the 1909 trial. In particular, the defence team took exception to the judge's oration when he said that Oscar Slater ' ... had maintained himself by the ruin of men and on the ruin of women, living for years past in a way that many blackguards would scorn to live'.[99] Then, as if that particular piece of scene setting was not sufficiently prejudicial, he had gone on to say:

> A man of that kind has **not the presumption of innocence in his favour** which is a form in the case of every man, but a reality in the case of an ordinary man. Not only is every man presumed to be innocent, but the ordinary man, in a case of brutal ferocity like the present, has a strong presumption in his favour.[100]

In the view of the defence team, by directing the jury in this way the judge had ' ... confused the presumption of innocence with a presumption of good character which

---

[95] Ibid.
[96] Roughead, *Trial of Oscar Slater*, pp. xlv.
[97] NRS, Justiciary Court, Criminal Case File 1927–1976: Oscar Slater, Transcript of Appeal Hearing, June–July 1928, HH16/112.
[98] Ibid.
[99] Ibid. The Oxford English Dictionary defines a 'blackguard' as a man who behaves in a dishonourable or contemptible way – see https://www.lexico.com/en (accessed 11 July 2019).
[100] NRS, Justiciary Court, Criminal Case File 1927–1976: Oscar Slater, Transcript of Appeal Hearing, June–July 1928, HH16/112. [Author's emphasis added.]

it is not. It is a presumption that a man is innocent *quoad* the particular crime with which he is charged.'[101]

The decision of the appeal court was announced on the 20th of July 1928. The five judges made it plain that in hearing the appeal they were looking to answer four questions:

(1) Whether the jury's verdict was unreasonable or unsupported by evidence;
(2) Whether any new facts had been disclosed material to the issue;
(3) Whether the appellant had suffered prejudice by non-disclosure of evidence known to the Crown; and
(4) Whether the verdict was vitiated in respect of misdirection by the presiding judge.[102]

In their summation, the judges declared that they did not find that the new evidence presented to them during the hearing materially affected the decision made in this case, and consequently it was their belief that the original decision made by the jury remained reasonable and supported by the evidence. However, the judges did acknowledge that:

> As the vital point of satisfactory proof of identity presented an unusually difficult narrow issue upon which the balance of judgement might be easily influenced, it was imperative that the jury should receive from the presiding judge the clearest and most unambiguous warning against being influenced by considerations at once so irrelevant and so prejudicial as the relations of the appellant with his female associates. But the directions of the judge not only did nothing to remove the erroneous impression which the opening passages of the speech for the Crown were likely to produce, but, on the contrary, they were calculated to confirm them. The direction that the appellant had not the benefit of ordinary presumption of innocence amounted, in the opinion of the Court, to a clear misdirection in law.[103]

The appeal thus succeeded on the fourth of the questions deliberated upon, and the conviction against Oscar Slater was quashed on a legal technicality, rather than on the strength of evidence presented regarding the weaknesses and inconsistencies of the witness testimonies provided. This decision also ignored the patent problems associated with the material evidence considered, and the fundamental prejudices and irregularities evident in the investigative procedures employed by the Glasgow Police Force. On the 4th of August 1927, Oscar Slater was awarded £6,000 compensation for his wrongful conviction by the Secretary of State for Scotland. Slater accepted the

---

[101] Ibid.
[102] NRS, Justiciary Court, Criminal Case File 1927–1976: Oscar Slater, Appeal Court Decision, 20th July 1928, HH16/112.
[103] Ibid.

payment without consulting his lawyers, only to discover that the costs of the appeal (approximately £1500) fell upon him, rather than the state. This meant, in effect, that Oscar Slater was awarded a paltry £250 in reparation for every year he was wrongly incarcerated.[104] Oscar Slater lived the remainder of his life peacefully, marrying a Scottish woman of German descent (Lina Wilhelmina Schad) in 1936 and the couple settled in Ayrshire where Slater repaired and sold antiques. He died at his home, of natural causes, on the 31st of January 1948 at the age of seventy-six.[105]

The persecution of John Thomson Trench

Although Marion Gilchrist was the undoubted victim in this case, it could also be argued that alongside Oscar Slater, another individual suffered significantly as a result of the botched investigation, the flawed procedural approaches adopted in the prosecution of this case and the single-minded prejudices of the authorities involved: Detective-Lieutenant John Thomson Trench.

Figure 7.5 Newspaper Photograph of Detective-Lieutenant John Thomson Trench, 1914.[106]

---

[104] NRS, Justiciary Court, Criminal Case File 1927–1976: Oscar Slater, Letter from the Secretary of State for Scotland to Oscar Slater, 4th August 1927, HH16/112.
[105] See *Glasgow Herald*, 2nd February 1948.
[106] SL, William Roughead Collection, R+343.1.S1.15/v2527, *Daily Record and Mail*, 2nd May 1914.

John Thomson Trench (seen in Figure 7.5) joined the City of Glasgow Police Force in May 1893 and had risen to the position of Detective-Lieutenant.[107] At the time of the Gilchrist murder in 1908, he was considered by his superiors to be a ' ... trustworthy, capable and efficient officer' achieving not only their respect, but a series of regular promotions throughout his career.[108] By 1914, Trench had won the King's Police Medal in 1914 for distinguished service and the gallantry he had displayed in bringing justice to bear on the most violent and hardened of Scottish criminals.[109] Evidently, Detective-Lieutenant Trench was held in high regard. However, just a few months later in that same year, 1914, things changed dramatically. As has been alluded to above, it was at this time that John Thomson Trench went to visit his friend, the solicitor David Cook, to seek his counsel. The detective told Cook that he remained adamant, even five years after the trial which convicted Oscar Slater, that on the night of the Gilchrist murder, the servant Helen Lambie had named another suspect (someone she knew) as the individual she had seen leaving the residence.[110] Trench was thus convinced of the innocence of Oscar Slater then languishing in Peterhead Prison, and although technically the case was officially closed, he felt he could not let things lie. David Cook agreed persuading him that it was in the interests of justice for him to reveal all that he knew and to do so publicly.[111]

Trench was well aware of the potential ramifications of the information he felt he needed to declare, especially as far as his own career and his loyalty to the police force were concerned, and so with the help of David Cook, he sought some ' ... guarantee of personal safety' from the authorities.[112] The two men persuaded a third party, Dr Devon who was then one of the H.M. Prison Commissioners for Scotland to write to the Secretary of State for Scotland asking how best to proceed. Mr McKinnon Wood replied in February of 1914 asking Trench to provide a written statement of the evidence he knew and that on receipt of this, he as the Secretary of State would give ' ... the matter my best consideration'.[113] Trench took this correspondence to provide the personal assurances he needed and he accordingly submitted his evidence. Evidently, as it was to turn out, this was an error of judgement.

The evidence Trench submitted to 'The Secret Inquiry' in 1914 made clear that as far as he was concerned, the chief suspect in the case was someone whom he identified by the initials A.B., and that this individual was *not* Oscar Slater.[114] He testified that he was given instructions by Chief Superintendent John Ord to visit a Miss Margaret

---

[107] NRS, Justiciary Court, Criminal Case File 1914–1948: Oscar Slater, Evidence heard at the Inquiry held by the Sheriff of Lanarkshire, 23rd–25th of April 1914, HH16/111.

[108] See ibid for the personal history of John Thomson Trench as well as GUA FM Case Files 1906–1969 – Oscar Slater, Memo to the City of Glasgow Police by John Ord, 22nd April 1914, 2B/5/1.

[109] See Anonymous (1965) 'A Policeman to Remember: I. Detective Lieutenant John Thomson Trench', *Police Journal*, 38, pp. 356–9 at p. 356 and Roughead, *Trial of Oscar Slater*, pp. xxx.

[110] Ibid.

[111] Ibid.

[112] Ibid., pp. xxx–xxxi.

[113] Ibid.

[114] NRS, Justiciary Court, Criminal Case File 1914–1948: Oscar Slater, Evidence heard at the Inquiry held by the Sheriff of Lanarkshire, 23rd–25th of April 1914, Testimony of Detective John Thomson Trench, HH16/111, p. 3.

Dawson Birrell (niece of the victim Marion Gilchrist) at 19 Blythswood Drive on the 23rd of December 1908 to ask her what Helen Lambie told her with regard to A.B. on the night of the murder, when she paid her a visit. He did as instructed, and the witness confirmed that Lambie had said to her 'I think it was A.B. I am sure that it was A.B.' Miss Birrell also told Trench that Detectives Pyper and Dornan had also visited her and told her that Lambie had named the same suspect to them.[115] Trench claimed that these two detectives, alongside Superintendent Douglas, had accordingly drove to the house of A.B. to make enquiries, but he did not know what had transpired with regard to their investigation.[116] Trench said he had handed Miss Birrell's statement to Chief Superintendent Ord and was told that Superintendent Douglas had told his superior officer that he ' … was convinced that A.B. had nothing to do with it'.[117]

Trench then testified that he went to see Helen Lambie on the 3rd of January 1909 to see if she could identify Oscar Slater from a sketch, which he considered was a 'fair representation' of him. She could not. She said plainly that she ' … did not know him'. Rather, she still maintained that A.B. was the culprit saying, 'It's gey [considerably] funny if it wasn't him I saw ….'[118] Trench then explained to the Inquiry that he believed Helen Lambie dropped the notion that A.B. was the killer because no-one would support her contention. However, from his perspective, the notion that A.B. was the killer explained why the culprit was able to get access to the house when Lambie had left the premises locked when she went on her errand; he was a known and frequent visitor, and Miss Gilchrist had allowed him inside.[119]

Trench also submitted additional damning testimony which demonstrated the investigative failings in this case. He stated that the key prosecution witness Mary Barrowman had lied, either in her original statement to him or in her trial testimony, as the two were completely different.[120] Furthermore, he could provide evidence from Colin Maccallum, Barrowman's employer, which proved that she did *not* deliver a package to an address on the night of the murder, an errand which she claimed situated her near the crime scene. Rather, she had made that delivery three days earlier and was instead, at a Band of Hope meeting, nowhere near the Queen's Terrace area.[121] Trench advised the makeshift courtroom that Mr Maccallum had been told by Detective Pyper (in his presence) not to say anything about this evidence to anyone, ' … as it would upset the whole case, and he might get into trouble about it'.[122] It was thus Detective-Lieutenant Trench's view that Mary Barrowman's testimony which had been so pivotal in the identification and subsequent conviction of Oscar Slater was ' … a cock-and-bull story of a young girl who was somewhat late in getting home and who wished to take the edge off by a little sensationalism'.[123]

---

[115] Ibid.
[116] Ibid.
[117] Ibid.
[118] Ibid., p. 5. Author's addition in parenthesis.
[119] Ibid.
[120] Ibid., p. 6.
[121] Ibid.
[122] Ibid., pp. 12–13.
[123] Ibid., p. 6.

Despite Trench's robust testimony, his professional credentials and his untarnished reputation, his evidence at 'The Secret Inquiry' unravelled and came to be seriously undermined by the testimony of various other individuals. Both Helen Lambie and Margaret Dawson Birrell flatly denied saying to Detective-Lieutenant Trench that A.B. had any involvement in the murder of Miss Gilchrist.[124] Indeed Helen Lambie was vehement about this, telling the Commissioner

> there is absolutely not one word of truth in it ... the whole story is false ... I wish to make it quite clear that neither to the Procurator Fiscal, nor to the police, nor to anyone else, did I make the statement that A.B. was the man I saw leaving the house.[125]

Moreover, the denials of the two women were corroborated by a further witness, Charles Frederick Cowan, who was with Miss Birrell when Helen Lambie visited her house on the night of the murder.[126] Then, came the testimony of Detective Inspector Andrew Nisbet of the Central Division of the Glasgow Police, who worked with Detective-Lieutenant Trench on the investigation into the Gilchrist murder. Detective Inspector Nisbet explained that he and Trench visited Helen Lambie in January of 1909 *on their own initiative* and not as ordered by their superior officers. He further testified that he had no recollection of his colleague showing the witness a sketch of Oscar Slater and that ' ... there was not such a word said in my presence' about A.B. being the man she saw leaving the Gilchrist residence.[127] Finally, came the testimony of Mary Barrowman's employer, Colin Maccallum. Although he no longer had the order books from 1908, he testified that Mary Barrowman *had* delivered the package on the night of the murder and this statement was reinforced by corroboratory evidence submitted by the recipient of the package, James Howat. Mr Maccallum said he had never made any statement to Detective-Lieutenant Trench and that his evidence on this matter was thus ' ... absolutely false'.[128]

Logically, we might consider why John Thomson Trench went to such lengths to submit this evidence if it was at best unsubstantiated or at worst false. For the purposes of this particular chapter, it is more important to consider the aftermath of his testimony

---

[124] NRS, Justiciary Court, Criminal Case File 1914–1948: Oscar Slater, Evidence heard at the Inquiry held by the Sheriff of Lanarkshire, 23rd–25th of April 1914, Testimony of Margaret Dawson Birrell, HH16/111, pp. 14–15.

[125] NRS, Justiciary Court, Criminal Case File 1914–1948: Oscar Slater, Evidence heard at the Inquiry held by the Sheriff of Lanarkshire, 23rd–25th of April 1914, Testimony of Helen Lambie, HH16/111, pp. 15–16.

[126] NRS, Justiciary Court, Criminal Case File 1914–1948: Oscar Slater, Evidence heard at the Inquiry held by the Sheriff of Lanarkshire, 23rd–25th of April 1914, Testimony of Charles Frederick Cowan, HH16/111, p. 15.

[127] NRS, Justiciary Court, Criminal Case File 1914–1948: Oscar Slater, Evidence heard at the Inquiry held by the Sheriff of Lanarkshire, 23rd–25th of April 1914, Testimony of Detective Inspector Andrew Nisbet, HH16/111, pp. 16–17.

[128] NRS, Justiciary Court, Criminal Case File 1914–1948: Oscar Slater, Evidence heard at the Inquiry held by the Sheriff of Lanarkshire, 23rd–25th of April 1914, Testimony of Colin Maccallum and Testimony of James Howat, HH16/111, p. 18 and p. 19, respectively.

and the personal cost of his revelations. Detailed testimony was provided at 'The Secret Inquiry' by Trench's superior officer, Chief Superintendent John Ord, about the 'alleged report' concerning Helen Lambie's statement regarding her recognition of the suspect. In a memo dated the 22nd of April 1914 and reiterated again at the Inquiry, Ord said that the first time he heard anything about this claim was on the 29th of March 1914 and not before. This was after he had read a *Daily Record* article some five days before, containing information that only someone in the original investigation would have been privy to. He then became determined to discover what the source of the leak to the press had been. Initially, Ord had been told that the mole was an officer who had since left the force, but he wanted to confirm this, and so wrote a private note to Detective-Lieutenant Trench requesting a meeting.[129] This took place on the 29th of March 1914 and Ord charged Trench to investigate the source of the leak.

At this request, Trench tried to convince Ord that Helen Lambie ' ... *had* made a statement to Miss Birrell on the night of the murder to the effect that man she saw leaving Miss Gilchrist's house was like Doctor Charteris'.[130] We can conclude from this revelation that presumably, Dr Francis James Charteris (a distant relative by marriage of the victim Marion Gilchrist) was the individual identified by the authorities as A.B. However, Chief Superintendent Ord corrected Trench and told him that this was ' ... altogether wrong', and that it was the lawyer Mr Archibald Hamilton Charteris (brother of Dr Charteris) whose name had somehow got connected with the case, but that in any event, this information had not come from Miss Gilchrist's servant.[131] Trench then reminded Ord that he had formerly provided him with all this evidence back in 1908/9 and that Ord had telephoned Superintendent Douglas to get his view on the matter, eventually reassuring him that there was no evidence linking any members of the Charteris family to the murder.[132]

Ord utterly disputed Trench's recollections, saying he was making a mistake, and he was adamant that as far as he was concerned ' ... I never heard Doctor Charteris name mentioned in connection with the murder'.[133] Changing tack, Ord then reported to Trench that two officers from New Scotland Yard had been leaking information to the solicitor David Cook and the press. On hearing this Detective-Lieutenant Trench ' ... became very uneasy' and exited their meeting.[134] Evidently John Ord was bemused and confused by this encounter. In any event, a few weeks later, on the 14th of April 1914, the Chief Superintendent attended a meeting in which John Thomson Trench was specifically named as the source of the leak. Taken by surprise,

---

[129] GUA FM Case Files 1906–1969 – Oscar Slater, Memo to the City of Glasgow Police by John Ord, 22nd April 1914, 2B/5/1. See also NRS, Justiciary Court, Criminal Case File 1914–1948: Oscar Slater, Evidence heard at the Inquiry held by the Sheriff of Lanarkshire, 23rd–25th of April 1914, Testimony of Chief Superintendent John Ord, HH16/111, pp. 31–2.

[130] NRS, Justiciary Court, Criminal Case File 1914–1948: Oscar Slater, Evidence heard at the Inquiry held by the Sheriff of Lanarkshire, 23rd–25th of April 1914, Testimony of Chief Superintendent John Ord, HH16/111, pp. 31–2.

[131] Ibid.
[132] Ibid.
[133] Ibid.
[134] Ibid.

initially Ord tried to defend his officer from the allegations being made, but the individuals present said that they had it on good authority that Detective-Lieutenant Trench was indeed the mole.[135] Ord challenged Trench about this later that night in a heated telephone conversation asking directly whether he had given David Cook any information relating to the Gilchrist case. Trench denied this vehemently.[136] However, in his testimony at 'The Secret Inquiry' Chief Superintendent Ord stated that it *was* Trench who supplied the information to external parties, explaining his officer's actions by saying: 'I know his weakness for notoriety.'[137] By structuring his testimony in this way, and in reaching this conclusion, Ord had skilfully moved the Inquiry and its Commissioner away from any meaningful consideration of this sensational new information and the potential of an alternative suspect to Oscar Slater. Thus rather than the Inquiry challenging the procedural aspects of the investigation of this case and the subsequent prosecution, its efforts had become diverted towards the discreditation, humiliation and persecution of the apparent quisling, Detective-Lieutenant Trench.

This initiative began almost instantaneously as at the Inquiry, Trench's personal history was utilized to portray him as an individual with a chequered past, undermining contemporary notions of him as a gallant, dutiful officer. The Commissioner heard that Trench had been born into relative poverty at Lasswade, Midlothian, in January 1869 and had become familiar with the Scottish justice system when he was convicted of theft at the age of eleven, although dismissed with an admonition (reprimand).[138] He joined the Royal Highlanders (the 'Black Watch') in January 1886 when he was just seventeen (after lying to the enrolment officer, saying he was nineteen) but his service record was littered with reprimands for being ill-kempt, for being late, but most typically, for being drunk and creating a disturbance. He was regularly fined and confined to barracks for his bad behaviour.[139] Trench lost all his stripes and his merit badges, but none of these disciplinary measures restrained him as he then went absent without leave, much to the fury of his commanding officers. This escapade earned him a sentence of imprisonment at hard labour for twenty-one days with stoppages (presumably of pay and food).[140] Despite this incarceration, Trench's bad behaviour continued and he was eventually transferred to the army reserve early in 1893, shortly before joining Glasgow's police force just a few months later. Even there, the Inquiry were told, although his habitual waywardness dissipated to a large extent, it did not disappear entirely as he was fined 5s. on the 24th of September 1896 for disorderly conduct.[141] These insalubrious details, together with the various rebuttals of his

---

[135] Ibid.
[136] Ibid.
[137] Ibid.
[138] NRS, Justiciary Court, Trial of Oscar Slater, 1908–1928, Papers relating to the 1914 Inquiry, AD21/15/6.
[139] Ibid.
[140] Ibid.
[141] Ibid. The Inquiry documentation also noted that John Thomson Trench's brother, Robert, was dismissed from the Police Force in Glasgow for obtaining a reward by false statement. He was latterly convicted of theft. The family history of Mr John Thomson Trench was tracked using records found at www.ancestry.com (accessed 19 July 2019).

testimony, and the evidence he had leaked sensitive information to third parties, all formed part of a government white paper stemming from the Inquiry in June 1914, and must have done much to tarnish the detective's reputation.

Indeed, by September of 1914, Trench was clearly in trouble. Chief Constable James V. Stevenson sent a report to the Magistrate's Committee in the early days of the month notifying them that he had suspended Detective-Lieutenant Trench ' ... for the offence of communicating to a person who is not a member of the Glasgow Police Force ... '.[142] As Chief Constable Stevenson explained:

> Detective-Lieutenant Trench did not ask or receive my permission to communicate information or copies of documents to DC or to any other person, and I had no knowledge that he had done so until I was informed by the Sheriff immediately before his inquiry ...

> It was a great surprise and disappointment to me to learn that any officer of the Glasgow police, and particularly an officer of such rank, and one so trusted as Lieutenant Trench, should have entered into secret communication with a person outside the force, and should have taken advantage of the access to official records which his position of trust afforded him, to secretly copy and dispose of documents which he well knew to be confidential.[143]

Although Stevenson had been shown the letter that Trench had from the Secretary of State for Scotland asking him to submit his evidence, the Chief Constable dismissed this saying: 'No person except the Chief Constable could give such authority, and the production of this letter is an attempt to over-ride the authority of the Chief Constable.'[144] Stevenson also challenged Trench, that if he thought this information so pertinent, he should have raised it at the trial in 1908. Stevenson concluded by saying that Trench's actions were:

> a deliberate act of gross indiscipline and as subversive of authority. Moreover, his action is destructive of the confidence that should subsist between officers of the detective department in carrying out their duties to the public.[145]

When the Magistrates' Committee met to discuss the fate of Trench's career just a few weeks later, the detective tried to defend his actions to them, saying that in twenty-one years of service in the police force, he had never questioned the act of a superior and had never once been charged with ' ... an infringement of discipline'.[146] More

---

[142] NRS, Justiciary Court, Criminal Case File 1914–1948: Oscar Slater, HH16/111.
[143] SL, William Roughead Collection, R+343.1.S1.15/v2526, scrap book of documentation relating to the suspension of John Thomson Trench from the Police Force, September 1914.
[144] Ibid.
[145] Ibid.
[146] NRS, Justiciary Court, Criminal Case File 1914–1948: Oscar Slater, HH16/111.

importantly, whilst he acknowledged that although ' ... there was nothing in the A.B. incident', he maintained that all he was trying to do was ' ... remedy a terrible wrong'. He restated his belief that ' ... there may be something amiss' in relation to the Oscar Slater case as he did not think that the hammer was the murder weapon and he declared himself 'satisfied' of the man's innocence from his ' ... appearance and demeanour'.[147] Despite the fervent nature of his pleas, the senior magistrate Baillie Thomas McMillan recounted:

> As a Court we could do nothing but dismiss Lieutenant Trench in the interests of the discipline of the Force, and the meeting was unanimous. As a Bench we were sorry for Lieutenant Trench, but we had a duty, no matter how painful, to discharge, and we discharged that responsibility.[148]

As if this shameful, career-ending reprimand was not enough, more ignominy was set to befall Mr Trench just a few months later. For, after re-enlisting in the army and just as his regiment was about to leave for Gallipoli in May 1915, he was arrested on a charge of reset (or the selling or holding of stolen goods). As Trench himself later commented ' ... it seemed as if an attempt was being made to blast my life altogether'.[149]

What can arguably only be described as a 'vindictive' indictment on the part of the Scottish authorities was brought on the 7th of August 1915 at the High Court in Edinburgh. It charged three men – John McArthur, John Thomson Trench and David Cook (Thomson Trench's erstwhile confidante) – that 'acting in concert' on the 19th of January 1914 at 5 Annfield Place, Dennistoun, Glasgow,

> ... you did reset 24 alberts (chains), 627 rings, four curb bracelets, 28 bangles, 24 necklets, two pairs of sleeve links, nine sets of studs, 20 medals, 299 brooches, eight expanding wrist watches, 43 watches, 73 lockets, 95 charms, 29 pendants, eight scarf pins, one pair of ear-rings, one fob, and two necklets/pendants to the value of £535 15s 5d.[150]

There were three other charges in the indictment, but as they were directed specifically at John McArthur and he had absconded from justice, only the first charge applied against Trench and Cook. Both men pleaded not guilty.

Trench's declaration to the authorities made on the 14th May 1915 was read out in court as part of the trial proceedings and gave his version of what had transpired. Early in 1914, Trench was asked by Detective Sergeant Montgomery to investigate a burglary at Reis the jewellers in Jamaica Street, Glasgow. When he arrived at the scene, the then Detective-Lieutenant ' ... saw that the premises had been entered by cutting a hole in the ceiling from an Umbrella Makers' premises above'. On the basis of this,

---

[147] Ibid.
[148] Ibid.
[149] Ibid. See also Anonymous, 'A Policeman to Remember', p. 358 and Hunt, *Oscar Slater*, p. 183.
[150] NRS, Justiciary Court, Process Papers, Indictment, JC26/2925/205.

he had concluded ' ... that the burglary was the work of an expert gang'.[151] He then followed usual procedure in terms of getting a sense of what had been taken and its value and description, which he subsequently circulated via communication with the Central Police Office. He learned from the jeweller, Mr Reis, ' ... that a large quantity of jewellery had been taken ... it ran to something like £1700'.[152] After approximately four or five days, with the investigation going nowhere, Trench suggested to his fellow officer Detective Sergeant George Dickie (whilst the two were off-duty) whether their informant John McArthur should be approached for his help. Dickie said to his colleague, 'If it doesn't do any good it can't do any harm.'[153] Consequently, the two officers went off in search of McArthur and eventually found him in Crown Street. The Detective-Lieutenant asked McArthur for his help in tracing the thieves. McArthur said he didn't know anything about the matter and hadn't heard anything about it either, but promised that if he heard anything he would let them know.[154]

John Thomson Trench met McArthur a few days later. McArthur asked the detective if there was a reward being offered in the matter and the Detective-Lieutenant said that the Mr Buchanan of Guardian Assurance Company had offered one as his company were ' ... very anxious to recover the stolen property'.[155] McArthur said ' ... there was a party who he thought could give some information' but that he wanted to meet the insurance man first.[156] Trench subsequently took McArthur to Buchanan's house. McArthur told Buchanan that ' ... the articles could be recovered on making payment of the sum of £400'. Buchanan thought the sum unproblematic but added that he would need to consult with his Head Office before agreeing. The individuals present also discussed who would be the person responsible for returning the stolen goods. David Cook's name was mentioned at this point but when questioned, Trench could not recall who said this.[157] Out of the earshot of McArthur, the Detective-Lieutenant said to Buchanan that this arrangement was problematic due to his ' ... position as a Police Officer' and told the insurance man that as well as contacting his Head Office for permission, he would also need to have this cleared by Superintendent Lindsay in charge of the department and ' ... to consult with him for guidance in this matter'. Buchanan agreed to do this first thing in the morning.[158]

Detective-Lieutenant Trench briefed the Superintendent prior to Buchanan's arrival the next morning. The Superintendent was clearly uncertain about how to proceed in this matter and so referred the issue to the Chief Constable and the four men met together. Mr Buchanan pressed upon the Police Officers present the need for this deal to work out, because ' ... it was a serious thing for them and that they couldn't afford to let a thing like that slip past as it meant a saving of a good few hundred pounds to

---

[151] NRS, Justiciary Court, Process Papers, Declaration of Detective-Lieutenant John Thomson Trench, JC26/1915/105.
[152] Ibid.
[153] Ibid.
[154] Ibid.
[155] Ibid.
[156] Ibid.
[157] Ibid.
[158] Ibid.

his Company'.[159] This was because the arrangement would evidently reduce Reis's claim against the insurers of the jewellery. The Chief Constable understood the insurance man's position, but wished that McArthur had gone straight to Buchanan, so that the police had not become involved. He said in conclusion ' … he was afraid that Mr Buchanan would require to carry the matter through himself as the Police could not assist him in a matter of that kind'.[160] Despite hearing the Chief Constable's advice, Trench went to see David Cook immediately afterwards. After hearing the story, the lawyer said that ' … he could see nothing to prevent *him* as a Law Agent assisting in this matter'. The money was then handed to Cook who counted it and the men arranged to meet McArthur at 3 pm that day at the corner of Bath and Elmbank Street.[161]

John Thomson Trench and David Cook met McArthur and went to pub opposite the King's Theatre. They started discussions about the deal but Trench soon left because McArthur ' … was reluctant to say much in the presence of the police'.[162] Trench met up again with Cook at the Central Police Office about 8 or 9 pm that night, when the lawyer was able to report that Mr Buchanan had ' … recovered the stuff' and that it had been sent to valuators.[163] The next morning the Detective-Lieutenant reported everything to Superintendent Lindsay and asked what he should do in the matter, with reference to appropriating the stolen property. Lindsay told his officer to go to see the Fiscal, Mr Hart. There, Trench was told that ' … there was no use taking possession of such a mass of stolen property unless I was going to use it as productions against some person'. Mr Hart then recommended that the officer ' … keep up the enquiry and that if I got any evidence to connect the thieves with the stolen property to report to him further'.[164] The Detective-Lieutenant reported all this to his senior officer.[165]

Aside from Detective-Lieutenant Trench retaining a superficial involvement in the 'arrangement' that transpired against the advice of his superior officer, there seems to have been little evidence of illegality on his part in the testimony heard in court. This led some newspapers to describe the trial as one which had occurred ' … under circumstances in some respects almost akin to comic opera' and made Sir Arthur Conan Doyle describe the affair as a 'persecution' rather than a 'prosecution' of John Thomson Trench.[166] It seems that comparatively similar views were held by the prosecution in this case too! Although the Lord Advocate began his charge to the jury by emphasizing how serious a charge this was, especially when made against ' … men in the positions

---

[159] Ibid.
[160] Ibid.
[161] Ibid.
[162] Ibid.
[163] Ibid.
[164] Ibid.
[165] The contents of this declaration were all corroborated by the testimony of David Cook, who went as far as saying that if he was guilty of any crime, then his co-accused should be J.V. Stevenson, the Chief Constable of Glasgow, who knew of the matter – see NRS, Justiciary Court, Process Papers, Declaration of David Cook, Writer, JC26/1915/105.
[166] See *The Sunday Post*, 27th November 1927 and SL, William Roughead Collection, R+343.1.S1.15/v2526, scrapbook of documentation relating to the suspension of John Thomson Trench from the Police Force, September 1914.

which the accused have held and still hold', he then went on to problematize the case he and his legal team had made against the two men standing in the dock.[167]

First, he admitted that it is tricky to prove a charge of reset as you have to demonstrate that the individuals *knew* the goods to be stolen when they received them. He then noted that the crime was said to have occurred in January 1914 but as no charges were brought until May 1915, a lot of the witnesses brought to court to testify could not recollect the details associated with the events.[168] The Lord Advocate then referred to a letter dated the 20th of January 1914 which had been sent to the Chief Constable by Mr Buchanan informing the officer that the stolen property had been recovered intact. Buchanan wanted to write to ' … express my appreciation of the good offices of Detective Trench, as I am aware that without his assistance the matter could not have been carried through'. Mr Buchanan then said in the same correspondence that the company directors would undoubtedly want to recognize Trench's efforts on this matter.[169] This letter made plain that senior police officers knew of the arrangement that had been made with the informant and the insurance company. This was further corroborated by the production of a report written by John Thomson Trench to his immediate superiors and to the Procurator Fiscal on the 21st of January 1914.[170] Although various individuals (including the said Fiscal Mr Hart) had testified in court that they had *not* met with Trench about this case, the Lord Advocate asked the court to consider why the former detective would lie about these meetings in an official report to his superiors two days after the crime.[171]

The Lord Advocate concluded his summation by saying that ' … according to my judgement, there is no law that would justify you in finding the crime of reset has been committed under the circumstances disclosed here'. He went on to suggest the heart of what occurred when he said:

If a man received stolen goods for the purpose of handing them back to their owner, accepted a fee and carried out that purpose, you could not call that man a resetter. This is because in law, the resetters has to take possession of goods in order to prevent them being returned to their rightful owner. Thus, if there is anyone guilty of reset in this case, it is actually Mr Buchanan, who, according to the Lord Advocate: ' … took the goods away; he kept them for a night and then handed them over'. However, he did all this with the explicit purpose of returning the goods to the owner, so in Scots law this would not constitute reset.[172] Thus in sum I think nothing has been put that would justify you in bringing in a conviction against these two accused persons.[173]

---

[167] Glasgow City Archives, The Mitchell Library, Papers relating to Oscar Slater (1872–1948) Victim of Miscarriage of Justice, The Lord Justice Clerk's Charge to the Jury in the Trial of John Thomson Trench (1915), TD1560/5/9.
[168] Ibid.
[169] Ibid.
[170] Ibid.
[171] Ibid.
[172] It should be noted that in English law these actions may well equate with the Common Law offence of compounding a felony.

The jury, unsurprisingly after that direction *from the prosecution*, ' ... returned a unanimous verdict of not guilty in favour of both pannels [accused].'[174]

William Roughead's view of what had transpired against John Thomson Trench since his appearance at 'The Secret Inquiry' was to note that although the police are sometimes criticized for the nature of their involvement in a specific case, to him, there was ' ... no incident more deplorable than what occurred here' in relation to this farcical trial which seemed to have occurred purely to demean and humiliate the erstwhile police officer.[175] In any event, after being dismissed from the police force and in the aftermath of the trial against him, Trench returned to his regiment, the fifth Battalion Royal Scots Fusiliers and served sporadically in Egypt and in France during the First World War, being invalided home on several occasions. Evidently, his health had been undermined by his various experiences, and Quartermaster-Sergeant John Thomson Trench died on the 13th of May 1919 at the age of fifty.[176]

Conclusion: Who did kill Marion Gilchrist?

If we can now assume that Oscar Slater was innocent of any involvement in the murder of Miss Marion Gilchrist, then it is evident that her killer was not brought to justice. So do we have any indication as to who the murderer might have been? Well it is evident that the police did, in fact, consider and interview a range of potential suspects, other than Slater, at least in the immediate aftermath of the murder.[177] Police informants also came forward with a range of individuals they believed capable of the crime, although this typically occurred when the named individual owed the informant money![178] One man, George Ewart, was even arrested for the crime, although subsequently released and two other individuals confessed to their involvement in the murder of Miss Gilchrist, but were quickly eliminated from police enquiries.[179] Officers did pay considerable attention to a man called Patrick Nugent purported to be the paramour

---

[173] Ibid.

[174] Ibid.

[175] Roughead, *Trial of Oscar Slater*, p. xiii.

[176] See ibid as well as Anonymous, 'A Policeman to Remember', p. 359. David Cook died just a few years later on the 3rd of October 1921. He was just forty-eight. See *The Sunday Post*, 11th December 1927.

[177] From a detailed analysis of the paperwork related to the early days of the police investigation individuals such as Elias Cohen and Harry Harper had their photocards confiscated and were kept under surveillance. Other named suspects included Robert Moffat, James Bow, William Proudfoot, James Armstrong and Dr J. Spencer-Daniell. See GUA FM Case Files 1906–1969 – Oscar Slater, 2B/5/1/111; 2B/5/1/116 and 2B/5/1/132.

[178] A good example of a suspect derived in this way is William Goodfellow – see GUA FM Case Files 1906–1969 – Oscar Slater, 2B/5/3/22.

[179] For the arrest of George Ewart on the 23rd of December 1908, see GUA FM Case Files 1906–1969 – Oscar Slater, 2B/5/1. For confessions made, see that of Robert Johnstone and a detailed letter sent to the *Glasgow Weekly Mail* in June 1909 by an evidently Irish individual – see respectively GUA FM Case Files 1906-1969 – Oscar Slater, 2B/5/3/149 and SL, William Roughead Collection, R+343.1.S1.15/v2527/191.

of Helen Lambie, Miss Gilchrist's domestic servant, but they found no evidence which materially linked him to the crime or its aftermath.[180]

The main reason that these particular individuals became linked to the murder at Queen's Terrace, and indeed the reason that Oscar Slater came to be associated with that crime, was the supposition that the murder was committed in order to expedite an act of robbery or theft. Most of the named suspects were small-time crooks or petty thieves who knew the value of stolen goods. However, if we consider the fact that only a single brooch was seemingly taken, when there was an opportunity to steal much more in the way of jewellery, plate, silverware, artwork, furniture and other items, an acquisitive motive seems perhaps implausible.[181] Moreover, given the care which Miss Gilchrist paid to her own personal security and possessions, how would anyone on the outside know the value of goods in her apartment, unless they had already observed it? Indeed, a closer examination of the crime scene evidence suggests that it was documentation of some sort that the intruder was looking for, rather than any plunder.[182] Next if we consider the nature of the debased assault on Marion Gilchrist, we might assume that it was an episode of homicidal brutality. Yet, surely such a crazed individual would have been easily identifiable to the authorities or would have likely tried to kill again in the same fashion. It is more likely that the demise of Miss Gilchrist began with a personal altercation which escalated into unadulterated rage and prolonged savagery. Cumulatively, this supposition, and the mystery of how the killer gained access to the premises, suggests that the killer and victim knew one another, or they were related. This coincides with Helen Lambie's acknowledgement to some parties, in the immediate aftermath of the murder, that she recognized the man she saw leaving her mistress's apartment.

It is clear that various male relatives of Miss Gilchrist *were* considered suspects. Indeed, only a few days after the murder, Detective-Lieutenant John Thomson Trench noted that three separate sets of families, all related to Marion Gilchrist, had been investigated and their photographs shown to the key witnesses in the case.[183] According to an anonymous letter sent to the Chief Constable of Glasgow Police on the 25th of December 1908, just a few days after the murder, some of Marion Gilchrist's family were 'wild' at her getting all of the money in her father's will when he died and they

---

[180] See GUA FM Case Files 1906–1969 – Oscar Slater, 2B/5/4/231 and NRS, Justiciary Court, Criminal Case File 1909: Oscar Slater, Letter to the Secretary of State for Scotland, 18th May 1909, HH16/109/1. One of the papers alleges that Patrick Nugent was an alias for Hugh Cameron, one of the witnesses for the defence in the Oscar Slater trial who was a friend of Slater and who substantiated his alibi. It suggested that as Cameron was married, but wanted to 'step out' with Helen Lambie, he used the name Patrick Nugent to cover his tracks. If true, this would link Helen Lambie with Oscar Slater, but there is no evidence to substantiate the suggestion that Nugent and Cameron were one and the same man.

[181] See NRS, Justiciary Court, Process Papers, Inventory of Possessions, JC34/1/32/9.

[182] See Roughead, *Trial of Oscar Slater*, pp. xxviii; Hunt, *Oscar Slater*, p. 148 and Park (1927) *The Truth about Oscar Slater*, p. 44.

[183] See SL, William Roughead Collection, Excerpt from Glasgow Police Archives, R+343.1.S1.15/v2527/473.

had '... bore her a grudge ever after'.[184] Attention soon focussed further after this, not on the Charteris brothers seemingly identified by Helen Lambie, or on the Lee brothers from another side of the family, but on the four Birrell brothers, nephews of Miss Gilchrist who were the sons of her sister Janet from her marriage to Walter Birrell.[185] Other anonymous letters subsequently arrived and pointed the finger specifically at one of the nephews who '... seemed to put the fear of death into others' and who '... everyone was warned not to turn their back on'.[186] Two of the nephews – William and Wingate – had strong alibis for the night of the murder[187] and another, James Aitken Birrell claimed, when interviewed, that he had '... never met the victim or conversed with her'.[188]

This left the police to concentrate on George Gilchrist Birrell. He admitted in a statement to the police in January 1909 that he had sent his wife to visit his aunt when they were '... in straightened circumstances' to ask for her assistance. She refused. However, he did remember his wife telling him, after her visit, that Miss Gilchrist was well off as she saw her wearing '... a good many rings' and was '... gorgeously dressed'. He also acknowledged his family's bitterness about Miss Gilchrist receiving more than her share of her father's estate, but noted his own father did not want to contest the matter.[189] Interestingly, archival research has revealed evidence

---

[184] See GUA FM Case Files 1906-1969 – Oscar Slater, 2B/5/1/28. This grudge seems to be more evident amongst the men in the family, rather than the women and that supposition is borne out by Marion Gilchrist's will, where only female relatives benefitted and explicit instructions were provided to ensure that the male relations of the beneficiaries were not to have access to any of the monies bequeathed, nor to dictate or in any way control what the women spent the money on – see NRS, Justiciary Court, Process Papers, Last Will and Testament of Miss Marion Gilchrist, JC34/1/32/18 and *The Scotsman*, 29th December 1908, p. 4.

[185] There were six boys born into the Birrell family: John, Walter, William, Windgate, George and James, who was the oldest. There are no records of the whereabouts of John or Walter and they may have died in childbirth. The family history of the Birrell family was tracked using records found at www.ancestry.com (accessed 20 July 2019). It should be noted that there is no evidence of the existence of an Austin Birrell, the co-protagonist (along with Dr Francis Charteris) in Jack House's investigation into the Gilchrist murder – see J. House (2002) *Square Mile of Murder* (Edinburgh: Black and White Publishing), pp. 140-84.

[186] See, for instance, GUA FM Case Files 1906-1969 – Oscar Slater, 2B/5/1/119 and GUA FM Case Files 1906-1969 – Oscar Slater, 2B/5/3/48.

[187] A telegraph sent to Glasgow City Police from Superintendent Cameron of Limehouse, London notes that William Birrell was seen by witnesses at his home in North Woolwich (London) on the night of the murder – see GUA FM Case Files 1906-1969 – Oscar Slater, 2B/5/1. A letter dated 31st of December 1908 written by Policeman Charles Hatton of North Woolwich (London) to Glasgow City Police notes that in the days and nights around the murder, Windgate Birrell was too ill with consumption to have travelled to Glasgow – see GUA FM Case Files 1906-1969 – Oscar Slater, 2B/5/1/135. An interesting but largely implausible theory suggesting that Dr Francis Charteris and Windgate Birrell worked together to kill Marion Gilchrist in order to get hold of her will is presented in T. Toughill (1993) *Oscar Slater: The Mystery Solved* (Edinburgh: Canongate Press). The involvement of either the Charteris or the Birrell family is roundly rejected through the detailed research evident in R. Whittington-Egan (2001) *The Oscar Slater Murder Story: New Light on a Classic Miscarriage of Justice* (Glasgow: Neil Wilson Publishing).

[188] The original precognitions taken from the Birrell brothers were included in the papers of 'The Secret Inquiry'; see NRS, Justiciary Court, Trial of Oscar Slater, 1908-1928, Papers relating to the 1914 Inquiry – Testimony of James Aitken Birrell, AD21/15/6.

[189] NRS, Justiciary Court, Trial of Oscar Slater, 1908-1928, Papers relating to the 1914 Inquiry – Testimony of George Gilchrist Birrell, AD21/15/6.

from two other witnesses which arguably intensifies the spotlight on George Birrell as a potential suspect. The first was an interview conducted with the servant of Marion Gilchrist's sister Elizabeth, Margaret Fraser, who told the police that George Gilchrist visited her mistress on a few occasions and ' ... was always very debauched in appearance' and typically begged for money. Elizabeth Gilchrist her mistress ' ... was very much afraid of him' and asked Margaret to do her best not to admit him. Specifically the servant was told by her mistress that ' ... she was in terror of him pouncing upon her when he was in'.[190] The second interesting piece of evidence is from another police interview in January 1909, but with William J. Oliver, who knew George Gilchrist and recalled him talking about a wealthy old aunt that he had, who refused to help him when he was down on his luck. Gilchrist said to Oliver, 'If I get a chance, I will smash her to pulp.'[191]

The reason George Gilchrist Birrell was not pursued is that by January 1909, the police were already convinced that Oscar Slater was the chief – and only – suspect worth pursuing for the murder of Marion Gilchrist. Their wilfulness in this regard, concentrated their efforts solely on bringing *him* to justice and ensuring that the little evidence they had, could be aligned to *him* as the culprit. They felt vindicated and victorious, when the Edinburgh Police reported during the trial (on the 6th of May 1909) that once, when they escorted Oscar Slater from the dock back to the cells, he confessed to having being involved – *with another* – in the murder of Miss Gilchrist.[192] Curiously, given that this confession was said in front of three police officers, it is strange that not more was made of this, by the press or the prosecution at the time.[193] This may have something to do with the fact that the three men gave completely contradictory statements regarding what Oscar Slater actually said when they were each later interviewed by their Glaswegian counterparts.[194] Given everything that we know about this case and the lengths the authorities would go to in order to 'save face', was this supposed confession just another fabrication and manipulation to that end?

It is clear that well over a century after Marion Gilchrist was murdered in her own home, a swathe of unanswered questions remain about this tragic and brutal event. Perhaps most importantly of all, it would seem that no-one has been brought to justice for this crime; however, we are not even entirely sure of that! What we can be certain of is that this chapter has shown the investigation into the murder of Miss Gilchrist to be the most flawed, prejudicial and mismanaged in the history of British justice. The rotten tentacles of the deliberate negligence displayed had a significant reach as it involved and impacted upon family members of the victim as well as her friends who may have

---

[190] See a memo from Glasgow CID regarding police interviews conducted on the 7th of January 1909 with various individuals – GUA FM Case Files 1906–1969 – Oscar Slater, 2B/5/5.

[191] Ibid.

[192] See the memo notifying Detective Superintendent John Ord of Slater's confession – GUA FM Case Files 1906–1969 – Oscar Slater, 2B/5/6/1. See also Hunt, *Oscar Slater*, p. 126.

[193] I can only find the confession mentioned in two newspaper reports; see *The Scotsman*, 8th May 1909, p. 8 and *Fife Free and Kirkcaldy Guardian*, 8th May 1909, p. 2.

[194] Further detailed scrutiny of the interview transcripts of the three police officers who heard the confession highlighted significant differences between them – see ibid as well as SL, William Roughead Collection, R+343.1.S1.15/v2527/135.

known more about the murder than they admitted; suspects who may or may not have been innocent; witnesses (including apparent 'experts') who may or may not have been accurate or honest in their testimony; and even police officers and other authority figures, some of whom were prepared to question what had transpired and speak out in the interests of truth and others who were clearly capable of corruption, bloody mindedness and vindictiveness in order to maintain the façade of their infallibility both in 1908 and in the two decades to follow. Did they close ranks to protect slipshod serving officers? Did they react to a burdensome pressure to get results? Or, was there an element of institutionalized anti-Semitism? Whilst their reasons remain unclear, the failure to bring these latter authority figures to book and to make them accountable for the shameful practices evident in the Gilchrist investigation is nothing less than a scandalous embarrassment and a blatant, inescapable example of injustice laid bare for Scottish and indeed British society. The fact that this remains as true today as the first third of the twentieth century is a further stain on the memory of the blameless, vulnerable victim in this case, Miss Marion Gilchrist (1826–1908).[195]

---

[195] The family history of Miss Marion Gilchrist was tracked using records found at www.ancestry.com (accessed 16 June 2019).

8

'Police Fiasco', 'The Black Army', 'Devil Dodgers' and 'Humbug': The Apparent 'Inevitably' of Unfair Blasphemy Trials up to 1922

David Nash
Oxford Brookes University

Introduction

This chapter investigates the cases of blasphemous libel brought against Ernest Pack, Thomas William Stewart and John William Gott in the Edwardian period and beyond. These are seen as the culmination of both problems for authorities charged with applying and administering the law, as opportunities for defendants to point out the problems with the conception and application of the law and the enduring problems that surrounded attempts to prosecute for the crime of blasphemous libel. These issues had been endemic throughout the nineteenth century, but came to a head in the first quarter of the twentieth century. The chapter ends by suggesting how this 'culmination' was responsible for initiating the twentieth-century campaigns for reform of the law of blasphemy in England.

Context

The crime of blasphemy has always produced judicial proceedings that could readily be made to appear to be steadfastly out of the ordinary. Its antecedent crime of heresy regularly courted the harsh judgement of contemporaries and posterity alike, as the twin imperatives of new orthodoxies or growing toleration regularly turned them into unfortunate and inhumane anachronisms of a previous age. The late seventeenth-century blasphemy trials in England were also tied up with issues of religious dissent and individual struggle against tyrannical state oppression. Famously, the trial of James Nayler, drawn out during the 1650s under the regime of the Commonwealth, degenerated into a profound discussion about whether the very judicial procedures themselves even existed to try him, all conducted while the unfortunate Nayler languished in a less than salubrious prison cell.[1] Such episodes, strung out over four centuries and more, constituted fertile ground for the caustic examination of blasphemy trials and persecution in a later pantheon of libertarian struggle for freedom of opinion.[2]

Such problems were exacerbated by the end of the eighteenth century when governmental action could be painted as oppression of legitimate opinion in the shape of Jacobin ideas. The forces of conservativism that sought to combat this tide were unwieldy and scarcely polished in their application of judicial power. So often they chose defenceless unpopular targets, or appeared embarrassingly tight lipped or foolish in the face of the articulate, learned or defiant. The prosecuting council, Thomas Erskine, in 1797 famously showed sympathy for the humble salesman of Paine's *Age of Reason* who had been made a hapless victim by draconian action.[3] In 1817 the government also got its fingers badly burned from its attempt to prosecute William Hone. In this instance, an erudite and skilled writer and orator clearly enjoyed himself in demonstrating the clumsiness of the case against him. From this debacle, the government emerged as intellectually underpowered, humourless and even institutionally philistine.[4]

By the time Richard Carlile and his shopmen became a veritable conveyor belt of cases throughout the 1820s and early 1830s, the concept of the inevitably unfair trial for blasphemy was becoming well established. Throughout these trials, Carlile and later his wife, sister and other fellow defendants turned the courtroom into an arena of struggle. It became a place where they attempted to discredit the cases they were called to answer and all proceedings therein. Judges who rashly sought to silence offenders were rounded on and their actions publicized beyond the court to an eager radically inclined public. The right to mount a legitimate defence, when questioned, was turned into pamphlets publicizing a so-called Suppressed Defence.[5] Similarly the actions of the government to prosecute were exposed as simultaneously tyrannical and cowardly, since it chose to hide behind the thinly veiled ineptitude of the Society for the Suppression of Vice.[6] Supposedly independent witnesses who had purchased blasphemous material from Carlile's shop were exposed as in the pay of the government; others could readily be persuaded to admit that they had not read the publications in question, nor had they been morally compromised by their contents.[7]

---

[1] D.S. Nash (2007) *Blasphemy in the Christian World: A History* (Oxford: Oxford University Press), pp. 119–23.

[2] See H. Bradlaugh-Bonner (1934) *Penalties upon Opinion* (London: Watts and Company), *passim* and D.S. Nash (1999) *Blasphemy in Modern Britain 1789 to the Present* (Aldershot: Ashgate), *passim*.

[3] L. Levy (1993) *Blasphemy: Verbal Offense Against the Sacred from Moses to Salman Rushdie* (New York: Knopf), pp. 336–8

[4] For more on William Hone, see F.M. Hackwood (1912) *William Hone: His Life and Times* (London: Fisher Unwin). See also Nash, *Blasphemy in Modern Britain*, pp. 80–4.

[5] Anonymous (1821) *Suppressed Defence: The Defence of Mary Anne Carlile to the Vice Society's Indictment against the Appendix to the Theological Works of Thomas Paine* (London: R. Carlile).

[6] For more on this, see P. Harling (2001) 'The Law of Libel and the Limits of Repression, 1790–1832', *Historical Journal*, 44, 1, pp. 107–34.

[7] R. Carlile (1822) *Report of the Trial of Mrs Susannah Wright for Publishing, in His Shop, the Writings and Correspondence of R. Carlile; before Chief Justice Abbott, and a Special Jury in the Court of King's Bench, Guildhall, London, on Monday, July 8, 1822: Indictment at the instance of the Society for the Suppression of Vice* (London: R. Carlile).

Beyond these assaults on procedure, such defendants were also dangerously adept at displaying apparently honest motives, since they frequently offered to withdraw such material from the public gaze if it could be demonstrated to be harmful.

Martyrdom was here worn like a well-tailored coat, and the Carlile agitations established something of a blueprint in communicating the nature of blasphemy prosecutions to the reading public at large. Blasphemy 'cases' and court appearances were contested territory, as the defendants became skilful and erudite in 'writing up' and narrativizing these. One particularly crucial effect of this was to outrage and motivate a sympathetic readership. The other side of this narrative was, however, on many occasions almost entirely missing. The agents of authority, prosecution and particularly judgement and punishment were largely silent on the matter. Whilst the public face of such prosecutions was a picture of sustained injustice and folly, it is frequently only the historian who has access to the Home Office files and opinions who can unravel the motivations of authority, both in general and at significant junctures in high-profile cases. In truth, the significant achievement of defendants was not to flout the law, or even occasionally to get the better of it, but instead their creation of a conduit through which stories of injustice and overly biased procedural operation could be disseminated. This was their greatest weapon with which to damage the law.[8] It is possible to argue that this phenomenon significantly influenced the wider cultural reception of blasphemy cases and the public profile of the offence in general. With only one side of the argument evident in public discourse, a picture of anti-intellectual tyranny was sometimes painted almost effortlessly, aided by the 'opposition's' apparent preference for silence.

The middle of the nineteenth century witnessed the draconian and ill-judged case against Thomas Pooley. This individual had scrawled godless graffiti over fences and gateposts in rural Devon. The court proceedings marooned an insane man, with diminished responsibility, to abortively defend his own interests in a courtroom peopled with some of the finest legal brains in the land. This case, which occurred in 1857, attracted the attention of J.S. Mill who saw this as an example of the sustained barbarism that still undermined freedom and democracy in England.[9] The early 1880s saw George William Foote turn the case against him and the *Freethinker* into a drawn out and sustained martyrdom that was written up and syndicated through his newspapers and pamphlets. His focus on the trial proceedings took opinion down a,

---

[8] This was commenced by Richard Carlile with numerous pamphlets circulating in the 1820s. This was echoed later by Holyoake. It was arguably recast into an art form by the later cases against George William Foote in which the trials and Foote's subsequent imprisonment and release were both drip-fed to his weekly readership of the *Freethinker* and subsequently written up at exhaustive length to become free standing and widely sold pamphlets. See, for example, G.W. Foote (1932 edition) *Defence of Free Speech, Being a Three Hours' Address to the Jury in the Court of Queen's Bench before Lord Coleridge on April 24, 1883 – New Edition with and Introduction by H. Cutner* (London: Progressive Publishing Co.) and G.W. Foote (1886) *Prisoner for Blasphemy* (London: Progressive Publishing Co.)

[9] T. Toohey (1987) 'Blasphemy in Nineteenth Century England: The Pooley Case and its Background', *Victorian Studies*, XXX, 3, pp. 315–33. The Pooley case, as noted by Toohey, prompted Mill's assault upon the verdict and how it was emblematic of many wider issues which tainted contemporary British culture.

by now, well-trodden path illuminated with dangerous partiality, anomalies, malice and injustice. In 1908 the case against Harry Boulter was portrayed as the Common Law of Blasphemous Libel, singling out the unpolished plebeian street corner rebel rouser, whilst cynically leaving the intellectually polished (and published) blasphemer to escape the attentions of the law.[10]

Whilst we might expect such defendants to play to the gallery, pitching the shining forces of enlightenment against irrationally devious darkness, it is apparent that these episodes all also tell us something else. From the perspective of the authorities, dealing with the crime of blasphemy was scarcely easy and contained a plethora of pitfalls for the careless, nervous, over confident or unwary. First, the apparent malice and premeditation that defendants found so easy to invoke were only episodic rather than sustained and concerted policy. The authorities at any given moment were equally susceptible to being stung by public pressure to do something about blasphemy. This was generally conceived of in the public mind (or that of self-appointed agents of morality) as intervention of some kind. Either publications ought to be confiscated, or street corner oratory circumscribed. What preoccupied the public mind were intense incidents of outrage and the casual encounter with such material, although it is equally possible that providential concerns may conceivably have additionally motivated some.[11]

But equally what were those placed in charge of gatekeeping dangerous religious opinion supposed to do? Attempts to restrict such opinion were often counterproductive and indeed, on occasion, farcical, having been sprung from misunderstanding and ineptitude. The latter was largely explained by the infrequency of the law's application which itself became recast as a grievance by defendants indicting it as the former. Blasphemous material circulated in Carlile's time at a far faster rate than normal, since the decision to deny such material the protection of copyright rendered it spectacularly fair game and profitable for the producers of pirated editions![12] Likewise, when pounced upon, the attention of seizure and the road to prosecution exposed such activities to the oxygen of publicity. This, in itself, fed the free speech arguments of defendants. If it was to your taste, you could consume the publications deemed blasphemous, alongside the highly coloured reports highlighting their nature and the legal proceedings against them drafted by defendants. The sustained power of this notoriously backfired on the Home Secretary Sir William Harcourt (1827–1904) in the early 1880s with his ill-judged treatment of George William Foote's prosecution and subsequent custodial sentence.[13] After this, Home Office Civil Servants regularly worried about Harcourt's appetite for intervention, constructively working to ensure that the *Freethinker* was thereafter left alone and denied further publicity. Given how

---

[10] For an account of the Boulter case, see Nash (1999) *Blasphemy in Britain*. For the Home Office view of the pitfalls of dealing with Harry Boulter, see also the National Archives, Home Office Papers (hereafter HO), Registered Papers, Prosecutions for Blasphemy, 144/871/160552.

[11] See D.S. Nash (2008) '"To Prostitute Morality, Libel Religion, and Undermine Government": Blasphemy and the Strange Persistence of Providence in Britain since the Seventeenth Century', *Journal of Religious History*, 32, 4, pp. 439–56.

[12] See Nash (1999) *Blasphemy in Britain*, chapter Three.

[13] See ibid., chapter Four.

sustained and sophisticated defendant narratives had become, this readily explains how policing agencies often defaulted to evading the prosecution process entirely, or attempted to minimize the antagonization of individuals at every stage of the judicial investigation.[14]

There was also the thoroughly problematic issue of what a definition of victory looked like for the authorities. Sometimes it might have seemed even temporarily silencing them was enough. If the authorities in their various forms ever hoped that blasphemy prosecutions proved to be a forcible deterrent this was, to say the least, scarcely proven. This of course was a 'dark figure' and could never be measured. In the long run it was never clear whether blasphemy prosecutions proved to be incentive or deterrent. Skilled defendants could paint such laws as both either and both, according to their own taste and situation. Thus, the apparent logic of when to proceed against blasphemy or when to encourage others to do so was never nearly as logical as it seemed.

The defendants in such cases also had a number of factors running in their favour which could serve to make blasphemy prosecutions problematic. Blasphemy as an offence always contained within it an especially murky relationship with the concept of *Mens Rea*. Whilst admitting to publishing such works, or vending them unwittingly to government servants was instinctively what prosecutions tried to focus on, it was nonetheless difficult to prove that the individuals concerned possessed 'guilty minds'. This issue regularly provoked free speech/liberty narratives as well as enlightenment-inspired ones of undertaking work of cultural and social value to the population at large. The last of these were the speciality of Richard Carlile and Susannah Wright who further ensured that their respective orations of such ideals were publicized far and wide.[15]

Despite regularly painting the offence, and its prosecution, as being arbitrary, blasphemers had a considerable degree of discretion in 'arranging' for themselves to be prosecuted when it suited them. Progressively lowering the tone and increasing the vehemence of the blasphemous content could eventually result in prosecution – as was the case with George William Foote in 1882–1883. Changing the mode, means and place of sale could also escalate the application of the legal process. This last action

---

[14] This did prevent a considerable number of prosecutions going forward where evading publicity became the prime motive for inaction. Such a motive could spread as far as managing the incarceration of the convicted. Sir William Harcourt arguably miscalculated in bringing the full force of detention down upon George William Foote. However, subsequent authorities were much more scrupulous in ensuring that 'prisoners for blasphemy' were not singled out for special forms of treatment, nor denied any legitimate privileges offered by the prison system. This was precisely to avoid feeding narratives of iniquitous treatment in prison. See, for example, the later imprisonment of Harry Boulter in the Edwardian period. In this episode the Home Office took considerable pains to ensure the prison chaplain had not antagonized a potentially dangerous adversary. See National Archives, HO, Registered Papers, Prosecutions for Blasphemy, 144/871/160552. See also National Archives, HO, Registered Papers, Prosecutions for Blasphemy, 144/114/A25454 which noted that even Sir William Harcourt, the militant opponent of secularists and their blasphemies, was concerned at the conduct of the prison governor whose negligence almost prevented Foote and his compatriot Ramsey form conferring between their first and second trial.

[15] See Nash (1999) *Blasphemy in Britain*, Chapter Three.

would occasionally bounce local policing authorities into action. This intervention in matters of 'religious doctrine' was often undertaken with the utmost reluctance, an attitude often appreciated with considerable relish by would-be blasphemers. As such blasphemy appears in the nineteenth century to have been a strange offence, analogous to other forms of radical publishing where defendants would actively contemplate serial transgression with wider goals and targets in view.[16] This sometimes meant that there was not so much a single definitive case in each instance, but instead often a series of cases where prosecution and defence arguments built upon one another. It was also true that the serial nature of these cases meant that procedural issues and problems were transferred from case to adjacent case on a regular basis.[17]

The conduct of judges was also a lingering grievance which could regularly be dusted down for the creation of an 'unfair trial' narrative. It was relatively easy to depict individual judges as unscrupulous agents of covert Christian vested interests. More ambitiously, they could also be cast as explicit agents of state repression. This came especially easy to radicals who were able to cite the primary piece of jurisprudence in the area. This had come from Sir Matthew Hale (1609–1676) in the case against John Taylor in 1678 where he had pronounced that 'Christianity was part and parcel of the law of the land' and that assaults upon one of these entities constituted an assault upon the other.[18] This typecast judges as defenders of their own vested interest in each and every blasphemy case.

The preceding assumption could gain wider and deeper credibility when the precise actions of individual judges and law enforcement agents were scrutinized. Many blasphemers realized this scrutiny was an opportunity and made considerable efforts to ensure the prosecuted works and opinions contained therein were extensively aired in court. These frequently had the visible impact of strong antipathy demonstrated by judges and often also by prosecuting counsel. Such reactions were commonplace in the numerous prosecutions of Richard Carlile and his shopmen and shopwomen.[19] Intervention to prevent defendants continuing to disseminate their opinions featured regularly in these trials and was circumvented and criticized at every opportunity. This was a battle between defendants reaching out to wider Britain by utilizing the mechanism of court reporting, whilst judges sought to snuff out this oxygen of publicity.

On other occasions defendants would consciously publicize incidents and decisions by judges that placed them at a considerably material disadvantage. George

---

[16] This profile certainly fits offenders like Richard Carlile, Susannah Wright and George William Foote. However, it is interesting to note that major secularist leaders were more circumspect. Charles Bradlaugh used his legal ingenuity to avoid prosecution for blasphemy when his enemies intended it. This may have been convenient but also suggests the blasphemy prosecutions would have provided him with perhaps ambivalent publicity, since he consciously refuted other accusations about his declarations and beliefs. G.J. Holyoake made much of his prosecution for blasphemy but notably never transgressed or sought such notoriety beyond this one incident.

[17] See the parallels between the issues raised here and those contained in the chapter by Lesley Hall in Chapter VI of this volume.

[18] See Levy, *Blasphemy*, pp. 220–4,

[19] See Nash (1999) *Blasphemy in Britain*, Chapter Three. See also J. Wiener (1983) *Radicalism and Freethought in Nineteenth-Century Britain: The Life of Richard Carlile* (Westport, CONN: Greenwood Press).

William Foote noted that he was given inadequate time to prepare his defence and that his eventual sentence had been deliberately enhanced and aggravated by the addition of 'hard labour'. Even when this sentence had just been pronounced Foote eagerly quipped that the sentence had been motivated by religious malice and told the judge that it had been 'worthy of his creed'.[20] It was also possible to indict the judge's own beliefs as serving a material function in such cases. The fact that prosecutions almost invariably happened as a result of the English Common Law Offence of Blasphemous Libel meant that all resulting jurisprudence and verdicts were inevitably judge-made law. Thus, it became easy to 'read' the highly personal opinions of judges regarding religion and morality into the verdicts and outcomes of the cases they presided over.

The very law of blasphemous libel itself was also indicted as having evolved to produce dangerous, anomalous and vindictively partial proceedings. The outcome of the final Foote case of 1883 had been a moral victory for Foote. This was partly because the presiding judge, John Duke Coleridge, had been prepared to set aside the Hale judgement and actively declare that Christianity should no longer be considered either 'part and parcel' or the law of the land. This meant that criticism of it was now legally possible, but the cornerstone of this new pronouncement was that the 'manner' of the quasi blasphemous pronouncement would be the test of its offensiveness. Manner at last seemed to address elements of *Mens Rea* since the 'manner' of such pronouncements was likely to be seen as *prima facie* evidence of the direct intention to offend. If polite philosophical disagreement would escape the scrutiny of the law, then the presumption that occasions where confrontational language was used would involve the courts. Whilst this at first sight seemed to be a liberalization of the law, many argued that this introduced an unwelcome and unjust class bias around how the law would operate. As was suggested, skilled operators of rhetoric and argument could do considerable damage to religious belief and yet escape unscathed. Conversely, the unlettered and equally sincere street corner orator or publisher of coarse yet popular literature that denigrated religion would much more readily fall foul of this interpretation of blasphemous libel. Such anomalies were to be both noted and ruthlessly exploited by defendants in the years after the Foote case and into the twentieth century. Thus, by the last years of Victoria's reign a considerable variety of factors had conspired to enable trials for Blasphemous Libel to seem, and be actively cast, as the quintessential unfair trial. This accumulated case law of unfairness and infamy was available to the key defendants of Edwardian society, the last to receive custodial punishment in England before the law's repeal in 2008.

The cases against Gott, Stewart and Pack

The Edwardian period in England witnessed some of the ripples of anarchist activity which had spread both from the United States and from continental Europe.[21] As we

---

[20] *Daily Telegraph*, 6th March 1883.
[21] See also the chapter by Lesley Hall in this volume.

have noted, blasphemy trials and 'cases' generally did not happen as single or 'one off' affairs. They were often the product of campaigns engineered and operated by both sides. Agitators could influence successors whose actions would create subsequent cases, all with the intention of creating specific social and political effects.

As we also know, campaigns from various forms of authority could also assume many shapes. Moral reformers would often assume the authority to act on behalf of their vision of the entire moral and God fearing community. Policing authorities would, on occasion, seek to stamp out what they perceived as the arrival of nuisances within their locality. As such, the serial nature of prosecutions was a concerted attempt to damage, and/or remove, individuals who were a threat to public order. Occasionally both motives would blend seamlessly as policing agencies would be pressed into expressing their opinion on the issues they were dealing with.

Agitators often saw that they had a gift in the wording of indictments and summonses against them. These frequently betrayed opinions on the nature and effect of blasphemy pronouncements as part of the summons. These were regularly later reproduced by defendants as part of their own 'indictment' of proceedings. Many of these motifs and narratives, alongside the others outlined in the introduction, came together in the cases against Gott, Pack and Stewart. These cases span the period 1903 until 1912 – although there were later cases and John William Gott was notorious for being the last man to serve a custodial sentence for blasphemy in England. He died shortly after having served his sentence in 1922. Nonetheless these cases (or 'extended case') represent both an accumulation and culmination of the airing of defendant grievances and the mixed history of prosecution responses.

The precise issues surrounding this case began in November 1903 when John William Gott and George Weir received summonses for having 'published a certain scandalous and impious blasphemy' in their newspaper *The Truthseeker*. The matter in question was a spoof article advertising a prize fight between 'G. Hovah' and 'B.L. Zebub'. This contained some obviously popular contemporary references, but also noted some sections of the Bible which had provoked mirth before – namely Foote's ribald misappropriation of the Exodus text for which he had been prosecuted in 1883.[22] They noted that the prosecution was really a culmination of attempts to stamp out the nuisance these embodied. However, the publication (and the occasion that the authorities had chosen in this instance) constituted a problem of credibility for the prosecution. As the defendants stated the precise material indicted had appeared in the *Freethinker* some fifteen years previously. As they also noted this had been published and had been ignored, indicating that the defence could make some capital out of indicting the opinions and proclivities of those seeking to prosecute.[23] This could also be painted as the capricious and arbitrary nature of opinion altering through a changed atmosphere or periodic moral panic – something any 'publisher' of opinions could never be certain of, appearing to be a manifestation of injustice.

---

[22] The text is Exodus xxxiii, 21–3 'And the Lord said ... I will put thee in a cleft in the rock ... and thou shalt see my back parts: but my face shall not be seen.'

[23] E. Pack (1912) *The Trial and Imprisonment of J.W. Gott* (Bradford: Freethought Socialist League), p. 2.

Harassing previously unprosecuted material could also be suggestively portrayed as the exertion of malice at the behest of powerful individuals.

Ernest Pack noted that these proceedings were hastily dropped when a realization of the previously unhindered circulation of these opinions dawned upon the authorities; a motif that was to reoccur. Perhaps fancifully this was pounced upon as evidence that partiality, skulduggery or incompetence had all either been exposed or somehow defeated by the forces of discussion and reason.[24] The ignominious end to the case gave Pack the opportunity to note that other radical pamphleteers such as the anti-vaccinationists were left well alone and that such a judgement could only be painted as a manifestation of partiality and malice. Certainly the end of this particular episode seems to have produced a situation where prosecutions for blasphemy fell, at least for a time, off the agenda. However, the Bradford Socialists scarcely relaxed their campaign or the potency of their publications and propaganda.[25]

Pack and his compatriots suggested that after this incident, policing authorities grew wary of escalating their action to the level of prosecution. This meant that the motive for this period of inaction in the north of England could readily be painted by would-be blasphemers as evidence of fear, or bias, or indeed once prosecution was resumed, as a subsequent episode of incompetence, recklessness, or out-and-out malice. The Bradford Socialists as a group wrote as though their whole unified campaign was considered a danger that should not be confronted lightly. However, the Home Office files reveal a rather different story. They suggest that Gott had been in their sights for some time and, whilst a thorough nuisance, he did not on his own arouse the imperative to take substantial and immediate action. It seems that it was the arrival of Thomas William Stewart (and the eye and ear catching Dr Nikola persona) which was regarded as increasing the inflammatory nature of these outdoor campaigns.[26] Another conceivable motivation for increased scrutiny comes from examining the close connection between international events and some of these set piece meetings.

Police surveillance of large public gatherings had increased in the previous three years in response to a conceivably more enhanced threat from anarchism. The Home Office had received a number of reports about how radical rhetoric blended with delight at the consequences of anarchist direct action against international statesmen which had proved fatal.[27] Subsequent moves against the Bradford Socialists thus began again in August 1911 when a summons was served on the new menace Stewart (under his platform pseudonym Dr Nikola). This was for speaking, and thereby publishing, ' ... scandalous, impious, blasphemous and profane matters things of and concerning the Holy Scriptures and the Christian Religion against the peace of Our Sovereign Lord

---

[24] Ibid., p. 3.
[25] Ibid.
[26] National Archives, HO, Registered Papers, Prosecutions for Blasphemy, 45/10665/216120 item 6 – Report from the Leeds Chief Constable 10 December 1911.
[27] See National Archives, HO, Registered Papers, Prosecutions for Blasphemy, 144/871/160552 item 20 – Letter from Chief Constable of Birmingham, C.H. Rafter, 10 February 1908. This communication noted assaults upon council buildings and a meeting in which the assassination of the King of Portugal was actively lauded and celebrated.

the King, His Crown and Dignity'.[28] As Ernest Pack noticed, such a charge squarely reinforced the enduring logic behind blasphemy as a Common Law and as a statutory offence – namely that religion was closely regarded as ' ... part and parcel of the law of the land'. Police evidence suggested that the sentiments were likely to have been ' ... most offensive and distressing to respectable persons passing by'.[29] On the same day, a similar summons was presented to Gott, but this time it was more specific implicating the comic pamphlet *Rib Ticklers*. This was a compendium of irreverent and semi-puerile jokes and profane stories making light of biblical events and central figures – alongside some rehashing of anti-clerical themes and stereotypes.[30]

At the initial examination of the case against Stewart, the defendant believed he had actively succeeded in establishing that apparently verbatim notes of his speech, which had prompted the summons, had been irregularly tampered with. These appeared to have been edited and subsequently 'completed' in ink. Moreover, a policemen who had testified that Pack had described Jesus as 'a dirty fellow' in his speech was unable to find corroborating evidence in the original notes he had taken, although they appeared in those subsequently written up as evidence for the hearing. The Bradford Socialists saw the adjournment of this case (*sine die*) merely as evidence of bungling. However the Home Office subsequently believed this had been a legitimate and calculated shot across their bows, one that ought to have been heeded and something undertaken so that the public nuisance would cease.[31]

Whatever their reading of the failure of this case to proceed, Gott and Stewart continued to lecture and a second round of summonses was the inevitable result. The indictment followed a speech given by Stewart on 20th August 1911. This concentrated upon a particular diatribe against the Christian doctrine of forgiveness, something which was a great favourite of Victorian and Edwardian secularist speakers and writers. This aimed at feeding a perceived moral repugnance at the idea that the worst of sinners could be saved whilst the most virtuous might find themselves damned. One of Foote's most sophisticated cartoons from 1882, entitled 'Going to Glory' pursued this theme with a depiction of a murdered man descending to hell, whilst his murderer is forgiven by a priest and admitted to heaven. Given Gott and Pack's familiarity with Foote's publications, they conceivably used this cartoon as the inspiration for this particular diatribe against forgiveness.[32]

Pack actively elaborated upon this critique and gave it a profoundly contemporary feel – citing Dr Crippen as the murderer in his rejuvenated story. Crippen was allowed into heaven whilst others (including Pack himself who offered a sincere denial of the scriptures) were not. This possibly suggests a further and clearer adaptation of the story with the murderer (in this case Crippen) portrayed as a devout Christian and

---

[28] Pack, *The Trial and Imprisonment of J.W. Gott*. p 6.
[29] National Archives, HO, Registered Papers, Prosecutions for Blasphemy, 45/10665/216120 item 6 – Report from the Leeds Chief Constable 10 December 1911.
[30] Anonymous (1900) *Rib Ticklers OR Questions for Parsons* (Bradford: J.W Gott).
[31] See respectively Pack, *The Trial and Imprisonment of J.W. Gott*. P. and National Archives, HO, Registered Papers, Prosecutions for Blasphemy, 45/10665/216120 item 6.
[32] See *Freethinker*, 3rd September 1882.

the victim as an honest freethinker. This manifestly apparent and moral injustice led Pack to conclude that ' ... God is not respectable company for a man like me'. Throughout this, and indeed all these prosecutions, the Bradford socialists believed themselves to be protected by the essence of the Coleridge dictum, drawn from the resolution of the last case against Foote, that had concluded with Justice John Duke Coleridge unravelling the belief that Christianity was ' ... part and parcel of the law of the land'.[33] Yet this also contradicted their earlier assertion that the doctrine was alive and well.

The arrival of the defendants in court became the opportunity for them to invoke a commonplace of blasphemy trials. They made efforts to size up the jury and readily concluded that they were 'the twelve apostles'. Moreover, they seemed obviously unlikely to be sympathetic to their case and the issues at stake – at least those pertaining to the exercise of free speech.[34] Levity was introduced into such discussions when Ernest Pack afterwards speculated that it was likely that they were less than assiduous in their duties. He noted that a local cattle show was more likely to have drawn their attention, and similarly that Leeds juries were similarly notorious for failing to retire to the jury-room when asked to consider their verdicts.

Pack's case was heard first and he proceeded to follow a, by now, established line of cross-examining the policemen charged with compiling evidence in the trial. His questioning sought to suggest that the policemen present were given careful instructions to note down potentially offensive material. This was scarcely surprising in itself, especially given the previous summons and the defendants' avowed commitment to continue the propaganda activity. However, this became the prelude to Stewart seeking to establish that his material deemed most blasphemous and offensive had been uttered in response to frequent interruptions from members of his audience. This ostensibly led to an accusation that agent provocateurs had been placed in the audience as a calculated act of incitement. Stewart scored a very cheap point by explaining the meaning of that term to the policeman before him, whilst also illuminating further that the uneducated were expected by the offence of blasphemy to adjudicate in theological matters. This line of argument led nowhere and intended to signal forms of oppression to an audience beyond the courtroom. In truth, establishing the existence of agent provocateurs was irrelevant to the case. The authorities were within their rights to continue to scrutinize the meetings of the Bradford socialists. Even if agent provocateurs had been involved, they could justifiably argue that they were motivated by religious conviction (or organized by religious organizations), rather than any malignant motive aimed at curtailing individual freedom. Stewart, during the course of cross-examining a second policeman, again reiterated the suggestion that the notes taken of his speeches were not verbatim and memory of their precise nature could be blurred from the original context. This line of thought was also an attempt to destabilize the idea of exact expressions being the basis of prosecution. If

---

[33] Nash, *Blasphemy in Modern Britain*, p. 183.
[34] Pack, *The Trial and Imprisonment of J.W. Gott*. p. 30.

they were deemed harmful to the ideas of others, these needed to be examined with precision in a court that had chosen to prosecute them.

After this, Stewart returned to the matter in question behind the original 1911 case which had been postponed and then dropped. Precisely how was it that local authorities presumed to prosecute ideas and beliefs that had been routinely published in the past? To enable this defence, Stewart called Ernest Pack himself to the witness stand and succeeded in establishing that the sentiments he expressed had been published in a book by the leading nineteenth-century American freethinker Colonel Robert Ingersoll. Pack then asked further questions to establish Ingersoll's reputation and the scope of the audience he had reached since publication.[35] The judge, Justice Thomas Gardner Horridge, must have sat up in his seat at this and recognized that this might constitute a legitimate evidence. He ordered that such evidence would be considered admissible if the relevant book could be produced in court.[36] Unluckily for Stewart, this did not run in his favour since it became obvious that finding the work would prove difficult in the circumstances.

Stewart, however, did have better luck when the judge asked the witness how frequently blasphemy had been prosecuted and Pack was able to reply citing the Foote case (artfully forgetting the Boulter case that should have been fresh in the memory).[37] Things improved still further when he called to the stand another secularist sympathizer George Weir. What transpired also trod a path well established by previous secularist defendants when accused of blasphemy. Foote in his 1883–1884 case had suggested that the unprovoked and, to him, unwelcome outbursts of the evangelical street preaching of the Salvation Army was anathema to him. It was vulgar and many of the sentiments appeared, to his finely tuned disposition, calculated to offend him and any other rational citizen.[38] Weir was similarly eagerly invited to note that the 1903 incident had (allegedly) been accompanied by a religious speaker who had spoken to the crowd before Weir had arrived. Upon being asked, he recalled that the speaker had quoted the biblical passage 2 Kings 18 v 27.[39] Stewart histrionically asked Weir if he was willing to discuss his reaction to this text. Weir replied that he would refuse to repeat these words in court and that he had upbraided the Christian preacher for being what he termed 'a dirty fellow', to find that portions of the audience were in complete agreement with Weir and his opinion. This may or may not have been a contrived and fictional narrative, nevertheless it did have the desired effect. When laughter cascaded through the court Justice Horridge stifled this immediately, anxious to regain an atmosphere of seriousness.[40]

---

[35] National Archives, HO, Registered Papers, Prosecutions for Blasphemy, 45/10665/216120 item 18.
[36] Ibid.
[37] Ibid.
[38] See the *Freethinker* 4th August 1881, 4th December 1881, 3rd September 1882 and 1st October 1882 for Foote's assaults upon the Salvation Army.
[39] The King James Bible renders this as 'But Rabshakeh said unto them, Hath my master sent me to thy master, and to thee, to speak these words? *hath he* not *sent me* to the men which sit on the wall, that they may eat their own dung, and drink their own piss with you?'
[40] National Archives, HO, Registered Papers, Prosecutions for Blasphemy, 45/10665/216120 item 18 – Shorthand notes of the trial.

Weir noted that the police had taken no action against this speaker and that the Freethought Socialist League's speeches delivered by Stewart had only received one complaint about their atheist sentiments, and not explicitly against any utterance or publication. When Weir had left the stand, Stewart proceeded with the task of putting two and two together. Building upon the presence of police, their note taking and their failure to behave similarly in the presence of a potentially offensive Christian speaker, Stewart suggested that all of this constituted a form of calculated entrapment. Citing the ignominious so-called failure of the first case against himself and Gott, Stewart described this latter case as 'deliberately worked up ... to hide the bungling in the first case'.[41] Even if true, this was unlikely to elicit sympathy from those in court. What was arguably more serious was his suggestion that the summonses had been incorrectly worded. The wording of the summons suggested that the precise words spoken and indicted were said to be contrary to the 9 & 10 William III Blasphemy Statute of 1698, which implied precise doctrines were under attack and were here being protected by law established. Yet paradoxically the prosecution opened the case in court by suggesting Stewart's words were contrary to the Common Law, and thus were indictable for causing offence because of the reaction they might provoke.[42] Such anomalies would regularly emerge in blasphemy cases and lack of experience and familiarity with the law would contribute to their frequency. Further sympathetic witnesses were called and their evidence trawled far and wide both geographically and chronologically. This searched supposedly in vain for any other evidence of disgust and outrage from Stewart's lecturing style and content in other localities. Looking backwards in time, one witness could recall Charles Bradlaugh lecturing and using similar language to Stewart and escaping prosecution around twenty years earlier.[43]

Stewart's own appearance in the witness box proved inconclusive. He reiterated the evidence about the apparently uncontroversial nature of his lectures elsewhere, and his belief that he was ostensibly protected by the logic of the Coleridge dictum in the Foote case of 1883. He was, however, caught slightly unawares by the judge who questioned him about a collection taken at the meeting, again a constant motif in the criticism offered by authorities both local and national, which maintained a belief that individuals who were accused of blasphemy were frequently following nefarious economic motives.[44]

Justice Horridge approached his summing up to the jury by acknowledging Stewart's invocation of the Coleridge judgement, and informing the jury that the law of blasphemy had evolved in recent years. He made it clear that the manner of expression had become the supreme test of offence. But, importantly, some of what the judge had to say departed from the logic of this judgement. Horridge noted that

---

[41] Ibid.
[42] Ibid.
[43] Ibid.
[44] See National Archives, HO, Registered Papers, Prosecutions for Blasphemy, 45/10665/216120 item 11 – Letter to Sir Edward Troup (Home Office) from Chief Constable of Leeds 13 December 1911 which describes the Bradford Socialists as ' ... making money out of sensationalism'.
[45] National Archives, HO, Registered Papers, Prosecutions for Blasphemy, 45/10665/216120 item 18 – Shorthand notes of the trial.

individuals had the right to say what they liked concerning religion but ought to be much more circumspect when talking about morals.[45] This line of argument was never followed up by the judge, but might conceivably have referred to the association with neo-Malthusianism which attended Stewart, Gott and Pack.

Beyond this, the summing up also further departed in some interesting ways from the 'manner'-based logic of the Coleridge judgement; ways which influenced the law's profile for the rest of the twentieth century. Horridge had new issues to deal with when faced with Stewart. Coleridge's judgement in the Foote case had followed Foote's ribald newspaper publication, and the judge here may have thought the offensive material could be assimilated and overlooked with a degree of contemplation. Horridge had speakers at a public meeting to contend with, and thus began to consider how the law would, and ought to work in a context much more closely linked to public order. The inherent problems of ruling on this case were laid bare by Horridge's relief at the fact that he was ' ... always glad that a jury has to decide these questions, because they have not got to give reasons for their decisions. They have not got to justify them in arguments.'[46] Although he suggested that 'common sense' would be their guide, it was still not clear precisely how a jury were supposed to decide between ' ... fair discussion on a religious subject' or ' ... a malicious abusive attack'.[47] Given this it emerges as scarcely surprising that Horridge reminded the jury that they did not have to give reasons for their eventual decision. Nonetheless, Horridge also proceeded to rehearse the language used, asking the jury to consider very carefully their judgement of its character. He also made an explicit point of reminding the jury that they had to administer the law of the land, and should not be considering whether it was prudent to be prosecuting for the offence of blasphemy or not.[48]

After conferring, the jury found Stewart guilty and without invitation, the foreman of the jury declared: 'We consider that he went beyond the bounds of decency in his language.'[49] The judge sentenced Stewart to three months' imprisonment at hard labour. Taking his imitation of Foote to the ultimate degree, Stewart quipped back, 'The sentence is worthy of your religion, my Lord, and great may be your reward in Heaven.'[50]

The Assizes then moved on to consider the case against Gott. This summons had been laid upon him in respect of his publication *Rib Ticklers*. Gott quite readily admitted to having published this work alongside a great many others. Following the lead of Stewart, Gott likewise decided to play to the gallery with his interrogation of members of the local constabulary. Beyond asking the policeman whether a complainant ' ... fastened his collar at the *back of his neck*', Gott's parade of witnesses and questions mirrored those previously utilized by Stewart.[51] The well-established and widespread

---

[46] Ibid.
[47] Ibid.
[48] Ibid.
[49] Ibid.
[50] Ibid.
[51] Pack, *The Trial and Imprisonment of J.W. Gott*, pp. 13–15.

circulation of Gott's works and the failure to generate complaints from successive audiences were both stories retold for the benefit of the jury.

However, one particular addition to this is worthy of some note. Gott continually reiterated that he was prepared to repurchase any of his publications if they failed to satisfy in any way. This was rather more than the guarantee that it seemed, since it also served as a rudimentary and crude species of warning sign to would-be purchasers warning of the nature of his publications.[52] Whether wittingly or unwittingly, Gott was addressing some of the thinking behind blasphemous libel being a Common Law offence. This flexibility meant the application of the law was intended to ensure it adapted to changing elements of public taste and sensibility. When questioned, Gott might have legitimately argued that he had done everything possible and reasonable to ensure that he was selling his wares to an aware and responsible niche audience, and thus not offending anyone beyond this grouping. This approach of placing legal responsibility with the consumers of such culture was an important principle in subsequent legislation in many European countries. Whilst not wholly indemnifying writers, artists and publishers he was further adding a greater cultural respect to the concept of free speech and free expression. As Gott put it:

> I have always made it perfectly clear when offering it for sale that it was an Anti-Christian pamphlet. My usual cry being that it was the new plan for getting rid of the Black Army, the Sky Pilots, the Devil Dodgers, the Fakers and the Humbugs – the parsons.[53]

From this point onwards, Gott found himself on ground that was more familiar and had been well-trodden by defendants during the course of the nineteenth century. Since he was talking about a publication, this was more familiar territory in which to argue that publications could be the subject of changing elements of taste and sensibility. Gott started by invoking a cultural relativism which tried to undermine the idea that an objective standard of what was precisely blasphemous could realistically be achieved. He asked, quite legitimately, whether it was conceivable that those who flourished without God could actually be accused of blasphemy.[54]

The standard invocation of moral revolt followed with Gott railing against the Bible as an obscene book ' … deliberately thrust into the unsuspecting hands of innocent children, who are requested to read, mark, learn, and inwardly digest it.'[55] He likewise pursued an enduring suggestion that Christianity quite readily profited financially from prosecutions for blasphemy. The nature of sentences passed against the convicted was the next link in the chain of Gott's argument. These seemed in many respects arbitrary, but notably there appeared to be a reduction in their severity over recent time. This was offered as evidence that society was becoming more enlightened.

---

[52] Ibid., p. 17.
[53] Ibid.
[54] Ibid., p. 16.
[55] Ibid., p. 17.

This theme was enhanced by Gott seeking to quote from Robert Blatchford's *God and My Neighbour*.[56] This investigated the truth of the New Testament, ironically by subjecting it to the scrutiny of a court of law. This noted that the messages of the New Testament and the persons mentioned in in its events would not successfully satisfy the laws of evidence, as understood by a court in England. Quoting this also had the benefit of exposing those in the court to material that had remained in circulation unmolested, yet it was apparently more offensive than anything Gott had published.[57] After further digressions, Gott wound up with a plea to the jury to defend the principle of free speech, hoping for a verdict of not guilty since he demonstrated ' … confidence in this enlightened age'.[58] In the event, this 'optimism' whether sarcastic or otherwise, was to be dashed since Gott was convicted and the judge sentenced him to four months' imprisonment.

Evidently some lessons had been learned from the case against Stewart and his infringement upon public order, since a small flurry of cases followed. In 1912 a case against an E. Stephens (who went under the alias of S.E. Bullock) was brought at the Leeds Assizes for using blasphemous language at a meeting in Rotherham. Stephens was a stridently apostate member of the Church Army who chose this meeting to rail against his former faith. It seems his repentance in court was as vehement as his proselytizing, yet this did not save him from a three months' prison sentence.[59]

Stephens could be dismissed as a youthful hothead, and seeking to police such meetings seemed to be bearing fruit. Certainly the police authorities were actively profiting from their experience. In this same year a further prosecution was aimed at another Bradford Socialist, Thomas Jackson. This one was notable for a change of tactic when he was charged under Section 28 of the 1847 Town Police Clauses Act. In particular he was indicted for ' … using profane or obscene language'. Jackson claimed the Act did not apply to him, thereby disputing the definition of 'profane'. The judge disagreed and Jackson received a sentence of fourteen days. Hypatia Bradlaugh-Bonner believed that this had been the first time this Act had ever been used against secularist or freethought speakers.[60] She also declared that religious offences, under an Act of 1842, were mandated to be tried at the assizes. From this it looked likely that the use of the Town Police Clauses Act of 1847 was an expedient to avoid such proceedings.[61] Jackson, like Stewart and Gott before him, refused to give undertakings to amend his behaviour and he underwent a similar term of brief imprisonment that came to resemble a 'cat and mouse' game akin to the frequent prosecution, detention and release of numerous Suffragettes.

---

[56] Ibid., pp. 21–3
[57] Ibid., p. 18.
[58] Ibid., p. 25.
[59] Bradlaugh-Bonner, *Penalties upon Opinion*, p. 124.
[60] Ibid.
[61] Pack, *The Trial and Imprisonment of J.W. Gott*. P 35.

The 'problem' of blasphemy at governmental levels

On the face of it, these blasphemy prosecutions appeared to have at least partly fulfilled their function. Despite the occasional false start, none of the defendants succeeded in escaping the law and its attempts to prosecute them and thereby combat a public nuisance. As far as the police in Leeds and Bradford were concerned, they had addressed and pacified local public opinion that had been opposed to the public meetings. They had thereby also, for the moment, prevented the circulation of advanced literature and the potentially unwelcome opportunity to accidentally hear views expressed which would inflame religious and moral sensibilities. They might even feel, perversely, that they had satisfied the quest of Gott, Pack, Stewart and Jackson for both their sustained mini-martyrdom and their episodic days in court. Yet this also was the Achilles heel of blasphemy prosecutions against the determined. Stewart was again lecturing upon his release and the Home office continued to receive reports and verbatim notes of his lectures from all over the country. His diatribes now included material he had obviously worked up during his imprisonment. He was prosecuted once more in Wolverhampton in September 1913 and Stafford in November 1913, again receiving a sentence of hard labour.[62]

However, these local victories, even though they were inevitably short-lived, were overshadowed by the ripples these prosecutions had caused in the wider cultural landscape of England. These trials effectively kick-started the modern twentieth-century movements for the repeal of the blasphemy laws. The Rationalist Press Association submitted a petition to the Home Secretary, Reginald McKenna (1863–1943) seeking the release of Gott and Stewart. The petition carefully stated that 'blasphemy' was a pejorative legal label placed upon the phenomenon of religious denial when it suited certain authorities. It then proceeded to suggest that ' ... the prosecution of which would not now be tolerated by public opinion and indeed according to the generally received view such denial is not a crime at all'.[63] McKenna also had to confront the particularly cogent intervention of the noted Freethinker politician John MacKinnon Robertson who was keen to ensure McKenna knew that many took a dim view of the prosecutions.[64] Robertson was well known as a determined intellectual heavyweight and his involvement certainly made the Home Office wary and circumspect.

The reaction of Home Secretary McKenna is informative in the context of these particular cases. The idea of blasphemy repeal had been aired before the 1911 crescendo of cases against the Bradford Socialists. Just after the cases had been heard, McKenna received a letter from the MP George Greenwood drawing his attention to Justice James Fitzjames Stephen's celebrated opposition to the Coleridge judgement, and how this had been enshrined in the 1894 edition of his *Digest*. McKenna was unimpressed and suggested that this had survived into the 1894 edition solely as a

---

[62] National Archives, HO, Registered Papers, Prosecutions for Blasphemy, 45/10665/216120 item 55 and 45/10665/216120 item 51.
[63] National Archives, HO, Registered Papers, Prosecutions for Blasphemy, 45/10665/216120 item 12.
[64] National Archives, HO, Registered Papers, Prosecutions for Blasphemy, 45/10665/216120 item 21.

result of it being updated by Stephens' own son.[65] This was suggesting that at this point Mckenna believed the law and its operation, as he understood it, functioned quite adequately at the local level.

However as events unfolded after this point, Mckenna was forced to concede ground and allow his civil servants to investigate the issue of repeal. One aspect of this process may have been caused by public ignorance. In reply to Sir Arthur Quiller-Couch, Mckenna noted how frequently he had to reiterate that the proceedings for prosecution were instigated by local agencies and were not the implementation of centrally operated statute law.[66] This indicates several things that stand out as important in understanding this episode and its subsequent influence on the wider history of blasphemy under English Common Law. Public understanding of the law presumed that a national statute was the means to prosecute whether fairly or unfairly. It also indicated a gulf between this and the public understanding of what Common, and thus judge-made law was seeking to achieve in this area. The Home Office had addressed those who would comment on the procedural elegance of the law directly. Civil servants had long believed that judges in individual cases would be guided by their interpretation of the moral outlook of the age. This was a clear and elegant safeguard to impress on both sides of the argument. Such interpretation by judges effectively reflected contemporary opinion, thereby arguing that the law was not obsolete. But this supposed elegance had merely a small informed audience and such elegance was so frequently lost on outside observers with other concerns and agendas.[67] The gulf between local action and disdainful distant opinion of such actions contrasted metropolitan relaxed complacency with urgent provincial fears. This had both advantages and disadvantages to government and its observers. Detachment from initiating such action could readily become a useful expedient. Righteous disappointment or chagrin could be displayed by the Home Secretary, even if private opinions argued otherwise. Yet distancing the Home Secretary from the implementation of the law was thoroughly capable of quickly calling the law itself into question. Certainly the Pack/Gott episode of 1911/12 inevitably drew the Home Secretary into debating the wisdom of repealing both the 9 & 10 William c 35 Blasphemy statute and the Common law of Blasphemous Libel – presumably as the defendants in this flurry of cases must have hoped.

By the end of 1914, Home Office opinion was rapidly mellowing and seemed to have retreated to a prepared defensive position. The ongoing and problematic nature of the cases against the Bradford Socialists had, at the very least, called into question the supposed purpose of a blasphemy law. Whatever their public defence of the law in response to letters of complaint, the Home Office was privately, but persistently, worn down by the determination of the offenders and the outcry they elicited from

---

[65] National Archives, HO, Registered Papers, Prosecutions for Blasphemy, 45/24619/217459 item 2 – Letter from George Greenwood to Reginald McKenna 26 December 1911.

[66] National Archives, HO, Registered Papers, Prosecutions for Blasphemy, 45/10665/216120 item 83 – Letter from Reginald McKenna to Sir Arthur Quiller-Couch 3rd February 1914.

[67] The Attorney General Sir John Simon called the existing law ' ... a striking instance of the Common Law adapting itself to the times and changing in accordance with a general change of view in regard to religious matters.' National Archives, HO, Registered Papers, Prosecutions for Blasphemy, 45 10665/216120 item 86.

concerned liberals at large. Certainly when the matter reached the tabling of a Blasphemy Laws Amendment Bill in 1913 and in 1914 their response was pragmatic. The experiences of the previous four years had crystallized their belief that the sole virtue of the existing blasphemy laws was the protection they afforded to elements of public order. This meant that all subsequent commentary that emanated from the Home Office on the subject of blasphemy repeal sought to ensure that public order was protected. Such sentiments were echoed in the words of one Civil Servant who responded to the Blasphemy Laws Amendment Bill of 1913 by suggesting:

> Public blasphemy is on much the same footing as public exposure of the person. Any one may expose his person or utter blasphemy in the privacy of his own home but when he offends the feelings of others by his public displays his acts should be criminal. It is plainly impossible at present to amend the law of blasphemy on the right lines – and to abolish it would lead to public scandals. It is never used now except in cases where blasphemy amounts to a public outrage. And no one would be the better for its repeal except those who want to make themselves offensive to their neighbours.[68]

Conclusion

Blasphemy cases throughout the long nineteenth century had a reputation for unfairness cultivated around them. The very subjective nature of the offence, as it developed over the course of the nineteenth century (especially after the Coleridge pronouncement in the Foote case), was a root cause of this. Proceedings could easily be painted as biased, as well as portrayed as motivated by a strange mixture of fear and malice. The diversity of court proceedings and attempts to supposedly stifle free expression, both in and out of court, provided important and influential journalistic and pamphleteering copy for the radicals who gamely took on the blasphemy laws and the authorities. Their success at this made the concept of an unfair blasphemy trial something of a commonplace.

The law itself was clearly something of a series of anomalies that could be made to look embarrassing in court. The ideas of individuals found themselves on trial like nowhere else in the legal canon and, in such instances, indicting the opposition with accusations of bias and malice was inevitably a result. Government itself regularly fought shy of being centrally involved in prosecution and much preferred outside agencies to take the lead in such matters. This, on occasions, led to bungling and mistakes. Procedural anomalies instigated by judges could very easily be portrayed as the exercise of premeditated malice, and a calculated means of circumventing free expression and a fair trial. This malice appeared still more stark when defendants regularly reminded themselves and the courtroom that Blasphemy prosecutions

---

[68] National Archives, HO, Registered Papers, Prosecutions for Blasphemy, 45/17459/8 – Commentary on the Blasphemy Laws Amendment Bill 1915 and Comment by 'C.J.' 20 June 1913.

almost invariably were brought under the Common Law of Blasphemous Libel. This ensured that all law that was practised was judge-made law and, whether drawing upon the past or exercising new initiatives in the present, the legal bias of the Christian ages seemed to inevitably cling to these proceedings. Because of this, defendants in blasphemy cases could easily problematize such proceedings by suggesting that they unfolded invariably following the bias and personal opinions of the presiding judge.

The flurry of cases against Gott, Stewart, Pack and Jackson were effectively the culmination of nineteenth-century radical secularist defendants seeking to bring the blasphemy law into spectacular disrepute. Many of the defences, lines of argument, narratives, loopholes and counter accusations that these earlier defendants had used were revisited in these cases. The words and sentiments of their prosecuted forebears provided a miscellany of ways in which to paint prosecutions for blasphemy, and the courtroom proceedings attached to them, as intrinsically unfair.

Yet many of these elements scarcely disappeared from blasphemy trials right up to repeal in 2008. During the *Gay News* case of 1977/8 the defence counsels found themselves regularly wrong-footed by the procedural decisions taken by the judge Justice Alan King-Hamilton. Geoffrey Robertson and John Mortimer's defence case was immediately destabilized when the judge departed from the established practice of allowing both the prosecution and the defence to address the jury at the outset. This meant the prosecution case was heard without respite, allowing calumny to be heaped upon calumny. King-Hamilton also ruled theological and academic evidence to be inadmissible, commenting in court upon the text of the poem that was effectively on trial. In his instructions to the jury, the judge also showed the innate power of judges in a Common Law case, spontaneously departing from the Coleridge dictum by suddenly declaring that the motives of those who wrote and those who published the poem were irrelevant. Reaching back to Justice Horridge and those civil servants in the Home Office in 1914, King-Hamilton focussed upon the public order element of individuals being suddenly faced with a poem which he declared to be ' ... blasphemous on its face'.[69]

Blasphemy cases from 1800, right through to 1978, represented a series of incidents where the partiality and bias inherent within legal proceedings against defendants were exposed for each generation. In secularist and liberal circles, radical reputations were carefully constructed around being a defendant in such proceedings. Yet for all its apparent power and the track record of successful prosecution that resulted, policing authorities, legal authorities and law itself were regularly damaged by such actions. These, arguably, drip-fed the call for reform and repeal which itself served to alter policing priorities in favour of public order issues. Yet as the *Gay News* case demonstrated, even these apparently clear uncertainties could be instantly overturned by a judge with a new agenda.

---

[69] G. Robertson (1999) *The Justice Game* (London: Vintage), pp. 138–51.

9

The Bobbed-Haired Bandit and the Smash-and-Grab Raider

Alyson Brown
Edge Hill University

Introduction

This chapter considers the criminal careers of two offenders, 'Ruby' Spark and Lilian Goldstein and illuminates how press coverage of their exploits was made to conform, as far as possible, to media-created stereotypes and tropes. Ultimately, the chapter argues this constituted an unfair trial by journalism that served the needs of popular culture rather than the legal system or of those of justice itself.

Spark and Goldstein were a couple whose relationship was both criminal and intimate, although it is the 'trials' of Goldstein that will be foregrounded. Lilian Goldstein became identified as the British bobbed-haired or bobbed hair bandit, after an earlier New York-based American female criminal. The ascription of that epithet reflects not only the nature of her offending and her role as one half of a criminal couple but also the era in which they became minor celebrities. While the colourful characterizations of this couple in the press may have attracted readers, those stories simplified and sometimes speculated about their experiences and activities. Coverage of the British bobbed-haired bandit was highly gendered, moralistic but sometimes sympathetic. That coverage formed an important part of the context of their trial in 1940, which was the last before they ended their partnership. At that trial, Spark was convicted for being an escaped convict on the run and he received twelve months' imprisonment, to run concurrently with the six years' penal servitude he still had to serve for previous offences. Goldstein was given a six-month prison sentence for harbouring him. However, her sentence was almost immediately commuted, and she was bound over for three years.

The lenient, and indeed what could be perceived as merciful treatment she received, at that point proved to be the catalyst that ended her criminal activities and her relationship with Spark. She was perceived as a woman under the influence, and possibly coercion, of her lover and someone who needed a fair trial and a chance to enable her to change her future path. Through an analysis of this criminal couple, the chapter contributes to the growing body of academic work on inter-war criminality and the role of the press in the growth and commodification of crime celebrity. This work will also consider the influence of the press in constructing tropes about the modern woman, her perceived transgressions and immorality, and the extent to which that constituted a particular form of unfair trial.

John Carter Wood observes that the 1920s and 1930s were ' … a golden age for press spectacles: increasing literacy, advances in printing technology and expanding consumer opportunities (and the advertising they brought) gave newspapers unprecedented social, political and economic influence'.[1] More specifically, it was a golden age for the human-interest story including ' … first-person revelations of a life of crime'.[2] Crime was popular entertainment in a way that operated to intensify a plethora of social fears that dogged the era: 'returning war veterans', 'foreign gangsters', 'hooligans', 'motor bandits', 'razor gangs' and 'dope fiends'.[3] Anxieties and uncertainties about the effects and implications of these phenomena created fertile ground for the press to capitalize on crime stories and a readership responsive to the emotive dramas encapsulated within them. Criminal trials, with their narratives of ' … crime, mystery, detection, sex and punishment' were 'perfect copy'.[4] Female criminality figured prominently in such narratives as a reflection of the dark side of the New Woman in the modern age. Indeed, the period has been depicted as one in which female criminality was reconceptualized in Britain. Wildman has suggested that women career criminals ' … challenged traditional gendered patterns of law-breaking, appropriated wider notions of fashionable modernity and transgressed social and geographical boundaries as poorer women embraced new opportunities for masquerade and used crime for upward social mobility'.[5] Long-held certainties, at least in public narratives, about gender identities were questioned in multiple ways and were reflected visibly, for example, in the way in which masculine dress for women became fashionable.[6]

Contemporary insecurities were exacerbated by the transmission of American culture into British society, through colourful stories about gangsters in the prohibition era glorified in immensely popular movies such as *Little Caesar* (1930) and *Scarface* (1932) which provided, as Andrew Davies has pointed out, a point of reference and means to understand British gang and gang-related activity. Whether on ' … newsprint or on screen the Chicago gangster was a compelling cultural icon in Britain'.[7] The depiction of American society as infinitely more violent and dangerous in many

---

[1] J. Carter Wood (2012) *'The Most Remarkable Woman': Poison, Celebrity and the Trials of Beatrice Pace* (Manchester: Manchester University Press), p. 68.
[2] M. Houlbrook (2013) 'Commodifying the Self Within: Ghosts, Libels, and the Crook Life Story in Inter-war Britain', *The Journal of Modern History*, 85, pp. 321–63 at p. 326.
[3] C. Emsley (2005) *Hard Men: Violence in England since 1750* (London: Hambledon, 2005), p. 20.
[4] L. Bland (2013) *Modern Women on Trial: Sexual Transgression in the Age of the Flapper* (Manchester: Manchester University Press), p. 8.
[5] C. Wildman (2016) 'Miss Moriarty, the Adventuress and the Crime Queen: The Rise of the Modern Female Criminal in Britain, 1918–1939', *Contemporary British History*, 30, 1, pp. 73–98 at p. 73.
[6] L.K. Doan (1998) 'Passing Fashions: Reading Female Masculinities in the 1920s', *Feminist Studies*, 24, 3, pp. 663–700.
[7] A. Davies (2007) 'The Scottish Chicago? From "Hooligans" to "Gangsters" in Inter-war Glasgow', *Cultural & Social History*, 4, 4, pp. 511–27 at p. 512.

respects served to highlight the reassuring relative stability of British society, but this perception of stability was subject to challenge. Reports about the racecourse gangs of the 1920s highlighted violent gang conflicts between the Sabini's and the Birmingham Boys and revealed a level of social dislocation and anxiety.[8] Matt Houlbrook asserts that many Britons experienced the inter-war years as a period 'of profound dislocation that threatened to destabilize the boundaries between classes, sexes, and races on which the nation's stability depended'.[9]

Ruby Spark was a well-known offender, 'smash-and-grab raider', 'motor bandit' and 'gangster', linked most famously to the Dartmoor Prison riot of January 1932 and to his later successful escape from that prison in 1940.[10] Up to that latter date, this was the longest period (over five months between the 10th of January and 28th of June 1940) an escaped convict had ever been on the run from Dartmoor. This feat was described later by Sir Gerald Dodson, the judge before whom Spark appeared when he was apprehended, as 'remarkable'.[11] Heralded in alarmist terms as a new kind of criminal, Jerry White has pointed out that the 'Smash-and-grab' by 'motor bandits' became 'the stuff of legend between the wars'.[12] Enhanced mobility offered by the motor-car seemed to suggest greater planning, resources and co-ordination and also potentially a greater and more violent threat. Clive Emsley observes that these 'new' criminals were seen as skilfully using the expanding opportunities provided by new technology and came to be seen as more 'professional' criminals.[13] In many senses, the motor bandit and the smash-and-grab raider represented wider concerns about the 'modern' age which also extended to the cultural shock posed by the New Woman in her criminal guises. Hence, some of the coverage about Ruby Spark is shadowed, and occasionally even over-shadowed, by his partner Lilian Rose Kendall Goldstein who at times supported Spark as a getaway driver, usually a masculine role.

The female criminal persona of the bobbed-haired bandit that appeared in a series of true crime exposés published in the *Sunday Pictorial*, companion to the *Daily Mirror*, between January and July 1940, and the way in which that related to the coverage of the woman who appeared sporadically in press reports of her courtroom trials, reflects differing media dimensions of Lilian Goldstein. Central to the *Sunday Pictorial*

---

[8] H. Shore (2014) 'Rogues of the Racecourse: Racing Men and the Press in Inter-war Britain', *Media History*, 20, 4, pp. 352–67.

[9] M. Houlbrook (2007) '"The Man with the Powder Puff" in Inter-war London', *Historical Journal*, 50, 1, pp. 145–71 at p. 160.

[10] It should be noted that in a range of historical sources Spark is more often recorded as Sparks, Sparkes or indeed by a number of aliases he also used. His own ghost-written autobiography gives his name as 'Ruby Sparks', although it is clear Ruby is a nickname relating to his criminal activities. See R. Sparks [ghost-written by Norman Parker] (1961) *Burglar to the Nobility* (London: Arthur Barker Limited). However, his birth certificate gives his full name as Charles John Spark. My thanks to his family for clarifying this issue.

[11] Sir Gerald Dodson (1967) *Consider Your Verdict: The Memoirs of Sir Gerald Dodson* (London: Hutchinson), p. 102.

[12] J. White (2001) *London in the 20th Century* (London: The Bodley Head), p. 265.

[13] See C. Emsley (2011) *Crime and Society in Twentieth-Century England* (Harlow: Longman), p. 87. The *Oxford English Dictionary* defined motor-bandit simply as 'a person who commits a crime using, or in connection with, a motor vehicle'.

coverage was the bobbed-haired bandit's relationship, both criminal and personal, with her partner and lover Ruby Spark. Goldstein is not named at that point. Before then the broader press reporting around their criminal trials highlighted Spark and Goldstein as individuals, with what could be portrayed as glamourous and exciting criminal lifestyles, but also as a romanticized package. Yet, surprisingly Lilian Goldstein was not confirmed publicly to be the bobbed-haired bandit. In July 1940 the identity of Lilian Goldstein attracted national notoriety as she gained even greater attention as Sparks's partner and associated fellow bandit.

The public identity of the British bobbed-haired bandit was a malleable press construct in which contemporary fears and tropes could be played out. It was an image that was manipulated to the best commercial effect by the press but, intriguingly, possibly also by the woman to whom it was appended. This chapter suggests that for Lilian Goldstein, unlike criminals who courted public attention, her public depictions may have been unwanted and constituted an unfair trial by the media. However, ultimately the press construction of the British bobbed-haired bandit may have served her as a means to align herself with narratives that were useful and familiar within contemporary gender norms but without threatening to reveal her identity. Before July 1940 the media trial had largely been waged against the bobbed-haired bandit and not Lilian Goldstein. The bobbed-haired bandit constructed by the press was alluring, fashionable, audacious, intelligent, wild, and knew how to use a gun and drive a getaway car: good copy as well as a dangerous social problem.

The press and the bobbed-haired bandit

Houlbrook notes that the 'ephemeral world of inter-war newspaper lives' often drew upon dubious sources, was often 'ventriloquized by a ghost-writer' and framed by one or more editors.[14] He further observes that the 'task of commodifying the self within was never taken in isolation'.[15] Nor was it at this time a practice limited to a few, there was what has been called a 'seemingly endless line of ex-crooks who made their way from the prison gates to the editor's office between the wars' and indeed into the early 1940s and beyond.[16] Some of these representations, such as that of Josephine O'Dare, examined by Houlbrook, appear to have been a means to exert control over their public identity from behind the prison gates. In the case of Spark and Goldstein in the *Sunday Pictorial*, this can be extended to an attempt to influence press representation while Spark was on the run. O'Dare's account was a 'narrative of redemptive suffering'.[17] A similar tone was evident in articles on Spark and the bobbed-haired bandit in the *Sunday Pictorial*, although Spark's tone was coloured as much by promoting his resilience, toughness and even humour under duress. His articles were a means not

---

[14] Houlbrook, 'Commodifying the Self Within', p. 325.
[15] Ibid., p. 327. See also Carter Wood, '*The Most Remarkable Woman in England*', p. 19.
[16] Houlbrook, 'Commodifying the Self Within', p. 322.
[17] Ibid., p. 335.

only to cash in on their past but also to deflect the taint of violence.[18] However, the strength of Spark's character, its tough masculinity and the threat of latent but not explicit aggression *are* foregrounded in the articles supposedly by the bobbed-haired bandit, whose actions were seemingly determined by love and loyalty to her man, although with a suggestion of potential coercion. This was a familiar trope but during the inter-war years was enhanced by its use as a critique of modern women seeking sexual and other pleasures.[19] This had been very publicly played out in the context of early 1920s New York and in relation to the distinctive cultural figure of the original bobbed-haired-bandit.

The original bobbed-haired bandit was a woman represented as loyal to her man though thick and thin. Celia Cooney, who supported her husband holding up local stores toting a gun, became a national phenomenon inextricably linked to the new shorter hairstyles in the 1920s that represented the more morally daring women.[20] In reality, aside from her criminal activities, Cooney was far from posing a threat to contemporary morality. However, the bobbed hair style she wore associated her with the modern woman and challenging conventions. Actors Clara Bow and Louise Brooks, as well as designer Coco Chanel, were prominently sporting the 'bob' in the early 1920s. It was a dramatic change in style which quickly became associated with wider social changes for women. Gold states that in the United States, 'vociferous debates featured in news items and editorial pages' which suggested that 'both defenders and detractors understood the haircut was as much a declaration of women's liberation as of style, and a symbol, for better or worse, of the modern era and women's place in it'.[21]

During the 1920s the bobbed-haired flapper was for some in England and the United States a dangerous modern woman: youthful, assertive and provocative.[22] Bobbed-hair represented increasing independence on the part of women workers which employers sometimes tried to restrain.[23] This occasionally came to light in advertisements for domestic situations vacant. One advertisement for a head housemaid in *The Times* from 1929 stated that the individual should be ' … experienced and capable of supervising' but also stipulated 'no bobbed hair'.[24] The 'modern' woman 'represented modernity, mobility, new opportunities, a brave new world … Above all, she represented female

---

[18] See various editions of the *Sunday Pictorial* 21st January 1940, p. 16, 25th February 1940, pp. 8–9, 3rd March 1940, pp. 8–9, 17th March 1940, pp. 20–1, 30th June 1940, p. 4, 21st July 1940, pp. 14–15, 28th July 1940, p. 13 and 4th August 1940, p. 15. See also his ghost-written autobiography published later, Sparks, *Burglar to the Nobility, passim*.

[19] For example, see in relation to miscegenation, Bland, *Modern Women on Trial*, chapter Four.

[20] S. Duncombe and A. Mattson (2006) *The Bobbed Haired Bandit: A True Story of Crime and Celebrity in 1920s New York* (New York: New York University Press).

[21] D. Gold (2015) '"Whose Hair Is It, Anyway?" Bobbed Hair and the Rhetorical Fashioning of the Modern American Woman', *Peitho Journal*, 17, 2, pp. 172–98 at p. 171.

[22] See, for example, Bland (2013) *Modern Women on Trial*, chapter Three. The 'modern' young woman was an 'obsessive focus' of the press at this time. See also Carter Wood (2012) 'The Most Remarkable Woman', p. 394 and Bland (2013) *Modern Women on Trial*, p. 1.

[23] S. Todd (2014) *The People: The Rise and fall of the Working Class* (London: John Murray), p. 31.

[24] *The Times*, 20th March 1929, p. 3 and p. 44.

youthfulness and the future'.²⁵ One of the problems was perceived to be how that newly discovered sexual freedom was to be contained.²⁶

In 1924, the case of New York robbers Celia Cooney and her husband Edward attracted extensive media coverage and the public's imagination. On the 23rd of April 1924, the *New York Herald Tribunal* asserted that 'the adventures of the original bobbed-haired bandit are entitled to be ranked among the minor masterpieces of outlawry'.²⁷ Even at that point, the use of the word 'original' implies recognition that the phrase would be attached to other female criminals. William Randolph Hearst's *New York American* paid Celia Cooney a thousand dollars to write her memoirs which were serialized as the 'Bobbed-Hair Bandit's Own Story'. The subject of competing narratives, Celia Cooney became a glamorized, dramatic and romantic heroine at the centre of a press generated ' … tried and true formula of controversy, outrage, and a pinch of fear … a contest between a wily female bandit and the keystone cops'.²⁸ The case of Celia Cooney was also covered in Britain.

By the mid-1920s in Britain, depictions of the modern bobbed-haired woman criminal were prominent in mass consumer culture, much of which was imported from the United States. These depictions connected female emancipation, social disruption and desires for consumer goods with criminality.²⁹ The generic bobbed-haired bandit, the woman robber often wielding a gun, became a central character in numerous film portrayals. On the 15th, 16th and 17th of October 1925, the Central Picture Theatre, Folkestone, screened the silent motion picture, *In Bad Company*, with prominent actor Madge Kennedy as the bobbed-haired bandit.³⁰ Almost a year later at the Electric Theatre, Folkestone, the film *Go Straight* was shown which revolved around the adventures of a beautiful bobbed-haired bandit and her endeavours to, as the title denotes, 'Go straight'.³¹ In 1926 the Palladium in Gloucester showed the silent movie *Silk Stocking Sal* the ' … story of a beautiful little bobbed-haired bandit' who 'went straight'.³² The Royal Electric Theatre in Hartlepool showed a two-act silent slapstick comedy, *Bobbed Hair and Bandits,* in January 1928.³³ In these movies, the

---

²⁵ Bland, *Modern Women on Trial*, p. 3.
²⁶ P. Tinkler (2000) 'Women and Popular Literature' in J. Purvis (ed.) *Women's History: Britain 1850–1945 – An Introduction* (London: Routledge), pp. 131–56 at p. 143 cited in Carter Wood (2012) 'The Most Remarkable Woman', p. 394.
²⁷ Cited in Duncombe and Mattson (2006) *The Bobbed Haired Bandit*, p. 3.
²⁸ See ibid., p. 8.
²⁹ See A. Miller (2011) 'Bloody Blondes and Bobbed Haired Bandits: Executing Justice and Constructing Celebrity Criminals in the 1920s Popular Press' in D. Negra and S. Holmes (eds) *In the Limelight and under the Microscope: Forms and Functions of Female Celebrity* (London: Continuum), pp. 61–81 at p. 69.
³⁰ See Anonymous (1923) 'Memories on My Own Screen', *Picture-Play Magazine*, January, pp. 18–20 available at http://www.archive.org/stream/Picture-playMagazineJan.1923/PicturePlay0123#page/n19/mode/1up (accessed 16 February 2018). Also widely advertised including *Folkestone, Hythe, Sandgate and Cheriton Herald*, 10th October 1925, p. 8.
³¹ *Folkestone, Hythe, Sandgate and Cheriton Herald*, 11th September 1926, p. 10.
³² *Gloucestershire Chronicle*, 23rd April 1926, p. 10.
³³ *Hartlepool Northern Daily Mail*, 21st January 1928, p. 1. This last film has been lost but appears not to include a woman bandit but rather to have capitalized on the contemporary association between bobbed-hair and female banditry. See https://www.lost-films.eu/films/show/id/4427 (accessed 23 June 2017).

redemptive narrative dramatized the plot lines offering a positive outcome for love and a return to appropriate gender roles.

The newsprint media repeatedly utilized cinematic language and associations. On the 26th of August 1926 an article in the *Leeds Mercury* described a 'twenty years old bobbed-haired girl' involved as the car driver in a 'smash-and-grab raid with male associates'. It notes that around London recently ' ... women have been involved in cases of burglary, house-breaking, hold-ups, black-mail'.[34] In September 1926 the *Yorkshire Post and Leeds Intelligencer* described a crime (breaking and entering and theft) in Hampstead involving a 'girl motor bandit' and specifically mentioned she had bobbed hair.[35] Two days later the headline 'GIRL BANDIT HUE AND CRY' was used in the *Lancashire Evening Post*.[36] Significantly, the article concerned a search for the identity of *the* 'bobbed-haired bandit', a daring woman known to have taken part in at least seven motor car raids in London. However, the article notes that the police are not sure that is 'her natural state of hair dressing'. It is surmised that this woman may be leading a 'Jekyll and Hyde existence' which enables her to exit her haunts, so increasing the mystery and dark allure of her identity. It was contended that she was able to ' ... cast off her role of motor bandit and become, instead, a young woman of fashion in London' hence retaining the association with modern lifestyles.

The article emphasizes her elusiveness, an elusiveness which has also been reflected in the very limited attention she has received from historians. This is due no doubt to a belief, asserted by Jerry White, that her identity was never revealed. He states, 'Ruby Sparks's female companion was the celebrated Bobbed-haired Bandit, an immensely skilled driver who captured the nation's headlines from the late 1920s to the early 1930s. She, though, was never captured.'[37] While early usage of terms such as 'girl motor bandit' may have had a more generic flavour about them, the image of the bobbed-haired bandit was eventually to solidify and become attached principally to one woman. However, by the time the bobbed-haired bandit had become firmly aligned to Lilian Goldstein, the trial by the press of this constructed criminal woman had already been conducted. The final step was to unite them into the form of a modern, attractive, fashionable and young woman who had sought excitement and pleasure in the arms of a notorious criminal, even become his accomplice. But, the trope continued, her essential feminine vulnerability, the loss of her reputation and fearfulness of his aggressive tendencies brought her to the realization of her dreadful mistake while also torn by her loyalty to her man. This unfair trial was a lesson for women to remain on the right moral pathway. The means of uniting the constructed bobbed-haired bandit and the 'real' one was the criminal trial of July 1940, but that also

---

[34] *Leeds Mercury*, 26th August 1926, p. 5.
[35] *Yorkshire Post and Leeds Intelligencer*, 2nd September 1926, p. 9. Also see, for example, an article in the *Dundee Evening Telegraph*, 12th November 1926, p. 1 in which a woman 'bandit' involved in a mail van robbery in Worcester was referred to as having 'dark bobbed hair'.
[36] *Lancashire Evening Post*, 4th September 1926, p. 2.
[37] White, *London in the 20th Century*, p. 265. In many historical accounts, including my own (2013) *Inter-war Penal Policy and Crime in England* (Basingstoke: Palgrave), Ruby Sparks was believed to be his correct name. This is the name which is used by the police and the press at the time. However, his birth certificate gives Spark as his correct surname. The digitization of newspapers has, of course, facilitated close research into individual offenders.

signalled the demise of the former. After 1940 the term 'bobbed-haired' or 'bobbed hair bandit' was rarely used in the press. A brief revival in July–August 1961 in *The People* was the serialization of Ruby Spark's book, *Burglar to the Nobility*, where Lil or Lily as the bobbed-haired bandit is often mentioned.[38]

Lilian Goldstein

As suggested by White's reference to the bobbed-haired bandit, it is through press coverage of Ruby Spark that Lilian Goldstein first emerges into the public limelight. She is named in the press from quite an early point, although her identification as the bobbed-haired bandit comes later. In 1927 an article in *The Scotsman* reported on the capture of Ruby 'Sparks' along with Victor Kendall for a series of robberies in the Liverpool and Manchester areas. Lilian Rose Goldstein, 'stated to be Kendall's sister', is accused of 'unlawful possession of stolen property' (receiving stolen goods).[39] A headline in the *Sunday Post* on the 5th of June 1927 reads, 'GIRL AND MOTOR BANDITS' and Lilian Goldstein is described as ' … a bobbed-haired girl in her early twenties' believed to be a native of London, ' … of dark features and distinctly good looking'. These and other articles invariably refer to her physical attractiveness. She is described as 'haughty' and as a 'woman bandit'.[40] In another article she is described as 'fashionably dressed' and a 'smartly dressed married woman', her marital status posing an incongruous challenge to the full realization of the modern woman criminal stereotype.[41] She apparently ' … smiled as she left the dock for the cells' (when the case was transferred from Liverpool to Southport jurisdiction). She was later discharged but at that point is again referred to as a 'woman bandit', aged twenty-five.[42] Later that year Goldstein helped Ruby Spark escape successfully from Strangeways Prison in Manchester, although he was soon apprehended.

The differing tone of reporting suggests uncertainty as to how to represent her at this stage, as she had not yet been convicted of any offence known to the press: was she a criminal, a bandit or a respectable married woman unknowingly caught up in events? Another problem is the looseness of press terminology so that not every vague reference to women criminals being bandits can be associated with Goldstein, albeit

---

[38] *The People*, 30th July 1961, p. 6, p. 13 and p. 20 and 27th August 1961 and also Spark, *Burglar to the Nobility*, passim.

[39] *The Scotsman*, 6th June, 1927, p. 11. Also see, B. McDonald (2015) *Alice Diamond and the Forty Elephants: Britain's First Female Crime Syndicate* (Croydon: Milo Books) for an account of some of Goldstein's activities and associations.

[40] *Yorkshire Post and Leeds Intelligencer*, 6th June 1927, p. 9.

[41] *Manchester Evening News*, 7th July 1927, p. 5 and *Yorkshire Post and Leeds Intelligencer*, 11th June 1927, p. 15.

[42] *The Scotsman*, 8th July 1927, p. 5 and *Yorkshire Post and Leeds Intelligencer*, 8th July 1927, p. 5. She appeared in the dock at Liverpool, but the offences with which the goods were connected occurred outside the Liverpool jurisdiction so she was to be handed over to the Southport Police and the case before the Liverpool court was withdrawn. At a later trial she was discharged.

that she was active alongside Spark so that some of these articles must indeed have referred to her.[43] In May 1932 Lilian Goldstein comes to light during police evidence given at the trial of convicts for offences relating to the Dartmoor Prison riot of the 24th of January 1932. Because of his perceived prominence in that riot, Ruby Spark is one of the defendants and unsurprisingly there is extensive coverage of the trial in the press. The riot was one of the biggest press stories of the year.[44] In police evidence prior to sentencing it was stated that a woman known as the 'bobbed haired bandit' had attempted to help Ruby 'Sparks' escape from Wandsworth Prison in 1930 but she is not named. She had not been apprehended for the offence and so her identity could not be proven. Interestingly, Ruby Spark is recorded as responding in court that the 'stuff' about the bobbed-haired bandit was 'entirely a lot of rot'.[45] However, many years later when he collaborated on the ghost-written account of his life, *Ruby Sparks, Burglar to the Nobility* (1961), he assumed a different, no doubt more commercial, line and Lilian Goldstein is referred to numerous times throughout the book as the bobbed-haired bandit.[46]

It is not until 1933, when Ruby Spark is in prison, that Lilian Goldstein is reported as appearing in court again. Under the headline, 'WOMAN SHOP THIEF SUSPECTED', the *Daily Mail* asserts about 'Mrs Lilian Goldstein, aged thirty, of Bedford Hill, Balham S.W' that she is ' … strongly suspected of being the woman described as the bobbed-haired bandit, and as such she was put up for identification, but was not picked out'. She was also believed to be 'associating with reputed thieves'.[47] She was sent to prison for four months for stealing articles worth £10 from a West End milliner's shop. Mr Claude Hornby, for the defence, stated at that point that Mrs Goldstein had been married for thirteen years, but was separated from her husband, and had one child. He had endeavoured without success to represent her as an honest woman of 'good-class' who had been subject to an instance of irresistible temptation: no common shop-lifter but a middle-class kleptomaniac.[48] This was a tenuous defence given that, according to one paper, she was apprehended with the following concealed about her person: '13 nightdresses, two pairs of pyjamas, two lady's slips, six pairs of knickers, seven chemises, and one bodice'.[49]

---

[43] See The National Archives (hereafter TNA), Metropolitan Police, Office of the Commissioner, Correspondence and Papers, Special Series, MEPO 3/481.
[44] See R. Murphy (1993) *Smash and Grab: Gangsters in the London Underworld* (London: Faber and Faber) and also A. Brown (2007) 'The Amazing Mutiny at the Dartmoor Convict Prison', *British Journal of Criminology*, 47, 2, pp. 276–92.
[45] TNA, Assizes: Western Circuit – Miscellaneous Books, Criminal Depositions and Case Papers, *Rex v Beadles*, ASSI 24/18/4.
[46] Ruby Spark gets intermittent further attention from the press during his life, especially in *The People* in August 1961 as a result of the publication of *Burglar to the Nobility*.
[47] *Daily Mail*, 12th July 1933, p. 5.
[48] *Illustrated Police News*, 20th July 1933, p. 7. Also see, E.S. Abelson (1989) 'The Invention of Kleptomania', *Signs*, 15, 1, pp. 123–43.
[49] *Liverpool Echo*, 11th July 1933, p. 8. According to Brian McDonald, Lilian Goldstein had joined a shoplifting gang from a young age. See, McDonald (2015) *Alice Diamond and the Forty Elephants*, p. 194.

The information given in court in 1933 about Goldstein's background was accurate. In October 1920, Lilian Rose Kendall married Henry Goldstein, a jeweller, at the St Martins Register Office.[50] The marriage certificate states that she was twenty-two years of age although in fact she was only eighteen; Henry Goldstein, it records, as twenty-four years old. About three months earlier, he had appeared in court charged with 'living wholly or in part on the earnings of prostitution'. Rose Kendall, as she was referred to (Kendall being her maiden name), was described as formerly being in the employment of the Ministry of Pensions, presumably during the war. In evidence, she stated she had met Goldstein in September or October 1918.[51] She was aged sixteen years old.[52] She then lived with him at various addresses and ' ... she used to give him money'. 'In reply to Mr Wilberforce, the witness said that she left him about three weeks ago because she was jealous of another girl. Mr Hornby, for Goldstein, said that the defendant was in regular employment, and did not know the life the girl was leading. The defendant was remanded.' Coverage in the *Illustrated Police News* was, predictably, more explicit and made it clear that Henry Goldstein's version of events had not been believed by the court. Under the headline, 'THE PERFECT BEAST' the article included the judge's description of this as a 'most pathetic case', involving Lilian Rose Kendall, who was 'not yet eighteen years of age'.[53]

> Kendall's story was that she made the acquaintance of the prisoner [Henry Goldstein] in October, 1918, when [he was] working as a jeweller at Hatton Gardens, and she was living with a girl friend. She subsequently went to live with him. He fell out of work, had no money, and in February, 1919, suggested that she should go on the streets. She did so, giving her earnings to him. The prisoner, on oath, said he met the girl in the streets and spent the evening and night with her. He took a liking to the girl, from whose story of herself took it she had reformed. He was in work during the whole of his association with the girl, and she had never given him a penny. Mr. Wilberforce imposed sentence of three months' hard labour, with an additional month in default of payment of ten guineas costs.

After her court appearances in 1920, 1927 (when she was discharged) and 1933, 'Lilian Kendall, alias Goldstein' is reported as being in court again in August 1934 when she and a woman companion were charged at Carlisle with stealing two fur coats.[54] Her alibi was that she was ' ... following her employment in London as a canvasser for a hosiery firm'. The case was dismissed due to insufficient evidence. By the end of 1934, when she was thirty-two years of age, Lilian Rose Goldstein had appeared in court at least four times during her chequered young life.

[50] St Martins Register Office, 'Henry Goldstein and Lilian Rose Kendall' (1920) certified copy of marriage certificate, 4 January 2018, application number 8825697/1.
[51] *The Times*, 5th July 1920, p. 11. Unfortunately, there is no report on the outcome of this trial in *The Times*.
[52] Wandsworth Register Office, 'Lilian Rose Kendall' (1902) certified copy of birth certificate for Lilian Rose Kendall, 3 July 1902, application number 8395796-1.
[53] *Illustrated Police News*, 27th July 1920, p. 7.
[54] *Manchester Guardian*, 18th August 1934, p. 12. However, she was defended by a London barrister, Mr G.L. Hardy.

Prison escape and on trial 1940

In January 1940 Ruby Spark escaped from Dartmoor Prison and remained on the run for an unprecedented five months. Upon his recapture by police late in June 1940, Lilian Rose Kendall Goldstein was also charged with harbouring him, although she denied the charge stating, 'I have not seen the man, and don't wish to'.[55] The bobbed-haired bandit also gained perhaps her greatest notoriety and public attention during the time Spark was on the run from prison. Yet prior to Spark's re-arrest, a series of prominent full or half-page supposedly confessional exposures by the 'bobbed-haired bandit' had appeared in the *Sunday Pictorial*.[56] Surprisingly the confessor was not Goldstein but a woman giving her name as Joyce Alexandra Powys-Wilson, who claimed to be a minor aristocrat even signing her statements to the paper, alongside the assertion 'I confess, I was the bobbed-haired bandit'.[57]

Joyce Powys-Wilson

The series of articles in the *Sunday Pictorial* focused initially on Ruby Spark, thereafter on the bobbed-haired bandit until the final articles return to Spark. She was described retrospectively as having slipped out of the court in Manchester following his conviction in 1927, 'slim, blonde, dressed in red. She had bobbed hair'.[58] She was dramatized as ' ... the famous Bobbed Haired Bandit, the girl smash-and-grab raider whom the police could never lay hands on'. Ruby's ' ... chief assistant, look-out and driver ... the blonde bobbed haired bandit, the girl in red'. 'Fair, with small features, blue eyes, slim build'. Red was apparently her lucky colour. As the bobbed-haired bandit she was commodified and judged as ' ... one of the outstanding stories of the underworld in the last generation', the woman who 'Got Him Out of Gaol Twice ... Has She Succeeded This Time?'[59] Despite linking the bobbed-haired bandit to Spark's appearance in court in 1927 and related press coverage which had named Lilian Goldstein, Joyce Alexandra Powys-Wilson was accepted, seemingly without question, as the notorious woman bandit.

These 'confessions' fit the mould of a genre that has been identified by other writers (see, for example, Houlbrook on Netley Lucas and Josephine O'Dare), including highlighting efforts of self-reformation and seeking to escape 'social marginalization rather than endure a life of crime.'[60] For example, on the 25th of February 1940, in

---

[55] *Evening Despatch*, 29th June 1940, p. 1.
[56] The *Sunday Pictorial* became the *Sunday Mirror* in 1963.
[57] Statement and signature from the *Sunday Pictorial*, 25th February 1940, p. 8.
[58] *Sunday Pictorial*, 21st January 1940, p. 16.
[59] Ibid.
[60] J. Carter Wood (2014) 'The Constables and the "Garage Girl"', *Media History*, 20, 4, pp. 384–99 at p. 394.

supposedly the last letter the bobbed-haired bandit wrote to Ruby Spark ('My last letter to "Public Enemy No.1"') she declared, 'I owe you nothing and you owe nothing to me … I am through with you and the old life forever. I never want to see you again. I said that then and I mean it more than ever now.' The popular combination of romance, social reform and (to use a modern term) 'misery memoir' identified by John Carter Wood comes through.[61] Of course, the irony is the yawning social chasm between a supposed minor member of the aristocracy and the background of Lilian Goldstein who was the daughter of a journeyman house painter, Henry Kendall, and was prostituting herself before she had reached the age of eighteen.[62] The image of the 1920s 'modern woman cum-flapper' may have played with the boundaries between respectable and working women, or women of a 'certain class', which was, as Bland points out, a coded phrase for prostitutes, but in practice the distinction remained and was inscribed in the differences between this construction of the bobbed-haired bandit and Goldstein's experiences.[63]

The *Sunday Pictorial* depicts the bobbed-haired bandit's love for a man 'Scotland Yard regards as the most dangerous criminal in Britain'. Through love and devotion as well as the thrill and excitement he offered, she became involved in his life of crime, 'Twice I tried to help him escape from gaol'.[64] She professed her desire to leave her life of crime behind her and, in true moral reportage, warned against other women following her example: 'I will tell the truth in these articles because I want to finish with the life that has brought me degradation. I have associated with infamous criminals, but I am going to tell all I know, even if I have to face punishment at the hands of the law.'[65] Now at the age of thirty-eight, which was indeed Lilian Goldstein's age at the time, 'I want to leave my past behind me and lead a decent life.'[66] Thus, she composed a major moral lesson of the times, a modern woman gone bad but desperate to return to the moral fold.

The articles contextualize the development of her relationship with Spark against a backdrop of post-war freedoms and alleviation of wartime constraints: hence fitting into an existing and well-known narrative about the demoralizing and destabilizing impact of war. According to Spark's ghost-written account he met and began a relationship with Goldstein, Lily, whom he describes as 'his first girl-friend', in 1920–1921 when he was nineteen or twenty and she was eighteen or nineteen years old.[67] The bobbed-haired bandit in the *Sunday Pictorial* is seduced by the excitement and romance of Spark. In dramatic, if unlikely, shades, 'I threw away the chance of marrying a wealthy young peer – for the excitement and thrills of fighting the law.'[68] At a party in Maida

---

[61] Ibid.
[62] Her father's occupation is given on her birth certificate, Wandsworth Register Office, 'Lilian Rose Kendall' (1902) certified copy of birth certificate for Lilian Rose Kendall, 3 July 1902, application number 8395796-1.
[63] Bland, *Modern Women on Trial*, p. 5.
[64] Successfully from Strangeways Prison in 1927 and unsuccessfully from Wandsworth Prison in 1930.
[65] *Sunday Pictorial*, 25th February 1940, pp. 8–9.
[66] Ibid.
[67] Sparks, *Burglar to the Nobility*, pp. 25–8.
[68] Ibid., p. 8.

Vale, she met, according to one article, ' ... a whole crowd of strange, adventurous-looking men. To me they looked like film stars and they talked about the most exciting things.' She meets Ruby Spark described as 'about her own age', ' ... brown haired, rosy-cheeked, and agile looking, with an expression that was as sharp as a razor'. From that brief meeting, 'I decided that Ruby was just the man for me. He was cut out for an exciting life, and he soon singled me out for his special attention. It was a case of "love at first sight" to me'.[69] The meaning of the term 'special attention' is clear as she then states that she went home with him that night. Despite their criminal involvement and the morality-challenging speed of their becoming lovers, their relationship is also in part depicted and articulated through a narrative of conventional romance and passion. 'Sparkes [sic] treated me as a gentleman would have done.' Yet once she became aware of him being a 'desperate criminal', she was a threat, 'I realised that if I showed my horror and threatened to leave him, Ruby would turn on me and for his own safety, do something desperate to keep me in his clutches. Besides, at that time I honestly believed I loved him.'[70] The language and air of sexual danger would have sat comfortably in a Hollywood movie script.

The bobbed-haired bandit who confessed in the *Sunday Pictorial* put her waywardness down to the 'madness of the dizzy days in London at the end of the last war' just as Charlotte Wildman's Miss Moriarty was 'identified by the press as an inevitable product of women's wartime experiences' as well as a ' ... broader sense of chaos around gender roles'.[71] Wildman emphasizes the depiction of such women ' ... as active, entrepreneurial agents of crime, rather than as victims or as reluctant accomplices of male offenders'.[72] Certainly the bobbed-haired bandit professes to be a willing partner in crime and indeed to have pressed the reluctant Spark to allow her to become involved. Yet the narrative also conforms to conservative notions of an affectionate romantic relationship dominated by masculine power and the varying fortunes of his criminal career. There is a discernible strain as the coverage attempts to walk the line between sometimes conflicting narratives of drama and condemnation, romanticization and moral judgement.

The successful attempt to break Ruby Spark out of Strangeways Prison in 1927, albeit he was quickly apprehended, is outlined under the heading 'GAOL-BREAK' as ' ... one of the most daring and idiotic things ever done by a woman' and in order to heighten the drama is followed by the assertion that Ruby Spark's earlier release from prison supposedly coincided with one of the greatest crime waves in Britain, of 'smash-and-grab raiders' and 'car bandits'. 'I was behind the scenes of this great crime wave.' Again, there are correlations with other evidence about the criminal career of Ruby Spark. In 1925 he was indeed wanted by police in relation to smash-and-grab raids across the country, including London, Birmingham and Manchester.[73]

---

[69] *Sunday Pictorial*, 25th February 1940, pp. 8–9.
[70] Ibid., p. 9.
[71] Wildman, 'Miss Moriarty, the Adventuress and the Crime Queen', pp. 73–98.
[72] Ibid., p. 74.
[73] See TNA, Metropolitan Police, Office of the Commissioner, Correspondence and Papers, Special Series, MEPO 3/481.

Significantly, the next relevant article in the *Sunday Pictorial* was a fairly short piece in a more standard news format, the title 'WOMAN ACCUSED OF HIDING RUBY (ESCAPE) SPARKES [sic]'.[74] Lilian Goldstein had appeared at Hendon Police Court charged with harbouring Ruby Spark from the 10th of January to 6th of June 1940: 'Dressed in a black hat and coat trimmed with fox-fur Goldstein, who is fair-haired, fingered a platinum wedding ring during the few minutes she stood in the dock.' The reference to her wedding ring is interesting and suggests not only her nervousness but also a questioning about her marital status: other articles refer to her as being 'independent'. Her statement, 'I don't think it is fair. I am not guilty of the charge and know nothing about it' was reported but there is no mention of the bobbed-haired bandit. The paper is silent on the bobbed-haired bandit from then onwards and makes no mention of the articles in which a Joyce Powys-Wilson posed as that daring female criminal. Instead on the 21st of July 1940 the newspaper includes a double-page article by Ruby Spark in which 'RUBY SPARK TELLS ALL' about the ordeal of his escape.[75] The article does include a photograph, which unfortunately cannot be verified, that it asserts is Mrs Lilian Goldstein, Spark's lover. However, the photograph looks remarkably like those used in the previous articles about the bobbed-haired bandit aka Joyce Alexandra Powys-Wilson.

An intriguing possibility surrounds the articles by Powys, although it must be said that the source is not corroborated and cannot therefore be substantiated. According to Frankie Fraser, a career criminal who met Ruby Spark in Wandsworth Prison in 1943, when the police were hunting for Spark on the run from Dartmoor Prison in 1940, Lilian Goldstein set up a 'really good smokescreen'.[76] The smokescreen was to get a woman ' ... to write to the papers saying how she's abandoned Ruby and begging him to give himself up – and all the while he was staying at her place in North London!'[77] This possibility would explain the level of accuracy in the newspaper reports and, given the circumstances, it was likely that Lilian Goldstein would not want to put herself in the limelight of press attention. These articles by an impostor may well have operated as a deflection and disincentive to journalists from delving further into Goldstein's identity and location, which she was then sharing with Spark. Joyce Powys-Wilson cannot be located and was probably a pseudonym. According to Spark's account, he and Goldstein were short of money while he was on the run and this ploy could have been a means of obtaining funds. Communications between the police and the press must have been weak about this escaped convict on the run. Detective Superintendent Robert Higgins states that the police captured Spark by following Goldstein and so were aware of their association. A special squad was set up with the specific aim of capturing Spark, so they would not have wanted to pass on information about Goldstein's identity to journalists who might endanger their operation.

Ruby Spark's ghost-written account ultimately trades on the aspects of his life which attracted the most public interest, including the bobbed-haired bandit and

---

[74] *Sunday Pictorial*, 30th June 1940, p. 4.
[75] *Sunday Pictorial*, 21st July 1940, pp. 14–15.
[76] F. Fraser with J. Morton (1997) *Mad Frank and Friends* (London: Warner Books), p. 7.
[77] Ibid.

the criminal activities for which they were known together. Dramatically, the smash-and-grab raider, Ruby, who escaped from prison and of Dartmoor riot fame loved the bobbed-haired bandit from a young age and was loved in return. They became glamourized, commodified and judged together as well as individually.[78] Following his escape from Dartmoor, Spark's account suggests that his bobbed-haired bandit lost her nerve.[79] Central Criminal Court records show indictments against Lilian that she knowingly harboured an escaped felon and that she ' ... did receive, comfort, harbour, assist and maintain the said Charles John Sparkes [sic]' hence concealing the commission of a felony.[80] In court Goldstein claimed that since Spark's conviction in 1939 she had been living with a man called Jim Duggan as his wife, that she had not seen Spark since then and did not want to see him.[81] That defence was not supported by the fact that the flat they lived in had not been rented until 18 May 1940. In addition, Goldstein, Spark (using the name Harry) and Jim Duggan were seen together in public and seemed to be on friendly terms.[82] Goldstein maintained she did not see Spark until April and she asked him to stay away. One newspaper reported, 'At this point Mrs Goldstein broke down and sobbed, saying she was afraid of Sparkes. Sparkes went to her flat while she was out, and sometimes had food there. He never stayed the night. Asked why she did not report Sparkes, Mrs Goldstein said that he had threatened to kill her on two occasions.' Spark did not deny this saying he did not find Lilian until two months after his escape, ' ... she begged him to leave her, saying she was living with a straight man. Sparkes said he told her that was all right and he did not want to spoil her life.'[83] According to press reports, Spark agreed that he had threatened 'Mrs Goldstein'.[84]

The historical evidence will not allow us to determine whether violence or threats of violence had formed a part of their relationship at any point, but this narrative of forced help was one that fed easily into Spark's masculine criminality and Goldstein's feminine vulnerability: his guilt and her ultimate, if self-inflicted, victimhood had already been determined through trial by media. Ruby Spark had no convictions specifically for physically violent offences, although smash-and-grab raiding could certainly be seen as an aggressive enterprise, nevertheless his raider-cum-bandit-cum-gangster identity no doubt evoked ready-made stereotypes of the assertive masculinity

---

[78] As Houlbrook notes about inter-war accounts, '... the crook life story's temporal specificity reflected the particular conjunction of social, cultural, political, and economic contexts within which it took shape'. It was a reworking of older and newer forms, the rising influence of the marketplace. See Houlbrook, 'Commodifying the Self Within', p. 327.
[79] Sparks, *Burglar to the Nobility*, p. 36.
[80] The case appeared before the Central criminal Court on the 16th of July 1940. 'Charles John Sparkes' was charged with 'Being at large, contrary to section 3 of the Penal Servitude Act 1857' and Lilian Goldstein was charged with 'Accessory after the fact to the same offence'. See TNA, Central Criminal Court, Depositions, CRIM 1/1215.
[81] Ibid.
[82] Ibid., *see the* evidence of Mary Margaret Cahill.
[83] *Coventry Evening Telegraph*, 18th July 1940. The case was widely reported across the London and provincial press, for example, *Daily Mirror*, 19th July 1940 and *Liverpool Evening Express*, 18th July 1940.
[84] *Liverpool Evening Express*, 18th July 1940.

of American gangsters ' … laced with explicit and implicit violence'.[85] At first sight this seems to be a damaging admission; however, the indictment against Spark was for being an escaped felon 'at large'. The manner of his behaviour while at large was not part of the indictment. On the other hand, Goldstein had much to gain by depicting herself as a victim, as a woman who was endeavouring to reform and move beyond previous criminal associations but prevented forcefully from doing so.

This was not the first occasion on which Ruby Spark may have acted to defend Goldstein from criminal conviction. In June 1927, Spark, under one of his alias's, John Wilson, appeared in court with three other men, one of whom was Victor Kendall, Lilian's brother, for breaking and entering and stealing from dwelling houses at Southport, in Lancashire. Alongside them Lilian Rose Goldstein was charged with receiving stolen goods. All the prisoners pleaded not guilty and were committed for trial at the next Manchester Assizes. However, one report of the proceedings noted that their defence solicitor claimed a detective had stated to Wilson 'that if he [Spark] would admit it they would do their best to help Lily'.[86] When the defendants appeared before the Manchester Assize in July the three men pleaded guilty, the prosecution did not proceed with the charge against Goldstein and she was discharged.[87]

Goldstein fought hard to stay out of prison mustering a range of elements in her defence. These included accusations, denied by detectives in court, that when they came to her flat to arrest her and she was changing out of her nightgown and dressing gown, at least one of them did not leave the room. She also claimed that she was inhibited or blocked from contacting her solicitor.[88] It was admitted by Detective Constable Matthew Brinnand that the police searched her flat without having a search warrant but in the end her defence failed and she was sentenced to six months' imprisonment.[89] However, following the verdict of the jury, the response of the judge, Gerald Dodson, suggests that she had succeeded in portraying herself as deserving of sympathy, despite the moral trial already conducted in the newspapers. The judge had remained open-minded as to whether coercion had been involved. In his memoirs Dodson left only a passing reference to Goldstein's appearance in court with Spark in 1940; ' … the prisoner was finally caught and appeared before me charged with prison-breaking, accompanied in the dock by a woman who had been harbouring him. She received a short sentence, but the man returned sorrowfully to complete his sentence in his residence on the Moor.'[90] For Lilian Goldstein, however, the verdict and subsequent action by the judge were significant and possibly life-changing. Her criminal experiences finally ended for her, it seems, when she received unexpected

---

[85] C. Potter Bond (1995) '"I'll Go the Limit and Then Some": Gun Molls, Desire and Danger in the 1930s', *Feminist Studies*, 21, 1, pp. 41–66, p. 55.

[86] *Manchester Guardian*, 16th June 1927, specifically 'POLICE QUESTIONS TO PRISONER: Alleged Bargain to Secure Confession.'

[87] *Manchester Guardian*, 8th July 1927.

[88] See TNA, Central Criminal Court, Depositions, CRIM 1/1215 and *Yorkshire Evening Post*, 8th July 1940.

[89] TNA, Central Criminal Court, Depositions, CRIM 1/1215.

[90] Dodson (1967) *Consider Your Verdict*, p. 103.

mercy in court. Her sentence of six months was commuted, she served only three weeks and was then put on probation.[91] The *Evening Despatch* of the 23rd of July 1940 reported the Recorder as telling her,

> You followed a very natural womanly instinct in trying to succour and protect this man with whom you had intimate relations over a period of years ... Make the best use of this chance, because although you have broken the law and assisted this man perhaps unwittingly and because you were compelled to do so, you obstructed the police and gave a lot of trouble. Now you can break away from your past association and there may be some hope for you in the future.

Spark's own account concurs that this unexpected mercy was a catalyst for Lilian Goldstein, 'The Bobbed Haired Bandit had finished with crime, anyway, and this unexpected – well, I suppose the only word is mercy – really did it. It shook me a bit too.'[92]

Conclusion

Unlike so many who journeyed from the prison gates to the editor's office between the wars, Goldstein never sought celebrity status.[93] Her narrative presents the intriguing possibility that she commodified and used to her own advantage the trial by the press and the constructed identities of the bobbed-haired bandit, and indeed Lilian Goldstein. The identity of the bobbed-haired bandit was, in many respects, fixed in time – exciting, fashionable, glamourous and, of course, always young – unlike Lilian Goldstein who aged and tired of criminality and who was given an opportunity by the court to change the direction of her life. While the press judged her as a modern, confident and immoral woman who went too far in seeking out excitement, the courtroom drew on the depiction of her as vulnerable and fearful: an image she herself may have played a part in constructing.

On the 7th of March 1944 she posted a notice in the *London Gazette* stating that LILIAN ROSE GOLDSTEIN of Wembley Park Drive, Middlesex, ' ... intends to renounce and abandon the surname of Goldstein and to assume and on all occasions whatsoever and at all times to sign and use and to be called and known by the surname of Kendall in lieu of and in substitute for the surname of Goldstein'. This was a clear attempt to disassociate herself from her married name and public image as Lilian Goldstein and was the final addendum to the narrative of Goldstein as criminal bandit. The fair trial she received in court enabled her to distance herself from past criminal activities and move beyond the stories about the woman bandit who fascinated readers with adventure, glamour, youth and romance but whose narrative was reassuring in its ultimate re-establishment of conservative female norms and priorities.[94]

[91] Ibid., p. 137.
[92] Sparks, *Burglar to the Nobility*, p. 137.
[93] Houlbrook, 'Commodifying the Self Within', p. 322.
[94] 'Joyce Powys-Wilson' and Lilian Goldstein have been the subject of further research forthcoming: See C.Davies (forthcoming 2021) *Queens of the Underworld* (London: The History Press).

Bibliography

Primary Sources

Unpublished Primary Sources

British Library (London)

British Library, Department of Manuscripts, Havelock Ellis Papers,
'Havelock Ellis to F.H. Perry-Coste, 1897–1899', Additional Manuscripts, 70524.
'Havelock Ellis to Edward Carpenter, 17 December 1892: Copy', Additional Manuscripts 70536.

Glasgow City Archives (The Mitchell Library, Glasgow)

Papers relating to Oscar Slater (1872–1948) Victim of Miscarriage of Justice, TD1560/5/9

Glasgow University Archives

Records of the Department of Forensic Medicine and Science, Case Files 1906–1969 – Oscar Slater, 2B/5/1-6

London Metropolitan Archives

Bow Street Court Register: Court of Summary Jurisdiction Records (31st May 1898), PS/BOW/A1/6
Calendar of Prisoners and North London Sessions, ILS/B/45/001
Greater London Burial Index, City of London Burials 1754–1855, P60.531 HAN
Quarter and General Sessions held at North London (10th April 1890), LJ/SR/155
Middlesex Sessions' records, Coroner's Inquest, 12 May 1827, MJ/SPC, E 3309

National Archives (Kew, Surrey)

Assizes,
Northern and North-Eastern Circuits: Criminal Depositions and Case Papers, ASSI 45/74
Northern and North-Eastern Circuits: Indictment Files, ASSI 44/180
Northern and North-Eastern Circuit: Miscellanea, ASSI 47/47
Western Circuit: Miscellaneous Books, Criminal Depositions and Case Papers, ASSI 24/18/4
Central Criminal Court,
Court Books, CRIM 6/8
Depositions, CRIM 1/1215
Home Office, Registered Papers,

Hundred: Ossulstone (Tower Division) Parish: Christ Church Spitalfields, Census Returns 1841, HO107/710, book 10
Prosecutions for Blasphemy, 45/17459/8, 45/10665/216120, 45/24619/217459, 144/114/A25454, 144/871/160552
Supplementary regarding Indecent Publications – Homogenic Love 1909–1910, 144/1043/183473
Home Office and Prison Commission,
Series 1, Newcastle upon Tyne Gaol: Calendar of Trials at Quarter Sessions and Assizes for the Town and County of Newcastle upon Tyne, PCOM 2/344
Metropolitan Police,
Office of the Commissioner, Correspondence and Papers, Special Series, MEPO 3/481
Treasury Solicitor and HM Procurator General: Law Officers' and Counsel's Opinions
Regina v William Palmer, Application for Jury Member Remuneration, TS 25/927
Treasury Solicitor and HM Procurator General Papers,
Regina v William Palmer, Central Criminal Court, TS 11/430-434

National Library of Ireland (Dublin)

'Lines Written on the Liberation of Barrett', Ms. LO 4051/112.

National Records of Ireland (Dublin)

Chief Secretary Papers, Inquiry into the Execution of Myles Joyce, NAI/CSORP/1883/189.
Queen v Barrett, 1869–1870, CCS/1870/197, Boxes 1-3.
Queen v Joyce – Transcript of Proceedings, CRF/1902/J13/18/7 and CRF/1902/J13/29.
Return of Outrages Specially Reported to the Constabulary Office: Homicides Reported in 1882, CSO/ICR/2/1882/8.

National Records of Scotland (Edinburgh)

Justiciary Court,
Criminal Case File 1909: Oscar Slater, HH16/109
Criminal Case File 1909–1921: Oscar Slater, HH16/110
Criminal Case File 1914–1948: Oscar Slater, HH16/111
Criminal Case File 1927–1976: Oscar Slater, HH16/112
Minute Book, JC9/7
Process Papers, JC26/1915/105, JC26/2925/205, JC34/1/32/2, JC34/1/32/4-6, JC34/1/32/9, JC34/1/32/11, JC34/1/32/18, JC34/1/32/27
Precognition Papers, AD21/5-6, AD21/17/7, AD21/18/13, AD21/19/16
Prisoner Record 1909–1927: Oscar Slater, HH15/20/1
Prisoner Record 1909–1928: Oscar Slater, HH15/20/3
Trial of Oscar Slater (Murder), AD21/14/7/2-3
Trial of Oscar Slater, 1908–1928, Papers relating to the 1914 Inquiry, AD21/15/6

Registry Offices

St Martins Register Office,

'Henry Goldstein and Lilian Rose Kendall' (1920) certified copy of marriage certificate, 4 January 2018, application number 8825697/1
Wandsworth Register Office,
'Lilian Rose Kendall' (1902) certified copy of birth certificate for Lilian Rose Kendall, 3 July 1902, application number 8395796-1

Sheffield City Archives

Papers of Edward Carpenter, 'Havelock Ellis to Edward Carpenter, 17 May 1907', MSS357/14

Signet Library (Edinburgh)

William Roughead Collection, R+343.1.S1.15/Volumes 2526-2528

Published Primary Sources

Official Documents and Publications (in chronological order)

Parliamentary Papers, Administration of Justice (Language) Act 1737 (11 Geo. 2, c.6).
R v. Leach (1789) 1 Leach 500, 502.
Parliamentary Papers, Select Committee on Criminal Laws relating to Capital Punishment in Felonies: Report, Minutes of Evidence, Appendix, 1819, 585, VIII, 1.
R v. Mead (1824) 2 Barn & Cress 605, 608.
R v. Sheehan (1826) Jebb CC 54.
Parliamentary Papers, Criminal Law (Ireland) Act 1828 (9 Geo. 4, c.54, s.9).
Parliamentary Papers, Central Criminal Court Act 1834 (4 & 5 Will IV c.36).
Parliamentary Papers, Prisoners' Counsel Act 1836 (6 & 7 Will. 4, c.14).
Parliamentary Papers, Select Committee on Metropolis Police Offices: Report, Minutes of Evidence, Appendix, Index, 1837, 451, XII, 176.
R v. Farlar (1837) 8 C & P 106.
Parliamentary Papers, A Copy of the Instructions given to the Respective Crown Solicitors on each Circuit, respecting the Challenging of Jurors in Crown Cases, 1842, 171, 1.
R v. Mooney (1851) 5 Cox CC 318.
R v. Dunne (1852) 5 Cox CC 507.
Parliamentary Papers, Report from the Select Committee on Outrages (Ireland), 1852, 438, XIV, 1.
Parliamentary Papers, Select Committee on Public Prosecutors – Report, 1854–55, 481, 1818.
Hansard: House of Commons Debates, 140, 25 February 1856, c1311/
Hansard: House of Commons Debates, 140, 3 March 1856, cc1768–70/
Hansard: House of Commons Debates, 140, 10 March 1856, cc2194–200/
Parliamentary Papers, The Central Criminal Court Act 1856 (19 & 20 Vict, c.16).
Parliamentary Papers, Judicial Statistics, Part I, England and Wales, Police – Criminal Proceedings – Prisons; Returns for the Year 1856.
R v. Burke (1858) 8 Cox CC 44.
Parliamentary Papers, Irish Church Act 1869 (32 & 33 Vic., c. 42).

Parliamentary Papers, Return of Outrages Reported to Constabulary Office in Ireland, 1869, C. 60 (forthcoming).
Hansard: House of Lords Debates, 199, 15 February 1870: 333.
Hansard: House of Lords Debates, 199, 28 February 1870: 876.
Hansard: House of Lords Debates, 200, 17 March 1870: 81-83
Hansard: House of Lords Debates, 200, 22 March 1870: 429
Hansard: House of Lords Debates, 200, 22 March 1870: 441
Parliamentary Papers, Landlord and Tenant (Ireland) Act 1870 (33 & 34 Vic., c. 46).
R v Barrett (1870) Ir Rep 4 CL 285-287.
Parliamentary Papers, Shorthand Writers' Notes of Judgment of Mr Justice Keogh on Trial of Galway County Election Petition, 1872, 241, XLVVIII, 17, 71, 14.
Parliamentary Papers, Select Committee on Juries (Ireland), First, Second and Special Reports, 1873, 283, 1746–47.
Parliamentary Papers, The Juries Procedure (Ireland) Act 1876 (39 & 40 Vic., c.78).
Parliamentary Papers, Return of Appeals on behalf of Persons convicted of Capital Offences to Home Secretary, for Exercise of Royal Prerogative of Pardon or Mitigation of Sentence 1861–80, 1881, 437, LXXVI, 391.
Parliamentary Papers, Report from the Select Committee of the House of Lords on the Operation of the Irish Jury Laws as regards Trial by Jury in Criminal Cases, 1881, 430, XI, 1.
Parliamentary Papers, Summary Jurisdiction (Process) Act 1881 (44 & 45 Vic., c.4).
Parliamentary Papers, Prevention of Crimes (Ireland) Act 1882 (45 & 46 Vic., c.25).
R v Hynes (1882) Dublin Commission Court (Francis Hynes), 1882, 408, LV, 167.
Hansard: House of Commons Debates, 13 August 1883, col. 283 and 294-95.
Hansard: House of Commons Debates, 24 October 1884, col. 225.
Parliamentary Papers, Poor Prisoners Defence Act 1903.
R v. Lee Kun (1916) 1 KB 337.
Parliamentary Papers, Offences against the State Act 1939.
Parliamentary Papers, Juries Act 1949 (12, 13 & 14 Geo VI c.27).
Parliamentary Papers, Legal Aid and Advice Act 1949.
Parliamentary Papers, Juries Act 1974.
Parliamentary Papers, Contempt of Court Act 1981.
Parliamentary Papers, Court and Court Officers Act 1995.
Parliamentary Papers, The Human Rights Act 1998.

Newspapers and Periodicals

Aberdeen Press and Journal, 6th February 1856
Belfast Newsletter, 21st February 1870
Berrow's Worcester Journal, 23rd February 1856
British Medical Journal, 5th November 1898, 26th June 1909
Clare Journal and Ennis Advertiser, 21st February 1870
Coventry Evening Telegraph, 18th July 1940
Daily Alta California, 26th July 1870
Daily Chronicle, 1st November 1898
Daily Mail, 12th July 1933
Daily Mirror, 19th July 1940
Daily News, 10th August 1898, 18th November 1927

Daily Telegraph, 6th March 1883, 19th February 1870
Devizes and Wiltshire Gazette, 24th January 1856
Dublin Daily Express, 21st February 1870
Dublin Evening Mail, 20 August 1869, 6th September 1869, 23rd September 1869, 21st February 1870
Dublin Weekly Nation, 2nd October 1869, 9th October 1869
Dundee Evening Telegraph, 12th November 1926
Edinburgh Evening News, 6th May 1909
Empire News, 28th March 1926, 23rd October 1927, 13th November 1927
Evening Despatch, 29th June 1940
Evening Mail, 25th January 1856, 30th January 1856
Evening Standard, 22nd June 1898
Folkestone, Hythe, Sandgate and Cheriton Herald, 11th September 1926, 10th October 1925
Fife Free Press and Kirkcaldy Guardian, 8th May 1909
Fifeshire Advertiser, 11th December 1909
Freedom: Supplement, July 1898
Freeman's Journal, 20th November 1882
Freethinker, 4th August 1881, 4th December 1881, 3rd September 1882, 1st October 1882, 12th June 1898
Glasgow Herald, 2nd February 1948
Glasgow Sentinel, 17th May 1856
Gloucestershire Chronicle, 23rd April 1926
Goulburn Herald, 16th May 1863
Hampshire Telegraph and Sussex Chronicle, 27th December 1851
Hartlepool Northern Daily Mail, 21st January 1928
Illustrated Police News, 27th July 1920, 20th July 1933
Illustrated Times, 2nd February 1856
Irish Independent, 9th July 2015
Irish Times, 28th September 1869, 2nd October 1869, 15th January 1870, 19th February 1870, 21st February 1870, 20th May 2016, 4th April 2018
Lancashire Evening Post, 4th September 1926
Lancaster Gazette, 19th May 1827
Leeds Mercury, 26th August 1926
Liverpool Echo, 11th July 1933
Liverpool Evening Express, 18th July 1940
Manchester Evening News, 7th July 1927
Manchester Guardian, 16th June 1927, 8th July 1927, 18th August 1934
Manchester Times, 27th December 1851
Morning Chronicle, 12th May 1827, 14th May 1827, 2nd June 1827, 14th July 1827, 16th July 1827, 29th November 1834, 2nd June 1837, 29th June 1837, 4th March 1840
Morning Post, 12th May 1827, 2nd June 1827, 20th September 1827
Morpeth Herald, 10th January 1863, 7th March 1863
Newcastle Courant, 6th March 1863
Newcastle Daily Journal, 11th October 1851, 2nd January 1863, 27th February 1863, 28th February 1863
Newcastle Guardian, 3rd January 1863, 28th February 1863, 21st March 1863
Oxford Chronicle and Reading Gazette, 12th January 1856
Pall Mall Gazette, 4th September 1869, 21st February 1870

Perthshire Advertiser, 1st April 1914, 18th April 1915
Political Examiner, 22nd July 1827
Poor Man's Guardian, 29th September 1832
Preston Guardian, 27th December 1851
Reynolds's Newspaper, 27th October 1850, 3rd April 1898, 5th June 1898, 12th June 1898, 19th June 1898, 6th November 1898
Saturday Review, 25th June 1898, 16th July 1898, 5th November 1898
South Wales Echo, 8th June 1898
St James's Gazette, 22nd June 1898
Sunday Chronicle, 18th November 1927
Sunday Pictorial 21st January 1940, 25th February 1940, 3rd March 1940, 17th March 1940, 30th June 1940, 21st July 1940, 28th July 1940 and 4th August 1940
The Adult, July 1898, August 1898, October 1898, December 1898
The Champion, 26th March 1837, 2nd April 1837
The Cork Examiner, 19th February 1870
The Derby Mercury, 19th March 1856
The Derry Journal, 23rd February 1870
The Era, 21st December 1851
The Evening Freeman, 17th February 1870, 19th February 1870, 21st February 1870
The Evening Telegraph (*Dundee*), 1st June 1898
The Examiner, 22nd July 1827, 22nd June 1834, 27th December 1851
The Flag of Ireland, 2nd October 1869, 2nd July 1870
The Freeman's Journal, 29th September 1869, 30th September 1869, 2nd October 1869, 12th October 1869, 15th October 1869, 17th January 1870, 18th February 1879, 21st February 1870, 1st July 1870, 4th July 1870, 9th July 1870, 12th July 1870, 16th July 1870, 31st January 1875
The Galway Express, 17th July 1869, 21st July 1869, 7th August 1869, 26th September 1869, 2nd October 1869, 19th February 1870, 26th February 1870, 25th June 1870, 2nd July 1870
The Galway Vindicator, 11th August 1869, 23rd August 1869, 25th August 1869, 16th October 1869, 19th February 1870, 23rd February 1870, 25th May 1870, 19th July 1870
The Globe, 7th January 1856, 7th June 1898
The Irish Canadian, 20th July 1870
The Irishman, 2nd July 1870
The Lancet, 2nd February 1856, 19th November 1898, 26th November 1898
The Malthusian, September 1898
The Mid Cumberland and North Westmorland Herald, 18th June 1898
The Morning Advertiser, 30th January 1856, 6th February 1856
The Morning Post, 9th June 1856, 1st June 1898, 14th June 1898, 17th June 1899
The New Age, 23rd June 1898
The Newcastle Daily Chronicle and Northern Counties Advertiser, 2nd January 1863, 3rd January 1863, 27th February 1863, 28th February 1863, 31st January 1863, 14th March 1863, 7th April 1863
The Newry Examiner and Louth Advertiser, 19th January 1856
The Northern Star, 27th December 1851
The People, 30th July 1961, 27th August 1961
The Reformer, 15th November 1898
The Scotsman, 29th December 1908, 4th–8th May 1909, 6th June, 1927, 8th July 1927
The Sketch, 2nd November 1898

The Standard, 11th July 1827, 14th July 1827, 17th July 1827, 16th August 1827, 16th September 1842, 22nd December 1851, 1st June 1898, 3rd June 1898
The Sunday Mail, 20th November 1927
The Sunday Post, 27th November 1927, 11th December 1927
The Times, 14th May 1827, 7th June 1827, 14th June 1827, 13th July 1827, 17th September 1827, 25th March 1837, 2nd June 1837, 10th June 1837, 28th June 1837, 13th November 1838, 25th January 1856, 29th February 1856, 28th May 1856, 9th June 1856, 6th August 1863, 31st January 1902, 21st March 1902, 20th March 1929, 5th July 1920, 4th January 2012
The Westmorland Gazette and Kendal Advertiser, 26th January 1856
The Worcestershire Chronicle, 30th January 1856
Tuam Herald, 19th February 1870
Warder and Dublin Evening Mail, 19th February 1870
Weekly Dispatch, 13th November 1927
Yorkshire Evening Post, 8th July 1940
Yorkshire Post and Leeds Intelligencer, 2nd September 1926, 6th June 1927, 11th June 1927, 8th July 1927

Other Works

(1866) *Report of the Capital Punishment Commission: Together with the Minutes of Evidence and Appendix; Presented to Both Houses of Parliament* (London: HMSO).
(1866) *Royal Commission on Capital Punishment – Report of the Capital Punishment Commission: Together with the Minutes of Evidence and Appendix* (London: HMSO).
Anonymous (1834) *The Annals of Crime and the Newgate Calendar* (London: Berger).
Anonymous (1898) 'The Bedborough Case (A Sequel to the Bradlaugh-Besant Prosecutions)', *The Malthusian*, XXII, 8, p. 62.
Anonymous (1898) 'The Bedborough Case', *Journal of Mental Science*, 44, 184, pp. 122–3.
Anonymous (1889) 'H.A. Allbutt v. the General Medical Council', *British Medical Journal*, II, p. 88.
Anonymous (1856) *Illustrated and Unabridged Edition of The Times Report of the Trial of William Palmer, for Poisoning John Parsons Cook, at Rugeley; from the Short-hand Notes Taken in the Central Criminal Court from Day to Day* (London: Ward & Lock).
Anonymous (1856) *Illustrated Life and Career of William Palmer of Rugeley* (London: Ward and Lock).
Anonymous (1898) 'Prosecution of George Bedborough', *The Agnostic Journal*, 11 June, p. 380.
Anonymous (1870) *The Queen against Peter Barrett: Report of the Third Trial of Peter Barrett for Shooting at with Intent to Murder Captain Thomas Eyre Lambert on Sunday the 11th of July 1869* (Dublin: Alexander Thom).
Anonymous (1856) *The Queen v. Palmer. Verbatim Report of the Trial of William Palmer at the Central Criminal Court, Old Bailey, London, May 14, and Following Days, 1856, before Lord Campbell, Mr Justice Cresswell, and Mr Baron Alderson. Transcribed from the Short-hand Notes of Mr Angelo Bennett* (London: J. Allen).
Anonymous (1898) 'Random Jottings', *Literary Guide and Rationalist Review – New Series*, 25, 1 July, p. 105.
Anonymous (1898) Response to 'Letter to the Editor: Free Love in England', *The Agnostic Journal*, 9 July 1898, pp. 29–30.

Bibliography

Anonymous (1900) *Rib Ticklers or Questions for Parsons* (Bradford: J.W Gott).
Anonymous (1821) *Suppressed Defence: The Defence of Mary Anne Carlile to the Vice Society's Indictment against the Appendix to the Theological Works of Thomas Paine* (London: R. Carlile).
Anonymous (1856) *The Trial of William Palmer for the Alleged Rugeley Poisonings* (London: Henry Lea).
Archbold, J.F. (1860) *A Complete Practical Treatise on Criminal Procedure, Pleading and Evidence, in Indictable* Cases, *Vol. 1* (London: Banks and Brothers).
Astor Singer, G., M.A. Pseud. [I.e. George Ferdinand Springmuhl von Weissenfeld] (1899) *Judicial Scandals and Errors* (London: The University Press).
Bentham, J. (1827 edition) *Rationale of Judicial Evidence as Applied to English Practice* [edited by J.S. Mill] (London: Hunt and Clarke).
Beccaria, C. (1764), *Dei Delitti e Delle Pene [On Crimes and Punishments]* (London: R. Bell).
Burn, R. (1831 edition) *The Justices of the Peace and Parish Officer* (London: S. Sweet).
Carlile, R. (1822) *Report of the Trial of Mrs Susannah Wright for Publishing, in His Shop, the Writings and Correspondence of R. Carlile; before Chief Justice* Abbott, *and* a Special Jury in the Court of King's Bench, Guildhall, London, on Monday, *July 8, 1822: Indictment at the Instance of the Society for the Suppression of Vice* (London: R. Carlile).
Carrington, F.A. and J. Payne (1827) *Reports of Cases Argued and Ruled at Nisi Prius, in the Courts of King's Bench, Common Please, and Exchequer, Together with Cases Tried on the Circuits and at the Old Bailey* (London: S. Sweet and R. Pheney).
Carrington, F.A. and J. Payne (1833) *Reports of Cases Argued and Ruled at Nisi Prius, in the Courts of King's Bench & Common Pleas, and on the Circuit* (London: S. Sweet).
Carrington, F.A. and J. Payne (1837) *Reports of Cases Argued and Ruled at Nisi Prius, in the Courts of Kings Bench, Common Pleas, & Exchequer; Together with Cases Tried on the Circuits and in the Central Criminal Court* (London: S. Sweet).
Eden, E. (1919) *Miss Eden's Letters, Edited by her Great Niece, Violet Dickenson* (London: Macmillan).
Ellis, H. (1898) *A Note on the Bedborough Trial* (London: University Press Ltd).
Foote, G.W. (1932 edition) *Defence of Free Speech, Being a Three Hours' Address to the Jury in the Court of Queen's Bench before Lord Coleridge on April 24, 1883 – New Edition with and Introduction by H. Cutner* (London: Progressive Publishing Co.).
Foote, G.W. (1886) *Prisoner for Blasphemy* (London: Progressive Publishing Co.).
Fraser, F. with J. Morton (1997) *Mad Frank and Friends* (London: Warner Books).
Hale, M. (1736) *History of the Pleas of the Crown – Volume II* (London: E. Rider).
Hayes, E. (1843 edition) *Crimes and Punishments, or a Digest of the Criminal Statute Law of Ireland* (Dublin: Hodges and Smith).
Knapp, A. and W. Baldwin (1826) *The Newgate Calendar* (London: J. Robins).
Lathom Browne, G. and C.G. Stewart (1883) (eds) *Reports of Trials for Murder by Poisoning* (London: Stevens and Sons).
Madame Tussaud and Sons' Exhibition (1869) *Catalogue Containing Biographical and Descriptive Sketches of the Distinguished Characters Which Compose the Unrivalled Exhibition and Historical gallery of Madame Tussaud and Sons* (London: Printed for G. Cole).
Palmer, T. (1856) *A Letter to the Lord Chief Justice Campbell: Containing Remarks upon the Conduct of the Prosecution and the Judges, with Strictures on the Charge Delivered to the Jury, Illustrative of Its Dangerous Tendencies to the Long-enjoyed Rights and Privileges of Englishmen* (London: T. Taylor).

Russell, W.O. and C.S. Greaves (1843) *A Treatise on Crimes and Misdemeanours*, Vol. 1 (London: Saunders and Benning).
Sergeant, T. and C.J. Lowber (1839) *Reports of Cases Argued and Determined in the English Courts of Common Law* (Philadelphia: Atwood and Culve).
Sparks, R. [ghost-written by Norman Parker] (1961) *Burglar to the Nobility* (London: Arthur Barker Limited).
Sprack, J. (2011 edition) *A Practical Approach to Criminal Procedure* (Oxford: Oxford University Press).
Stead, W.T. (1898) 'The Police and the Press: Scotland Yard Censorship', *The Review of Reviews*, XVIII, August, p. 162.
Stephen, J.F. (1860) 'Criminal Law and the Detection of Crime', *Cornhill Magazine*, II, pp. 697–708.
Stephen, J.F. (1883) *History of the Criminal Law of England – Volume I* (London: Macmillan and Co.).
Tilstone, W.J., K.A. Savage and L.A. Clark (2006) *Encyclopaedia of Forensic Science: An Encyclopaedia of History, Methods and Techniques* (London: ABC Clio).
Wharton, F. (1849) *Precedents of Indictments and Pleas, Adapted to the Use Both of the Courts of the United States and Those of All the Several States* (London: J. Kay).

Secondary Sources

Monographs and Key Edited Collections

Altick, R.D. (1970) *Victorian Studies in Scarlet* (London: J M Dent and Sons), p. 10.
Bates, S. (2014) *The Poisoner: The Life and Crimes of Victorian England's Most Notorious Doctor* (New York: Overlook Duckworth).
Beattie, J.M. (1986) *Crime and the Courts in England 1660–1800* (Princeton: Princeton University Press).
Beattie, J.M. (2012) *The First English Detectives: The Bow Street Runners and the Policing of London, 1750–1840* (Oxford: Oxford University Press).
Beattie, J.M. (2001) *Policing and Punishment in London 1660–1750* (Oxford: Oxford University Press).
Bentley, D. (1998) *English Criminal Justice in the Nineteenth Century* (London: Hambledon Press).
Burney, I.A. (2006) *Poison, Detection, and the Victorian Imagination* (Manchester: Manchester University Press).
Bew, P. (1991) *Charles Stewart Parnell* (Dublin: Gill and Macmillan).
Blackstone, W. (1979 edition) *Commentaries on the Laws of England – Volume IV* (Chicago: University of Chicago Press).
Bland, L. (2013) *Modern Women on Trial: Sexual Transgression in the Age of the Flapper* (Manchester: Manchester University Press).
Bloch, I. (1908) *The Sexual Life of Our Time in Its Relations to Modern Civilization – Translated from the Sixth German Edition by M. Eden Paul* (London: Rebman).
Bloom, M.E. (2003) *Waxworks: A Cultural Obsession* (Minneapolis: University of Minnesota Press).
Borchard, E.M. (1932) *Convicting the Innocent: Errors of Criminal Justice* (New Haven: Yale University Press).

Boyle, T. (1989) *Black Swine in the Sewers of Hampstead: Beneath the Surface of Victorian Sensationalism* (New York: Viking).
Bradlaugh-Bonner, H. (1934) *Penalties upon Opinion* (London: Watts and Company).
Brady, S. (2005) *Masculinity and Male Homosexuality in Britain, 1861–1913* (Basingstoke: Palgrave Macmillan).
Bristow, E. (1977) *Vice and Vigilance: Purity Movements in Britain since 1700* (Dublin: Gee & Macmillan).
Brome, V. (1979) *Havelock Ellis, Philosopher of Sex: A Biography* (London: Routledge and Kegan Paul).
Brown, A. (2013) *Inter-war Penal Policy and Crime in England* (Basingstoke: Palgrave).
Calder-Marshall, A. (1959) *Havelock Ellis: A Biography* (London: Rupert Hart-Davis).
Carter Wood, J. (2012) *'The Most Remarkable Woman': Poison, Celebrity and the Trials of Beatrice Pace* (Manchester: Manchester University Press).
Chandrasekhar, S. (1981) *'A Dirty Filthy Book': The Writings of Charles Bradlaugh and Annie Besant on Reproductive Physiology and Birth Control, and an Account of the Bradlaugh-Besant Trial* (Berkeley, CA: University of California Press).
Chapman, P. (1984) *Madame Tussaud's Chamber of Horrors* (London: HarperCollins).
Conan Doyle, A. (1912) *The Case of Oscar Slater* (New York: Hodder & Stoughton).
Conley, C. (2007) *Certain Other Countries: Homicide, Gender and National Identity in Late-Nineteenth Century England, Ireland, Scotland and Wales* (Columbus, OH: Ohio State University Press).
Costello, K. and N. Howlin (2020) (eds) *Law and Religion in Ireland, 1695–1950* (Basingstoke: Palgrave).
Cottrell, L. (1965) *Madame Tussaud* (London: Evans Brothers).
Cox, D.J. (2010) *A Certain Share of Low Cunning: A History of the Bow Street Runners, 1792–1839* (Abingdon: Willan).
Crilly, D. (1887) *Jury Packing in Ireland, as Illustrated by the Prosecution of J. Dillon* (Oxford: Oxford University Press).
Crone, R. (2012) *Violent Victorians: Popular Entertainment in Nineteenth Century London* (Manchester: Manchester University Press).
Cronin, M. (2012) *Agrarian Protest in Ireland 1750–1960* (Dublin: Economic and Social History Society of Ireland).
Curtis, L.P. (1963) *Coercion and Conciliation in Ireland 1880–1892: A Study in Conservative Unionism* (Princeton, NJ: Princeton University Press).
Davies, O. (2005) *Murder, Magic, Madness: The Victorian Trials of Dove and the Wizard* (Harlow: Pearson Education).
D'Cruze, S., S. Walklate and S. Pegg (2006) *Murder: Social and Historical Approaches to Understanding Murder and Murderers* (Abingdon: Willan).
Doan, L. (2001) *Fashioning Sapphism: The Origins of a Modern English Lesbian Culture* (New York: Columbia University Press).
Dodson, Sir G. (1967) *Consider Your Verdict: The Memoirs of Sir Gerald Dodson* (London: Hutchinson).
Duncombe, S. and A. Mattson (2006) *The Bobbed Haired Bandit: A True Story of Crime and Celebrity in 1920s New York* (New York: New York University Press).
Elias, N. (2000 edition) *The Civilising Process* (London: Wiley Blackwell).
Ellis, H. (1939) *My Life* (London: William Heinemann Ltd).
Emsley, C. (2011) *Crime and Society in Twentieth-Century England* (Harlow: Longman).
Emsley, C. (2005) *Hard Men: Violence in England since 1750* (London: Hambledon, 2005).

Flanders, J. (2011) *The Invention of Murder: How the Victorians Revelled in Death and Detection and Created Modern Crime* (London: Harper Press).

Fletcher, G. (1925) *The Life & Career of Dr William Palmer of Rugeley* (London: T. Fisher Unwin).

Fox, M. (2018) *Conan Doyle for the Defence: A Sensational Murder, the Quest for Justice and the World's Greatest Detective Writer* (London: Profile Books).

Fryer, P. (1965) *The Birth Controllers* (London: Secker & Warburg).

Gantt, J. (2010) *Irish Terrorism in the Atlantic Community, 1865–1922* (Basingstoke: Palgrave).

Golan, T. (2004) *Laws of Med and Laws of Nature: The History of Scientific Expert Testimony in England and America* (Cambridge, MA: Harvard University Press).

Goldberg, I. (1926) *Havelock Ellis: A Biographical and Critical Survey* (New York: Simon and Schuster).

Grosskurth, P. (1980) *Havelock Ellis: A Biography* (London: Allen Lane).

Hackwood, F.M. (1912) *William Hone: His Life and Times* (London: Fisher Unwin).

Hammond, J.L. (1938) *Gladstone and the Irish Nation* (London: Longmans).

Harrington, T.C. (1884) *The Maamtrasna Massacre: Impeachment of the Trials* (Dublin: Nation Office).

Hay, D., P. Linebaugh, J. Rule, E.P. Thompson and C. Winslow (2011 edition) *Albion's Fatal Tree: Crime and Society in Eighteenth Century England* (London: Verso).

Hilliard, C. (2017) *The Littlehampton Libels: A Miscarriage of Justice* (Oxford: Oxford University Press).

Horder, J. (2012) *Homicide and the Politics of Law Reform* (Oxford: Oxford University Press).

Hostettler, J. (2009) *A History of Criminal Justice in England and Wales* (Hook: Waterside Press).

House, J. (2002) *Square Mile of Murder* (Edinburgh: Black and White Publishing).

Howlin, N. (2017) *Juries in Ireland: Laypersons and Law in the Long Nineteenth Century* (Dublin: Four Courts Press).

Hunt, P. (1951) *Oscar Slater: The Great Suspect* (London: Carroll & Nicholson).

Jackson, A. (1999) *Ireland 1798–1998* (Oxford: Blackwell).

Jeffrey, R. (2013) *Peterhead: The Inside Story of Scotland's Toughest Prison* (Edinburgh: Black and White Publishing).

Jenkins, B. (2008) *The Fenian Problem: Insurgency and Terrorism in a Liberal State 1858–1874* (Montreal: McGill-Queen's University Press).

Kelleher, M. (2018) *The Maamtrasna Murders* (Dublin: UCD Press).

King, P. (2000) *Crime, Justice and Discretion in England 1740–1820* (Oxford: Oxford University Press).

Knott, G.H. (1912) (ed.) *Trial of William Palmer* (Calcutta: Butterworth & Co.).

Legg, M.L. (1999) *Newspapers and Nationalism: The Irish Provincial Press 1850–1892* (Dublin: Four Courts Press).

Lemmings, D. (2012) (ed.) *Crime, Courtrooms and the Public Sphere in Britain, 1700–1850* (Farnham: Ashgate).

Levy, L. (1993) *Blasphemy: Verbal Offense against the Sacred from Moses to Salman Rushdie* (New York: Knopf).

May, A.N. (2003) *The Bar and the Old Bailey, 1750–1850* (Chapel Hill, NC: The University of North Carolina Press).

McDonald, B. (2015) *Alice Diamond and the Forty Elephants: Britain's First Female Crime Syndicate* (Croydon: Milo Books).

McGrath, D. (2005) *Evidence* (Dublin: Thompson Round Hall).
McKenzie, A. (2007) *Tyburn's Martyrs: Execution in England, 1675–1775* (London: Hambledon).
Molony, S. (2006) *The Phoenix Park Murders: Conspiracy, Betrayal and Retribution* (Cork: Mercier Press).
Murphy, R. (1993) *Smash and Grab: Gangsters in the London Underworld* (London: Faber and Faber).
Nash, D.S. (1999) *Blasphemy in Modern Britain 1789 to the Present* (Aldershot: Ashgate).
Nash, D.S. (2007) *Blasphemy in the Christian World: A History* (Oxford: Oxford University Press).
Nottingham, C. (1999) *The Pursuit of Serenity: Havelock Ellis and the New Politics* (Amsterdam: Amsterdam University Press).
O'Regan, F. (1999) *The Lamberts of Athenry* (Athenry: Lambert Project Society).
Pack, E. (1912) *The Trial and Imprisonment of J.W. Gott* (Bradford: Freethought Socialist League).
Park, W. (1927) *The Truth about Oscar Slater (with the Prisoner's Own Story)* (London: The Psychic Press).
Parry, L.A. (1976 edition) *Some Famous Medical Trials* (Fairfield, NJ: Augustus M. Kelley).
Penfold-Mounce, R. (2009) *Celebrity Culture and Crime: The Joy of Transgression* (Basingstoke: Palgrave Macmillan).
Peterson, H. (1929) *Havelock Ellis: Philosopher of Love* (London: George Allen and Unwin).
Pilbeam, P. (2003) *Madame Tussaud and the History of Waxworks* (New York: Hambledon and London).
Richards, F. (1904) (ed.) *At Scotland Yard: Being the Record of Twenty-Seven Years' Service of John Sweeney, late Detective-Inspector, Criminal Investigation Department Scotland Yard* (London: Grant Richards).
Roberts, M.J.D. (2004) *Making English Morals: Voluntary Associations and Moral Reform in England, 1787–1886* (Cambridge: Cambridge University Press).
Robertson, G. (1999) *The Justice Game* (London: Vintage).
Rolph, C.H. (1961) (ed.) *The Trial of Lady Chatterley: Regina v. Penguin Books Ltd: The Transcript of the Trial* (Harmondsworth: Penguin).
Roome, H.D. and R.E. Ross (1922) (eds) *Archbold's Pleading, Evidence and Practice in Criminal Cases, by Sir John Jervis*, 26th edition (London: Sweet and Maxwell).
Roughead, W. (1950 edition) (ed.) *Trial of Oscar Slater* (Edinburgh: William Hodge and Co.).
Rowbotham, J., K. Stevenson and S. Pegg (2014) *Crime News in Modern Britain: Press Reporting and Responsibility, 1820–2010* (London: Palgrave).
Rowbotham, S. (2008) *Edward Carpenter: A Life of Liberty and Love* (London: Verso).
Shore, H. (1999) *Artful Dodgers: Youth and Crime in Nineteenth Century London* (Woodbridge: Boydell).
Shore, H. (2015) *London's Criminal Underworlds, c.1720–c.1930: A Social and Cultural History* (Basingstoke: Palgrave Macmillan).
St Aubyn, G. (1971) *Infamous Victorians: Palmer and Lamson, Two Notorious Poisoners* (London: Constable).
Taylor, D. (1998) *Crime Policing and Punishment in England, 1750–1914* (London: Palgrave).
Todd, S. (2014) *The People: The Rise and Fall of the Working Class* (London: John Murray).
Toughill, T. (1993) *Oscar Slater: The Mystery Solved* (Edinburgh: Canongate Press).

Travis, A. (2000) *Bound and Gagged: A Secret History of Obscenity in Britain* (London: Profile Books, 2000).
Vaughan, W.E. (2009) *Murder Trials in Ireland, 1836–1914* (Dublin: Irish Legal History Society).
Waldron, J. (1992) *Maamtrasna: The Murders and the Mystery* (Dublin: Edmund Burke).
Walker, C. and K. Starmer (1999) (eds) *Miscarriages of Justice: A Review of Justice in Error* (Oxford: Oxford University Press).
Warner, M. (2006) *Phantasmagoria* (Oxford: Oxford University Press).
Watson, K. (2004) *Poisoned Lives: English Poisoners and Their Victims* (London: Hambledon and London).
Weight, G. (1840) 'Statistics of St. George the Martyr, Southwark', *Journal of the Statistical Society of London*, 3, 1, pp. 50–71.
White, J. (2001) *London in the 20th Century* (London: The Bodley Head).
Whittington-Egan, R. (2001) *The Oscar Slater Murder Story: New Light on a Classic Miscarriage of Justice* (Glasgow: Neil Wilson Publishing).
Wiener, J. (1983) *Radicalism and Freethought in Nineteenth-Century Britain: The Life of Richard Carlile* (Westport, CONN: Greenwood Press).
Wiener, J.H. (2011) *The Americanization of the British Press, 1830–1914* (Basingstoke: Palgrave Macmillan).
Wilton, G.W. (1938) *Fingerprints: History, Law and Romance* (London: William Hodge).

Journal Articles

Abelson, E.S. (1989) 'The Invention of Kleptomania', *Signs*, 15, 1, pp. 123–43.
Anonymous (1912) 'The Case of Oscar Slater', *The Spectator*, 28th September 1912, pp. 8–10.
Anonymous (1914) 'The Case of Oscar Slater', *The Spectator*, 17th October 1914, pp. 10–11.
Anonymous (1923) 'Memories on My Own Screen', *Picture-Play Magazine*, January, pp. 18–20.
Anonymous (1965) 'A Policeman to Remember: I. Detective Lieutenant John Thomson Trench', *Police Journal*, 38, pp. 356–9.
Ardill, A. (2000) 'The Right to a Fair Trial: Prejudicial Pre-trial Media Publicity', *Alternative Law Journal*, 25, 1, pp. 3–9.
Baston, K. (2012) 'Oscar Slater: Presumed Guilty', *Signet Magazine*, 2, pp. 13–16.
Blake, R.B. (2004) '"A Delusion, a Mockery, and a Snare": Array Challenges and Jury Selection in England and Ireland, 1800–1850', *Canadian Journal of History*, 39, 1, pp. 2–26.
Braber, B. (2003) 'The Trial of Oscar Slater (1909) and Anti-Jewish Prejudices in Edwardian Glasgow', *History*, 88, 290, pp. 262–79.
Brown, A. (2007) 'The Amazing Mutiny at the Dartmoor Convict Prison', *British Journal of Criminology*, 47, 2, pp. 276–92.
Carter Wood, J. (2014) 'The Constables and the "Garage Girl"', *Media History*, 20, 4, pp. 384–99.
Christianson, G.E. (1972) 'Secret Societies and Agrarian Violence in Ireland, 1790–1840', *Agricultural History*, 46, 2, pp. 369–84.

Corker, D. and M. Levi (1996) 'Pre-trial Publicity and Its Treatment in the English Courts', *Criminal Law Review*, September, pp. 622–632.

Davies, A. (2007) 'The Scottish Chicago? From "Hooligans" to "Gangsters" in Inter-war Glasgow', *Cultural & Social History*, 4, 4, pp. 511–27.

Devereaux, S. (2017) 'Execution and Pardon at the Old Bailey 1730–1837', *American Journal of Legal History*, 57, pp. 447–94.

Doan, L.K. (1998) 'Passing Fashions: Reading Female Masculinities in the 1920s', *Feminist Studies*, 24, 3, pp. 663–700.

Faust, F. (1994) 'Hadley v. Baxendale: An Understandable Miscarriage of Justice', *Journal of Legal History*, 15, pp. 41–72.

Gold, D. (2015) '"Whose Hair Is It, Anyway?" Bobbed Hair and the Rhetorical Fashioning of the Modern American Woman', *Peitho Journal*, 17, 2, pp. 172–98.

Hanly, C. (2016) 'The 1916 Proclamation and Jury Trial in the Irish Free State', *Dublin University Law Journal*, 39, 2, pp. 373–404.

Harling, P. (2001) 'The Law of Libel and the Limits of Repression, 1790–1832', *Historical Journal*, 44, 1, pp. 107–34.

Hobbs, A. (2009) 'When the Provincial Press Was the National Press (c.1836–c.1900)', *International Journal of Regional and Local History*, 5, pp. 16–43.

Honess, T.M., S. Barker, E. Charman and M. Levi (2002) 'Empirical and Legal Perspectives on the Impact of Pre-trial Publicity', *Criminal Law Review*, September, pp. 719–27.

Hope, L., A. Memon and P. McGeorge (2004) 'Understanding Pre-trial Publicity Pre-decisional Distortion of Evidence by Mock Jurors', *Journal of Experimental Psychology: Applied*, 10, 2, pp. 111–19.

Houlbrook, M. (2013) 'Commodifying the Self Within: Ghosts, Libels, and the Crook Life Story in Inter-war Britain', *The Journal of Modern History*, 85, pp. 321–63.

Houlbrook, M. (2007) '"The Man with the Powder Puff" in Inter-war London', *Historical Journal*, 50, 1, pp. 145–71.

Howlin, N. (2009) 'Controlling Jury Composition in Nineteenth-Century Ireland', *Journal of Legal History*, 30, 3, pp. 227–61.

Howlin, N. (2014) 'Irish Jurors: Passive Observers or Active Participants?', *Journal of Legal History*, 35, 2, pp. 143–71.

Hunter, J. (1984) 'The Development of the Rule against Double Jeopardy', *Journal of Legal History*, 5, pp. 3–19.

Johnson, D. (1996) 'Trial by Jury in Ireland 1860–1914', *Journal of Legal History*, 17, 3, pp. 270–93.

Johnson, D.S. (1985) 'The Trials of Sam Gray: Monaghan Politics and Nineteenth Century Irish Criminal Procedure', *Irish Jurist – New Series*, 20, pp. 109–34.

Junyk, I. (2008) 'Spectacles of Virtue: Classicism, Waxworks and the Festivals of the French Revolution', *Early Popular Visual Culture*, 6, 3, pp. 281–304.

Kornmeier, U. (2008) 'The Famous and the Infamous: Waxworks as Retailers of Renown', *International Journal of Cultural Studies*, 11, 3, pp. 276–88.

Langbein, J. (1983) 'Albion's Fatal Flaws', *Past and Present*, 98, pp. 96–120.

Langford, I. (2009) 'Fair Trial: The History of an Idea', *Journal of Human Rights*, 8, 1, pp. 37–52.

MacGilp, M. (2014) 'Springthorpe: Waxworks, Views, Concerts, Marionettes', *Theatre Notebook*, 68, 1, pp. 2–18.

Manchester, C. (1979) 'Wives as Crown Witnesses', *Cambridge Law Journal*, 37, pp. 249–51.

Nagy, V.M. (2014), 'Narratives in the Courtroom: Female Poisoners in Mid-Nineteenth Century England', *European Journal of Criminology*, 11, pp. 213–27.

Nash, D.S. (2008) '"To Prostitute Morality, Libel Religion, and Undermine Government": Blasphemy and the Strange Persistence of Providence in Britain since the Seventeenth Century', *Journal of Religious History*, 32, 4, pp. 439–56.

Otto, A.L., S. Penrod and H.R. Dexter (1994) 'The Biasing Impact of Pretrial Publicity on Juror Judgments', *Law and Human Behavior*, 18, 4, pp. 453–69.

Pilbeam, P. (2002) 'Madame Tussaud and Her Waxworks', *History Today*, 52, 12, pp. 6–7.

Potter Bond, C. (1995) '"I'll Go the Limit and Then Some": Gun Molls, Desire and Danger in the 1930s', *Feminist Studies*, 21, 1, pp. 41–66.

Roberts, M.J.D. (1985) 'Morals, Art, and the Law: The Passing of the Obscene Publications Act, 1857', *Victorian Studies*, 28, pp. 609–29.

Rowbotham, J. (2007) 'Miscarriage of Justice? Postcolonial Reflections on the "Trial" of the Maharajah of Baroda, 1875', *Liverpool Law Review*, 28, 3, pp. 377–403.

Ruva, C.L. and M.A. LeVasseur (2012) 'Behind Closed Doors: The Effect of Pre-trial Publicity on Jury Deliberations', *Psychology, Crime and Law*, 18, 5, pp. 431–52.

Sandford-Couch, C. and H. Rutherford (2018) 'From the Death of a Female Unknown to the Life of Margaret Dockerty: Rediscovering a Nineteenth Century Victim of Crime', *Law, Crime and History*, 8, 1, pp. 21–37.

Shore, H. (2014) 'Rogues of the Racecourse: Racing Men and the Press in Inter-war Britain', *Media History*, 20, 4, pp. 352–67.

Sigler, J.A. (1963) 'A History of Double Jeopardy', *The American Journal of Legal History*, 7, 4, pp. 283–309.

Smith, B.P. (2005) 'Did the Presumption of Innocence Exist in Summary Proceedings', *Law and History Review*, 23, 1, pp. 191–9.

Smith, B.P. (2005) 'The Presumption of Guilt and the English Law of Theft, 1750–1850', *Law and History Review*, 23, 1, pp. 133–171.

Stead, W.T. (1898) 'The Police and the Press: Scotland Yard Censorship', *The Review of Reviews*, XVIII, August, p. 162.

Thomas, C. (2010) *Are Juries Fair?* Ministry of Justice Bulletin, 39, pp. 40–2.

Toohey, T. (1987) 'Blasphemy in Nineteenth Century England: The Pooley Case and Its Background', *Victorian Studies*, XXX, 3, pp. 315–33.

Watson, K.D. (2006) 'Medical and Chemical Expertise in English Trials for Criminal Poisoning, 1750–1914', *Medical History*, 50, pp. 373–90.

Wiener, M.J. (1999) 'Judges v. Jurors: Courtroom Tensions in Murder Trials and the Law of Criminal Responsibility in Nineteenth-Century England', *Law and History Review*, 17, 3, pp. 467–506.

Wiener, M.J. (1999) 'The Sad Story of George Hall: Adultery, Murder and the Politics of Mercy in Mid-Victorian England', *Social History*, 24, 2, pp. 174–95.

Wildman, C. (2016) 'Miss Moriarty, the Adventuress and the Crime Queen: The Rise of the Modern Female Criminal in Britain, 1918–1939', *Contemporary British History*, 30, 1, pp. 73–98.

Wilson, P.W. (1928) 'But Who Killed Miss Gilchrist?', *The North American Review*, 226, 5, pp. 531–44.

'W.S.R.' (1898) 'The Prosecuted Volume', *The Agnostic Journal*, 18 June, p. 391.

Various (1991) 'Who Killed Miss Gilchrist?', *Murder Casebook: Investigations into the Ultimate Crime*, 5, 67, pp. 2379–411.

Various (1998) 'Oscar Slater', *Murder in Mind: The Killers, The Crimes, Their Psychology*, 35, pp. 1–37.

Chapters from Edited Collections

Brown, M. and E. Carrabine (2017) 'Introducing Visual Criminology' in M. Brown and E. Carrabine (eds) *Routledge International Handbook of Visual Criminology* (Oxford and New York: Routledge), pp. 1–10.

Comerford, R.V. (2010) 'Gladstone's First Irish Enterprise, 1864–70' in W.E. Vaughan (ed.) *A New History of Ireland: Volume V – Ireland under the Union 1801–70* (Oxford: Oxford University Press), pp. 431–51.

Crone, R. (2012) 'Publishing Courtroom Drama for the Masses, 1820–1855' in D. Lemmings (ed.) *Crime, Courtrooms and the Public Sphere in Britain, 1700–1850* (Farnham: Ashgate), pp. 193–216.

Donohue, L. (2003) 'Civil Liberties, Terrorism and Liberal Democracy: Lessons from the United Kingdom' in A. Howitt and R. Pangi (eds) *Countering Terrorism: Dimensions of Preparedness* (Cambridge, MA: MIT Press), pp. 411–46.

Finnane, M. (2006) 'Irish Crime without the Outrage' in N.M. Dawson (ed.) *Reflections on Law and History* (Dublin: Irish legal History Society), pp. 203–22.

Hewitt, M. (2017) 'The Law and the Press' in J. Shattock (ed.) *Journalism and the Periodical Press in Nineteenth Century Britain* (Cambridge: Cambridge University Press), pp. 147–64.

Howlin, N. (2008) 'Merchants and Esquires: Special Juries in Dublin 1725–1833' in G. O'Brien and F. O'Kane (eds) *Georgian Dublin* (Dublin: Four Courts Press), pp. 97–109.

Joyce, J. (1959) 'Ireland at the Bar' in E. Mason and R. Ellmann (eds) *The Critical Writings of James Joyce* (London: Faber & Faber), pp. 197–200.

Lemmings, D. (2012) 'Introduction: Criminal Courts, Lawyers and the Public Sphere' in D. Lemmings (ed.) *Crime, Courtrooms and the Public Sphere in Britain, 1700–1850* (Farnham: Ashgate), pp. 1–21.

Miller, A. (2011) 'Bloody Blondes and Bobbed Haired Bandits: Executing Justice and Constructing Celebrity Criminals in the 1920s Popular Press' in D. Negra and S. Holmes (eds) *In the Limelight and under the Microscope: Forms and Functions of Female Celebrity* (London: Continuum), pp. 61–81.

Robbins, K. (2020) 'The Disestablishment of the Church of Ireland' in K. Costello and N. Howlin (eds) *Law and Religion in Ireland, 1695–1950* (Basingstoke: Palgrave).

Shoemaker, R. (2012) 'Representing the Adversary Criminal Trial: Lawyers in the Old Bailey Proceedings, 1770–1800' in D. Lemmings (ed.) *Crime, Courtrooms and the Public Sphere in Britain, 1700–1850* (Farnham: Ashgate), pp. 71–91.

Smyth, W.J. (2017) 'Conflict, Reaction and Control in Nineteenth-Century Ireland: The Archaeology of Revolution' in J. Crowley et al. (eds) *Atlas of the Irish Revolution* (Cork: Cork University Press), pp. 21–55.

Stepansky, P.E. (1980) 'A Footnote to the History of Homosexuality in Britain: Havelock Ellis and the Bedborough Trial of 1898' in E.R. Wallace and L.C. Pressley (eds) *Essays in the History of Psychiatry: A Tenth Anniversary Supplementary Volume to the Psychiatric Forum Columbia* (Columbia, SC: WM. S. Hall), pp. 72–102.

Ward, T. (2005) 'A Mania for Suspicion: Poisoning, Science, and the Law' in J. Rowbotham and K. Stevenson (eds) *Criminal Conversations: Victorian Crimes, Social Panic, and Moral Outrage* (Columbus: Ohio State University Press), pp. 40–56.

Unpublished Theses and Dissertations

Phelan, M. (2013) *Irish Language Court Interpreting, 1801–1922*, Unpublished Ph.D dissertation, Dublin City University.

On-line Publications

Ellison, J.M. and P.K. Brennan (2014) 'Prejudicial Pretrial Publicity', *The Encyclopedia of Criminology and Criminal Justice*, pp. 1–5 found at: http://onlinelibrary.wiley.com/doi/10.1002/9781118517383.wbeccj462/

The Law Commission (Law Com No. 267), *Double Jeopardy and Prosecution Appeals: Report on Two References under Section 3 (1)(e)of the Law Commissions Act 1965* found at: https://s3-eu-west-2.amazonaws.com/lawcom-prod-storage-11jsxou24uy7q/uploads/2015/03/lc267__Double_Jeopardy_Report.pdf

The Law Commission (Law Com No. 156), *Double Jeopardy: A Consultation Paper* found at: http://www.lawcom.gov.uk/app/uploads/2015/04/CP156.pdf

Macpherson, W. (1999) *The Stephen Lawrence Inquiry: Report of an Inquiry by Sir William Macpherson of Cluny* found at: https://assets.publishing.service.gov.uk/government/uploads/system/uploads/attachment_data/file/277111/4262.pdf

Key Websites

http://ballads.bodleian.ox.ac.uk/
https://hansard.parliament.uk
www.ancestry.com
www.dib.cambridge.org
www.exclassics.com/newgate/
www.lexico.com/en
www.oxforddnb.com/
www.oldbaileyonline.org
www.stephenlawrence.org.uk

Index

Adams, John 149
Albion's Fatal Tree 6
Allbutt, Henry 118
   The Wife's Handbook 118
America 5, 62
   American crime films, influence of 196–7, 200–1
   Juries in 62
   Law in 5
Amnesty Association (Ireland) 74, 87
Autrefois acquit (double jeopardy) 12, 18, 23–8
   Law Commission Report (2001)
   Macpherson report, opinion of double jeopardy 32–3

Banks, Charles Henry 27
Barrett, Peter 13, 73–97
   background 75–6, 80
   cost of prosecution 94–6
   defence case 80–1
   first trial 76–83
   jurors 84–5, 87–9, 91, 92–3
   jury packing 78–9, 87–8, 91
   press reaction to trials 76–85, 88–90, 93–4, 96–7
   public reaction 84–5, 89–90, 93–4, 96
   second trial 83–90
   third trial 90–3
Barrowman, Mary 147, 150, 154
Barry, Charles 78, 86
Beatttie, J.M. 2
Beccaria, Cesare 26
Bedborough, George 14, 117–36
   defence case 122, 124–5
   press reaction to the case 122, 124, 126–33
   presence of women in courtroom 123–4
   prosecution case 122–3, 125
Bentham, Jeremy 26

Bentley, David 25, 36, 56, 63
Besant, Annie 118–19, 124, 133
Birrell, George Gilchrist 171–2
Blackstone 18
Blackwell, Benjamin Bruton 56, 57–8, 60, 62–6, 68, 70–1
Bland, Lucy 206
Blasphemy 10–11, 15, 175–94
   attempts at repeal 193
   Common Law 181, 194
   Coleridge 'judgement' 181, 185, 187–8, 191–3
   'Gay News' case 194
   government discussion of the legal position 191–3
   Hale 'judgement' 180–1
   mens rea 179, 181
   narrativisation of 177–9, 185–6
   Statute (9 & 10 William c 35) 187, 192
Blasphemy Laws Amendment Bill (1913) 193
Blatchford, Robert 190
Bloch, Iwan 134
Bolton, George 101, 110
Bradford Socialist League 183, 184, 191
Bradlaugh, Charles 118–19, 124, 133, 187
Bradlaugh, Hypatia 190
Brande, William 47
Broadbridge, Sally 32
Burke, J.H. 95–6
Butt, Isaac 74, 78, 86–9, 91–2, 93, 96

Calder-Marshall, Arthur 134
Carlile, Richard 176–7, 180
Campbell, John Baron (Lord Chief Justice) (1779–1861) 44, 48, 49, 52
Carlile, Richard 176–7, 180
Carpenter, Edward 119, 124, 128, 129, 134–5
Casey, Michael, 101
Casey, Thomas Archbishop of Tuam 101

Central Criminal Court Act (Trial of Offences Act) (1856) 36, 40–1, 44, 105
Christison, Robert 47
Class 8–10
Cockburn, Sir Alexander (1802–1880) 45, 117–18
Coleridge, John Duke 181
Comerford, R.V. 74–5
Conan Doyle, Sir Arthur 151, 153, 167
Concannon, Henry 78, 95
Cook, David 159–63, 165, 167
Cook, J.P. 39, 46, 47, 49, 52
Cooney, Celia 199–200
Coroner's Inquests 23
Courtroom 11, 13
    performance of counsel in 11, 13, 22
Cox, David 20
Crilly, Daniel 111
Criminal Appeal (Scotland) Act 1926 155
Criminal Law Act (1826) 25
Criminal Law Amendment Act (1885) 119, 130
Criminal Trials
    characteristics of 2–4, 6–10, 12, 13–16, 17–34, 69–71, 101, 105–7, 111–14

Davies, Andrew 196
De Villiers, Roland 120, 126, 133–4
Devereux, Simon 25
Docherty, Margaret 53, 56, 57, 64–6, 71–2
Dodson, Justice Sir Gerald 197, 210
Doherty, Justice John Beaver Henry Blacker 106–7
Dublin (Ireland) 84–8, 93–4, 100, 103, 105, 108, 110, 114

Elias, Norbert (1897–1990) 5, 6
Ellis, Havelock 14, 118–22, 124, 126–31
    Contemporary Science series 119
    Sexual Inversion 14, 118–24, 126–8, 132, 134–5
    Studies in the Psychology of Sex 119
Emsley, Clive 197
Erskine, Thomas 176
ethnicity 9
expert witness testimony 36, 48–9

Fitzgerald, Justice John David 90–1, 104
Fletcher, George 47
    account of poisoning symptoms 47
Foote, George William 124–5, 128, 177–8, 179–81, 184, 186, 187, 193
The Freethinker 182, 184
Foucault, Michel (1926–1984) 6, 7
Free Press Defence Committee 122, 124–6, 133
Freethought Socialist League 187

Galt, Hugh 140–2, 149
Galway, Ireland 13, 73–97, 99–115
Gender 8–9, 123–4
    press creation of stereotypes 195–211
Gilchrist, Marion 137–73
    character of 138–9
    murder of 138–44
Gilmour, Sir John (Secretary of State for Scotland) 153–5
Gladstone, William Ewart 74, 89, 96, 102–3
    Land Act 96–7
Glaister, John 140–2, 149
Glasgow 14–15, 137–73
Golding, Frederick Arthur 28
Goldstein, Lillian ('bob haired bandit') 15, 195–211
    background 204
    relationship with Spark 195, 201, 205–10
    press depictions of 'bob haired bandit' persona 197–208, 211
    American crime films influence of 196–7, 200–1
    repentance of 210–11
    shoplifting charges 203–5
    verdict and sentence 210–11
Gott, John William 15, 175, 181–90
    defence of pre publicity 189
    first case 182, 188–90
    Rib Ticklers 184, 188
    The Truthseeker 182
    Verdict 190
Gray, John 78
Greenwood, George 191
Guthrie, Lord Charles 144

Habermas, Jurgen 5–6
Hale, Sir Matthew (1609–76) 180

Hall, Edward Marshall 151–2
Hall, Radclyffe 136
Harrington, Tim 101–2, 111–13
Hepburn, Minnie 153
Heron, Denis Caulfield QC 78–9, 80–1, 86
historiography 1, 2, 6, 11–12, 20, 25, 30, 32, 36, 47, 55, 56, 60, 63, 74–5, 134, 180, 195–8, 201–2, 205–6
homosexuality 119–20
Hone, William 176
Horridge, Justice Thomas Gardner 186, 188–9, 194
    summing up in case against Stewart 187–9
Houlbrook, Matthew 198, 205
Houssart, Lewis 23

identity parades 10
Ireland 13–14, 73–97, 99–115
    jury 'packing' 13, 78–9, 87–8, 91, 109–11, 114
    Land League 102
    'Land War' 13–14, 74–5, 102–3

Jackson, Thomas 190, 194
Joyce, Myles 14, 99–115
    approver testimony 101, 105–7, 114–15
    defence case 100
    inadmissibility of evidence 111–13
    Jury 'packing' 109–11, 114
    language issues in court 107–8
    posthumous pardon of (2018) 115
    press reaction to case 100–2, 108–10, 113
    prosecution case 105–7
    trial 100–13
Joynt, William Lane 84
Judgement of Death Act (1823) 25
juries 62, 64, 69–71, 78–9, 83–4, 87, 94, 109–11
justice 5, 7, 11
    approver testimony 101, 105–7
    conceptions of 5, 7
    'failed' justice 17–34

King, Peter 1
King-Hamilton Justice Alan 194

Knowlton, Charles 118
Fruits of Philosophy 118
Kornmeier 59

Lady Chatterley's Lover 123
Lambert, Captain Thomas Eyre 73, 74–6, 79, 80–1, 83, 85–6, 88–9, 91–2, 96
Lambie, Helen 139, 142–3, 147–8, 150, 153, 155–6, 160–1, 170–1
Landsteiner, Karl 33
Langford, I. 55
Leeds Vigilance Association 118
Lees, Edith 119
Legitimation League 118, 121–2, 135
    police surveillance of 121–2
London 2, 12, 13, 17–34, 36–7, 80, 127
London Society for the Protection of Young Females 30

Maamtrasna, Galway (Ireland) 99–115
MacDermot, Hugh 78, 82
MacDonald, Ramsay 153
MacGilp, M. 60
Magna Carta 4–5
Manion, Patrick 54, 63, 67–8, 70
Marx, Karl 6
Marxist historians 6
Massingham, H.W. 131
Mayo, Ireland 14
McKenna, Reginald (Home Secretary) 191–2
McKenzie, Andrea 1
microstudies 11–12
Mill, J.S. 177
moral panics 3, 9, 74
Mortimer, John 194
Madame Tussard's 59
May, Allyson 2
Metropolitan Police Act (1829) 20
murder 12–15, 17–34, 35–52, 53–72

National Vigilance Association 118
Nayler, James 175–6
Newcastle 13, 53–72
Northern Ireland 5
Nugent, Patrick 169–70

Obscene Publications 10, 14
Obscene Publications Act (1857) 14, 117–18
O'Dare, Josephine 198, 205

Pack, Ernest 15, 175, 181–90
Palmer, Anne 39, 47
Palmer, William 13, 35–52
   affidavits in the case 42–3
   background 37–9, 49–51
   cost of prosecution 45
   defence case 36–7, 45–6
   financial problems 39–41, 47
   press reaction 36, 39–41
   prosecution case 46–7
   sentence 48
Park, William 153
Peace Preservation (Ireland) Act (1870) 96–7
Penfold-Mounce, Ruth 30
'Penny Dreadfuls' 4
Phoenix Park murders 103
poisoning 13, 36, 39, 46–7
policing 6–8, 10
   failure of 11, 15
Pooley, Thomas 177
Poor Man's Guardian 28–9
popular culture 4, 9
Powys-Wilson, Alexandra 205, 208
Prevention of Crime (Ireland) Act (1882) 104–5
Protection of Persons and Property (Ireland) Act (1881) 103
Prisoners' Counsel Act (1836) 2, 63

Rationalist Press Association 191
Rex v Glennon, Toole and McGrath 106
Rex v Hicklin (1868) 118
Rex v Parry, Rea and Wright (1837) 26–7
Rex v Phelan and Phelan 104
Rex v Plant and Birchenough (1836) 26–7
Rex v Reaney and Reddish 112
Robertson, J.M. 131, 191
Robertson, Geoffrey 16, 194
Roughhead, William 14, 137, 141, 145, 149, 150, 152, 169
Rowbotham, Judith 55
Royal Commission on capital Punishment 57
Royal Irish Constabulary (RIC) 103–4

Scotland 14–15, 137–73
Seymour, Henry 127
Seymour, William Digby 62

Sheen, William 12, 17–34
   first trial 21–2
   hunt for 20–1
   press reaction 24–5, 28, 30–2, 34
   public reaction to 27–9
   second trial 23–6
   subsequent career 29–32
   testimony in case 19–20
Shoemaker, Robert 6
Sinclair, John Lord Pentland (Secretary of State for Scotland) 151
Slater Oscar 14, 137–173
   appeal against conviction 155–8
   character of 146–7
   defence case 144–51
   press reaction to the case 162
   prosecution case 144–51
   public reaction 150–1
   subsequent investigation of the case 152–7
   witness identification of 143–4, 147–9, 153–4, 157, 159–60
Spark, Charles John 'Ruby' 195–210
   Burglar to the Nobility 203
   escape from prison 205
Spencer, John Pointz Earl, Lord Lieutenant of Ireland 100–1, 103, 115
Staffordshire 35–7, 42, 45–6
Stead, W.T. 129–30
Stephen Lawrence case 32
Stephens, E. 190
Stewart, Thomas William 15, 175, 181–90
   case against (august 1911) 183–4, 185–6
   Dr Nikola (pseudonym) 183–4
   public speeches 184–5, 187, 191
   summing up in case against Stewart 187–8
Sullivan, John (Attorney-General) 78, 79, 84, 86
Symonds, John Addington 120

Tallack, William 57–8, 60–1
Taylor, Alfred Swaine (1806–1880) 36, 45
Taylor, John 180
Torrens, Justice Robert 106, 107
Town Police Clauses Act (1847) 190
Trench, John Thompson 14–15, 137–8, 152, 153, 158–70

background 159, 163–5
charged with Reset (Receiving stolen goods) 165–9
intervention in Oscar Slater case 159–65
'Secret Inquiry' 163–4

'Unfair' Trials 2–4, 7–15, 17–34, 40–1, 45–8, 52, 53–72, 99–115, 137–73, 175–94, 195–211
media interest in 3–4, 7–9, 15, 19–22, 24–5, 31–2, 36, 53–7, 59, 61–2, 66–7, 71, 78, 100–2
public interest in 3, 15
wrongful conviction 4
Ure, Alexander (Lord Advocate) 144, 151

Vass, George 13, 53–72
defence case 54, 56–8
press reaction to case 53–7, 59, 66–7, 72
pre-trial reporting 56–7, 61–2, 69–72
trial of 63–72
verdict 68
waxworks images of 57–63
Vizetelly, Henry 118, 133

Wales 20–1, 30
Watford University Press 14, 120, 128, 133–4
The Adult 120, 125, 127, 135
Waxworks 4, 57–63
Weir, George 182, 186, 187
Whistle-blowers 12
White, Jerry 197, 201–2
Whiteside, Justice James 78, 86, 87, 94
Wiener, Martin 55, 63
Wilde, Oscar 117, 119
Wildman, Charlotte 196
Wood, John-Carter 196
Wood, Thomas Mackinnon (Secretary of State for Scotland) 152, 159
Wright, Susannah, 179

www.ingramcontent.com/pod-product-compliance
Lightning Source LLC
Chambersburg PA
CBHW072147290426
44111CB00012B/2002